THE
RIVER
OF THE
WEST

BY FRANCES FULLER VICTOR

Originally published in 1870
R. W. BLISS & Co.
Hartford, Connecticut

*An Edition of Fifteen Hundred Copies
Republished in 1974*

BROOKS-STERLING COMPANY
815 East Fourteenth Street
Oakland, Calif. 94604

Library of Congress Catalog Card No. 74-83523
ISBN 0-914418-02-5

Joseph L. Meek

THE RIVER OF THE WEST.

LIFE AND ADVENTURE

IN THE

ROCKY MOUNTAINS AND OREGON;

EMBRACING EVENTS IN THE LIFE-TIME OF A

MOUNTAIN-MAN AND PIONEER:

WITH THE

EARLY HISTORY OF THE NORTH-WESTERN SLOPE,

INCLUDING

AN ACCOUNT OF THE FUR TRADERS, THE INDIAN TRIBES, THE OVERLAND IMMIGRA-
TION, THE OREGON MISSIONS, AND THE TRAGIC FATE OF
REV. DR. WHITMAN AND FAMILY.

ALSO, A DESCRIPTION OF THE COUNTRY,

ITS CONDITION, PROSPECTS, AND RESOURCES; ITS SOIL, CLIMATE, AND SCENERY;
ITS MOUNTAINS, RIVERS, VALLEYS, DESERTS, AND PLAINS; ITS
INLAND WATERS, AND NATURAL WONDERS.

WITH NUMEROUS ENGRAVINGS.

BY MRS. FRANCES FULLER VICTOR.

PUBLISHED BY SUBSCRIPTION ONLY.

HARTFORD, CONN.:
COLUMBIAN BOOK COMPANY.
BLISS & CO., NEWARK, N. J.;   W. E. BLISS & CO., TOLEDO, O.:
R. J. TRUMBULL & CO., SAN FRANCISCO, CAL.
1870.

WE FIND THEM, ACCORDINGLY, HARDY, LITHE, VIGOROUS, AND ACTIVE, EXTRAVAGANT IN WORD, IN THOUGHT, AND DEED: HEEDLESS OF HARDSHIP, DARING OF DANGER; PRODIGAL OF THE PRESENT, AND THOUGHTLESS OF THE FUTURE.—*Irving*.

INTRODUCTION.

When the author of this book has been absorbed in the elegant narratives of Washington Irving, reading and musing over *Astoria* and *Bonneville*, in the cozy quiet of a New York study, no prescient motion of the mind ever gave prophetic indication of that personal acquaintance which has since been formed with the scenes, and even with some of the characters which figure in the works just referred to. Yet so have events shaped themselves that to me Astoria is familiar ground; Forts Vancouver and Walla-Walla pictured forever in my memory; while such journeys as I have been enabled to make into the country east of the last named fort, have given me a fair insight into the characteristic features of its mountains and its plains.

To-day, a railroad traverses the level stretch between the Missouri River and the Rocky Mountains, along which, thirty years ago, the fur-traders had worn a trail by their annual excursions with men, pack-horses, and sometimes wagons, destined to the Rocky Mountains. Then, they had to guard against the attacks of the Savages; and in this respect civilization is behind the railroad, for now, as then, it is not safe to travel without a sufficient escort. To-day, also, we have new Territories called by several names cut out of the identical hunting-grounds of the fur-traders of thirty years ago; and steamboats plying the rivers where the mountain-men came to set their traps for beaver; or cities growing up like mushrooms from a soil made quick by gold, where the hardy mountain-hunter pursued the buffalo herds in search of his winter's supply of food.

The wonderful romance which once gave enchantment to stories of hardship and of daring deeds, suffered and done in these then distant wilds, is fast being dissipated by the rapid settlement of the new Territories, and by the familiarity of the public mind with tales of stirring adventure encountered in the search for glittering ores. It was, then, not without an emotion of pleased surprise that I first encountered in the fertile plains of Western Oregon the subject of this biography, a man fifty-eight years of age, of fine appearance and buoyant temper, full of anecdote, and with a memory well stored with personal recollections of all the men of note who have formerly visited the old Oregon Territory, when it comprised the whole country west of the Rocky Mountains lying north of California and south of the forty-ninth parallel. This man is *Joseph L. Meek*, to whose stories of mountain-life I have listened for days together; and who, after having figured conspicuously, and not without considerable fame, in the early history of Oregon, still prides himself most of all on having been a "mountain-man."

Most persons are familiar with the popular, celebrated Indian pictures of the artist Stanley; and it cannot fail to interest the reader to learn that in one of these Meek is represented as firing his last shot at the pursuing Savages. He was also the hero of another picture, painted by an English artist. The latter picture represents him in a contest with a grizzly bear, and has been copied in wax for the benefit of a St. Louis Museum, where it has been repeatedly recognized by Western men.

It has frequently been suggested to Mr. Meek, who has now come to be known by the familiar title of "Uncle

Joe" to all Oregon, that a history of his varied adventures would make a readable book, and some of his neighbors have even undertaken to become his historian, yet with so little well-directed efforts that the task after all has fallen to a comparative stranger. I confess to having taken hold of it with some doubts as to my claims to the office; and the best recommendation I can give my work is the interest I myself felt in the subject of it; and the only apology I can offer for anything incredible in the narrative which it may contain, is that I "tell the tale as 'twas told to me," and that I have no occasion to doubt the truth of it.

Mr. Meek has not attempted to disguise the fact that he, as a mountain-man, "did those things which he ought not to have done, and left undone those things which he ought to have done." It will be seen, by referring to Mr. Irving's account of this class of men, as given him by Capt. Bonneville, that he in no wise differed from the majority of them in his practical rendering of the moral code, and his indifference to some of the commandments. Yet, no one seeing Uncle Joe in his present aspect of a good-humored, quiet, and not undignified citizen of the " Plains," would be likely to attribute to him any very bad or dangerous qualities. It is only when recalling the scenes of his early exploits in mountain life, that the smouldering fire of his still fine eyes brightens up with something suggestive of the dare-devil spirit which characterized those exploits, and made him famous even among his compeers, when they were such men as Kit Carson, Peg-Leg Smith, and others of that doughty band of bear-fighters.

Seeing that the incidents I had to record embraced a period of a score and a half of years, and that they extended over those years most interesting in Oregon history, as well as of the history of the Fur Trade in the West, I have concluded to preface Mr. Meek's adventures with a sketch of the latter, believing that the information thus conveyed to the reader will give an additional degree of interest to their narration. The impression made upon my own mind as I gained a knowledge of the facts which I shall record in this book relating to the early occupation of Oregon, was that they were not only profoundly romantic, but decidedly unique.

In giving Mr. Meek's personal adventures I should have preferred always to have clothed them in his own peculiar language could my memory have served me, and above all I should have wished to convey to the reader some impression of the tones of his voice, both rich and soft, and deep, too; or suddenly changing, with a versatile power quite remarkable, as he gave with natural dramatic ability the perfect imitation of another's voice and manner. But these fine touches of narrative are beyond the author's skill, and the reader must perforce be content with words, aided only by his own powers of imagination in conjuring up such tones and subtile inflexions of voice as seem to him to suit the subject. Mr. Meek's pronunciation is Southern. He says "thar," and "whar," and "bar," like a true Virginian as he is, being a blood relation of one of our Presidents from that State, as well as cousin to other one-time inmates of the White House. Like the children of many other slave-holding planters he received little attention, and was allowed to frequent the negro quarters, while the alphabet was neglected. At the age of sixteen he could not read. He had been sent to a school in the neighborhood, where he had the alphabet set for him on a wooden "paddle;" but not liking this method of instruction he one day "hit the teacher over the head with it, and ran home," where he was suffered to disport himself among his black associates, clad like themselves in a tow frock, and guiltless of shoes and stockings. This sort of training was not without its advantages to the physical man; on the contrary, it produced, in this instance, as in many others, a tall, broad-shouldered, powerful and handsome man, with plenty of animal courage and spirit, though somewhat at the expense of the inner furnishing which is supposed to be necessary to a perfect development. In this instance, however, Nature had been more than usually kind, and distinguished her favorite with a sort of inborn grace and courtesy which, in some phases of his eventful life, served him well.

Mr. Meek was born in Washington Co., Virginia, in 1810, one year before the settlement of *Astoria*, and at a period when Congress was much interested in the question of our Western possessions and their boundary. "Manifest destiny" seemed to have raised him up, together with many others, bold, hardy, and fearless men, to become sentinels on the outposts of civilization, securing to the United States with comparative ease a vast extent of territory, for which, without them, a long struggle with England would have taken place, delaying the settlement of the Pacific Coast for many years, if not losing it to us altogether. It is not without a feeling of genuine self-congratulation, that I am able to bear testimony to the services, hitherto hardly recognized, of the "mountain-men" who have settled in Oregon. Whenever there shall arise a studious and faithful historian, their names shall not be excluded from honorable mention, nor least illustrious will appear that of Joseph L. Meek, the Rocky Mountain Hunter and Trapper.

SUNSET AT THE MOUTH OF THE COLUMBIA.

There sinks the sun; like cavalier of old,
　　Servant of crafty Spain,
He flaunts his banner, barred with blood and gold,
　　Wide o'er the western main;
A thousand spear heads glint beyond the trees
　　In columns bright and long,
While kindling fancy hears upon the breeze
　　The swell of shout and song.

And yet not here Spain's gay, adventurous host
　　Dipped sword or planted cross;
The treasures guarded by this rock-bound coast
　　Counted them gain nor loss.
The blue Columbia, sired by the eternal hills
　　And wedded with the sea,
O'er golden sands, tithes from a thousand rills,
　　Rolled in lone majesty—

Through deep ravine, through burning, barren plain,
　　Through wild and rocky strait,
Through forest dark, and mountain rent in twain
　　Toward the sunset gate;
While curious eyes, keen with the lust of gold,
　　Caught not the informing gleam,
These mighty breakers age on age have rolled
　　To meet this mighty stream.

Age after age these noble hills have kept,
　　The same majestic lines;
Age after age the horizon's edge been swept
　　By fringe of pointed pines.
Summers and Winters circling came and went,
　　Bringing no change of scene;
Unresting, and unhasting, and unspent,
　　Dwelt Nature here serene !

Till God's own time to plant of Freedom's seed,
  In this selected soil ;
Denied forever unto blood and greed,
  But blest to honest toil.
There sinks the sun ; Gay cavalier no more !
  His banners trail the sea,
And all his legions shining on the shore
  Fade into mystery.

The swelling tide laps on the shingly beach,
  Like any starving thing ;
And hungry breakers, white with wrath, upreach,
  In a vain clamoring.
The shadows fall ; just level with mine eye
  Sweet Hesper stands and shines,
And shines beneath an arc of golden sky,
  Pinked round with pointed pines.

A noble scene ! all breadth, deep tone, and power,
  Suggesting glorious themes ;
Shaming the idler who would fill the hour
  With unsubstantial dreams.
Be mine the dreams prophetic, shadowing forth
  The things that yet shall be,
When through this gate the treasures of the North
  Flow outward to the sea.

ILLUSTRATIONS.

	PAGE.
PORTRAIT OF JOSEPH L. MEEK.—*Frontispiece.*	
THE ENLISTMENT,	42
THE SUMMER RENDEZVOUS,	48
BEAVER-DAM,	66
THE THREE "BARES,"	92
THE WRONG END OF THE TREE,	94
BRANDING CATTLE,	150
THE MULE FORT,	155
THE FREE TRAPPER'S INDIAN WIFE,	177
DESCENDING THE BLUE MOUNTAINS,	211
THE BEAR IN CAMP,	219
SATISFIED WITH BEAR FIGHTING,	221
THE TRAPPER'S LAST SHOT,	229
THE SQUAW'S ESCAPE,	231
A BUFFALO HUNT,	246
THE MISSIONARY WEDGE,	274
WRECKED IN THE RAPIDS,	336
THE CASCADE MOUNTAIN ROAD-HUNTERS,	374
MASSACRE OF DR. WHITMAN AND FAMILY, OF THE PRESBYTERIAN MISSION,	410
MEEK AS STEAMBOAT RUNNER,	441
"TAKE CARE KNOX,"	451
A MOUNTAIN-MAN IN CLOVER,	461
GOV. LANE AND MARSHAL MEEK EN ROUTE TO OREGON,	476
OREGON BEAVER-MONEY,	485
MEEK AS UNITED STATES MARSHAL,	498
MT. RANIER FROM PUGET SOUND,	561
SHERIDAN'S FIRST BATTLE-GROUND, COLUMBIA RIVER,	568
CASTLE ROCK,	569
HORSE-TAIL FALL,	570
VIEW ON THE COLUMBIA,	571
MT. HOOD FROM THE DALLES,	573

CONTENTS.

PREFATORY CHAPTER.

PAGE.

Astoria—Fort Vancouver—Its isolated Position—Precautions against In-
dians—The Hudson's Bay Company—Its Policy and Intercourse with
the Indians—The Arrival of the "Brigade"—Other Yearly Arrivals—
Punishment of Indian Offenders—Indian Strategy—A Hero—The
American Fur Companies—Their Dealings with the Indians—Ashley's
Expeditions to Green River—Attack on Smith's Party—Wyeth's Ex-
peditions—Fort Hall—Decline of the Fur Trade—Causes of the Indians'
Hostility—Dangers attending the Trapper's Life,   -   -   - 23

CHAPTER I.

Early Life of Meek—He leaves Home—Enlists in a Fur Company—On
the March—A Warning Voice—Frontier Sports—Last Vestige of Civilization—On the Plains—A first Adventure—A firm Front—A Parley—
The Summer Rendezvous—An enchanting Picture—The Free Trapper's Indian Wife—Wild Carousals—Routine of Camp Life—Smoked
Moccasins versus Green Ones—A "Trifling Fellow," -   -   - 41

CHAPTER II.

The Camp in Motion—A Trapping Expedition—Opposition to the Hud-
son's Bay Company—Beautiful Scenery—The Lost Leader Found—
Rejoicings in Camp—The "Luck" of the Trappers—Conference of
Leaders—The "Devil's Own"—Blackfoot Character—Account of the
Tribes,   -   -   -   -   -   -   -   -   - 57

CHAPTER III.

How Beaver are Taken—Beaver Dams—Formation of Meadows—Beaver
Lodges—"Bachelors"—Trapping in Winter—"Up to Trap"—Black-
feet on the Trail—On Guard—The Trapper's Ruse—A disappointed
Bear—A Fight with Blackfeet—"Out of Luck —Alone in the Moun-
tains—Splendid Views—A Miserable Night—The last Luxury of Life—
The Awfulness of Solitude—A Singular Discovery—A Hell on Earth—
A Joyful Recognition—Hard Times in Camp—The Negro's Porcupine—
Craig's Rabbit—Deep Snows—What the Scout saw—Bighorn River—
"Colter's Hell"—An Alarm—Arrival at Wind River—Christmas,   - 64

CHAPTER IV.

Removal to Powder River—A Trapper's Paradise—The Transformation
in the Wilderness—The Encampment by Night—Meek takes to Study—

PAGE.

On the Move—Loss of Horses and Traps—Robbed and Insulted by a
Bear—Crossing the Yellowstone—A Novel Ferriage—Annoyance from
Blackfeet—A Cache Opened—A Comrade Killed—Rude Burial Serv-
ice—Return to Rendezvous—Gay Times—The old Partners take Leave,   82

CHAPTER V.

Grizzly Bears—An Adventure with a Grizzly—The Three "Bares"—
The Mountain-Man's Manners — Joking the Leaders—The Irishman
and the Booshway—How Sublette climbed a Tree and escaped a Bear—
Rival Trappers—Whisky as a Strong Card—Ogden's Indian Wife—
Her Courage and Escape—Winter Quarters—Crow Horse-Thieves—
An Expedition on Foot—Night Attack on the Indian Fort—Fitzpatrick
Missing—Destitution in Camp—A "Medicine-Man" consulted—"Mak-
ing Medicine"—A Vision Obtained—Fitzpatrick Found—Death of
Smith— An Expedition on Snow-Shoes,   -   -   -   -   90

CHAPTER VI

Annoying Competition — The Chief's Daughter — Sublette Wounded—
Forty Days of Isolation—Sublette and Meek captured by Snake Indians—A Solemn Council—Sentence of Death—Hope Deferred—A Rescue—The "Mountain Lamb"—An Obstinate Rival—Blackfeet Marauders—Fitzpatrick's Adventures in the Mountains—"When the Pie
was opened the Birds began to Sing"—Rough Sports—A Man on Fire—
Brigades ready for the Start—Blackfeet Caravan—Peaceful Overtures—
The Half-Breed's Revenge—A Battle—Reinforcements—Death of Sinclair—Sublette Wounded—Greenhorns—A false Alarm—Indian Adroit-
ness—A Deserted Fort—Incident of the Blackfoot Woman—Murder of
a Party by Blackfeet, -   -   -   -   -   -   - 103

CHAPTER VII.

The March to the Humboldt—Scarcity of Game—Terrible Sufferings—
The Horrors of Thirst and Famine—Eating Ants, Crickets and Mules—
Return to Snake River—A lucky Discovery—A Trout Supper—The
Country of the Diggers—Some Account of Them—Anecdote of Wyeth
and Meek—Comparison of Indian Tribes—The Blackfeet—The Crows—
The Coast Tribes and the Mountain Tribes—The Columbia River
Indians—Their Habits, Customs, and Dress—Indian Commerce—The
Indians of the Plains—Their Dress, Manners, and Wealth—The Horses
of the Plains—Language—The Indian's Moral Nature—Hungry and
Hospitable Savages—A Trap set for a Rival—An Ambush—Death of
Vanderburg—Skirmish with Blackfeet—The Woman Interpreter taken
Prisoner—Bravery of her Husband—Happy Finale—Meek Rescues the
"Mountain Lamb"—Intense Cold—Threatened by Famine—The Den
of Grizzlys—Second Daniels,   -   -   -   -   - 119

CHAPTER VIII.

PAGE.

A Visit from Blackfeet—The Green River Rendezvous—A " Powerful Drunk"—Mad Wolf—A Friendly Warning—A Trip to the Salt Lake Country—Meek Joins Jo. Walker's California Expedition—Instinct of the Mule—On the Humboldt River—Massacre of Diggers at Mary's River—Vain Explorations—Crossing the Sierra Nevadas—Hardships and Sufferings—The Sacramento Valley—Delight of the Trappers— Meeting with Spanish Soldiers—A Parley—Escorted to Monterey—A Hospitable Reception—The Native Californians—Visit to the Mohave Village—Meeting with Trapp and Jervais—Infamous Conduct at the Moquis Village—The Return March,   -   -   -   -   - 141

CHAPTER IX.

In the Camanche Country—A Surprise and a Rapid Movement—The Mule Fort—A Camanche Charge—Sure Aim—Another Charge—More Dead Indians—Woman's Weapon, the Tongue—Fearful Heat and Sufferings from Thirst—The Escape by Night—The South Park—Death of Guthrie—Meeting with Bonneville—Indignant Reproaches, -   - 154

CHAPTER X.

Gossip at Rendezvous—Adventures in the Crow Country—Fitzpatrick Picked by the Crows and Flies from Them—Honor among Thieves— Unfair Treatment of Wyeth—Bonneville Snubbed at Walla-Walla— He Rejects good Counsel—Wyeth's Threat, and its Fulfillment—Division of Territory, -   -   -   -   -   -   -   - 160

CHAPTER XI.

In the Blackfoot Country—A Visit to Wyeth's Trappers—Sorry Experiences—Condolence and its Effect—The Visitors become Defenders— A Battle with Fire and Sword—Fighting for Life—The Trappers' Victory—A Trapping Excursion—Meek Plays a Trick and has one Played on Him—A Run to Camp—Taking up Traps—A Blackfoot Ambush— A Running Fire—A lucky Escape—Winter Camp on the Yellowstone— Interpretation of a Dream—A Buffalo Hunt and a Blackfoot Surprise— Meek's Mule Story,   -   —   -   -   -   -   - 166

CHAPTER XII.

Setting up as a Family Man—First Love—Cut out by the Booshway— Reward of Constancy—Beauty of Umentucken—Her Dress, Her Horse and Equipments—Anecdotes of the Mountain Lamb—Her Quarrel with The Trapper—Capture by Crows—Her Rescue—Meek Avenges an Insult—A Row in Camp—The Female Element—Death of Umentucken, 175

CHAPTER XIII.

PAGE.

Visitors at Rendezvous—Advent of Missionaries—What Brought Them—
Bonneville's account of the Nez Perces and Flatheads—An Enthusiastic
View of Their Characters—Origin of some of Their Religious Observances—An Indian's Idea of a God—Material Good Desired—Mistake
of the Missionaries—First Sermon in the Rocky Mountains—Interrupted
by Buffaloes—Precept and Example—Dr. Whitman's Character—The
Missionaries Separate—Dr. Whitman Returns to the States, -   - 181

CHAPTER XIV.

Meek Falls into the Hands of Crows—The Story as He tells It—He Packs
Moccasins, and Bears the Jeers of the Fair Sex—Bridger's Camp Dis-
covered and the Lie Found out—A Desperate Situation—Signaling the
Horse-Guard—A Parley with Bridger—Successful Strategy—Capture
of Little-Gun—Meek Set at Liberty with a New Name—A Fort Be-
sieged by Bears—A Lazy Trapper—The Decoy of the Delawares—
Winter Amusements — The Ishmaelite of the Wilderness — March
through the Crow Country—Return to Green River—Punishment of the
Bannacks—Consolidation—An Excursion—Intercepted by Crows—A
Scattered Camp—The Escape,   -   -   —   -   - 189

CHAPTER XV.

An Express from Fitzpatrick—The Approach of Missionaries Announced—The Caravan Welcomed by a Party of Trappers—Noisy Demonstrations—Curiosity of the Indians—The Missionary Ladies—Preparations
in the Indian Villages—Reception of the Missionaries by the Nez Perces
and Flatheads—Kind Treatment from the Hudson's Bay Company—
The Missionaries' Land of Promise—Visit to Fort Vancouver—Selection
of Missionary Stations,   -   -   -   -   -   - 201

CHAPTER XVI.

The Den of Rattlesnakes—The Old Frenchman—How to Keep Snakes
out of Bed—The Prairie Dog's Tenants at Will—Fight with Blackfeet—
Policy of War—A Duel Averted—A Run-away Bear—Meek's Best Bear
Fight—Winter Quarters on Powder River—Robbing Bonneville's Men, 214

CHAPTER XVII.

A Dissipated Camp—A Crow Carousal—Picked Crows—A Fight with
Blackfeet—Manhead Killed—Night Visit to the Blackfoot Village—
"Cooning a River"—Stanley the Indian Painter—Desperate Fight
with Blackfeet—"The Trapper's Last Shot"—War and Peace—In the
Wrong Camp—To Rendezvous on Wind River—Mr. Gray, and His
Adventures — Massacre of Indian Allies — Capt. Stuart Robbed by
Crows—Newell's Address to the Chiefs,   -   -   -   - 225

CHAPTER XVIII.

PAGE.

Decline of the Fur Trade—Wild Scenes at Rendezvous—A Missionary Party—Entertained by a War Dance—Meek in Armor—Deserted by his Indian Spouse—The Pursuit—Meek abuses a Missionary and Kidnaps his Wife—Meek's Black Eyed Daughter—Singing for a Biscuit—Trapping Again—A hot March, and Fearful Suffering from Thirst—The Old Flathead Woman—Water at Last, - - . - - 237

CHAPTER XIX.

A Chat about Buffalo Hunting—Buffalo Horses—The Start—The Pursuit—The Charge—Tumbles—Horsemanship—The Glory of Mountain Life—How a Nez Perce Village Hunts Buffalo—Kit Carson and the Frenchman on a Run—Mountain Manners, - - - - 246

CHAPTER XX.

The Solitary Trapper—A Jest—Among the Nez Perces—Their Eagerness to be Taught—Meek is Called upon to Preach—He modestly Complies—Asks for a Wife — Polygamy Defended — Meek Gets a Wife—The Preacher's Salary—Surprised by Blackfeet—Death of Allen—The Last Rendezvous—Anecdote of Shawnee Jim—The new Wife Missing—Meeting with Farnham—Cold and Famine—Succor and Food—Parties at Fort Crockett—Setting up in Trade—How Al. Saved His Bacon—Bad Times—War upon Horse Thieves—In Search of Adventures—Green River Canyon—Running Antelope—Gambling—Vain Hunt for Rendezvous—Reflections and Half-Resolves—The last Trapping Expedition, - - - - - - - - - 251

CHAPTER XXI.

A new Start in Life—Mountain-Men for Pioneers—Discovery of the Columbia River—What Capt. Gray Did—What Vancouver Did—The United States' Claim to Oregon—The Treaty of 1818—Plans for Colonizing Oregon—Yankee Enterprise—Hall J. Kelley—Ball and Tibbits—Execration of the H. B. Company—First Missionaries to the Wallamet—Their Reception—Three Points in the H. B. Co. Policy—The Political History of Oregon—Extracts from " Thirty Years in Congress "—Benton on the Oregon Claims—The Missionary Wedge—Character of Dr. John McLaughlin—Hospitalities of Fort Vancouver—The Mission Reinforced—Other Settlers in the Wallamet Valley—How they Regarded the Mission—The California Cattle Company—Distribution of Settlers, 264

CHAPTER XXII.

Westward Ho!—Opening Wagon Roads—Republicanism—Fat Pork for Preachers—Mission Work at Waiilatpu—Helen Mar—Off for the Wallamet—Wagons Left at Walla-Walla—The Dalles Mission — Indian

2

PAGE.

Prayers—The Missionaries and the Mountain-Men—The Impious Cana-
dian—Doing Penance—Down the Columbia—Trouble with Indians—
Arrival at the Wallamet—Hunger, and Dependence on Fort Vancouver—
Meeting Old Comrades—Settling on the Tualatin Plains—A disagreeable
Winter—Taking Claims—Who furnished the Seed Wheat,   -   - 279

CHAPTER XXIII.

Wealth of the Methodist Mission—Waste of Property—Influence on the
Indians—What the Mission Board Did for Oregon—A Natural Se-
quence—Policy of the Mission regarding Other Settlers—Memorial to
Congress—Trying Position of Dr. McLaughlin—How He Directed the
Power of the Hudson's Bay Company—Fear of Catholicism—The Mis-
sion Party and the American Party—The Story of Ewing Young—A
Historical Character—Some Opinions of the Writer—Position of the
Mountain-Men in Oregon.   -   -   -   -   -   - 288

CHAPTER XXIV.

Scarcity of Employment—Wilkes' Exploring Expedition—Meek Employed
as Pilot—Interchange of Courtesies at Vancouver—Unpleasant Re-
minder—Exploring the Cowelitz—Wilkes' Chronometer—Land Expedition to California—Meek Discharged—Gleaning Wheat—Fifty Miles
for an Axe—Visit to the New Mission—Praying for a Cow—The Great
Event of the Year—The "Star of Oregon"—Cargo of the "Thomas
Perkins"—Salvation of the Colony,   -   -   -   - 296

CHAPTER XXV.

The Brooding of Events—The Balance of Power—First Cargo for the
American Market—Fourth of July—An Indian Agent for Oregon—
Reception of Immigrants—Indian Agent no Governor—Dr. Whitman
Visits Washington—The "Ashburton Treaty"—Emigration from Missouri—Discontent of the Indians—Missionaries Threatened—Mrs. Whitman leaves Waiilatpu—Dr White Visits the Indians—A Code of Laws
for the Neż Perces—Cayuses avoid an Interview,   -   - 304

CHAPTER XXVI.

The Plot Thickens—Forms of Government Discussed—The Wolf Associa-
tion—Suspicions of the Canadians—A Committee Appointed—Their
Report Accepted—The Die Cast—Address of the Canadians—Officers
Elected—Meek Elected Sheriff—The Provisional Government—Notable
Laws—Indian Disturbances in the Upper Country—The Agent Leaves
for a Visit—Mr. Hines and Dr. McLaughlin—Dorio the wicked Half-
Breed—Account of the Indian Troubles—Particulars of the Indian Con-
ference—The Missionaries Warned,   -   -   -   - 316

CHAPTER XXVII.

PAGE.

Arrival of the Immigration at the Dalles—Wagons Abandoned—Condition of the People—Aid from the Hudson's Bay Company—Perils of the Columbia—Wreck of a Boat—Wonderful Escape—Trials of the New Colonists—The Generous Savage—The Barefoot Lawyer—Meek's Pumpkin—Privation of the Settlers—Going Shopping—No Mails—Education and Literary Societies—Attempt to Manufacture Ardent Spirits—Dilemma of the People—An Appeal to Dr. White—The Sheriff Destroys the Distillery—Anecdote of Dr. White and Madam Cooper—Meek Levies on Her Whisky—Meek and "The better Part of the Community"—First Official Act of the Sheriff, - - - - - 333

CHAPTER XXVIII.

Excitement about Indians—Dr. White's Flogging Law—Indian Revenge—Raid of the Klamaths—Massacre of Indians—Affray at the Falls—Death of Cockstock—Death of LeBreton and Rogers—Meek's Advice—His Policy with the Indians—Meek and the Agent—The Borrowed Horse—Success of the New Government—Ambitious Designs—Negroes and Liquors Interdicted—Taxation Opposed—Defeat of the Independent Party, - - - - - - - - - 347

CHAPTER XXIX.

The Oregon City Land-Claim—Enmity of the Mission to Dr. McLaughlin—His Possessory Rights—Attempts at a Settlement—Mr. Waller's Trifling—Double Dealings Extraordinary—Various Propositions—Ricord's Caveat—The Doctor's Devotions and Irritability—A Settlement Effected—The Several Parties—Uneasiness at Fort Vancouver—Desperate Characters—Dr. McLaughlin Asks for Protection—The Situation, 355

CHAPTER XXX.

The American Organization—Oath of Membership Modified—Dr. McLaughlin Unites with the Americans—Unwelcome Visitors at the Fort—The British Government Promise Protection—Disagreeable Results of Espionage—The English Officers—Wonderful Transformation—Temperance—Courts—Anecdote of Judge Nesmith—Memorial to Congress—Ludicrous Legislative Proceedings—Audacity Triumphant—Growth of Improvements—New Towns—Early Days of Portland—An Indian Carousal—Meek "Settles the Indians"—Reader's Query, and Answer—The Immigration of 1845—The Road-Hunters—Hunger and Peril—A Last Request—Succor at the Last Moment—A Reason for Patriotism, 364

CHAPTER XXXI.

Difficulty of Collecting Taxes—A Ponderous Currency—Dr. McLaughlin's Ox—An Exciting Year—Abrogation of the Treaty—The Boundary

PAGE.

Question—Fifty-Four-Forty or Fight—Caution of the Government—
War Vessels in the Columbia—Loss of the Shark—Meek Receives a
Salute—Schenck Arrested—The Color-Stand of the Shark—The Agony
Over—Terms of the New Treaty not Agreeable to the Oregonians—
Disappointment of the Hudson's Bay Company, -   -   -   - 377

CHAPTER XXXII.

Colonial Gossip—The Oregon Spectator—Overland Mail Special—Theat-
ricals on Board the Modeste—Literature of the Spectator—"The Adventures of a Columbia River Salmon"—History of the Immigration of
1846—Opening of the Southern Route—Tragic Fate of the California
Immigrants—Hardships of the Oregon Immigrants—The Cause—Tardy
Relief—Disappointment of the Colony—The Road-hunters Blamed—
Feuds in Consequence—Legislature for 1846—Meek and Newell Members—The Liquor Bill—Divorce Acts,   -   -   -   -   - 382

CHAPTER XXXIII.

The Beginning of Oregon Commerce—The Oregon Colony second only to
that of the Mayflower—The Foundations of a New State—Celebrating
the Fourth of July—Visit to the Ship Brutus—An Indignity Resented
with a Twelve-Pounder—Dr. McLaughlin Interferes—Re-election of
Meek—Large Immigration—Letter from Thomas H. Benton—Affray
between Immigrants and Indians at the Dalles—The Governor's Delegate to Congress—Manner of his Equipment—Stranded at San Juan—
Meeting of the Legislature—Falling of the Thunderbolt,   -   - 391

CHAPTER XXXIV.

The Up-Country Indians—Causes of Their Disquiet—Their Opinion of the
Americans—Their Feelings toward Dr. Whitman—Acts of Violence—
Influence of the Catholic Missionaries—What Provoked the Massacre—
Jo Lewis the Half-Breed—The Fatal Test—Sickness Among the Emi-
grants—Dr. Whitman's Family—Persons at the Mission and Mill—
Night Visit to the Umatilla—The Warning of Stickas and His Family—
The Death Song—Meeting with Brouillet—News of the Massacre—Mr.
Spalding's Night Journeys,   -   -   -   -   -   - 400

CHAPTER XXXV.

The Tragedy at Waiilatpu—Dr. Whitman's Arrival at Home—The Com-
mencement of the Massacre—Horrors of the Attack—Shooting of Mrs.
Whitman—Treachery of a Chief—Sufferings of the Children—The Two
Compassionate Indians—Escape of Mr. Osborne and Family—Escape
and Fate of Mr. Hall—Cruel Treatment of Fugitives—Sufferings of Mr.
Osborne's Family—Fears of McBean—Kindness of Stickas,   -   - 410

CHAPTER XXXVI.

PAGE.

Horrors of the Waiilatpu Massacre—Exemption of the Catholics—Charges of the Protestants—Natural Suspicions—Further Particulars of the Massacre—Cruelty to the Children—Fate of the Young Women—Miss Bulee and the Priests—Lapwai Mission—Arrival of Mr. Camfield—An Indian Trait—Heroism of Mrs. Spalding—Appeal to the Chiefs—Arrival of the News—Lapwai Plundered—Treachery of Joseph—Arrival of Mr. Spalding—Detained as Hostages—Ransomed by the H. B. Company— The "Blood of the Martyrs"—Country Abandoned to the Indians— Subsequent Return of Mr. Spalding to the Nez Perces, - - - 419

CHAPTER XXXVII.

The Call to Arms—Meetings and Speeches—Ways and Means of Defence—The first Regiment of Oregon Riflemen—Messenger to the Governor of California—Meek Chosen Messenger to the President of the United States—He Proceeds to the Dalles—The Army Marches to Waiilatpu—A Skirmish with the Des Chutes—Burial of the Victims— Meek Escorted to the Blue Mountains, - - - - - 428

CHAPTER XXXVIII.

Meek's Party—Precautions against Indians—Meeting with Bannacks— White Lies—Fort Hall—Deep Snows—Horses Abandoned—The Mountain Spirit Returning—Meeting with Peg-Leg Smith—A Mountain Revel—Meeting with An Old Leader—Reception at Fort Laramie— Passing the Sioux Village—Courtesy of a French Trader—Reflections on Nearing the Settlements—Resolve to Remain Joe Meek—Reception at St. Joseph—"The Quickest Trip Yet"—Arrival at St. Louis—Meek as Steamboat Runner—Interview with the Stage Agent at Wheeling— Astonishing the Natives—The Puzzled Conductor—Arrival at Washington, - - - - - - - - - 434

CHAPTER XXXIX.

Meek Dines at Coleman's—A Sensation—An Amusing Scene—Recognized by Senator Underwood—Visit to the President—Cordial Reception by the Family of Polk—Some Doubts of Himself—Rapid Recovery of Self-Possession—Action of the Friends of Oregon—The Two Oregon Representatives—The Oregon Bill in the Senate—Benton's Speech— Meek's Successful Debut in Society—Curiosity of Ladies—Kit Carson and the "Contingent Fund"—Meek's Remarkable Popularity—Invited to Baltimore by the City Council—Escorts the President—Visit to Lowell—The Factory Girls—Some Natural Regrets—Kindness of Mrs. Polk and Mrs. Walker—Commodore Wilkes—Oregon Lies—Getting Franked—Champagne Suppers, - - - - - 447

CHAPTER XL.

PAGE.

Mr. Thornton as Representative of Oregon—The Territorial Bill—How Obnoxious to the South—The Friends and Enemies of the Bill—The Land Bill—The Last Chance—Scene between Butler and Benton—Speech of Senator Foote—A Tedious Night—The Territorial Bill Passed—Failure of the Land Bill—What Became of It, - - - 463

CHAPTER XLI.

Meek Appointed U. S. Marshal for Oregon—"Home Sweet Home"—Pay of the Delegates—The Lion's Share—Meek's Interview with Gov. Lane—Buying out a Peddler—The Escort of Riflemen—The Start from St. Louis, and the Route—Meeting Price's Army—An Adventure and a Pleasant Surprise—Leaving the Wagons—Desertion of Soldiers—Drought—The Trick of the Yumas—Demoralization of the Train—Rumors of Gold—Gen. Lane's Coffee—The Writer's Reflection—The Party on Foot—Extreme Sufferings—Arrival at William's Ranch—Speculation in Silks and Jack-Knives—Miners at Los Angelos—Oregonians at San Francisco—Nat Lane and Meek Take the Gold Fever—Meek's Investment—The Governor and Marshal Quarrel—Pranks with a Jew—A Salute—Arrival in Oregon City, - - - 469

CHAPTER XLII.

If This Were a Novel—The Dropped Threads of Our Story—Gov. Lane's Proclamation—One Day under Polk—Condition of Oregon—The Honolulu and Her Captain—The Gold Excitement—Deserted Harvest Fields—Sudden Prosperity of Oregon—Gradual Relapse, and the Cause—The Three Parties—Resignation of Dr. McLaughlin—His Wish to Become an American Citizen—Complications of His Case—Mr. Thurston, Delegate to Congress—The Story of the Donation Act—Death of the Doctor, - - - - - - - 482

CHAPTER XLIII.

Lane's Course with the Cayuse Indians—Magnanimity of the Savages—Rebuke to Their Captors—Their Statements to Meek—The Puzzle of Indian Ethics—Incidents of the Trial and Execution—State of the Upper Country for A Term of Years—How Meek Was Received in Oregon—His Incurable Waggishness—Scene in a Court-Room—Contempt of Court—Judge Nelson and the Carpenters—Two Hundred Lies—An Excursion by the Oregon Court—Indians Tried for Murder—Proceedings of a Jury—Sentence and Execution of the Indians—The Chief's Wife—Cost of Proceedings—Lane's Career in Oregon—Gov. Davis, 493

CHAPTER XLIV.

PAGE.

Meek as U. S. Marshal—The Captain of the Melvin—The British Smuggler—Returning a Compliment—"Barly Enough for the Officers of the Court"—Misused Confidence—Indian Disturbances—The Indian War of 1855-6—Gen Wool and Gov. Curry—Officers of the War—How the Volunteers Fared—Meek as a Volunteer—Feasting and Fun—"Marking Time"—End of Meek's Public Career—His Stern Loyalty in Contrast with Lane's Disloyalty—His Present Life—Treatment of a "Preacher"—Hope of the Future, - - - - - - 503

CHAPTER XLV.

The Northern Pacific Railroad—WESTERN OREGON—The Wallamet River and Valley—The Falls of the Wallamet—The Umpqua Valley—The Rogue River Valley—The Coast Country—The Dairy Region of the Pacific Coast—Varieties of Soil—Climate and Temperature—Productions and Natural Resources — Fruit Growing—Native Grasses—Shrubbery—Price of Lands—Sheep Raising and Woolen Goods—Trees and Lumbering—Turpentine, Tar, and Rosin—Fish and Fisheries—Game—Salt—Coal—Iron—Lead—Copper—Gold and Silver—Grain—Flax and Hemp—Tobacco—Hops—Honey—EASTERN OREGON—Impressions of Early Emigrants—Aspect of the Country—Waste Lands—Sage Deserts—Valleys and Plains—The Blue Mountains—Soil and Productions—The Klamath Basin—Sprague's River Valley—Goose Lake Valley—Surprise Valley—Oases in the Desert—The Des Chutes, John Day, Umatilla, Grande Ronde, and Powder Rivers and Valleys—Climate and Resources of Eastern Oregon - - Stock-Ranches—Fruit Orchards—Vineyards—Corn and Sorghum—Flax and Wool—Mineral Wealth—Area and Population of Oregon, - - - - 513

CHAPTER XLVI.

WASHINGTON TERRITORY—Area and Population—The Cowelitz River—The Cascade Range—Mount Olympus—The Cowelitz Prairie—The Future of Washington—The Strait of San Juan De Fuca—Admiralty Inlet—Hood's Canal—PUGET SOUND—Its Advantages as a Great Naval Depot—Material for Ship Building—Ample Room and Safe Anchorage—The Lumbering Interests—Large Saw Mills—Immense Forests—Magnificent Trees—Coal Mines—Fisheries—The Coast Counties—Shoal Water Bay—Cape Hancock—Markets for Agricultural Products—A Great Maritime City to Grow up at the Terminus of the Northern Pacific Railroad—Southern and Eastern Washington—The Cowelitz, Lewis, and Lake River Valleys—Excellent Fruit, Grain, and Dairy Regions—The Walla-Walla Valley, - - - - 554

CONTENTS.

CHAPTER XLVII.

THE COLUMBIA RIVER—Its Scenery, Extent, and Resources—Point
Adams—Fort Stevens—The Bar—Astoria—Shipping of the Lower Co-
lumbia—Monticello—St. Helen—Junction with the Wallamet—Sauvies
Island—Vancouver—The Cascade Range — The Heart of the Moun-
tains—Railroad Portage—Magnificent Scenery—The Cascades—Castle
Rock — Indian Tradition — Stupendous Bluffs — Precipitous Cliffs—
Grandeur of the Mountains—A Terrible Passage—Wind Mountain—
Hood River—Mt. Hood—Mt. Adams—The Dalles of the Columbia—
Wildness of the Scenery—Dalles City—Second Railroad Portage—
Celilo—Immense Warehouses—The Rapids—The Des Chutes River—
Columbus — Umatilla — Wallula — The Walla-Walla River — Walla-
Walla City,—White Bluffs—Colville—Northern Branches of the Colum-
bia—A Region of Mineral and Agricultural Wealth—Lewiston, Idaho—
The Oregon Steam Navigation Company—Scenery of Snake River—
The American Falls—Tributaries of Snake River—Rich Mineral Dis-
tricts—Fertile Valleys, and Excellent Timber—Changing Aspect of the
Country—Facilities for Emigrants,   -   -   -   -   - 564

CHAPTER XLVIII.

MONTANA TERRITORY—First Discovery of Gold—Extract from the
Report of Gov. Stevens—The Valleys of the Cour d'Alene and Spokane—
The Cour d'Alene Prairie—The Bitter Root Valley—Hell Gate Pass—
Deer Lodge Prairie—The Little Blackfoot—Flint Creek—The Hell
Gate River—Flathead Lake—Clarke's Fork—Hot Spring Creek—
Pend d' Oreille Lake—Estimates of the Areas of Arable Land—A
Beautiful Country—Agricultural Advantages—The Climate—The Fa-
vorite Wintering Grounds of the Fur Hunters—Mineral and Lumbering
Resources,   -   -   -   -   -   -   -   - 582

CHAPTER XLIX.

General Remarks on the North-west—Varieties of Climate and Temperature
—The Mild Climate of the Rocky Mountains in Montana—Captain Mul-
lan's Theory Respecting It—The Isochimenal Line Across the Conti-
nent—Reclamation of Dry Lands by Irrigation—Productiveness of the
Soil—Gigantic Trees and Ferns—Unfailing Harvests—The Foot-Hills
of the Mountains—Meadows and Uplands—Elements of the Grand and
Wonderful—The Cascade Mountains—Their Solitary Wonders—Awful
Chasms—Description of a Mountain Lake—Unequalled Scenery—Com-
mercial Condition and Advantages—Need of Capital and Railroads—
Probable Railroad Routes—The Oregon Central Railroad—Proposed
Branch from the Union Pacific Railroad—The Northern Pacific Rail-
road,   -   -   -   -   -   -   -   -   - 589

PREFATORY CHAPTER.

AN ACCOUNT OF THE HUDSON'S BAY COMPANY'S INTERCOURSE WITH THE
INDIANS OF THE NORTH-WEST COAST; WITH A SKETCH OF THE DIFFER-
ENT AMERICAN FUR COMPANIES, AND THEIR DEALINGS WITH THE
TRIBES OF THE ROCKY MOUNTAINS.

IN the year 1818, Mr. Prevost, acting for the United States, received Astoria
back from the British, who had taken possession, as narrated by Mr. Irving,
four years previous. The restoration took place in conformity with the treaty
of Ghent, by which those places captured during the war were restored to their
original possessors. Mr. Astor stood ready at that time to renew his enterprise
on the Columbia River, had Congress been disposed to grant him the necessary
protection which the undertaking required. Failing to secure this, when the
United States sloop of war Ontario sailed away from Astoria, after having
taken formal possession of that place for our Government, the country was left to
the occupancy, (scarcely a joint-occupancy, since there were then no Americans
here,) of the British traders. After the war, and while negotiations were
going on between Great Britain and the United States, the fort at Astoria had
remained in possession of the North-West Company, as their principal establishment west of the mountains. It had been considerably enlarged since it had
come into their possession, and was furnished with artillery enough to have
frightened into friendship a much more warlike people than the subjects of old
king Comcomly; who, it will be remembered, was not at first very well disposed
towards the "King George men," having learned to look upon the "Boston
men" as his friends in his earliest intercourse with the whites. At this time
Astoria, or *Fort George*, as the British traders called it, contained sixty-five
inmates, twenty-three of whom were whites, and the remainder Candian half-
breeds and Sandwich Islanders. Besides this number of men, there were a few
women, the native wives of the men, and their half-breed offspring. The situation of Astoria, however, was not favorable, being near the sea coast, and not
surrounded with good farming lands such as were required for the furnishing
of provisions to the fort. Therefore, when in 1821 it was destroyed by fire, it
was only in part rebuilt, but a better and more convenient location for the head-
quarters of the North-West Company was sought for in the interior.

About this time a quarrel of long standing between the Hudson's Bay and
North-West Companies culminated in a battle between their men in the Red

River country, resulting in a considerable loss of life and property. This affair drew the attention of the Government at home; the rights of the rival companies were examined into, the mediation of the Ministry secured, and a compromise effected, by which the North-West Company, which had succeeded in dispossessing the Pacific Fur Company under Mr. Astor, was merged into the Hudson's Bay Company, whose name and fame are so familiar to all the early settlers of Oregon.

At the same time, Parliament passed an act by which the hands of the consolidated company were much strengenthed, and the peace and security of all persons greatly insured; but which became subsequently, in the joint occupancy of the country, a cause of offence to the American citizens, as we shall see hereafter. This act allowed the commissioning of Justices of the Peace in all the territories not belonging to the United States, nor already subject to grants. These justices were to execute and enforce the laws and decisions of the courts of Upper Canada; to take evidence, and commit and send to Canada for trial the guilty; and even in some cases, to hold courts themselves for the trial of criminal offences and misdemeanors not punishable with death, or of civil causes in which the amount at issue should not exceed two hundred pounds.

Thus in 1824, the North-West Company, whose perfidy had occasioned such loss and mortification to the enterprising New York merchant, became itself a thing of the past, and a new rule began in the region west of the Rocky Mountains. The old fort at Astoria having been only so far rebuilt as to answer the needs of the hour, after due consideration, a site for head-quarters was selected about one hundred miles from the sea, near the mouth of the Wallamet River, though opposite to it. Three considerations went to make up the eligibility of the point selected. First, it was desirable, even necessary, to settle upon good agricultural lands, where the Company's provisions could be raised by the Company's servants. Second, it was important that the spot chosen should be upon waters navigable for the Company's vessels, or upon tide-water. Lastly, and not leastly, the Company had an eye to the boundary question between Great Britain and the United States; and believing that the end of the controversy would probably be to make the Columbia River the northern limit of the United States territory, a spot on the northern bank of that river was considered a good point for their fort, and possible future city.

The site chosen by the North-West Company in 1821, for their new fort, combined all these advantages, and the further one of having been already commenced and named. Fort Vancouver became at once on the accession of the Hudson's Bay Company, the metropolis of the northwest coast, the center of the fur trade, and the seat of government for that immense territory, over which roamed the hunters and trappers in the employ of that powerful corporation. This post was situated on the edge of a beautiful sloping plain on the northern bank of the Columbia, about six miles above the upper mouth of the Wallamet. At this point the Columbia spreads to a great width, and is divided on the south side into bayous by long sandy islands, covered with oak, ash, and cotton-wood trees, making the noble river more attractive still by adding the charm of curiosity concerning its actual breadth to its natural and ordinary magnificence. Back of the fort the land rose gently, covered with forests of fir; and away to the east swelled the foot-hills of the Cascade range, then the mountains themselves, draped in filmy azure, and over-topped five thousand feet by the snowy cone of Mt. Hood.

In this lonely situation grew up, with the dispatch which characterized the acts of the Company, a fort in most respects similar to the original one at Astoria. It was not, however, thought necessary to make so great a display of artillery as had served to keep in order the subjects of Comcomly. A stockade enclosed a space about eight hundred feet long by five hundred broad, having a bastion at one corner, where were mounted three guns, while two eighteen pounders and two swivels were planted in front of the residence of the Governor and chief factors. These commanded the main entrance to the fort, besides which there were two other gates in front, and another in the rear. Military precision was observed in the precautions taken against surprises, as well as in all the rules of the place. The gates were opened and closed at certain hours, and were always guarded. No large number of Indians were permitted within the enclosure at the same time, and every employee at the fort knew and performed his duty with punctuality.

The buildings within the stockade were the Governor's and chief factors' residences, stores, offices, work-shops, magazines, warehouses, &c.

Year by year, up to 1835 or '40, improvements continued to go on in and about the fort, the chief of which was the cultivation of the large farm and garden outside the enclosure, and the erection of a hospital building, large barns, servants' houses, and a boat-house, all outside of the fort; so that at the period when the Columbia River was a romance and a mystery to the people of the United States, quite a flourishing and beautiful village adorned its northern shore, and that too erected and sustained by the enemies of American enterprise on soil commonly believed to belong to the United States: fair foes the author firmly believes them to have been in those days, yet foes nevertheless.

The system on which the Hudson's Bay Company conducted its business was the result of long experience, and was admirable for its method and its justice also. When a young man entered its service as a clerk, his wages were small for several years, increasing only as his ability and good conduct entitled him to advancement. When his salary had reached one hundred pounds sterling he became eligible to a chief-tradership as a partner in the concern, from which position he was promoted to the rank of a chief factor. No important business was ever intrusted to an inexperienced person, a policy which almost certainly prevented any serious errors. A regular tariff was established on the Company's goods, comprising all the articles used in their trade with the Indians; nor was the quality of their goods ever allowed to deteriorate. A price was also fixed upon furs according to their market value, and an Indian knowing this, knew exactly what he could purchase. No bartering was allowed. When skins were offered for sale at the fort they were handed to the clerk through a window like a post-office delivery-window, and their value in the article desired, returned through the same aperture. All these regulations were of the highest importance to the good order, safety, and profit of the Company. The confidence of the Indians was sure to be gained by the constancy and good faith always observed toward them, and the Company obtained thereby numerous and powerful allies in nearly all the tribes.

As soon as it was possible to make the change, the Indians were denied the use of intoxicating drinks, the appetite for which had early been introduced among them by coasting vessels, and even continued by the Pacific Fur Company at Astoria. It would have been dangerous to have suddenly deprived them of the coveted stimulus; therefore the practice must be discontinued by many wise arts and devices. A public notice was given that the sale of it would be stopped, and the reasons for this prohibition explained to the Indians. Still, not to come into direct conflict with their appetites, a little was sold to the chiefs, now and then, by the clerks, who affected to be running the greatest risks in violating the order of the company. The strictest secrecy was enjoined on the lucky chief who, by the friendship of some under-clerk, was enabled to smuggle off a bottle under his blanket. But the cunning clerk had generally managed to get his "good friend" into a state so cleverly between drunk and sober, before he entrusted him with the precious bottle, that he was sure to betray himself. Leaving the shop with a mien even more erect than usual, with a gait affected in its majesty, and his blanket tightened around him to conceal his secret treasure, the chuckling chief would start to cross the grounds within the fort. If he was a new customer, he was once or twice permitted to play his little game with the obliging clerk whose particular friend he was, and to escape detection.

But by-and-by, when the officers had seen the offence repeated more than once from their purposely contrived posts of observation, one of them would skillfully chance to intercept the guilty chief at whose comical endeavors to appear sober he was inwardly laughing, and charge him with being intoxicated. Wresting away the tightened blanket, the bottle appeared as evidence that could not be controverted, of the duplicity of the Indian and the unfaithfulness of the clerk, whose name was instantly demanded, that he might be properly punished. When the chief again visited the fort, his particular friend met him with a sorrowful countenance, reproaching him for having been the cause of his disgrace and loss. This reproach was the surest means of preventing another demand for rum, the Indian being too magnanimous, probably, to wish to get his friend into trouble; while the clerk affected to fear the consequences too much to be induced to take the risk another time. Thus by kind and careful means the traffic in liquors was at length broken up, which otherwise would have ruined both Indian and trader.

To the company's servants liquor was sold or allowed at certain times: to those on the sea-board, one half-pint two or three times a year, to be used as medicine,—not that it was always needed or used for this purpose, but too strict inquiry into its use was wisely avoided,—and for this the company demanded pay. To their servants in the interior no liquor was sold, but they were furnished as a gratuity with one pint on leaving rendezvous, and another on arriving at winter quarters. By this management, it became impossible for them to dispose of drink to the Indians; their small allowance being always immediately consumed in a meeting or parting carouse.

The arrival of men from the interior at Fort Vancouver usually took place in the month of June, when the Columbia was high, and a stirring scene it was. The chief traders generally contrived their march through the upper country, their camps, and their rendezvous, so as to meet the Express which annually came to Vancouver from Canada and the Red River settlements. They then descended the Columbia together, and arrived in force at the Fort. This annual fleet went by the name of Brigade—a name which suggested a military spirit in the crews that their appearance failed to vindicate. Yet, though there was nothing warlike in the scene, there was much that was exciting, picturesque, and even brilliant; for these *couriers de bois*, or wood-rangers, and the *voyageurs*, or boatmen, were the most foppish of mortals when they came to rendezvous. Then, too, there was an exaltation of spirits on their safe arrival at head-quarters, after their year's toil and danger in wildernesses, among Indians and wild beasts, exposed to famine and accident, that almost deprived them of what is called "common sense," and compelled them to the most fantastic excesses.

Their well-understood peculiarities did not make them the less welcome at Vancouver. When the cry was given—"the Brigade! the Brigade!"—there was a general rush to the river's bank to witness the spectacle. In advance came the chief-trader's barge, with the company's flag at the bow, and the cross of St. George at the stern: the fleet as many abreast as the turnings of the river allowed. With strong and skillful strokes the boatmen governed their richly laden boats, keeping them in line, and at the same time singing in chorus a loud and not unmusical hunting or boating song. The gay ribbons and feathers with which the singers were bedecked took nothing from the picturesqueness of their appearance. The broad, full river, sparkling in the sunlight, gemmed with emerald islands, and bordered with a rich growth of flowering shrubbery; the smiling plain surrounding the Fort; the distant mountains, where glittered the sentinel Mt. Hood, all came gracefully into the picture, and seemed to furnish a fitting back-ground and middle distance for the bright bit of coloring given by the moving life in the scene. As with a skillful sweep the brigade touched the bank, and the traders and men sprang on shore, the first cheer which had welcomed their appearance was heartily repeated, while a gay clamor of questions and answers followed.

After the business immediately incident to their arrival had been dispatched, then took place the regale of pork, flour, and spirits, which was sure to end in a carouse, during which blackened eyes and broken noses were not at all uncommon; but though blood was made to flow, life was never put seriously in peril, and the belligerent parties were the best of friends when the fracas was ended.

The business of exchange being completed in three or four weeks—the rich stores of peltries consigned to their places in the warehouse, and the boats re-laden with goods for the next year's trade with the Indians in the upper country, a parting carouse took place, and with another parade of feathers, ribbons, and other finery, the brigade departed with songs and cheers as it had come, but with probably heavier hearts.

It would be a stern morality indeed which could look upon the excesses of this peculiar class as it would upon the same excesses committed by men in the enjoyment of all the comforts and pleasures of civilized life. For them, during most of the year, was only an out-door life of toil, watchfulness, peril, and isolation. When they arrived at the rendezvous, for the brief period of their stay they were allowed perfect license because nothing else would content them. Although at head-quarters they were still in the wilderness, thousands of miles from civilization, with no chance of such recreations as men in the continual enjoyment of life's sweetest pleasures would naturally seek. For them there was only one method of seeking and finding temporary oblivion of the accustomed hardship; and whatever may be the strict rendering of man's duty as an immortal being, we cannot help being somewhat lenient at times to his errors as a mortal.

After the departure of the boats, there was another arrival at the Fort, of trappers from the Snake River county. Previous to 1832, such were the dangers of the fur trade in this region, that only the most experienced traders were suffered to conduct a party through it; and even they were frequently attacked, and sometimes sustained serious losses of men and animals. Subsequently, however, the Hudson's Bay Company obtained such an influence over even these hostile tribes as to make it safe for a party of no more than two of their men to travel through this much dreaded region.

There was another important arrival at Fort Vancouver, usually in mid-summer. This was the Company's supply ship from London. In the possible event of a vessel being lost, one cargo was always kept on store at Vancouver; but for which wise regulation much trouble and disaster might have resulted, especially in the early days of the establishment. Occasionally a vessel foundered at sea or was lost on the bar of the Columbia; but these losses did not interrupt the regular transaction of business. The arrival of a ship from London was the occasion of great bustle and excitement also. She brought not only goods for the posts throughout the district of the Columbia, but letters, papers, private parcels, and all that seemed of so much value to the little isolated world at the Fort.

A company conducting its business with such method and regularity as has been described, was certain of success. Yet some credit also must attach to certain individuals in its service, whose faithfulness, zeal, and ability in carrying out its designs, contributed largely to its welfare. Such a man was at the head of the Hudson's Bay Company's affairs in the large and important district west of the Rocky Mountains. The Company never had in its service a more efficient man than Gov. John McLaughlin, more commonly called Dr. McLaughlin.

To the discipline, at once severe and just, which Dr. McLaughlin maintained in his district, was due the safety and prosperity of the company he served, and the servants of that company generally; as well as, at a later period, of the emigration which followed the hunter and trapper into the wilds of Oregon.

Careful as were all the officers of the Hudson's Bay Company, they could not always avoid conflicts with the Indians; nor was their kindness and justice always sufficiently appreciated to prevent the outbreak of savage instincts. Fort Vancouver had been threatened in an early day; a vessel or two had been lost in which the Indians were suspected to have been implicated; at long intervals a trader was murdered in the interior; or more frequently, Indian insolence put to the test both the wisdom and courage of the officers to prevent an outbreak.

When murders and robberies were committed, it was the custom at Fort Vancouver to send a strong party to demand the offenders from their tribe; Such was the well known power and influence of the Company, and such the wholesome fear of the "King George men," that this demand was never resisted, and if the murderer could be found he was given up to be hung according to "King George" laws. They were almost equally impelled to good conduct by the state of dependence on the company into which they had been brought. Once they had subsisted and clothed themselves from the spoils of the rivers and forest; since they had tasted of the tree of knowledge of good and evil, they could no more return to skins for raiment, nor to game alone for food. Blankets and flour, beads, guns, and ammunition had become dear to their hearts: for all these things they must love and obey the Hudson's Bay Company. Another fine stroke of policy in the Company was to destroy the chieftain-ships in the various tribes; thus weakening them by dividing them and preventing dangerous coalitions of the leading spirits: for in savage as well as civilized life, the many are governed by the few.

It may not be uninteresting in this place to give a few anecdotes of the manner in which conflicts with the Indians were prevented, or offences punished by the Hudson's Bay Company. In the year 1828 the ship *William and Ann* was cast away just inside the bar of the Columbia, under circumstances which seemed to direct suspicion to the Indians in that vicinity. Whether or not they had attacked the ship, not a soul was saved from the wreck to tell how she was lost. On hearing that the ship had gone to pieces, and that the Indians had appropriated a portion of her cargo, Dr. McLaughlin sent a message to the chiefs, demanding restitution of the stolen goods. Nothing was returned by the messenger except one or two worthless articles. Immediately an armed force was sent to the scene of the robbery with a fresh demand for the goods, which the chiefs, in view of their spoils, thought proper to resist by firing upon the reclaiming party. But they were not unprepared; and a swivel was discharged to let the savages know what they might expect in the way of fire-arms. The argument was conclusive, the Indians fleeing into the woods. While making search for the goods, a portion of which were found, a chief was observed skulking near, and cocking his gun; on which motion one of the men fired, and he fell. This prompt action, the justice of which the Indians well understood, and the intimidating power of the swivel, put an end to the incipient war. Care was then taken to impress upon their minds that they must not expect to profit by the disasters of vessels, nor be tempted to murder white men for the sake of plunder. The *William and Ann* was supposed to have got aground, when the savages seeing her situation, boarded her and murdered the crew for the cargo which they knew her to contain. Yet as there were no positive proofs, only such measures were taken as would deter them from a similar attempt in future. That the lesson was not lost, was proven two years later, when the *Isabella*, from London, struck on the bar, her crew deserting her. In this instance no attempt was made to meddle with the vessel's cargo; and as the crew made their way to Vancouver, the goods were nearly all saved.

In a former voyage of the *William and Ann* to the Columbia River, she had been sent on an exploring expedition to the Gulf of Georgia to discover the mouth of Frazier's River, having on board a crew of forty men. Whenever the ship came to anchor, two sentries were kept constantly on deck to guard against any surprise or misconduct on the part of the Indians; so adroit, however, were they in the light-fingered art, that every one of the eight cannon with which the ship was armed was robbed of its ammunition, as was discovered on leaving the river! Such incidents as these served to impress the minds of the Company's officers and servants with the necessity of vigilance in their dealings with the savages.

Not all their vigilance could at all times avail to prevent mischief. When Sir George Simpson, Governor of the Hudson's Bay Company, was on a visit to Vancouver in 1829, he was made aware of this truism. The Governor was on his return to Canada by way of the Red River Settlement, and had reached the Dalles of the Columbia with his party. In making the portage at this place, all the party except Dr. Tod gave their guns into the charge of two men to prevent their being stolen by the Indians, who crowded about, and whose well-known bad character made great care needful. All went well, no attempt to seize either guns or other property being made until at the end of the portage the boats had been reloaded. As the party were about to re-embark, a simultaneous rush was made by the Indians who had dogged their steps, to get possession of the boats. Dr. Tod raised his gun immediately, aiming at the head chief, who, not liking the prospect of so speedy dissolution, ordered his followers to desist, and the party were suffered to escape. It was soon after discovered that every gun belonging to the party in the boat had been wet, excepting the one carried by Dr. Tod; and to the fact that the Doctor did carry his gun, all the others owed their lives.

The great desire of the Indians for guns and ammunition led to many stratagems which were dangerous to the possessors of the coveted articles. Much more dangerous would it have been to have allowed them a free supply of these things; nor could an Indian purchase from the Company more than a stated supply, which was to be used, not for the purposes of war, but to keep himself in game.

Dr. McLaughlin was himself once quite near falling into a trap of the Indians, so cunningly laid as to puzzle even him. This was a report brought to him by a deputation of Columbia River Indians, stating the startling fact that the fort at Nesqually had been attacked, and every inmate slaughtered. To this horrible story, told with every appearance of truth, the Doctor listened with incredulity mingled with apprehension. The Indians were closely questioned and cross-questioned, but did not conflict in their testimony. The matter assumed a very painful aspect. Not to be deceived, the Doctor had the unwelcome messengers committed to custody while he could bring other witnesses from their tribe. But they were prepared for this, and the whole tribe were as positive as those who brought the tale. Confounded by this cloud of witnesses, Dr. McLaughlin had almost determined upon sending an armed force to Nesqually to inquire into the matter, and if necessary, punish the Indians, when a detachment of men arrived from that post, and the plot was exposed! The design of the Indians had been simply to cause a division of the force at Vancouver, after which they believed they might succeed in capturing and plundering the fort. Had they truly been successful in this undertaking, every other trading-post in the country would have been destroyed. But so long as the head-quarters of the Company remained secure and powerful, the other stations were comparatively safe.

An incident which has been several times related, occurred at fort Walla-Walla, and shows how narrow escapes the interior traders sometimes made. The hero of this anecdote was Mr. McKinlay, one of the most estimable of the Hudson's Bay Company's officers, in charge of the fort just named. An Indian was one day lounging about the fort, and seeing some timbers lying in a heap that had been squared for pack saddles, he'ped himself to one and commenced cutting it down into a whip handle for his own use. To this procedure Mr. McKinlay's clerk demurred, first telling the Indian its use, and then ordering him to resign the piece of timber. The Indian insolently replied that the timber was his, and he should take it. At this the clerk, with more temper than prudence, struck the offender, knocking him over, soon after which the savage left the fort with sullen looks boding vengeance. The next day Mr. McKinlay, not being informed of what had taken place, was in a room of the fort with his clerk when a considerable party of Indians began dropping quietly in until there were fifteen or twenty of them inside the building. The first intimation of anything wrong McKinlay received was when he observed the clerk pointed out in a particular manner by one of the party. He instantly comprehended the purpose of his visitors, and with that quickness of thought which is habitual to the student of savage nature, he rushed into the store room and returned with a powder keg, flint and steel. By this time the unlucky clerk was struggling for his life with his vindictive foes. Putting down the powder in their midst and knocking out the head of the keg with a blow, McKinlay stood over it ready to strike fire with his flint and steel. The savages paused aghast. They knew the nature of the "perilous stuff," and also understood the trader's purpose. "Come," said he with a clear, determined voice, "you are twenty braves against us two: now touch him if you dare, and see who dies first " In a moment the fort was cleared, and McKinlay was left to inquire the cause of what had so nearly been a tragedy. It is hardly a subject of doubt whether or not his clerk got a scolding. Soon after, such was the powerful influence exerted by these gentlemen, the chief of the tribe flogged the pilfering Indian for the offence, and McKinlay became a great brave, a "big heart" for his courage.

3

It was indeed necessary to have courage, patience, and prudence in dealing with the Indians. These the Hudson's Bay officers generally possessed. Perhaps the most irascible of them all in the Columbia District, was their chief, Dr. McLaughlin; but such was his goodness and justice that even the savages recognized it, and he was *hyas tyee*, or great chief, in all respects to them. Being on one occasion very much annoyed by the pertinacity of an Indian who was continually demanding pay for some stones with which the Doctor was having a vessel ballasted, he seized one of some size, and thrusting it in the Indian's mouth, cried out in a furious manner, "pay, pay! if the stones are yours, take them and eat them, you rascal! Pay, pay! the devil! the devil!" upon which explosion of wrath, the native owner of the soil thought it prudent to withdraw his immediate claims.

There was more, however, in the Doctor's action than mere indulgence of wrath. He understood perfectly that the savage values only what he can eat and wear, and that as he could not put the stones to either of these uses, his demand for pay was an impudent one.

Enough has been said to give the reader an insight into Indian character, to prepare his mind for events which are to follow, to convey an idea of the influence of the Hudson's Bay Company, and to show on what it was founded. The American Fur Companies will now be sketched, and their mode of dealing with the Indians contrasted with that of the British Company. The comparison will not be favorable; but should any unfairness be suspected, a reference to Mr. Irving's *Bonneville*, will show that the worthy Captain was forced to witness against his own countrymen in his narrative of his hunting and trading adventures in the Rocky Mountains.

The dissolution of the Pacific Fur Company, the refusal of the United States Government to protect Mr. Astor in a second attempt to carry on a commerce with the Indians west of the Rocky Mountains, and the occupation of that country by British traders, had the effect to deter individual enterprise from again attempting to establish commerce on the Pacific coast. The people waited for the Government to take some steps toward the encouragement of a trans-continental trade; the Government beholding the lion (British) in the way, waited for the expiration of the convention of 1818, in the Micawber-like hope that something would "turn up" to settle the question of territorial sovereignty. The war of 1812 had been begun on the part of Great Britain, to secure the great western territories to herself for the profits of the fur trade, almost solely. Failing in this, she had been compelled, by the treaty of Ghent, to restore to the United States all the places and forts captured during that war. Yet the forts and trading posts in the west remained practically in the possession of Great Britain; for her traders and fur companies still roamed the country, excluding American trade, and inciting (so the frontiers-men believed), the Indians to acts of blood and horror.

Congress being importuned by the people of the West, finally, in 1815, passed an act expelling British traders from American territory east of the Rocky Mountains. Following the passage of this act the hunters and trappers of the old North American Company, at the head of which Mr. Astor still remained, began to range the country about the head waters of the Mississippi and the upper Missouri. Also a few American traders had ventured into the northern provinces of Mexico, previous to the overthrow of the Spanish Government; and after that event, a thriving trade grew up between St. Louis and Santa Fe.

At length, in 1823, Mr. W. H. Ashley, of St. Louis, a merchant for a long time engaged in the fur trade on the Missouri and its tributaries, determined to push a trading party up to or beyond the Rocky Mountains. Following up the Platte River, Mr. Ashley proceeded at the head of a large party with horses and merchandise, as far as the northern branch of the Platte, called the Sweetwater. This he explored to its source, situated in that remarkable depression in the Rocky Mountains, known as the South Pass—the same which Fremont *discovered* twenty years later, during which twenty years it was annually traveled by trading parties, and just prior to Fremont's discovery, by missionaries and emigrants destined to Oregon. To Mr. Ashley also belongs the credit of having first explored the head-waters of the Colorado, called the Green River, afterwards a favorite rendezvous of the American Fur Companies. The country about the South Pass proved to be an entirely new hunting ground, and very rich in furs, as here many rivers take their rise, whose head-waters furnished abundant beaver. Here Mr. Ashley spent the summer, returning to St. Louis in the fall with a valuable collection of skins.

In 1824, Mr. Ashley repeated the expedition, extending it this time beyond Green River as far as Great Salt Lake, near which to the south he discovered another smaller lake, which he named Lake Ashley, after himself. On the shores of this lake he built a fort for trading with the Indians, and leaving in it about one hundred men, returned to St. Louis the second time with a large amount of furs. During the time the fort was occupied by Mr. Ashley's men, a period of three years, more than one hundred and eighty thousand dollars worth of furs were collected and sent to St. Louis. In 1827, the fort, and all Mr. Ashley's interest in the business, was sold to the Rocky Mountain Fur Company, at the head of which were Jedediah Smith, William Sublette, and David Jackson, Sublette being the leading spirit in the Company.

The custom of these enterprising traders, who had been in the mountains since 1824, was to divide their force, each taking his command to a good hunting ground, and returning at stated times to rendezvous, generally appointed on the head-waters of Green River. Frequently the other fur companies, (for there were other companies formed on the heels of Ashley's enterprise,) learning of the place appointed for the yearly rendezvous, brought their goods to the same resort, when an intense rivalry was exhibited by the several traders as to which company should soonest dispose of its goods, getting, of course, the largest amount of furs from the trappers and Indians. So great was the competition in the years between 1826 and 1829, when there were about six hundred American trappers in and about the Rocky Mountains, besides those of the Hudson's Bay Company, that it was death for a man of one company to dispose of his furs to a rival association. Even a "free trapper"—that is, one not indentured, but hunting upon certain terms of agreement concerning the price of his furs and the cost of his outfit, only, dared not sell to any other company than the one he had agreed with.

Jedediah Smith, of the Rocky Mountain Fur Company, during their first year in the mountains, took a party of five trappers into Oregon, being the first American, trader or other, to cross into that country since the breaking up of Mr. Astor's establishment. He trapped on the head-waters of the Snake River until autumn, when he fell in with a party of Hudson's Bay trappers, and going with them to their post in the Flathead country, wintered there.

Again, in 1826, Smith, Sublette, and Jackson, brought out a large number of men to trap in the Snake River country, and entered into direct competition with the Hudson's Bay Company, whom they opposed with hardly a degree more of zeal than they competed with rival American traders : this one extra degree being inspired by a " spirit of '76 " toward anything British.

After the Rocky Mountain Fur Company had extended its business by the purchase of Mr. Ashley's interest, the partners determined to push their enterprise to the Pacific coast, regardless of the opposition they were likely to encounter from the Hudson's Bay traders. Accordingly, in the spring of 1827, the Company was divided up into three parts, to be led separately, by different routes, into the Indian Territory, nearer the ocean.

Smith's route was from the Platte River, southwards to Santa Fé, thence to the bay of San Francisco, and thence along the coast to the Columbia River. His party were successful, and had arrived in the autumn of the following year at the Umpqua River, about two hundred miles south of the Columbia, in safety. Here one of those sudden reverses to which the "mountain-man" is liable at any moment, overtook him. His party at this time consisted of thirteen men, with their horses, and a collection of furs valued at twenty thousand dollars. Arrived at the Umpqua, they encamped for the night on its southern bank, unaware that the natives in this vicinity (the Shastas) were more fierce and treacherous than the indolent tribes of California, for whom, probably, they had a great contempt. All went well until the following morning, the Indians hanging about the camp, but apparently friendly. Smith had just breakfasted, and was occupied in looking for a fording-place for the animals, being on a raft, and having with him a little Englishman and one Indian. When they were in the middle of the river the Indian snatched Smith's gun and jumped into the water. At the same instant a yell from the camp, which was in sight, proclaimed that it was attacked. Quick as thought Smith snatched the Englishman's gun, and shot dead the Indian in the river.

To return to the camp was certain death. Already several of his men had fallen ; overpowered by numbers he could not hope that any would escape, and nothing was left him but flight. He succeeded in getting to the opposite shore with his raft before he could be intercepted, and fled with his companion, on foot and with only one gun, and no provisions, to the mountains that border the river. With great good fortune they were enabled to pass through the remaining two hundred miles of their journey without accident, though not without suffering, and reach Fort Vancouver in a destitute condition, where they were kindly cared for.

Of the men left in camp, only two escaped. One man named Black defended himself until he saw an opportunity for flight, when he escaped to the cover of the woods, and finally to a friendly tribe farther north, near the coast, who piloted him to Vancouver. The remaining man was one Turner, of a very powerful frame, who was doing camp duty as cook on this eventful morning. When the Indians rushed upon him he defended himself with a huge firebrand, or half-burnt poplar stick, with which he laid about him like Sampson, killing four red-skins before he saw a chance of escape. Singularly, for one in his extremity, he did escape, and also arrived at Vancouver that winter.

Dr. McLaughlin received the unlucky trader and his three surviving men with every mark and expression of kindness, and entertained them through the winter. Not only this, but he dispatched a strong, armed party to the scene of the disaster to punish the Indians and recover the stolen goods ; all of which was done at his own expense, both as an act of friendship toward his American rivals, and as necessary to the discipline which they everywhere maintained among the Indians. Should this offence go unpunished, the next attack might be upon one of his own parties going annually down into California. Sir George Simpson, the Governor of the Hudson's Bay Company, chanced to be spending the winter at Vancouver. He offered to send Smith to London the following summer, in the Company's vessel, where he might dispose of his furs to advantage ; but Smith declined this offer, and finally sold his furs to Dr. McLaughlin, and returned in the spring to the Rocky Mountains.

On Sublette's return from St. Louis, in the summer of 1829, with men and merchandise for the year's trade, he became uneasy on account of Smith's protracted absence. According to a previous plan, he took a large party into the Snake River country to hunt. Among the recruits from St. Louis was Joseph L. Meek, the subject of the narrative following this chapter. Sublette not meeting with Smith's party on its way from the Columbia, as he still hoped, at length detailed a party to look for him on the head-waters of the Snake. Meek was one of the men sent to look for the missing partner, whom he discovered at length in Pierre's Hole, a deep valley in the mountains, from which issues the Snake River in many living streams. Smith returned with the men to camp, where the tale of his disasters was received after the manner of mountain-men, simply declaring with a momentarily sobered countenance, that their comrade has not been " in luck ; " with which brief and equivocal expression of sympathy the subject is dismissed. To dwell on the dangers incident to their calling would be to half disarm themselves of their necessary courage ; and it is only when they are gathered about the fire in their winter camp, that they indulge in tales of wild adventure and " hair-breadth 'scapes," or make sorrowful reference to a comrade lost.

Influenced by the hospitable treatment which Smith had received at the hands of the Hudson's Bay Company, the partners now determined to withdraw from competition with them in the Snake country, and to trap upon the waters of the Colorado, in the neighborhood of their fort. But " luck," the mountain-man's Providence, seemed to have deserted Smith. In crossing the Colorado River with a considerable collection of skins, he was again attacked by Indians, and only escaped by losing all his property. He then went to St. Louis for a supply of merchandise, and fitted out a trading party for Santa Fé; but on his way to that place was killed in an encounter with the savages.

Turner, the man who so valiantly wielded the firebrand on the Umpqua River, several years later met with a similar adventure on the Rogue River, in Southern Oregon, and was the means of saving the lives of his party by his courage, strength, and alertness. He finally, when trapping had become unprofitable, retired upon a farm in the Wallamet Valley, as did many other mountain-men who survived the dangers of their perilous trade.

After the death of Smith, the Rocky Mountain Fur Company continued its operations under the command of Bridger, Fitzpatrick, and Milton Sublette, brother of William. In the spring of 1830 they received about two hundred recruits, and with little variation kept up their number of three or four hundred men for a period of eight or ten years longer, or until the beaver were hunted out of every nook and corner of the Rocky Mountains.

Previous to 1835, there were in and about the Rocky Mountains, beside the "American" and "Rocky Mountain" companies, the St. Louis Company, and eight or ten "lone traders." Among these latter were William Sublette, Robert Campbell, J. O. Pattie, Mr. Pilcher, Col. Charles Bent, St. Vrain, William Bent, Mr. Gant, and Mr. Blackwell. All these companies and traders more or less frequently penetrated into the countries of New Mexico, Old Mexico, Sonora, and California; returning sometimes through the mountain regions of the latter State, by the Humboldt River to the head-waters of the Colorado. Seldom, in all their journeys, did they intrude on that portion of the Indian Territory lying within three hundred miles of Fort Vancouver, or which forms the area of the present State of Oregon.

Up to 1832, the fur trade in the West had been chiefly conducted by merchants from the frontier cities, especially by those of St. Louis. The old "North American" was the only exception. But in the spring of this year, Captain Bonneville, an United States officer on furlough, led a company of a hundred men, with a train of wagons, horses and mules, with merchandise, into the trapping grounds of the Rocky Mountains. His wagons were the first that had ever crossed the summit of these mountains, though William Sublette had, two or three years previous, brought wagons as far as the valley of the Wind River, on the east side of the range. Captain Bonneville remained nearly three years in the hunting and trapping grounds, taking parties of men into the Colorado, Humboldt, and Sacramento valleys; but he realized no profits from his expedition, being opposed and competed with by both British and American traders of larger experience.

But Captain Bonneville's venture was a fortunate one compared with that of Mr. Nathaniel Wyeth of Massachusetts, who also crossed the continent in 1832, with the view of establishing a trade on the Columbia River. Mr. Wyeth brought with him a small party of men, all inexperienced in frontier or mountain life, and destined for a salmon fishery on the Columbia. He had reached Independence, Missouri, the last station before plunging into the wilderness, and found himself somewhat at a loss how to proceed, until, at this juncture, he was overtaken by the party of William Sublette, from St. Louis to the Rocky Mountains, with whom he travelled in company to the rendezvous at Pierre's Hole.

When Wyeth arrived at the Columbia River, after tarrying until he had acquired some mountain experiences, he found that his vessel, which was loaded with merchandise for the Columbia River trade, had not arrived. He remained at Vancouver through the winter, the guest of the Hudson's Bay Company, and either having learned or surmised that his vessel was wrecked, returned to the United States in the following year. Not discouraged, however, he made another venture in 1834, despatching the ship *May Dacre*, Captain Lambert, for the Columbia River, with another cargo of Indian goods, traveling himself overland with a party of two hundred men, and a considerable quantity of merchandise which he expected to sell to the Rocky Mountain Fur Company. In this expectation he was defeated by William Sublette, who had also brought out a large assortment of goods for the Indian trade, and had sold out, supplying the market, before Mr. Wyeth arrived.

Wyeth then built a post, named Fort Hall, on Snake River, at the junction of the Portneuf, where he stored his goods, and having detached most of his men in trapping parties, proceeded to the Columbia River to meet the *May Dacre*. He reached the Columbia about the same time with his vessel, and proceeded at once to erect a salmon fishery. To forward this purpose he built a post, called Fort William, on the lower end of Wappatoo (now known as Sauvie's) Island, near where the Lower Wallamet falls into the Columbia. But for various reasons he found the business on which he had entered unprofitable. He had much trouble with the Indians, his men were killed or drowned, so that by the time he had half a cargo of fish, he was ready to abandon the effort to establish a commerce with the Oregon Indians, and was satisfied that no enterprise less stupendous and powerful than that of the Hudson's Bay Company could be long sustained in that country.

Much complaint was subsequently made by Americans, chiefly Missionaries, of the conduct of that company in not allowing Mr. Wyeth to purchase beaver skins of the Indians, but Mr. Wyeth himself made no such complaint. Personally, he was treated with unvarying kindness, courtesy, and hospitality. As a trader, they would not permit him to undersell them. In truth, they no doubt wished him away; because competition would soon ruin the business of either, and they liked not to have the Indians taught to expect more than their furs were worth, nor to have the Indians' confidence in themselves destroyed or tampered with.

The Hudson's Bay Company were hardly so unfriendly to him as the American companies; since to the former he was enabled to sell his goods and fort on the Snake River, before he returned to the United States, which he did in 1835.

The sale of Fort Hall to the Hudson's Bay Company was a finishing blow at the American fur trade in the Rocky Mountains, which after two or three years of constantly declining profits, was entirely abandoned.

Something of the dangers incident to the life of the hunter and trapper may be gathered from the following statements, made by various parties who have been engaged in it. In 1808, a Missouri Company engaged in fur hunting on the three forks of the river Missouri, were attacked by Blackfeet, losing twenty-seven men, and being compelled to abandon the country. In 1823, Mr. Ashley was attacked on the same river by the Arickaras, and had twenty-six men killed. About the same time the Missouri company lost seven men, and fifteen thousand dollars' worth of merchandise on the Yellowstone River. A few years previous, Major Henry lost, on the Missouri River, six men and fifty horses. In the sketch given of Smith's trading adventures is shown how uncertain were life and property at a later period. Of the two hundred men whom Wyeth led into the Indian country, only about forty were alive at the end of three years. There was, indeed, a constant state of warfare between the Indians and the whites, wherever the American Companies hunted, in which great numbers of both lost their lives. Add to this cause of decimation the perils from wild beasts, famine, cold, and all manner of accidents, and the trapper's chance of life was about one in three.

Of the causes which have produced the enmity of the Indians, there are about as many. It was found to be the case almost universally, that on the first visit of the whites the natives were friendly, after their natural fears had been allayed. But by degrees their cupidity was excited to possess themselves of the much coveted dress, arms, and goods of their visitors. As they had little or nothing to offer in exchange, which the white man considered an equivalent, they took the only method remaining of gratifying their desire of possession, and *stole* the coveted articles which they could not purchase. When they learned that the white men punished theft, they murdered to prevent the punishment. Often, also, they had wrongs of their own to avenge. White men did not always regard their property-rights. They were guilty of infamous conduct toward Indian women. What one party of whites told them was true, another plainly contradicted, leaving the lie between them. They were overbearing toward the Indians on their own soil, exciting to irrepressible hostility the natural jealousy of the inferior toward the superior race, where both are free, which characterizes all people. In short, the Indians were not without their grievances; and from barbarous ignorance and wrong on one side, and intelligent wrong-doing on the other, together with the misunderstandings likely to arise between two entirely distinct races, grew constantly a thousand abuses, which resulted in a deadly enmity between the two.

For several reasons this evil existed to a greater degree among the American traders and trappers than among the British. The American trapper was not, like the Hudson's Bay employees, bred to the business. Oftener than any other way he was some wild youth who, after an *escapade* in the society of his native place, sought safety from reproach or punishment in the wilderness. Or he was some disappointed man who, with feelings embittered towards his fellows, preferred the seclusion of the forest and mountain. Many were of a class disreputable everywhere, who gladly embraced a life not subject to social laws. A few were brave, independent, and hardy spirits, who delighted in the hardships and wild adventures their calling made necessary. All these men, the best with the worst, were subject to no will but their own; and all experience goes to prove that a life of perfect liberty is apt to degenerate into a life of license. Even their own lives, and those of their companions, when it depended upon their own prudence, were but lightly considered. The constant presence of danger made them reckless. It is easy to conceive how, under these circumstances, the natives and the foreigners grew to hate each other, in the Indian country; especially after the Americans came to the determination to "shoot an Indian at sight," unless he belonged to some tribe with whom they had intermarried, after the manner of the trappers.

On the other hand, the employees of the Hudson's Bay Company were many of them half-breeds or full-blooded Indians of the Iroquois nation, towards whom nearly all the tribes were kindly disposed. Even the Frenchmen who trapped for this company were well liked by the Indians on account of their suavity of manner, and the ease with which they adapted themselves to savage life. Besides most of them had native wives and half-breed children, and were regarded as relatives. They were trained to the life of a trapper, were subject to the will of the Company, and were generally just and equitable in their dealings with the Indians, according to that company's will, and the dictates of prudence. Here was a wide difference.

Notwithstanding this, there were many dangers to be encountered. The hostility of some of the tribes could never be overcome; nor has it ever abated. Such were the Crows, the Blackfeet, the Cheyennes, the Apaches, the Camanches. Only a superior force could compel the friendly offices of these tribes for any white man, and then their treachery was as dangerous as their open hostility.

It happened, therefore, that although the Hudson's Bay Company lost comparatively few men by the hands of the Indians, they sometimes found them implacable foes in common with the American trappers; and frequently one party was very glad of the others' assistance. Altogether, as has before been stated, the loss of life was immense in proportion to the number employed.

Very few of those who had spent years in the Rocky Mountains ever returned to the United States. With their Indian wives and half-breed children, they scattered themselves throughout Oregon, until when, a number of years after the abandonment of the fur trade, Congress donated large tracts of land to actual settlers, they laid claim, each to his selected portion, and became active citizens of their adopted state.

CHAPTER I.

As has been stated in the Introduction, Joseph L. Meek was a native of Washington Co., Va. Born in the early part of the present century, and brought up on a plantation where the utmost liberty was accorded to the "young massa;" preferring out-door sports with the youthful bondsmen of his father, to study with the bald-headed schoolmaster who furnished him the alphabet on a paddle; possessing an exhaustless fund of waggish humor, united to a spirit of adventure and remarkable personal strength, he unwittingly furnished in himself the very material of which the heroes of the wilderness were made. Virginia, "the mother of Presidents," has furnished many such men, who, in the early days of the now populous Western States, became the hardy frontiers-men, or the fearless Indian fighters who were the bone and sinew of the land.

When young Joe was about eighteen years of age, he wearied of the monotony of plantation life, and jumping into the wagon of a neighbor who was going to Louis- ville, Ky., started out in life for himself. He "reckoned they did not grieve for him at home;" at which conclu- sion others besides Joe naturally arrive on hearing of his heedless disposition, and utter contempt for the ordinary and useful employments to which other men apply them- selves. This truly Virginian and chivalric contempt for " honest labor " has continued to distinguish him through- out his eventful career, even while performing the most arduous duties of the life he had chosen.

Joe probably believed that should his father grieve for him, his step-mother would be able to console him; this step-mother, though a pious and good woman, not being one of the lad's favorites, as might easily be conjectured. It was such thoughts as these that kept up his resolution to seek the far west. In the autumn of 1828 he arrived in St. Louis, and the following spring he fell in with Mr. Wm. Sublette, of the Rocky Mountain Fur Company, who was making his annual visit to that frontier town to purchase merchandise for the Indian country, and pick up recruits for the fur-hunting service. To this experienced leader he offered himself.

THE ENLISTMENT.

"How old are you?" asked Sublette.

"A little past eighteen."

"And you want to go to the Rocky Mountains?"

"Yes."

"You don't know what you are talking about, boy. You'll be killed before you get half way there."

"If I do, I reckon I can die!" said Joe, with a flash of his full dark eyes, and throwing back his shoulders to show their breadth.

"Come," exclaimed the trader, eyeing the youthful candidate with admiration, and perhaps a touch of pity also; "that is the game spirit. I think you'll do, after all. Only be prudent, and keep your wits about you."

"Where else should they be?" laughed Joe, as he marched off, feeling an inch or two taller than before.

Then commenced the business of preparing for the journey—making acquaintance with the other recruits—enjoying the novelty of owning an outfit, being initiated into the mysteries of camp duty by the few old hunters who were to accompany the expedition, and learning something of their swagger and disregard of civilized observances.

On the 17th of March, 1829, the company, numbering about sixty men, left St. Louis, and proceeded on horses and mules, with pack-horses for the goods, up through the state of Missouri. Camp-life commenced at the start; and this being the season of the year when the weather is most disagreeable, its romance rapidly melted away with the snow and sleet which varied the sharp spring wind and the frequent cold rains. The recruits went through all the little mishaps incident to the business and to their inexperience, such as involuntary somersaults over the heads of their mules, bloody noses, bruises, dusty faces, bad colds, accidents in fording streams,—yet withal no very serious hurts or hindrances. Rough weather and severe exercise gave them wolfish appetites, which sweetened the coarse camp-fare and amateur cooking.

Getting up at four o'clock of a March morning to kindle

fires and attend to the animals was not the most delectable duty that our labor-despising young recruit could have chosen; but if he repented of the venture he had made nobody was the wiser. Sleeping of stormy nights in corn-cribs or under sheds, could not be by any stretch of imagination converted into a highly romantic or heroic mode of lodging one's self. The squalid manner of living of the few inhabitants of Missouri at this period, gave a forlorn aspect to the country which is lacking in the wilderness itself;—a thought which sometimes occurred to Joe like a hope for the future. Mountain-fare he began to think must be better than the boiled corn and pork of the Missourians. Antelope and buffalo meat were more suitable viands for a hunter than coon and opossum. Thus those very duties which seemed undignified, and those hardships without danger or glory, which marked the beginning of his career made him ambitious of a more free and hazardous life on the plains and in the mountains.

Among the recruits was a young man not far from Joe's own age, named Robert Newell, from Ohio. One morning, when the company was encamped near Boonville, the two young men were out looking for their mules, when they encountered an elderly woman returning from the milking yard with a gourd of milk. Newell made some remark on the style of vessel she carried, when she broke out in a sharp voice,—

"Young chap, I'll bet you run off from your mother! Who'll mend them holes in the elbow of your coat? You're a purty looking chap to go to the mountains, among them Injuns! They'll *kill* you. You'd better go back home!"

Considering that these frontier people knew what Indian fighting was, this was no doubt sound and disinterested advice, notwithstanding it was given somewhat sharply. And so the young men felt it to be; but it was not in the nature of either of them to turn back from a course because there was danger in it. The thought of home, and somebody to mend their coats, was, however, for the time strongly presented. But the company moved on, with undiminished numbers, stared at by the few inhabitants, and having their own little adventures, until they came to Independence, the last station before committing themselves to the wilderness.

At this place, which contained a dwelling-house, cotton-gin, and grocery, the camp tarried for a few days to adjust the packs, and prepare for a final start across the plains. On Sunday the settlers got together for a shooting-match, in which some of the travelers joined, without winning many laurels. Coon-skins, deer-skins, and bees-wax changed hands freely among the settlers, whose skill with the rifle was greater than their hoard of silver dollars. This was the last vestige of civilization which the company could hope to behold for years; and rude as it was, yet won from them many a parting look as they finally took their way across the plains toward the Arkansas River.

Often on this part of the march a dead silence fell upon the party, which remained unbroken for miles of the way. Many no doubt were regretting homes by them abandoned, or wondering dreamily how many and whom of that company would ever see the Missouri country again. Many indeed went the way the woman of the gourd had prophesied; but not the hero of this story, nor his comrade Newell.

The route of Captain Sublette led across the country from near the mouth of the Kansas River to the River Arkansas; thence to the South Fork of the Platte; thence on to the North Fork of that River, to where Ft. Laramie now stands; thence up the North Fork to the Sweetwater, and thence across in a still northwesterly direction to the head of Wind River.

The manner of camp-travel is now so well known through the writings of Irving, and still more from the great numbers which have crossed the plains since *Astoria* and *Bonneville* were written, that it would be superfluous here to enter upon a particular description of a train on that journey. A strict half-military discipline had to be maintained, regular duties assigned to each person, precautions taken against the loss of animals either by straying or Indian stampeding, etc. Some of the men were appointed as camp-keepers, who had all these things to look after, besides standing guard. A few were selected as hunters, and these were free to come and go, as their calling required. None but the most experienced were chosen for hunters, on a march; therefore our recruit could not aspire to that dignity yet.

The first adventure the company met with worthy of mention after leaving Independence, was in crossing the country between the Arkansas and the Platte. Here the camp was surprised one morning by a band of Indians a thousand strong, that came sweeping down upon them in such warlike style that even Captain Sublette was fain to believe it his last battle. Upon the open prairie there is no such thing as flight, nor any cover under which to conceal a party even for a few moments. It is always fight or die, if the assailants are in the humor for war.

Happily on this occasion the band proved to be more peaceably disposed than their appearance indicated, being the warriors of several tribes—the Sioux, Arapahoes, Kiowas, and Cheyennes, who had been holding a council to consider probably what mischief they could do to some other tribes. The spectacle they presented as they came at full speed on horseback, armed, painted, brandishing their weapons, and yelling in first rate Indian style, was one which might well strike with a palsy the stoutest heart and arm. What were a band of sixty men against a thousand armed warriors in full fighting trim, with spears, shields, bows, battle-axes, and not a few guns?

But it is the rule of the mountain-men to *fight*—and that there is a chance for life until the breath is out of the body; therefore Captain Sublette had his little force drawn up in line of battle. On came the savages, whooping and swinging their weapons above their heads. Sublette turned to his men. "When you hear my shot, then fire." Still they came on, until within about fifty paces of the line of waiting men. Sublette turned his head, and saw his command with their guns all up to their faces ready to fire, then raised his own gun. Just at this moment the principal chief sprang off his horse and laid his weapon on the ground, making signs of peace. Then followed a talk, and after the giving of a considerable present, Sublette was allowed to depart. This he did with all dispatch, the company putting as much distance as possible between themselves and their visitors before making their next camp. Considering the warlike character of these tribes and their superior numbers, it was as narrow an escape on the part of the company as it was an exceptional freak of generosity on the part of the savages to allow it. But Indians have all a great respect for a man who shows no fear; and it was most probably the warlike movement of Captain Sublette and his party which inspired a willingness on the part of the chief to accept a present, when he had the power to have taken the whole train. Besides, according to Indian logic, the present cost him nothing, and it might cost him many warriors to

4

capture the train.   Had there been the least wavering on Sublette's part, or fear in the countenances of his men, the end of the affair would have been different.   This adventure was a grand initiation of the raw recruits, giving them both an insight into savage modes of attack, and an opportunity to test their own nerve.

The company proceeded without accident, and arrived, about the first of July, at the rendezvous, which was appointed for this year on the Popo Agie, one of the streams which form the head-waters of Bighorn River.

Now, indeed, young Joe had an opportunity of seeing something of the life upon which he had entered.   As customary, when the traveling partner arrived at rendezvous with the year's merchandise, there was a meeting of all the partners, if they were within reach of the appointed place.   On this occasion Smith was absent on his tour through California and Western Oregon, as has been related in the prefatory chapter.   Jackson, the resident partner, and commander for the previous year, was not yet in; and Sublette had just arrived with the goods from St. Louis.

All the different hunting and trapping parties and Indian allies were gathered together, so that the camp contained several hundred men, with their riding and pack-horses.   Nor were Indian women and children wanting to give variety and an appearance of domesticity to the scene.

The Summer rendezvous was always chosen in some valley where there was grass for the animals, and game for the camp.   The plains along the Popo Agie, besides furnishing these necessary bounties, were bordered by picturesque mountain ranges, whose naked bluffs of red sandstone glowed in the morning and evening sun with a mellowness of coloring charming to the eye of the Virginia

THE SUMMER RENDEZVOUS.

recruit. The waving grass of the plain, variegated with wild flowers; the clear summer heavens flecked with white clouds that threw soft shadows in passing; the grazing animals scattered about the meadows; the lodges of the *Booshways,** around which clustered the camp in motley garb and brilliant coloring; gay laughter, and the murmur of soft Indian voices, all made up a most spirited and enchanting picture, in which the eye of an artist could not fail to delight.

But as the goods were opened the scene grew livelier. All were eager to purchase, most of the trappers to the full amount of their year's wages; and some of them, generally free trappers, went in debt to the company to a very considerable amount, after spending the value of a year's labor, privation, and danger, at the rate of several hundred dollars in a single day.

The difference between a hired and a free trapper was greatly in favor of the latter. The hired trapper was regularly indentured and bound not only to hunt and trap for his employers, but also to perform any duty required of him in camp. The Booshway, or the trader, or the partisan, (leader of the detachment,) had him under his command, to make him take charge of, load and unload the horses, stand guard, cook, hunt fuel, or, in short, do any and every duty. In return for this toilsome service he received an outfit of traps, arms and ammunition, horses, and whatever his service required. Besides his outfit, he received no more than three or four hundred dollars a year as wages.

There was also a class of free trappers, who were furnished with their outfit by the company they trapped for, and who were obliged to agree to a certain stipulated

* Leaders or chiefs—corrupted from the French of Bourgeois, and borrowed from the Canadians.

price for their furs before the hunt commenced. But the genuine free trapper regarded himself as greatly the superior of either of the foregoing classes. He had his own horses and accoutrements, arms and ammunition. He took what route he thought fit, hunted and trapped when and where he chose; traded with the Indians; sold his furs to whoever offered highest for them; dressed flauntingly, and generally had an Indian wife and half-breed children. They prided themselves on their hardihood and courage; even on their recklessness and profligacy. Each claimed to own the best horse; to have had the wildest adventures; to have made the most narrow escapes; to have killed the greatest number of bears and Indians; to be the greatest favorite with the Indian belles, the greatest consumer of alcohol, and to have the most money to spend, *i. e.* the largest credit on the books of the company. If his hearers did not believe him, he was ready to run a race with him, to beat him at "old sledge," or to fight, if fighting was preferred,—ready to prove what he affirmed in any manner the company pleased.

If the free trapper had a wife, she moved with the camp to which he attached himself, being furnished with a fine horse, caparisoned in the gayest and costliest manner. Her dress was of the finest goods the market afforded, and was suitably ornamented with beads, ribbons, fringes, and feathers. Her rank, too, as a free trapper's wife, gave her consequence not only in her own eyes, but in those of her tribe, and protected her from that slavish drudgery to which as the wife of an Indian hunter or warrior she would have been subject. The only authority which the free trapper acknowledged was that of his Indian spouse, who generally ruled in the lodge, however her lord blustered outside.

One of the free trapper's special delights was to take in

hand the raw recruits, to gorge their wonder with his boastful tales, and to amuse himself with shocking his pupil's civilized notions of propriety. Joe Meek did not escape this sort of "breaking in;" and if it should appear in the course of this narrative that he proved an apt scholar, it will but illustrate a truth—that high spirits and fine talents tempt the tempter to win them over to his ranks. But Joe was not won over all at once. He beheld the beautiful spectacle of the encampment as it has been described, giving life and enchantment to the summer landscape, changed into a scene of the wildest carousal, going from bad to worse, until from harmless noise and bluster it came to fighting and loss of life. At this first rendezvous he was shocked to behold the revolting exhibition of four trappers playing at a game of cards with the dead body of a comrade for a card-table! Such was the indifference to all the natural and ordinary emotions which these veterans of the wilderness cultivated in themselves, and inculcated in those who came under their influence. Scenes like this at first had the effect to bring feelings of home-sickness, while it inspired by contrast a sort of penitential and religious feeling also. According to Meek's account of those early days in the mountains, he said some secret prayers, and shed some secret tears. But this did not last long. The force of example, and especially the force of ridicule, is very potent with the young; nor are we quite free from their influence later in life.

If the gambling, swearing, drinking, and fighting at first astonished and alarmed the unsophisticated Joe, he found at the same time something to admire, and that he felt to be congenial with his own disposition, in the fearlessness, the contempt of sordid gain, the hearty merriment and frolicsome abandon of the better portion of the men about him.   A spirit of emulation arose in him to become as brave as the bravest, as hardy as the hardiest, and as gay as the gayest, even while his feelings still revolted at many things which his heroic models were openly guilty of. If at any time in the future course of this narrative, Joe is discovered to have taken leave of his early scruples, the reader will considerately remember the associations by which he was surrounded for years, until the memory of the pious teachings of his childhood was nearly, if not quite, obliterated.   To "nothing extenuate, nor set down aught in malice," should be the frame of mind in which both the writer and reader of Joe's adventures should strive to maintain himself.

Before our hero is ushered upon the active scenes of a trapper's life, it may be well to present to the reader a sort of *guide to camp life*, in order that he may be able to understand some of its technicalities, as they may be casually mentioned hereafter.

When the large camp is on the march, it has a leader, generally one of the Booshways, who rides in advance, or at the head of the column.   Near him is a led mule, chosen for its qualities of speed and trustworthiness, on which are packed two small trunks that balance each other like panniers, and which contain the company's books, papers, and articles of agreement with the men.   Then follow the pack animals, each one bearing three packs—one on each side, and one on top—so nicely adjusted as not to slip in traveling.   These are in charge of certain men called camp-keepers, who have each three of these to look after. The trappers and hunters have two horses, or mules, one to ride, and one to pack their traps.   If there are women and children in the train, all are mounted.   Where the country is safe, the caravan moves in single file, often stretching out for half or three-quarters of a mile.   At the end of the column rides the second man, or "little Booshway," as the men call him ; usually a hired officer, whose business it is to look after the order and condition of the whole camp.

On arriving at a suitable spot to make the night camp, the leader stops, dismounts in the particular space which is to be devoted to himself in its midst. The others, as they come up, form a circle ; the "second man" bringing up the rear, to be sure all are there. He then proceeds to appoint every man a place in the circle, and to examine the horses' backs to see if any are sore. The horses are then turned out, under a guard, to graze ; but before darkness comes on are placed inside the ring, and picketed by a stake driven in the earth, or with two feet so tied together as to prevent easy or free locomotion. The men are divided into messes : so many trappers and so many camp-keepers to a mess. The business of eating is not a very elaborate one, where the sole article of diet is meat, either dried or roasted. By a certain hour all is quiet in camp, and only the guard is awake. At times during the night, the leader, or the officer of the guard, gives the guard a challenge—"all's well ! " which is answered by "all's well ! "

In the morning at daylight, or sometimes not till sunrise, according to the safe or dangerous locality, the second man comes forth from his lodge and cries in French, " *leve, leve, leve, leve, leve !* " fifteen or twenty times, which is the command to rise. In about five minutes more he cries out again, in French, " *leche lego, leche lego !* " or turn out, turn out ; at which command all come out from the lodges, and the horses are turned loose to feed ; but not before a horseman has galloped all round the camp at some distance, and discovered every thing to be safe in the neighborhood. Again, when the horses have been

sufficiently fed, under the eye of a guard, they are driven
up, the packs replaced, the train mounted, and once more
it moves off, in the order before mentioned.

In a settled camp, as in winter, there are other regulations. The leader and the second man occupy the same
relative positions; but other minor regulations are observed. The duty of a trapper, for instance, in the trapping season, is only to trap, and take care of his own
horses. When he comes in at night, he takes his beaver
to the clerk, and the number is counted off, and placed to
his credit. Not he, but the camp-keepers, take off the
skins and dry them. In the winter camp there are six
persons to a lodge: four trappers and two camp-keepers;
therefore the trappers are well waited upon, their only
duty being to hunt, in turns, for the camp. When a piece
of game is brought in,—a deer, an antelope, or buffalo
meat,—it is thrown down on the heap which accumulates
in front of the Booshway's lodge; and the second man
stands by and cuts it up, or has it cut up for him. The
first man who chances to come along, is ordered to stand
still and turn his back to the pile of game, while the
"little Booshway" lays hold of a piece that has been cut
off, and asks in a loud voice—"who will have this?"—
and the man answering for him, says, "the Booshway,"
or perhaps "number six," or "number twenty"—meaning certain messes; and the number is called to come and
take their meat. In this blind way the meat is portioned
off; strongly reminding one of the game of "button,
button, who has the button?" In this chance game of
the meat, the Booshway fares no better than his men;
unless, in rare instances, the little Booshway should indicate to the man who calls off, that a certain choice piece
is designed for the mess of the leader or the second man.

A gun is never allowed to be fired in camp under any

provocation, short of an Indian raid; but the guns are frequently inspected, to see if they are in order; and woe to the careless camp-keeper who neglects this or any other duty. When the second man comes around, and finds a piece of work imperfectly done, whether it be cleaning the firearms, making a hair rope, or a skin lodge, or washing a horse's back, he does not threaten the offender with personal chastisement, but calls up another man and asks him, "Can *you* do this properly?"

"Yes, sir."

"I will give you ten dollars to do it;" and the ten dollars is set down to the account of the inefficient camp-keeper. But he does not risk forfeiting another ten dollars in the same manner.

In the spring, when the camp breaks up, the skins which have been used all winter for lodges are cut up to make moccasins: because from their having been thoroughly smoked by the lodge fires they do not shrink in wetting, like raw skins. This is an important quality in a moccasin, as a trapper is almost constantly in the water, and should not his moccasins be smoked they will close upon his feet, in drying, like a vice. Sometimes after trapping all day, the tired and soaked trapper lies down in his blankets at night, still wet. But by-and-by he is wakened by the pinching of his moccasins, and is obliged to rise and seek the water again to relieve himself of the pain. For the same reason, when spring comes, the trapper is forced to cut off the lower half of his buckskin breeches, and piece them down with blanket leggins. which he wears all through the trapping season.

Such were a few of the peculiarities, and the hardships also, of a life in the Rocky Mountains. If the camp discipline, and the dangers and hardships to which a raw recruit was exposed, failed to harden him to the service in one year, he was rejected as a " trifling fellow," and sent back to the settlement the next year. It was not prob- able, therefore, that the mountain-man often was detected in complaining at his lot. If he was miserable, he was laughed at ; and he soon learned to laugh at his own mis- eries, as well as to laugh back at his comrades.

CHAPTER II.

THE business of the rendezvous occupied about a month. In this period the men, Indian allies, and other Indian parties who usually visited the camp at this time, were all supplied with goods. The remaining merchandise was adjusted for the convenience of the different traders who should be sent out through all the country traversed by the company. Sublette then decided upon their routes, dividing up his forces into camps, which took each its appointed course, detaching as it proceeded small parties of trappers to all the hunting grounds in the neighborhood. These smaller camps were ordered to meet at certain times and places, to report progress, collect and cache their furs, and "count noses." If certain parties failed to arrive, others were sent out in search for them.

This year, in the absence of Smith and Jackson, a considerable party was dispatched, under Milton Sublette, brother of the Captain, and two other free trappers and traders, Frapp and Jervais, to traverse the country down along the Bighorn River. Captain Sublette took a large party, among whom was Joe Meek, across the mountains to trap on the Snake River, in opposition to the Hudson's Bay Company. The Rocky Mountain Fur Company had hitherto avoided this country, except when Smith had once crossed to the head-waters of the Snake with a small party of five trappers. But Smith and Sublette had determined to oppose themselves to the British traders who occupied so large an extent of territory presumed to be American; and it had been agreed between them to meet this year on Snake River on Sublette's return from St. Louis, and Smith's from his California tour. What befel Smith's party before reaching the Columbia, has already been related; also his reception by the Hudson's Bay Company, and his departure from Vancouver.

Sublette led his company up the valley of the Wind River, across the mountains, and on to the very head-waters of the Lewis or Snake River. Here he fell in with Jackson, in the valley of Lewis Lake, called Jackson's Hole, and remained on the borders of this lake for some time, waiting for Smith, whose non-appearance began to create a good deal of uneasiness. At length runners were dispatched in all directions looking for the lost Booshway.

The detachment to which Meek was assigned had the pleasure and honor of discovering the hiding place of the missing partner, which was in Pierre's Hole, a mountain valley about thirty miles long and of half that width, which subsequently was much frequented by the camps of the various fur companies. He was found trapping and exploring, in company with four men only, one of whom was Black, who with him escaped from the Umpqua Indians, as before related.

Notwithstanding the excitement and elation attendant upon the success of his party, Meek found time to admire the magnificent scenery of the valley, which is bounded on two sides by broken and picturesque ranges, and overlooked by that magnificent group of mountains, called the Three Tetons, towering to a height of fourteen thousand feet. This emerald cup set in its rim of amethystine mountains, was so pleasant a sight to the mountain-men that camp was moved to it without delay, where it remained until some time in September, recruiting its animals and preparing for the fall hunt.

Here again the trappers indulged in their noisy sports
and rejoicing, ostensibly on account of the return of the
long-absent Booshway. There was little said of the men
who had perished in that unfortunate expedition. "Poor
fellow! out of luck;" was the usual burial rite which
the memory of a dead comrade received. So much and
no more. They could indulge in noisy rejoicings over a
lost comrade restored; but the dead one was not mentioned. Nor was this apparently heartless and heedless
manner so irrational or unfeeling as it seemed. Everybody understood one thing in the mountains—that he must
keep his life by his own courage and valor, or at the least
by his own prudence. Unseen dangers always lay in
wait for him. The arrow or tomahawk of the Indian, the
blow of the grizzly bear, the mis-step on the dizzy or slippery height, the rush of boiling and foaming floods, freezing cold, famine—these were the most common forms of
peril, yet did not embrace even then all the forms in which
Death sought his victims in the wilderness. The avoid-
ance of painful reminders, such as the loss of a party of
men, was a natural instinct, involving also a principle of
self defence—since to have weak hearts would be the
surest road to defeat in the next dangerous encounter.
To keep their hearts "big," they must be gay, they must
not remember the miserable fate of many of their one-time
comrades. Think of that, stern moralist and martinet in
propriety! Your fur collar hangs in the gas-lighted hall.
In your luxurious dressing gown and slippers, by the
warmth of a glowing grate, you muse upon the depravity
of your fellow men. But imagine yourself, if you can, in
the heart of an interminable wilderness. Let the snow
be three or four feet deep, game scarce, Indians on your
track: escaped from these dangers, once more beside a
camp fire, with a roast of buffalo meat on a stick before it,

and several of your companions similarly escaped, and destined for the same chances to-morrow, around you. Do you fancy you should give much time to lamenting the less lucky fellows who were left behind frozen, starved, or scalped? Not you. You would be fortifying yourself against to-morrow, when the same terrors might lay in wait for you. Jedediah Smith was a pious man; one of the few that ever resided in the Rocky Mountains, and led a band of reckless trappers; but he did not turn back to his camp when he saw it attacked on the Umpqua, nor stop to lament his murdered men. The law of self-preservation is strong in the wilderness. "Keep up your heart to-day, for to-morrow you may die," is the motto of the trapper.

In the conference which took place between Smith and Sublette, the former insisted that on account of the kind services of the Hudson's Bay Company toward himself and the three other survivors of his party, they should withdraw their trappers and traders from the western side of the mountains for the present, so as not to have them come in conflict with those of that company. To this proposition Sublette reluctantly consented, and orders were issued for moving once more to the east, before going into winter camp, which was appointed for the Wind River Valley.

In the meantime Joe Meek was sent out with a party to take his first hunt for beaver as a hired trapper. The detachment to which he belonged traveled down Pierre's fork, the stream which watered the valley of Pierre's Hole, to its junction with Lewis' and Henry's forks where they unite to form the great Snake River. While trapping in this locality the party became aware of the vicinity of a roving band of Blackfeet, and in consequence, redoubled their usual precautions while on the march.

The Blackfeet were the tribe most dreaded in the Rocky Mountains, and went by the name of "Bugs Boys," which rendered into good English, meant "the devil's own." They are now so well known that to mention their characteristics seems like repeating a "twice-told tale;" but as they will appear so often in this narrative, Irving's account of them as he had it from Bonneville when he was fresh from the mountains, will, after all, not be out of place. "These savages," he says, "are the most dangerous banditti of the mountains, and the inveterate foe of the trapper. They are Ishmaelites of the first order, always with weapon in hand, ready for action. The young braves of the tribe, who are destitute of property, go to war for booty; to gain horses, and acquire the means of setting up a lodge, supporting a family, and entitling themselves to a seat in the public councils. The veteran warriors fight merely for the love of the thing, and the consequence which success gives them among their people. They are capital horsemen, and are generally well mounted on short, stout horses, similar to the prairie ponies, to be met with in St. Louis. When on a war party, however, they go on foot, to enable them to skulk through the country with greater secrecy; to keep in thickets and ravines, and use more adroit subterfuges and stratagems. Their mode of warfare is entirely by ambush, surprise, and sudden assaults in the night time. If they succeed in causing a panic, they dash forward with headlong fury; if the enemy is on the alert, and shows no signs of fear, they become wary and deliberate in their movements.

Some of them are armed in the primitive style, with bows and arrows; the greater part have American fusees, made after the fashion of those of the Hudson's Bay Company. These they procure at the trading post of the American Fur Company, on Maria's River, where they traffic their peltries for arms, ammunition, clothing, and trinkets. They are extremely fond of spirituous liquors and tobacco, for which nuisances they are ready to exchange, not merely their guns and horses, but even their wives and daughters. As they are a treacherous race, and have cherished a lurking hostility to the whites, ever since one of their tribe was killed by Mr. Lewis, the associate of General Clarke, in his exploring expedition across the Rocky Mountains, the American Fur Company is obliged constantly to keep at their post a garrison of sixty or seventy men."

"Under the general name of Blackfeet are comprehended several tribes, such as the Surcies, the Peagans, the Blood Indians, and the Gros Ventres of the Prairies, who roam about the Southern branches of the Yellowstone and Missouri Rivers, together with some other tribes further north. The bands infesting the Wind River Mountains, and the country adjacent, at the time of which we are treating, were Gros Ventres *of the Prairies*, which are not to be confounded with the Gros Ventres *of the Missouri*, who keep about the *lower* part of that river, and are friendly to the white men."

"This hostile band keeps about the head-waters of the Missouri, and numbers about nine hundred fighting men. Once in the course of two or three years they abandon their usual abodes and make a visit to the Arapahoes of the Arkansas. Their route lies either through the Crow country, and the Black Hills, or through the lands of the Nez Perces, Flatheads, Bannacks, and Shoshonies. As they enjoy their favorite state of hostility with all these tribes, their expeditions are prone to be conducted in the most lawless and predatory style; nor do they hesitate to extend their maraudings to any party of white men they meet with, following their trail, hovering about their camps, waylaying and dogging the caravans of the free traders, and murdering the solitary trapper. The consequences are frequent and desperate fights between them and the mountaineers, in the wild defiles and fastnesses of the Rocky Mountains." Such were the Blackfeet at the period of which we are writing; nor has their character changed at this day, as many of the Montana miners know to their cost.

5

CHAPTER III.

1830.   SUBLETTE's camp commenced moving back to the east side of the Rocky Mountains in October.   Its course was up Henry's fork of the Snake River, through the North Pass to Missouri Lake, in which rises the Madison fork of the Missouri River.   The beaver were very plenty on Henry's fork, and our young trapper had great success in making up his packs; having learned the art of setting his traps very readily.   The manner in which the trapper takes his game is as follows:—

He has an ordinary steel trap weighing five pounds, attached to a chain five feet long, with a swivel and ring at the end, which plays round what is called the *float*, a dry stick of wood, about six feet long.   The trapper wades out into the stream, which is shallow, and cuts with his knife a bed for the trap, five or six inches under water. He then takes the float out the whole length of the chain in the direction of the centre of the stream, and drives it into the mud, so fast that the beaver cannot draw it out; at the same time tying the other end by a thong to the bank.   A small stick or twig, dipped in musk or castor, serves for bait, and is placed so as to hang directly above the trap, which is now set.   The trapper then throws water plentifully over the adjacent bank to conceal any foot prints or scent by which the beaver would be alarmed, and going to some distance wades out of the stream.

In setting a trap, several things are to be observed with care:—first, that the trap is firmly fixed, and the proper distance from the bank—for if the beaver can get on shore with the trap, he will cut off his foot to escape: secondly, that the float is of dry wood, for should it not be, the little animal will cut it off at a stroke, and swimming with the trap to the middle of the dam, be drowned by its weight. In the latter case, when the hunter visits his traps in the morning, he is under the necessity of plunging into the water and swimming out to dive for the missing trap, and his game. Should the morning be frosty and chill, as it very frequently is in the mountains, diving for traps is not the pleasantest exercise. In placing the bait, care must be taken to fix it just where the beaver in reaching it will spring the trap. If the bait-stick be placed high, the hind foot of the beaver will be caught: if low, his fore foot.

The manner in which the beavers make their dam, and construct their lodge, has long been reckoned among the wonders of the animal creation; and while some observers have claimed for the little creature more sagacity than it really possesses, its instinct is still sufficiently wonderful. It is certainly true that it knows how to keep the water of a stream to a certain level, by means of an obstruction; and that it cuts down trees for the purpose of backing up the water by a dam. It is not true, however, that it can always fell a tree in the direction required for this purpose. The timber about a beaver dam is felled in all directions; but as trees that grow near the water, generally lean towards it, the tree, when cut, takes the proper direction by gravitation alone. The beaver then proceeds to cut up the fallen timber into lengths of about three feet, and to convey them to the spot where the dam is to be situated, securing them in their places by means of mud and stones. The work is commenced when the water is low, and carried on as it rises, until it

has attained the desired height. And not only is it made
of the requisite height and strength, but its shape is suited
exactly to the nature of the stream in which it is built.
If the water is sluggish the dam is straight; if rapid and
turbulent, the barrier is constructed of a convex form, the
better to resist the action of the water.

BEAVER-DAM.

When the beavers have once commenced a dam, its ex
tent and thickness are continually augmented, not only by
their labors, but by accidental accumulations; thus accom-
modating itself to the size of the growing community.
At length, after a lapse of many years, the water being
spread over a considerable tract, and filled up by yearly
accumulations of drift-wood and earth, seeds take root
in the new made ground, and the old beaver-dams become green meadows, or thickets of cotton-wood and
willow.

The food on which the beaver subsists, is the bark of
the young trees in its neighborhood; and when laying up
a winter store, the whole community join in the labor of
selecting, cutting up, and carrying the strips to their store-

houses under water. They do not, as some writers have affirmed, when cutting wood for a dam strip off the bark and store it in their lodges for winter consumption; but only carry under water the stick with the bark on.

" The beaver has two incisors and eight molars in each jaw; and empty hollows where the canine teeth might be. The upper pair of cutting teeth extend far into the jaw, with a curve of rather more than a semicircle; and the lower pair of incisors form rather less than a semicircle. Sometimes, one of these teeth gets broken and then the opposite tooth continues growing until it forms a nearly complete circle. The chewing muscle of the beaver is strengthened by tendons in such a way as to give it great power. But more is needed to enable the beaver to eat wood. The insalivation of the dry food is provided for by the extraordinary size of the salivary glands.

" Now, every part of these instruments is of vital importance to the beavers. The loss of an incisor involves the formation of an obstructive circular tooth; deficiency of saliva renders the food indigestible; and when old age comes and the enamel is worn down faster than it is renewed, the beaver is not longer able to cut branches for its support. Old, feeble and poor, unable to borrow, and ashamed to beg, he steals cuttings, and subjects himself to the penalty assigned to theft. Aged beavers are often found dead with gashes in their bodies, showing that they have been killed by their mates. In the fall of 1864, a very aged beaver was caught in one of the dams of the Esconawba River, and this was the reflection of a great authority on the occasion, one Ah-she-goes, an Ojibwa trapper: ' Had he escaped the trap he would have been killed before the winter was over, by other beavers, for stealing cuttings.'

When the beavers are about two or three years old, their teeth are in their best condition for cutting. On the Upper Missouri, they cut the cotton tree and the willow bush; around Hudson's Bay and Lake Superior, in addition to the willow they cut the poplar and maple, hemlock, spruce and pine. The cutting is round and round, and deepest upon the side on which they wish the tree to fall. Indians and trappers have seen beavers cutting trees. The felling of a tree is a family affair. No more than a single pair with two or three young ones are engaged at a time. The adults take the cutting in turns, one gnawing and the other watching; and occasionally a youngster trying his incisors. The beaver whilst gnawing sits on his plantigrade hind legs, which keep him conveniently upright. When the tree begins to crackle the beavers work cautiously, and when it crashes down they plunge into the pond, fearful lest the noise should attract an enemy to the spot. After the tree-fall, comes the lopping of the branches. A single tree may be winter provision for a family. Branches five or six inches thick have to be cut into proper lengths for transport, and are then taken home."

The lodge of a beaver is generally about six feet in diameter, on the inside, and about half as high. They are rounded or dome-shaped on the outside, with very thick walls, and communicate with the land by subterranean passages, below the depth at which the water freezes in winter. Each lodge is made to accommodate several inmates, who have their beds ranged round the walls, much as the Indian does in his tent. They are very cleanly, too, and after eating, carry out the sticks that have been stripped, and either use them in repairing their dam, or throw them into the stream below.

During the summer months the beavers abandon their lodges, and disport themselves about the streams, sometimes going on long journeys; or if any remain at home, they are the mothers of young families. About the last of August the community returns to its home, and begins preparations for the domestic cares of the long winter months.

An exception to this rule is that of certain individuals, who have no families, make no dam, and never live in lodges, but burrow in subterranean tunnels. They are always found to be males, whom the French trappers call "les parasseux," or idlers; and the American trappers, "bachelors." Several of them are sometimes found in one abode, which the trappers facetiously denominate "bachelor's hall." Being taken with less difficulty than the more domestic beaver, the trapper is always glad to come upon their habitations.

The trapping season is usually in the spring and autumn. But should the hunters find it necessary to continue their work in winter, they capture the beaver by sounding on the ice until an aperture is discovered, when the ice is cut away and the opening closed up. Returning to the bank, they search for the subterranean passage, tracing its connection with the lodge; and by patient watching succeed in catching the beaver on some of its journeys between the water and the land. This, however, is not often resorted to when the hunt in the fall has been successful; or when not urged by famine to take the beaver for food.

"Occasionally it happens," says Captain Bonneville, "that several members of a beaver family are trapped in succession. The survivors then become extremely shy, and can scarcely be "brought to medicine," to use the trappers' phrase for "taking the bait." In such case, the trapper gives up the use of the bait, and conceals his traps in the usual paths and crossing places of the household. The beaver being now completely "up to trap," approaches them cautiously, and springs them, ingeniously, with a stick. At other times, he turns the traps bottom upwards, by the same means, and occasionally even drags them to the barrier, and conceals them in the mud. The trapper now gives up the contest of ingenuity, and shouldering his traps, marches off, admitting that he is not yet "up to beaver."

Before the camp moved from the forks of the Snake River, the haunting Blackfeet made their appearance openly. It was here that Meek had his first battle with that nation, with whom he subsequently had many a savage contest. They attacked the camp early in the morning, just as the call to turn out had sounded. But they had miscalculated their opportunity: the design having evidently been to stampede the horses and mules, at the hour and moment of their being turned loose to graze. They had been too hasty by a few minutes, so that when they charged on the camp pell-mell, firing a hundred guns at once, to frighten both horses and men, it happened that only a few of the animals had been turned out, and they had not yet got far off. The noise of the charge only turned them back to camp.

In an instant's time, Fitzpatrick was mounted, and commanding the men to follow, he galloped at headlong speed round and round the camp, to drive back such of the horses as were straying, or had been frightened from their pickets. In this race, two horses were shot under him; but he escaped, and the camp-horses were saved. The battle now was to punish the thieves. They took their position, as usual with Indian fighters, in a narrow ravine; from whence the camp was forced to dislodge them, at a great disadvantage. This they did do, at last, after six hours of hard fighting, in which a few men were wounded, but none killed. The thieves skulked off, through the canyon, when they found themselves defeated, and were seen no more until the camp came to the woods which cover the western slope of the Rocky Mountains.

But as the camp moved eastward, or rather in a northeasterly direction, through the pine forests between Pierre's Hole and the head-waters of the Missouri, it was continually harrassed by Blackfeet, and required a strong guard at night, when these marauders delighted to make an attack. The weather by this time was very cold in the mountains, and chilled the marrow of our young Virginian. The travel was hard, too, and the recruits pretty well worn out.

One cold night, Meek was put on guard on the further side of the camp, with a veteran named Reese. But neither the veteran nor the youngster could resist the approaches of " tired Nature's sweet restorer," and went to sleep at their post of duty. When, during the night, Sublette came out of his tent and gave the challenge— " All's well!" there was no reply. To quote Meek's own language, " Sublette came round the horse-pen swearing and snorting. He was powerful mad. Before he got to where Reese was, he made so much noise that he waked him; and Reese, in a loud whisper, called to him, 'Down, Billy! Indians!' Sublette got down on his belly mighty quick. 'Whar? whar?' he asked.

" 'They were right there when you hollered so,' said Reese.

" 'Where is Meek?' whispered Sublette.

" 'He is trying to shoot one,' answered Reese, still in a whisper.

" Reese then crawled over to whar I war, and told me what had been said, and informed me what to do. In a few minutes I crept cautiously over to Reese's post, when Sublette asked me how many Indians had been thar, and I told him I couldn't make out their number. In the morning a pair of Indian moccasins war found whar Reese *saw the Indians*, which I had *taken care to leave there;* and thus confirmed, our story got us the credit of vigilance, instead of our receiving our just dues for neglect of duty."

It was sometime during the fall hunt in the Pine Woods, on the west side of the Rocky Mountains, that Meek had one of his earliest adventures with a bear. Two comrades, Craig and Nelson, and himself, while out trapping, left their horses, and traveled up a creek on foot, in search of beaver. They had not proceeded any great distance, before they came suddenly face to face with a red bear; so suddenly, indeed, that the men made a spring for the nearest trees. Craig and Meek ascended a large pine, which chanced to be nearest, and having many limbs, was easy to climb. Nelson happened to take to one of two small trees that grew close together; and the bear, fixing upon him for a victim, undertook to climb after him. With his back against one of these small trees, and his feet against the other, his bearship succeeded in reaching a point not far below Nelson's perch, when the trees

opened with his weight, and down he went, with a shock
that fairly shook the ground. But this bad luck only
seemed to infuriate the beast, and up he went again, with
the same result, each time almost reaching his enemy.
With the second tumble he was not the least discouraged;
but started up the third time, only to be dashed once
more to the ground when he had attained a certain height.
At the third fall, however, he became thoroughly dis-
gusted with his want of success, and turned and ran at
full speed into the woods.

"Then," says Meek, "Craig began to sing, and I began
to laugh; but Nelson took to swearing. 'O yes, you can
laugh and sing now,' says Nelson; 'but you war quiet
enough when the bear was around.' 'Why, Nelson,' I
answered, 'you wouldn't have us noisy before that distinguished guest of yours?' But Nelson damned the
wild beast; and Craig and I laughed, and said he didn't
seem wild a bit. That's the way we hector each other in
the mountains. If a man gets into trouble he is only
laughed at: 'let him keep out; let him have better luck,'
is what we say."

The country traversed by Sublette in the fall of 1829,
was unknown at that period, even to the fur companies,
they having kept either farther to the south or to the
north. Few, if any, white men had passed through it
since Lewis and Clarke discovered the head-waters of the
Missouri and the Snake Rivers, which flow from the opposite sides of the same mountain peaks. Even the toils
and hardships of passing over mountains at this season of
the year, did not deprive the trapper of the enjoyment
of the magnificent scenery the region afforded. Splendid
views, however, could not long beguile men who had
little to eat, and who had yet a long journey to accom-

plish in cold, and surrounded by dangers, before reaching the wintering ground.

In November the camp left Missouri Lake on the east side of the mountains, and crossed over, still northeasterly, on to the Gallatin fork of the Missouri River, passing over a very rough and broken country. They were, in fact, still in the midst of mountains, being spurs of the great Rocky range, and equally high and rugged. A particularly high mountain lay between them and the main Yellowstone River. This they had just crossed, with great fatigue and difficulty, and were resting the camp and horses for a few days on the river's bank, when the Blackfeet once more attacked them in considerable numbers. Two men were killed in this fight, and the camp thrown into confusion by the suddenness of the alarm. Capt. Sublette, however, got off, with most of his men, still pursued by the Indians.

Not so our Joe, who this time was not in luck, but was cut off from camp, alone, and had to flee to the high mountains overlooking the Yellowstone. Here was a situation for a nineteen-year-old raw recruit! Knowing that the Blackfeet were on the trail of the camp, it was death to proceed in that direction. Some other route must be taken to come up with them; the country was entirely unknown to him; the cold severe; his mule, blanket, and gun, his only earthly possessions. On the latter he depended for food, but game was scarce; and besides, he thought the sound of his gun would frighten himself, so alone in the wilderness, swarming with stealthy foes.

Hiding his mule in a thicket, he ascended to the mountain top to take a view of the country, and decide upon his course. And what a scene was that for the miserable boy, whose chance of meeting with his comrades again was small indeed! At his feet rolled the Yellow-

stone River, coursing away through the great plain to the
eastward.   To the north his eye follows the windings of
the Missouri, as upon a map, but playing at hide-and-seek
in amongst the mountains.   Looking back, he saw the
River Snake stretching its serpentine length through lava
plains, far away, to its junction with the Columbia.   To
the north, and to the south, one white mountain rose
above another as far as the eye could reach.   What a
mighty and magnificent world it seemed, to be alone in!
Poor Joe succumbed to the influence of the thought, and
wept.

Having indulged in this sole remaining luxury of life,
Joe picked up his resolution, and decided upon his course.
To the southeast lay the Crow country, a land of plenty,
— as the mountain-man regards plenty, — and there he
could at least live ; provided the Crows permitted him to
do so.   Besides, he had some hopes of falling in with one
of the camps, by taking that course.

Descending the mountain to the hiding-place of his
mule, by which time it was dark night, hungry and freezing, Joe still could not light a fire, for fear of revealing his
whereabouts to the Indians ; nor could he remain to perish with cold.   Travel he must, and travel he did, going
he scarcely knew whither.   Looking back upon the terrors
and discomforts of that night, the veteran mountaineer
yet regards it as about the most miserable one of his
life.   When day at length broke, he had made, as well as
he could estimate the distance, about thirty miles.   Traveling on toward the southeast, he had crossed the Yellowstone River, and still among the mountains, was obliged
to abandon his mule and accoutrements, retaining only
one blanket and his gun.   Neither the mule nor himself
had broken fast in the last two days.   Keeping a southerly course for twenty miles more, over a rough and

elevated country, he came, on the evening of the third day, upon a band of mountain sheep. With what eagerness did he hasten to kill, cook, and eat! Three days of fasting was, for a novice, quite sufficient to provide him with an appetite.

Having eaten voraciously, and being quite overcome with fatigue, Joe fell asleep in his blanket, and slumbered quite deeply until morning. With the morning came biting blasts from the north, that made motion necessary if not pleasant. Refreshed by sleep and food, our traveler hastened on upon his solitary way, taking with him what sheep-meat he could carry, traversing the same rough and mountainous country as before. No incidents nor alarms varied the horrible and monotonous solitude of the wilderness. The very absence of anything to alarm was awful; for the bravest man is wretchedly nervous in the solitary presence of sublime Nature. Even the veteran hunter of the mountains can never entirely divest himself of this feeling of awe, when his single soul comes face to face with God's wonderful and beautiful handiwork.

At the close of the fourth day, Joe made his lonely camp in a deep defile of the mountains, where a little fire and some roasted mutton again comforted his inner and outer man, and another night's sleep still farther refreshed his wearied frame. On the following morning, a very bleak and windy one, having breakfasted on his remaining piece of mutton, being desirous to learn something of the progress he had made, he ascended a low mountain in the neighborhood of his camp—and behold! the whole country beyond was smoking with the vapor from boiling springs, and burning with gasses, issuing from small craters, each of which was emitting a sharp whistling sound.

When the first surprise of this astonishing scene had

passed, Joe began to admire its effect in an artistic point
of view. The morning being clear, with a sharp frost, he
thought himself reminded of the city of Pittsburg, as he
had beheld it on a winter morning, a couple of years before. This, however, related only to the rising smoke and
vapor ; for the extent of the volcanic region was immense,
reaching far out of sight. The general face of the country was smooth and rolling, being a level plain, dotted
with cone-shaped mounds. On the summits of these
mounds were small craters from four to eight feet in diameter. Interspersed among these, on the level plain,
were larger craters, some of them from four to six miles
across. Out of these craters issued blue flames and molten
brimstone.

For some minutes Joe gazed and wondered. Curious
thoughts came into his head, about hell and the day of
doom. With that natural tendency to reckless gayety
and humorous absurdities which some temperaments are
sensible of in times of great excitement, he began to solilo-
quize. Said he, to himself, "I have been told the sun
would be blown out, and the earth burnt up. If this infernal wind keeps up, I shouldn't be surprised if the sun
war blown out. If the earth is *not* burning up over thar,
then it is that place the old Methodist preacher used to
threaten me with. Any way it suits me to go and see
what it's like."

On descending to the plain described, the earth was
found to have a hollow sound, and seemed threatening to
break through. But Joe found the warmth of the place
most delightful, after the freezing cold of the mountains,
and remarked to himself again, that "if it war hell, it war
a more agreeable climate than he had been in for some
time."

He had thought the country entirely desolate, as not a

living creature had been seen in the vicinity; but while he stood gazing about him in curious amazement, he was startled by the report of two guns, followed by the Indian yell. While making rapid preparations for defence and flight, if either or both should be necessary, a familiar voice greeted him with the exclamation, "It *is* old Joe!" When the adjective "old" is applied to one of Meek's age at that time, it is generally understood to be a term of endearment. "My feelings you may imagine," says the "old Uncle Joe" of the present time, in recalling the adventure.

Being joined by these two associates, who had been looking for him, our traveler, no longer simply a raw recruit, but a hero of wonderful adventures, as well as the rest of the men, proceeded with them to camp, which they overtook the third day, attempting to cross the high mountains between the Yellowstone and the Bighorn Rivers. If Meek had seen hard times in the mountains alone, he did not find them much improved in camp. The snow was so deep that the men had to keep in advance, and break the road for the animals; and to make their condition still more trying, there were no provisions in camp, nor any prospect of plenty, for men or animals, until they should reach the buffalo country beyond the mountains.

During this scarcity of provisions, some of those amusing incidents took place with which the mountaineer will contrive to lighten his own and his comrades' spirits, even in periods of the greatest suffering. One which we have permission to relate, has reference to what Joe Meek calls the "meanest act of his life."

While the men were starving, a negro boy, belonging to Jedediah Smith, by some means was so fortunate as to have caught a porcupine, which he was roasting before the fire. Happening to turn his back for a moment, to observe

something in camp, Meek and Reese snatched the tempting viand and made off with it, before the darkey discovered his loss.   But when it was discovered, what a wail
went up for the embezzled porcupine! Suspicion fixed
upon the guilty parties, but as no one would 'peach on
white men to save a "nigger's" rights, the poor, disappointed boy could do nothing but lament in vain, to the
great amusement of the men, who upon the principle that
"misery loves company," rather chuckled over than con-
demned Meek's "mean act."

There was a sequel, however, to this little story. So
much did the negro dwell upon the event, and the heart-
lessness of the men towards him, that in the following
summer, when Smith was in St. Louis, he gave the boy his
freedom and two hundred dollars, and left him in that city;
so that it became a saying in the mountains, that "the nigger got his freedom for a porcupine."

During this same march, a similar joke was played upon
one of the men named Craig. He had caught a rabbit
and put it up to roast before the fire—a tempting looking
morsel to starving mountaineers.   Some of his associates
determined to see how it tasted, and Craig was told that
the Booshways wished to speak with him at their lodge.
While he obeyed this supposed command, the rabbit was
spirited away, never more to be seen by mortal man.
When Craig returned to the camp-fire, and beheld the
place vacant where a rabbit so late was nicely roasting, his
passion knew no bounds, and he declared his intention of
cutting it out of the stomach that contained it.   But as
finding the identical stomach which contained it involved
the cutting open of many that probably did not, in the
search, he was fain to relinquish that mode of vengeance,
together with his hopes of a supper.   As Craig is still living, and is tormented by the belief that he knows the man

who stole his rabbit, Mr. Meek takes this opportunity of assuring him, upon the word of a gentleman, that *he* is not the man.

While on the march over these mountains, owing to the depth of the snow, the company lost a hundred head of horses and mules, which sank in the yet unfrozen drifts, and could not be extricated. In despair at their situation, Jedediah Smith one day sent a man named Harris to the top of a high peak to take a view of the country, and ascertain their position. After a toilsome scramble the scout returned.

" Well, what did you see, Harris?" asked Smith anxiously.

"I saw the city of St. Louis, and one fellow taking a drink!" replied Harris; prefacing the assertion with a shocking oath.

Smith asked no more questions. He understood by the man's answer that he had made no pleasing discoveries; and knew that they had still a weary way before them to reach the plains below. Besides, Smith was a religious man, and the coarse profanity of the mountaineers was very distasteful to him. " A very mild man, and a christian; and there were very few of them in the mountains," is the account given of him by the mountaineers themselves.

The camp finally arrived without loss of life, except to the animals, on the plains of the Bighorn River, and came upon the waters of the Stinking Fork, a branch of this river, which derives its unfortunate appellation from the fact that it flows through a volcanic tract similar to the one discovered by Meek on the Yellowstone plains. This place afforded as much food for wonder to the whole camp, as the former one had to Joe; and the men unanimously pronounced it the "back door to that country which divines

6

preach about." As this volcanic district had previously
been seen by one of Lewis and Clarke's men, named Colter, while on a solitary hunt, and by him also denominated
"hell," there must certainly have been something very
suggestive in its appearance.

If the mountains had proven barren, and inhospitably
cold, this hot and sulphurous country offered no greater
hospitality. In fact, the fumes which pervaded the air
rendered it exceedingly noxious to every living thing,
and the camp was fain to push on to the main stream of
the Bighorn River. Here signs of trappers became apparent, and spies having been sent out discovered a camp of
about forty men, under Milton Sublette, brother of Captain
William Sublette, the same that had been detached the
previous summer to hunt in that country. Smith and Sublette then cached their furs, and moving up the river joined
the camp of M. Sublette.

The manner of caching furs is this: A pit is dug to a
depth of five or six feet in which to stand. The men then
drift from this under a bank of solid earth, and excavate a
room of considerable dimensions, in which the furs are
deposited, and the apartment closed up. The pit is then
filled up with earth, and the traces of digging obliterated
or concealed. These caches are the only storehouses of
the wilderness.

While the men were recruiting themselves in the joint
camp, the alarm of "Indians!" was given, and hurried
cries of "shoot! shoot!" were uttered on the instant.
Captain Sublette, however, checked this precipitation, and
ordering the men to hold, allowed the Indians to approach,
making signs of peace. They proved to be a war party
of Crows, who after smoking the pipe of peace with the
Captain, received from him a present of some tobacco, and
departed.

As soon as the camp was sufficiently recruited for traveling, the united companies set out again toward the south, and crossed the Horn mountains once more into Wind River Valley; having had altogether, a successful fall hunt, and made some important explorations, notwithstanding the severity of the weather and the difficulty of mountain traveling. It was about Christmas when the camp arrived on Wind River, and the cold intense. While the men celebrated Christmas, as best they might under the circumstances, Capt. Sublette started to St. Louis with one man, Harris, called among mountain-men Black Harris, on snowshoes, with a train of pack-dogs. Such was the indomitable energy and courage of this famous leader!

CHAPTER IV.

1830. THE furs collected by Jackson's company were cached on the Wind River; and the cold still being very severe, and game scarce, the two remaining leaders, Smith and Jackson, set out on the first of January with the whole camp, for the buffalo country, on the Powder River, a distance of about one hundred and fifty miles. "Times were hard in camp," when mountains had to be crossed in the depth of winter.

The animals had to be subsisted on the bark of the sweet cotton-wood, which grows along the streams and in the valleys on the east side of the Rocky Mountains, but is nowhere to be found west of that range. This way of providing for his horses and mules involved no trifling amount of labor, when each man had to furnish food for several of them. To collect this bark, the men carried the smooth limbs of the cotton-wood to camp, where, beside the camp-fire, they shaved off the sweet, green bark with a hunting-knife transformed into a drawing-knife by fastening a piece of wood to its point; or, in case the cotton-wood was not convenient, the bark was peeled off, and carried to camp in a blanket. So nutritious is it, that animals fatten upon it quite as well as upon oats.

In the large cotton-wood bottoms on the Yellowstone River, it sometimes became necessary to station a double guard to keep the buffalo out of camp, so numerous were they, when the severity of the cold drove them from the prairies to these cotton-wood thickets for subsistence. It was, therefore, of double importance to make the winter camp where the cotton-wood was plenty ; since not only did it furnish the animals of the camp with food, but by attracting buffalo, made game plenty for the men.   To such a hunter's paradise on Powder River, the camp was now traveling, and arrived, after a hard, cold march, about the middle of January, when the whole encampment went into winter quarters, to remain until the opening of spring.

This was the occasion when the mountain-man "lived fat" and enjoyed life : a season of plenty, of relaxation, of amusement, of acquaintanceship with all the company, of gayety, and of "busy idleness."   Through the day, hunting parties were coming and going, men were cooking, drying meat, making moccasins, cleaning their arms, wrestling, playing games, and, in short, everything that an isolated community of hardy men could resort to for occupation, was resorted to by these mountaineers.   Nor was there wanting, in the appearance of the camp, the variety, and that picturesque air imparted by a mingling of the native element ; for what with their Indian allies, their native wives, and numerous children, the mountaineers' camp was a motley assemblage ; and the trappers themselves, with their affectation of Indian coxcombry, not the least picturesque individuals.

The change wrought in a wilderness landscape by the arrival of the grand camp was wonderful indeed.   Instead of Nature's superb silence and majestic loneliness, there was the sound of men's voices in boisterous laughter, or the busy hum of conversation ; the loud-resounding stroke of the axe ; the sharp report of the rifle ; the neighing of horses, and braying of mules ; the Indian whoop and yell ; and all that not unpleasing confusion of sound which accompanies the movements of the creature man.   Over the plain, only dotted until now with shadows of clouds, or the transitory passage of the deer, the antelope, or the bear, were scattered hundreds of lodges and immense herds of grazing animals. Even the atmosphere itself seemed changed from its original purity, and became clouded with the smoke from many camp-fires. And all this change might go as quickly as it came. The tent struck and the march resumed, solitude reigned once more, and only the cloud dotted the silent landscape.

If the day was busy and gleesome, the night had its charms as well. Gathered about the shining fires, groups of men in fantastic costumes told tales of marvelous adventures, or sung some old-remembered song, or were absorbed in games of chance. Some of the better educated men, who had once known and loved books, but whom some mishap in life had banished to the wilderness, recalled their favorite authors, and recited passages once treasured, now growing unfamiliar ; or whispered to some chosen confrere the saddened history of his earlier years, and charged him thus and thus, should ever-ready death surprise himself in the next spring's hunt.

It will not be thought discreditable to our young trapper, Joe, that he learned to read by the light of the camp-fire. Becoming sensible, even in the wilderness, of the deficiencies of his early education, he found a teacher in a comrade, named Green, and soon acquired sufficient knowledge to enjoy an old copy of Shakspeare, which, with a Bible, was carried about with the property of the camp.

In this life of careless gayety and plenty, the whole company was allowed to remain without interruption, until the first of April, when it was divided, and once more started on the march. Jackson, or "Davey," as he was called by the men, with about half the company, left

for the Snake country.   The remainder, among whom
was Meek, started north, with Smith for commander, and
James Bridger as pilot.

Crossing the mountains, ranges of which divide the
tributary streams of the Yellowstone from each other, the
first halt was made on Tongue River.   From thence the
camp proceeded to the Bighorn River.   Through all this
country game was in abundance,—buffalo, elk, and bear,
and beaver also plenty.   In mountain phrase, "times
were good on this hunt:" beaver packs increased in number, and both men and animals were in excellent condition.

A large party usually hunted out the beaver and frightened away the game in a few weeks, or days, from any
one locality.   When this happened the camp moved on ;
or, should not game be plenty, it kept constantly on the
move, the hunters and trappers seldom remaining out
more than a day or two.   Should the country be considered dangerous on account of Indians, it was the habit of
the men to return every night to the encampment.

It was the design of Smith to take his command into
the Blackfoot country, a region abounding in the riches
which he sought, could they only be secured without
coming into too frequent conflict with the natives: always
a doubtful question concerning these savages.   He had
proceeded in this direction as far as Bovey's Fork of the
Bighorn, when the camp was overtaken by a heavy fall
of snow, which made traveling extremely difficult, and
which, when melted, caused a sudden great rise in the
mountain streams.   In attempting to cross Bovey's Fork
during the high water, he had thirty horses swept away,
with three hundred traps: a serious loss in the business
of hunting beaver.

In the manner described, pushing on through an un-

known country, hunting and trapping as they moved, the
company proceeded, passing another low chain of mountains, through a pass called Pryor's Gap, to Clark's Fork
of the Yellowstone, thence to Rose-Bud River, and finally
to the main Yellowstone River, where it makes a great
bend to the east, enclosing a large plain covered with
grass, and having also extensive cotton-wood bottoms,
which subsequently became a favorite wintering ground
of the fur companies.

It was while trapping up in this country, on the Rose-
Bud River, that an amusing adventure befel our trapper
Joe. Being out with two other trappers, at some distance
from the great camp, they had killed and supped off a fat
buffalo cow. The night was snowy, and their camp was
made in a grove of young aspens. Having feasted themselves, the remaining store of choice pieces was divided
between, and placed, hunter fashion, under the heads of
the party, on their betaking themselves to their blanket
couches for the night. Neither Indian nor wild beast disturbed their repose, as they slept, with their guns beside
them, filled with comfort and plenty. But who ever
dreams of the presence of a foe under such circumstances ? Certainly not our young trapper, who was only
awakened about day-break by something very large and
heavy walking over him, and snuffing about him with a
most insulting freedom. It did not need Yankee powers
of guessing to make out who the intruder in camp might
be : in truth, it was only too disagreeably certain that it
was a full sized grizzly bear, whose keenness of smell had
revealed to him the presence of fat cow-meat in that
neighborhood.

" You may be sure," says Joe, " that I kept very quiet,
while that bar helped himself to some of my buffalo meat,
and went a little way off to eat it. But Mark Head, one

of the men, raised up, and back came the bar. Down
went our heads under the blankets, and I kept mine covered pretty snug, while the beast took another walk over
the bed, but finally went off again to a little distance.
Mitchel then wanted to shoot; but I said, 'no, no; hold
on, or the brute will kill us, sure.' When the bar heard
our voices, back he run again, and jumped on the bed as
before. I'd have been happy to have felt myself sinking
ten feet under ground, while that bar promenaded over
and around us! However, he couldn't quite make out our
style, and finally took fright, and ran off down the mountain. Wanting to be revenged for his impudence, I went
after him, and seeing a good chance, shot him dead.
Then I took my turn at running over him awhile!"

Such are the not infrequent incidents of the trapper's
life, which furnish him with material, needing little em-
bellishment to convert it into those wild tales with which
the nights are whiled away around the winter camp-fire.

Arrived at the Yellowstone with his company, Smith
found it necessary, on account of the high water, to construct Bull-boats for the crossing. These are made by
stitching together buffalo hides, stretching them over light
frames, and paying the seams with elk tallow and ashes.
In these light wherries the goods and people were ferried
over, while the horses and mules were crossed by swimming.

The mode usually adopted in crossing large rivers, was
to spread the lodges on the ground, throwing on them the
light articles, saddles, etc. A rope was then run through
the pin-holes around the edge of each, when it could be
drawn up like a reticule. It was then filled with the
heavier camp goods, and being tightly drawn up, formed a
perfect ball. A rope being tied to it, it was launched on
the water, the children of the camp on top, and the women swimming after and clinging to it, while a man, who

had the rope in his hand, swam ahead holding on to his horse's mane. In this way, dancing like a cork on the waves, the lodge was piloted across; and passengers as well as freight consigned, undamaged, to the opposite shore. A large camp of three hundred men, and one hundred women and children were frequently thus crossed in one hour's time.

The camp was now in the excellent but inhospitable country of the Blackfeet, and the commander redoubled his precautions, moving on all the while to the Mussel Shell, and thence to the Judith River. Beaver were plenty and game abundant; but the vicinity of the large village of the Blackfeet made trapping impracticable. Their war upon the trappers was ceaseless; their thefts of traps and horses ever recurring: and Smith, finding that to remain was to be involved in incessant warfare, without hope of victory or gain, at length gave the command to turn back, which was cheerfully obeyed: for the trappers had been very successful on the spring hunt, and thinking discretion some part at least of valor, were glad to get safe out of the Blackfoot country with their rich harvest of beaver skins.

The return march was by the way of Pryor's Gap, and up the Bighorn, to Wind River, where the cache was made in the previous December. The furs were now taken out and pressed, ready for transportation across the plains. A party was also dispatched, under Mr. Tullock, to raise the cache on the Bighorn River. Among this party was Meek, and a Frenchman named Ponto. While digging to come at the fur, the bank above caved in, falling upon Meek and Ponto, killing the latter almost instantly. Meek, though severely hurt, was taken out alive: while poor Ponto was "rolled in a blanket, and pitched into the river." So rude were the burial services of the trapper of the Rocky Mountains.

Meek was packed back to camp, along with the furs, where he soon recovered. Sublette arrived from St. Louis with fourteen wagons loaded with merchandise, and two hundred additional men for the service. Jackson also arrived from the Snake country with plenty of beaver, and the business of the yearly rendezvous began. Then the scenes previously described were re-enacted. Beaver, the currency of the mountains, was plenty that year, and goods were high accordingly. A thousand dollars a day was not too much for some of the most reckless to spend on their squaws, horses, alcohol, and themselves. For "alcohol" was the beverage of the mountaineers. Liquors could not be furnished to the men in that country. Pure alcohol was what they "got tight on;" and a desperate tight it was, to be sure!

An important change took place in the affairs of the Rocky Mountain Company at this rendezvous. The three partners, Smith, Sublette, and Jackson, sold out to a new firm, consisting of Milton Sublette, James Bridger, Fitzpatrick, Frapp, and Jervais; the new company retaining the same name and style as the old.

The old partners left for St. Louis, with a company of seventy men, to convoy the furs. Two of them never returned to the Rocky Mountains; one of them, Smith, being killed the following year, as will hereafter be related; and Jackson remaining in St. Louis, where, like a true mountain-man, he dissipated his large and hard-earned fortune in a few years. Captain Sublette, however, continued to make his annual trips to and from the mountains for a number of years; and until the consolidation of another wealthy company with the Rocky Mountain Company, continued to furnish goods to the latter, at a profit on St. Louis prices; his capital and experience enabling him to keep the new firm under his control to a large degree.

CHAPTER V.

1830.   THE whole country lying upon the Yellowstone and its tributaries, and about the head-waters of the Missouri, at the time of which we are writing, abounded not only in beaver, but in buffalo, bear, elk, antelope, and many smaller kinds of game.   Indeed the buffalo used then to cross the mountains into the valleys about the head-waters of the Snake and Colorado Rivers, in such numbers that at certain seasons of the year, the plains and river bottoms swarmed with them.   Since that day they have quite disappeared from the western slope of the Rocky Mountains, and are no longer seen in the same numbers on the eastern side.

Bear, although they did not go in herds, were rather uncomfortably numerous, and sometimes put the trapper to considerable trouble, and fright also; for very few were brave enough to willingly encounter the formidable grizzly, one blow of whose terrible paw, aimed generally at the hunter's head, if not arrested, lays him senseless and torn, an easy victim to the wrathful monster.   A gunshot wound, if not directed with certainty to some vulnerable point, has only the effect to infuriate the beast, and make him trebly dangerous.   From the fact that the bear always bites his wound, and commences to run with his head thus brought in the direction from which the ball comes, he is pretty likely to make a straight wake towards his enemy, whether voluntarily or not; and woe be to the hunter who is not prepared for him, with a shot for his

eye, or the spot just behind the ear, where certain death
enters.

In the frequent encounters of the mountain-men with
these huge beasts, many acts of wonderful bravery were
performed, while some tragedies, and not a few comedies
were enacted.

From something humorous in Joe Meek's organization,
or some wonderful "luck" to which he was born, or both,
the greater part of his adventures with bears, as with men,
were of a humorous complexion; enabling him not only
to have a story to tell, but one at which his companions
were bound to laugh. One of these which happened during the fall hunt of 1830, we will let him tell for himself:
"The first fall on the Yellowstone, Hawkins and myself
were coming up the river in search of camp, when we discovered a very large bar on the opposite bank. We shot
across, and thought we had killed him, fur he laid quite
still. As we wanted to take some trophy of our victory
to camp, we tied our mules and left our guns, clothes, and
everything except our knives and belts, and swum over to
whar the bar war. But instead of being dead, as we expected, he sprung up as we come near him, and took after
us. Then you ought to have seen two naked men run!
It war a race for life, and a close one, too. But we made
the river first. The bank war about fifteen feet high above
the water, and the river ten or twelve feet deep; but we
didn't halt. Overboard we went, the bar after us, and in
the stream about as quick as we war. The current war
very strong, and the bar war about half way between
Hawkins and me. Hawkins was trying to swim down
stream faster than the current war carrying the bar, and I
war a trying to hold back. You can reckon that I swam!
Every moment I felt myself being washed into the yawn-
ing jaws of the mighty beast, whose head war up the

stream, and his eyes on me. But the current war too strong
for him, and swept him along as fast as it did me. All this
time, not a long one, we war looking for some place to
land where the bar could not overtake us. Hawkins war
the first to make the shore, unknown to the bar, whose
head war still up stream; and he set up such a whooping
and yelling that the bar landed too, but on the opposite
side. I made haste to follow Hawkins, who had landed
on the side of the river we started from, either by design
or good luck: and then we traveled back a mile and more
to whar our mules war left—a bar on one side of the river,
and *two bares* on the other!"

Notwithstanding that a necessary discipline was observed
and maintained in the fur traders' camp, there was at the
same time a freedom of manner between the Booshways
and the men, both hired and free, which could not obtain
in a purely military organization, nor even in the higher
walks of civilized life in cities. In the mountain community, motley as it was, as in other communities more refined,
were some men who enjoyed almost unlimited freedom of
speech and action, and others who were the butt of everybody's ridicule or censure. The leaders themselves did
not escape the critical judgment of the men; and the estimation in which they were held could be inferred from
the manner in which they designated them. Captain Sublette, whose energy, courage, and kindness entitled him to
the admiration of the mountaineers, went by the name of
Billy: his partner Jackson, was called *Davey;* Bridger,
old Gabe, and so on. In the same manner the men distinguished favorites or oddities amongst themselves, and to
have the adjective *old* prefixed to a man's name signified
nothing concerning his age, but rather that he was an
object of distinction; though it did not always indicate,
except by the tone in which it was pronounced, whether
that distinction were an enviable one or not.

THE THREE "BARES."

Whenever a trapper could get hold of any sort of story reflecting on the courage of a leader, he was sure at some time to make him aware of it, and these anecdotes were sometimes sharp answers in the mouths of careless camp-keepers. Bridger was once waylaid by Blackfeet, who shot at him, hitting his horse in several places. The wounds caused the animal to rear and pitch, by reason of which violent movements Bridger dropped his gun, and the Indians snatched it up; after which there was nothing to do except to run, which Bridger accordingly did. Not long after this, as was customary, the leader was making a circuit of the camp examining the camp-keeper's guns, to see if they were in order, and found that of one Maloney, an Irishman, in a very dirty condition.

"What would you do," asked Bridger, "with a gun like that, if the Indians were to charge on the camp?"

"Be ——, I would throw it to them, and run the way ye did," answered Maloney, quickly. It was sometime after this incident before Bridger again examined Maloney's gun.

A laughable story in this way went the rounds of the camp in this fall of 1830. Milton Sublette was out on a hunt with Meek after buffalo, and they were just approaching the band on foot, at a distance apart of about fifty yards, when a large grizzly bear came out of a thicket and made after Sublette, who, when he perceived the creature, ran for the nearest cotton-wood tree. Meek in the meantime, seeing that Sublette was not likely to escape, had taken sure aim, and fired at the bear, fortunately killing him. On running up to the spot where it laid, Sublette was discovered sitting at the foot of a cotton-wood, with his legs and arms clasped tightly around it.

"Do you always climb a tree in that way?" asked Meek.

"I reckon you took the wrong end of it, that time, Milton!"

"I'll be —— , Meek, if I didn't think I was twenty feet up that tree when you shot;" answered the frightened Booshway; and from that time the men never tired of alluding to Milton's manner of climbing a tree.

THE WRONG END OF THE TREE.

These were some of the mirthful incidents which gave occasion for a gayety which had to be substituted for happiness, in the checkered life of the trapper; and there were like to be many such, where there were two hundred men, each almost daily in the way of adventures by flood or field.

On the change in the management of the Company which occurred at the rendezvous this year, three of the new partners, Fitzpatrick, Sublette, and Bridger, conducted a large party, numbering over two hundred, from the Wind River to the Yellowstone; crossing thence to Smith's River, the Falls of the Missouri, three forks of the Missouri, and to the Big Blackfoot River. The hunt proved very successful; beaver were plentiful; and the Blackfeet shy of so large a traveling party. Although so long in their country, there were only four men killed out of the whole company during this autumn.

From the Blackfoot River the company proceeded down the west side of the mountains to the forks of the Snake River, and after trapping for a short time in this locality, continued their march southward as far as Ogden's Hole, a small valley among the Bear River Mountains.

At this place they fell in with a trading and trapping party, under Mr. Peter Skeen Ogden, of the Hudson's Bay Company. And now commenced that irritating and reprehensible style of rivalry with which the different companies were accustomed to annoy one another. Accompanying Mr. Ogden's trading party were a party of Rockway Indians, who were from the North, and who were employed by the Hudson's Bay Company, as the Iroquois and Crows were, to trap for them. Fitzpatrick and associates camped in the neighborhood of Ogden's company, and immediately set about endeavoring to purchase from the Rockways and others, the furs collected for Mr. Ogden. Not succeeding by fair means, if the means to such an end could be called fair,—they opened a keg of whiskey, which, when the Indians had got a taste, soon drew them away from the Hudson's Bay trader, the regulations of whose company forbade the selling or giving of liquors to the Indians. Under its influence, the furs were disposed of to the Rocky Mountain Company, who in this manner obtained nearly the whole product of their year's hunt. This course of conduct was naturally exceedingly disagreeable to Mr. Ogden, as well as unprofitable also; and a feeling of hostility grew up and increased between the two camps.

While matters were in this position, a stampede one day occurred among the horses in Ogden's camp, and two or three of the animals ran away, and ran into the camp of the rival company. Among them was the horse of Mr. Ogden's Indian wife, which had escaped, with her babe hanging to the saddle.

7

Not many minutes elapsed, before the mother, following her child and horse, entered the camp, passing right through it, and catching the now halting steed by the bridle. At the same moment she espied one of her company's pack-horses, loaded with beaver, which had also run into the enemy's camp. The men had already begun to exult over the circumstance, considering this chance load of beaver as theirs, by the laws of war. But not so the Indian woman. Mounting her own horse, she fearlessly seized the pack-horse by the halter, and led it out of camp, with its costly burden.

At this undaunted action, some of the baser sort of men cried out "shoot her, shoot her!" but a majority interfered, with opposing cries of "let her go; let her alone; she's a brave woman: I glory in her pluck;" and other like admiring expressions. While the clamor continued, the wife of Ogden had galloped away, with her baby and her pack-horse.

As the season advanced, Fitzpatrick, with his other partners, returned to the east side of the mountains, and went into winter quarters on Powder river. In this trapper's "land of Canaan" they remained between two and three months. The other two partners, Frapp and Jervais, who were trapping far to the south, did not return until the following year.

While wintering it became necessary to send a dispatch to St. Louis on the company's business. Meek and a Frenchman named Legarde, were chosen for this service, which was one of trust and peril also. They proceeded without accident, however, until the Pawnee villages were reached, when Legarde was taken prisoner. Meek, more cautious, escaped, and proceeded alone a few days' travel beyond, when he fell in with an express on its way to St. Louis, to whom he delivered his dispatches, and returned

to camp, accompanied only by a Frenchman named Cabe-
neau; thus proving himself an efficient mountaineer at
twenty years of age.

1831. As soon as the spring opened, sometime in
March, the whole company started north again, for the
Blackfoot country. But on the night of the third day out,
they fell unawares into the neighborhood of a party of
Crow Indians, whose spies discovered the company's
horses feeding on the dry grass of a little bottom, and
succeeded in driving off about three hundred head. Here
was a dilemma to be in, in the heart of an enemy's country! To send the remaining horses after these, might be
"sending the axe after the helve;" besides most of them
belonged to the free trappers, and could not be pressed
into the service.

The only course remaining was to select the best men
and dispatch them on foot, to overtake and retake the
stolen horses. Accordingly one hundred trappers were
ordered on this expedition, among whom were Meek,
Newell, and Antoine Godin, a half-breed and brave fellow,
who was to lead the party. Following the trail of
the Crows for two hundred miles, traveling day and night,
on the third day they came up with them on a branch of
the Bighorn river. The trappers advanced cautiously,
and being on the opposite side of the stream, on a wooded
bluff, were enabled to approach close enough to look into
their fort, and count the unsuspecting thieves. There
were sixty of them, fine young braves, who believed that
now they had made a start in life. Alas, for the vanity
of human, and especially of Crow expectations! Even
then, while they were grouped around their fires, congratulating themselves on the sudden wealth which had descended upon them, as it were from the skies, an envious fate,
in the shape of several roguish white trappers, was laugh-

ing at them and their hopes, from the overhanging bluff
opposite them.   And by and by, when they were wrapped
in a satisfied slumber, two of these laughing rogues, Robert Newell, and Antoine Godin, stole under the very
walls of their fort, and setting the horses free, drove them
across the creek.

The Indians were awakened by the noise of the trampling horses, and sprang to arms.   But Meek and his fellow-
trappers on the bluff fired into the fort with such effect
that the Crows were appalled.   Having delivered their
first volley, they did not wait for the savages to recover
from their recoil.   Mounting in hot haste, the cavalcade
of bare-back riders, and their drove of horses, were soon
far away from the Crow fort, leaving the ambitious braves
to finish their excursion on foot.   It was afterwards ascertained that the Crows lost seven men by that one volley
of the trappers.

Flushed with success, the trappers yet found the back-
ward journey more toilsome than the outward; for what
with sleeplessness and fatigue, and bad traveling in melted
snow, they were pretty well exhausted when they reached
camp.   Fearing, however, another raid from the thieving
Crows, the camp got in motion again with as little delay
as possible.   They had not gone far, when Fitzpatrick
turned back, with only one man, to go to St. Louis for
supplies.

After the departure of Fitzpatrick, Bridger and Sublette
completed their spring and summer campaign without any
material loss in men or animals, and with considerable
gain in beaver skins.   Having once more visited the Yellowstone, they turned to the south again, crossing the
mountains into Pierre's Hole, on to Snake river; thence
to Salt river; thence to Bear river; and thence to Green
river. to rendezvous.

It was expected that Fitzpatrick would have arrived from St. Louis with the usual annual recruits and supplies of merchandise, in time for the summer rendezvous; but after waiting for some time in vain, Bridger and Sublette determined to send out a small party to look for him. The large number of men now employed, had exhausted the stock of goods on hand. The camp was without blankets and without ammunition; knives were not to be had; traps were scarce; but worse than all, the tobacco had given out, and alcohol was not! In such a case as this, what could a mountain-man do?

To seek the missing Booshway became not only a duty, but a necessity; and not only a necessity of the physical man, but in an equal degree a need of the moral and spiritual man, which was rusting with the tedium of waiting. In the state of uncertainty in which the minds of the company were involved, it occurred to that of Frapp to consult a great "medicine-man" of the Crows, one of those recruits filched from Mr. Ogden's party by whiskey the previous year.

Like all eminent professional men, the Crow chief required a generous fee, of the value of a horse or two, before he would begin to make "medicine." This peculiar ceremony is pretty much alike among all the different tribes. It is observed first in the making of a medicine man, i. e., qualifying him for his profession; and afterwards is practiced to enable him to heal the sick, to prophecy, and to dream dreams, or even to give victory to his people. To a medicine-man was imputed great power, not only to cure, but to kill; and if, as it sometimes happened, the relatives of a sick man suspected the medicine-man of having caused his death, by the exercise of evil powers, one of them, or all of them, pursued him to the death.   Therefore, although it might be honorable, it was not always safe to be a great "medicine."

The Indians placed a sort of religious value upon the practice of fasting; a somewhat curious fact, when it is remembered how many compulsory fasts they are obliged to endure, which must train them to think lightly of the deprivation of food.   Those, however, who could endure voluntary abstinence long enough, were enabled to become very wise and very brave.   The manner of making a "medicine" among some of the interior tribes, is in certain respects similar to the practice gone through with by some preachers, in making a convert.   A sort of camp-meeting is held, for several nights, generally about five, during which various dances are performed, with cries, and incantations, bodily exercises, singing, and nervous excitement; enough to make many patients, instead of one doctor.   But the native's constitution is a strong one, and he holds out well.   At last, however, one or more are overcome with the mysterious *power* which enters into them at that time; making, instead of a saint, only a superstitious Indian doctor.

The same sort of exercises which had made the Cree man a doctor were now resorted to, in order that he might obtain a more than natural sight, enabling him to see visions of the air, or at the least to endow him with prophetic dreams.   After several nights of singing, dancing, hopping, screeching, beating of drums, and other more violent exercises and contortions, the exhausted medicine-man fell off to sleep, and when he awoke he announced to Frapp that Fitzpatrick was not dead.   He was on the road; some road; but not the right one; etc., etc.

Thus encouraged, Frapp determined to take a party, and go in search of him.   Accordingly Meek, Reese, Ebarts, and Nelson, volunteered to accompany him.   This

party set out, first in the direction of Wind River; but
not discovering any signs of the lost Booshway in that
quarter, crossed over to the Sweetwater, and kept along
down to the North Fork of the Platte, and thence to the
Black Hills, where they found a beautiful country full of
game; but not the hoped-for train, with supplies. After
waiting for a short time at the Black Hills, Frapp's party
returned to the North Fork of the Platte, and were
rejoiced to meet at last, the long absent partner, with his
pack train. Urged by Frapp, Fitzpatrick hastened forward, and came into camp on Powder River after winter
had set in.

Fitzpatrick had a tale to tell the other partners, in explanation of his unexpected delay. When he had started
for St. Louis in the month of March previous, he had
hoped to have met the old partners, Capt. Sublette and
Jedediah Smith, and to have obtained the necessary supplies from them, to furnish the Summer rendezvous with
plenty. But these gentlemen, when he fell in with them,
used certain arguments which induced him to turn back,
and accompany them to Santa Fe, where they promised to furnish him goods, as he desired, and to procure
for him an escort at that place. The journey had proven
tedious, and unfortunate. They had several times been
attacked by Indians, and Smith had been killed. While
they were camped on a small tributary of the Simmaron
River, Smith had gone a short distance from camp to procure water, and while at the stream was surprised by an
ambush, and murdered on the spot, his murderers escaping
unpunished. Sublette, now left alone in the business,
finally furnished him; and he had at last made his way
back to his Rocky Mountain camp.

But Fitzpatrick's content at being once more with his
company was poisoned by the disagreeable proximity of a

rival company. If he had annoyed Mr. Ogden of the Hudson's Bay Company, in the previous autumn, Major Vanderburg and Mr. Dripps, of the American Company, in their turn annoyed him. This company had been on their heels, from the Platte River, and now were camped in the same neighborhood, using the Rocky Mountain Company as pilots to show them the country. As this was just what it was not for their interest to do, the Rocky Mountain Company raised camp, and fairly ran away from them; crossing the mountains to the Forks of the Snake River, where they wintered among the Nez Perces and Flathead Indians.

Some time during this winter, Meek and Legarde, who had escaped from the Pawnees, made another expedition together; traveling three hundred miles on snowshoes, to the Bitter Root River, to look for a party of free trappers, whose beaver the company wished to secure. They were absent two months and a half, on this errand, and were entirely successful, passing a Blackfoot village in the night, but having no adventures worth recounting.

CHAPTER VI.

1832. In the following spring, the Rocky Mountain Fur Company commenced its march, first up Lewis' Fork, then on to Salt River, thence to Gray's River, and thence to Bear River. They fell in with the North American Fur Company on the latter river, with a large lot of goods, but no beaver. The American Company's resident partners were ignorant of the country, and were greatly at a loss where to look for the good trapping grounds. These gentlemen, Vanderburg and Dripps, were therefore inclined to keep an eye on the movements of the Rocky Mountain Company, whose leaders were acquainted with the whole region lying along the mountains, from the head-waters of the Colorado to the northern branches of the Missouri. On the other hand, the Rocky Mountain Company were anxious to "shake the dust from off their feet," which was trodden by the American Company, and to avoid the evils of competition in an Indian country. But they found the effort quite useless; the rival company had a habit of turning up in the most unexpected places, and taking advantage of the hard-earned experience of the Rocky Mountain Company's leaders. They tampered with the trappers, and ferreted out the secret of their next rendezvous; they followed on their trail, making them pilots to the trapping grounds; they sold goods to the Indians, and what was worse, to the hired trappers. In this way grew up that fierce conflict of interests, which made it "as much as his life was worth" for a trapper to suffer himself to be inveigled into the service of a rival company, which about this time or a little later, was at its highest, and which finally ruined the fur-trade for the American companies in the Rocky Mountains.

Finding their rivals in possession of the ground, Bridger and Milton Sublette resolved to spend but a few days in that country. But so far as Sublette was concerned, circumstances ordered differently. A Rockway Chief, named Gray, and seven of his people, had accompanied the camp from Ogden's Hole, in the capacity of trappers. But during the sojourn on Bear River, there was a quarrel in camp on account of some indignity, real or fancied, which had been offered to the chief's daughter, and in the affray Gray stabbed Sublette so severely that it was thought he must die.

It thus fell out that Sublette had to be left behind; and Meek who was his favorite, was left to take care of him while he lived, and bury him if he died; which trouble Sublette saved him, however, by getting well. But they had forty lonesome days to themselves after the camps had moved off,—one on the heels of the other, to the great vexation of Bridger. Time passed slowly in Sublette's lodge, while waiting for his wound to heal. Day passed after day, so entirely like each other that the monotony alone seemed sufficient to invite death to an easy conquest. But the mountain-man's blood, like the Indians, is strong and pure, and his flesh heals readily, therefore, since death would not have him, the wounded man was forced to accept of life in just this monotonous form. To him Joe Meek was everything,—hands, feet, physician, guard, caterer, hunter, cook, companion, friend. What long talks they had, when Sublette grew better: what stories they told; what little glimpses of a secret chamber in their hearts, and a better than the every-day spirit, in their bosoms, was revealed,—as men will reveal such things in the isolation of sea-voyages, or the solitary presence of majestic Nature.

To the veteran mountaineer there must have been something soothing in the care and friendship of the youth of twenty-two, with his daring disposition, his frankness, his cheerful humor, and his good looks;—for our Joe was growing to be a maturely handsome man—tall, broad-shouldered, straight, with plenty of flesh, and none too much of it; a Southerner's olive complexion; frank, dark eyes, and a classical nose and chin. What though in the matter of dress he was ignorant of the latest styles?—grace imparts elegance even to the trapper's beaver-skin cap and blanket capote.

At the end of forty days, as many as it took to drown a world, Sublette found himself well enough to ride; and the two set out on their search for camp. But now other adventures awaited them. On a fork of Green River, they came suddenly upon a band of Snake Indians feeding their horses. As soon as the Snakes discovered the white men, they set up a yell, and made an instinctive rush for their horses. Now was the critical moment. One word passed between the travelers, and they made a dash past the savages, right into the village, and never slacked rein until they threw themselves from their horses at the door of the Medicine lodge. This is a large and fancifully decorated lodge, which stands in the centre of a village, and like the churches of Christians, is sacred. Once inside of this, the strangers were safe for the present; their blood could not be shed there.

The warriors of the village soon followed Sublette and Meek into their strange house of refuge. In half an hour it was filled. Not a word was addressed to the strangers; nor by them to the Indians, who talked among themselves with a solemn eagerness, while they smoked the medicine pipe, as inspiration in their councils. Great was the excitement in the minds of the listeners, who understood the Snake tongue, as the question of their life or death was gravely discussed; yet in their countenances appeared only the utmost serenity. To show fear, is to whet an Indian's appetite for blood: coolness confounds and awes him when anything will.

If Sublette had longed for excitement, while an invalid in his lonely lodge on Bear River, he longed equally now for that blissful seclusion. Listening for, and hearing one's death-warrant from a band of blood-thirsty savages, could only prove with bitter sharpness how sweet was life, even the most uneventful. For hours the council continued, and the majority favored the death-sentence. But one old chief, called the good *Gotia*, argued long for an acquittal: he did not see the necessity of murdering two harmless travelers of the white race. Nothing availed, however, and just at sunset their doom was fixed.

The only hope of escape was, that, favored by darkness, they might elude the vigilance of their jailers; and night, although so near, seemed ages away, even at sundown. Death being decreed, the warriors left the lodge one by one to attend to the preparation of the preliminary ceremonies. Gotia, the good, was the last to depart. As he left the Medicine lodge he made signs to the captives to remain quiet until he should return; pointing upwards to signify that there was a chance of life; and downwards to show that possibly they must die.

What an age of anxiety was that hour of waiting! Not a word had been exchanged between the prisoners since the Indians entered the lodge, until now; and now very little was said, for speech would draw upon them the vigilance of their enemy, by whom they desired most ardently to be forgotten.

About dusk there was a great noise, and confusion, and clouds of dust, in the south end of the village. Something was going wrong among the Indian horses. Immediately all the village ran to the scene of the disorder, and at the same moment Gotia, the good, appeared at the door of the Medicine lodge, beckoning the prisoners to follow him. With alacrity they sprang up and after him, and were led across the stream, to a thicket on the opposite side, where their horses stood, ready to mount, in the charge of a young Indian girl. They did not stop for compliments, though had time been less precious, they might well have bestowed some moments of it in admiration of *Umentucken Tukutsey Undewatsey*, the Mountain Lamb. Soon after, the beautiful Snake girl became the wife of Milton Sublette; and after his return to the States, of the subject of this narrative; from which circumstance the incident above related takes on something of the rosy hue of romance.

As each released captive received his bridle from the delicate hand of the Mountain Lamb, he sprang to the saddle. By this time the chief had discovered that the strangers understood the Snake dialect. "Ride, if you wish to live," said he: "ride without stopping, all night: and to-morrow linger not." With hurried thanks our mountain-men replied to this advice, and striking into a gallop, were soon far away from the Snake village. The next day at noon found them a hundred and fifty miles on their way to camp. Proceeding without further accident, they crossed the Teton Mountains, and joined the company at Pierre's Hole, after an absence of nearly four months.

Here they found the ubiquitous if not omnipresent American Fur Company encamped at the rendezvous of the Rocky Mountain Company. The partners being anx ious to be freed from this sort of espionage, and obstinate competition on their own ground, made a proposition to Vanderburg and Dripps to divide the country with them, each company to keep on its own territory. This proposition was refused by the American Company; perhaps because they feared having the poorer portion set off to themselves by their more experienced rivals. On this refusal, the Rocky Mountain Company determined to send an express to meet Capt. William Sublette, who was on his way out with a heavy stock of merchandise, and hurry him forward, lest the American Company should have the opportunity of disposing of its goods, when the usual, gathering to rendezvous began. On this decision being formed, Fitzpatrick determined to go on this errand himself; which he accordingly did, falling in with Sublette, and Campbell, his associate, somewhere near the Black Hills. To them he imparted his wishes and designs, and receiving the assurance of an early arrival at rendezvous, parted from them at the Sweetwater, and hastened back, alone, as he came, to prepare for business.

Captain Sublette hurried forward with his train, which consisted of sixty men with pack-horses, three to a man. In company with him, was Mr. Nathaniel Wyeth, a history of whose fur-trading and salmon-fishing adventures has already been given. Captain Sublette had fallen in with Mr. Wyeth at Independence, Missouri; and finding him ignorant of the undertaking on which he was launched, offered to become pilot and traveling companion, an offer which was gratefully accepted.

The caravan had reached the foot-hills of the Wind River Mountains, when the raw recruits belonging to both these parties were treated to a slight foretaste of what Indian fighting would be, should they ever have to encounter it. Their camp was suddenly aroused at midnight by the simultaneous discharge of guns and arrows, and the frightful whoops and yells with which the savages make an attack. Nobody was wounded, however; but on springing to arms, the Indians fled, taking with them a few horses which their yells had frightened from their pickets. These marauders were Blackfeet, as Captain Sublette explained to Mr. Wyeth, their moccasin tracks having betrayed them; for as each tribe has a peculiar way of making or shaping the moccasin, the expert in Indian habits can detect the nationality of an Indian thief by his foot-print. After this episode of the night assault, the leaders redoubled their watchfulness, and reached their destination in Pierre's hole about the first of July.

When Sublette arrived in camp, it was found that Fitzpatrick was missing. If the other partners had believed him to be with the Captain, the Captain expected to find him with them; but since neither could account to the other for his non-appearance, much anxiety was felt, and Sublette remembered with apprehension the visit he had received from Blackfeet. However, before anything had been determined upon with regard to him, he made his appearance in camp, in company with two Iroquois half-breeds, belonging to the camp, who had been out on a hunt.

Fitzpatrick had met with an adventure, as had been conjectured. While coming up the Green river valley, he descried a small party of mounted men, whom he mistook for a company of trappers, and stopped to reconnoitre; but almost at the same moment the supposed trappers, perceiving him, set up a yell that quickly undeceived him, and compelled him to flight. Abandoning his pack-horse, he put the other to its topmost speed, and succeeded in gaining the mountains, where in a deep and dark defile he secreted himself until he judged the

Indians had left that part of the valley. In this he was deceived, for no sooner did he emerge again into the open country, than he was once more pursued, and had to abandon his horse, to take refuge among the cliffs of the mountains. Here he remained for several days, without blankets or provisions, and with only one charge of ammunition, which was in his rifle, and kept for self-defense. At length, however, by frequent reconnoitering, he managed to elude his enemies, traveling by night, until he fortunately met with the two hunters from camp, and was conveyed by them to the rendezvous.

All the parties were now safely in. The lonely mountain valley was populous with the different camps. The Rocky Mountain and American companies had their separate camps; Wyeth had his; a company of free trappers, fifteen in number, led by a man named Sinclair, from Arkansas, had the fourth; the Nez Perces and Flatheads, the allies of the Rocky Mountain company, and the friends of the whites, had their lodges along all the streams; so that altogether there could not have been less than one thousand souls, and two or three thousand horses and mules gathered in this place.

"When the pie was opened then the birds began to sing." When Captain Sublette's goods were opened and distributed among the trappers and Indians, then began the usual gay carousal; and the "fast young men" of the mountains outvied each other in all manner of mad pranks. In the beginning of their spree many feats of horsemanship and personal strength were exhibited, which were regarded with admiring wonder by the sober and inexperienced New Englanders under Mr. Wyeth's command. And as nothing stimulated the vanity of the mountainmen like an audience of this sort, the feats they performed were apt to astonish themselves. In exhibitions of the kind, the free trappers took the lead, and usually carried off the palm, like the privileged class that they were.

But the horse-racing, fine riding, wrestling, and all the manlier sports, soon degenerated into the baser exhibitions of a "crazy drunk" condition. The vessel in which the trapper received and carried about his supply of alcohol was one of the small camp kettles. "Passing round" this clumsy goblet very freely, it was not long before a goodly number were in the condition just named, and ready for any mad freak whatever. It is reported by several of the mountain-men that on the occasion of one of these "frolics," one of their number seized a kettle of alcohol, and poured it over the head of a tall, lank, red-headed fellow, repeating as he did so the baptismal ceremony. No sooner had he concluded, than another man with a lighted stick, touched him with the blaze, when in an instant he was enveloped in flames. Luckily some of the company had sense enough left to perceive his danger, and began beating him with pack-saddles to put out the blaze. But between the burning and the beating, the unhappy wretch nearly lost his life, and never recovered from the effects of his baptism by fire.

Beaver being plenty in camp, business was correspondingly lively, there being a great demand for goods. When this demand was supplied, as it was in the course of about three weeks, the different brigades were set in motion. One of the earliest to move was a small party under Milton Sublette, including his constant companion, Meek. With this company, no more than thirty in number, Sublette intended to explore the country to the south-west, then unknown to the fur companies, and to proceed as far as the Humboldt river in that direction.

On the 17th of July they set out toward the south end of the valley, and having made but about eight miles the first day, camped that night near a pass in the mountains. Wyeth's party of raw New Englanders, and Sinclair's free trappers, had joined themselves to the company of Milton Sublette, and swelled the number in camp to about sixty men, many of them new to the business of mountain life.

Just as the men were raising camp for a start the next morning, a caravan was observed moving down the mountain pass into the valley. No alarm was at first felt, as an arrival was daily expected of one of the American company's partisans, Mr. Fontenelle, and his company. But on reconnoitering with a glass, Sublette discovered them to be a large party of Blackfeet, consisting of a few mounted men, and many more, men, women, and children, on foot. At the instant they were discovered, they set up the usual yell of defiance, and rushed down like a mountain torrent into the valley, flourishing their weapons, and fluttering their gay blankets and feathers in the wind. There was no doubt as to the warlike intentions of the Blackfeet in general, nor was it for a moment to be supposed that any peaceable overture on their part meant anything more than that they were not prepared to fight at that particular juncture; therefore let not the reader judge too harshly of an act which under ordinary circumstances would have been infamous. In Indian fighting, every man is his own leader, and the bravest take the front rank. On this occasion there were two of Sublette's men, one a half-breed Iroquois, the other a Flathead Indian, who had wrongs of their own to avenge, and they never let slip a chance of killing a Blackfoot. These two men rode forth alone to meet the enemy, as if to hold a "talk" with the principal chief, who advanced to meet them, bearing the pipe of peace. When the chief extended his hand, Antonio Godin, the half-breed, took it, but at the same moment he ordered the Flathead to fire, and the chief fell dead. The two trappers galloped back to camp, Antoine bearing for a trophy the scarlet blanket of his enemy.

This action made it impossible to postpone the battle, as the dead chief had meant to do by peaceful overtures, until the warriors of his nation came up. The Blackfeet immediately betook themselves to a swamp formed by an old beaver dam, and thickly overgrown with cotton-wood and willow, matted together with tough vines. On the edge of this dismal covert the warriors skulked, and shot with their guns and arrows, while in its very midst the women employed themselves in digging a trench and throwing up a breastwork of logs, and whatever came to hand. Such a defence as the thicket afforded was one not easy to attack; its unseen but certain dangers being sufficient to appal the stoutest heart.

Meantime, an express had been sent off to inform Captain Sublette of the battle, and summon assistance. Sinclair and his free trappers, with Milton Sublette's small company, were the only fighting men at hand. Mr. Wyeth, knowing the inefficiency of his men in an Indian fight, had them entrenched behind their packs, and there left them to take care of themselves, but charged them not to appear in open field. As for the fighting men, they stationed themselves in a ravine, where they could occasionally pick off a Blackfoot, and waited for reinforcements.

Great was the astonishment of the Blackfeet, who believed they had only Milton Sublette's camp to fight, when they beheld first one party of white men and then another; and not only whites, but Nez Perces and Flatheads came galloping up the valley. If before it had been a battle to destroy the whites, it was now a battle to defend themselves. Previous to the arrival of Captain Sublette, the opposing forces had kept up only a scattering fire, in which nobody on the side of the trappers had been either killed or wounded. But when the impetuous captain arrived on the battle-field, he prepared for less guarded warfare. Stripped as if for the prize-ring, and armed *cap-a-pie*, he hastened to the scene of action, accompanied by his intimate friend and associate in business, Robert Campbell.

At sight of the reinforcements, and their vigorous movements, the Indians at the edge of the swamp fell back within their fort. To dislodge them was a dangerous undertaking, but Captain Sublette was determined to make the effort. Finding the trappers generally disinclined to enter the thicket, he set the example, together with Campbell, and thus induced some of the free trappers, with their leader, Sinclair, to emulate his action. However, the others took courage at this, and advanced near the swamp, firing at random at their invisible foe, who, having the advantage of being able to see them, inflicted some wounds on the party.

The few white "braves" who had resolved to enter the swamp, made their wills as they went, feeling that they were upon perilous business. Sublette, Campbell, and Sinclair succeeded in penetrating the thicket without alarming the enemy, and came at length to a more open space from whence they could get a view of the fort. From this they learned that the women and children had retired to the mountains, and that the fort was a slight affair, covered with buffalo robes and blankets to keep out prying eyes. Moving slowly on, some slight accident betrayed their vicinity, and the next moment a shot struck Sinclair, wounding him mortally. He spoke to Campbell, requesting to be taken to his brother. By this time some of the men had come up, and he was given in charge to be taken back to camp. Sublette then pressed forward, and seeing an Indian looking through an aperture, aimed at him with fatal effect. No sooner had he done so, and pointed out the opening to Campbell, than he was struck with a ball in the shoulder, which nearly prostrated him, and turned him so faint that Campbell took him in his arms and carried him, assisted by Meek, out of the swamp. At the same time one of the men received a wound in the head. The battle was now carried on with spirit, although from the difficulty of approaching the fort, the firing was very irregular.

The mountaineers who followed Sublette, took up their station in the woods on one side of the fort, and the Nez Perces, under Wyeth, on the opposite side, which accidental arrangement, though it was fatal to many of the Blackfeet in the fort, was also the occasion of loss to themselves by the cross-fire. The whites being constantly reinforced by fresh arrivals from the rendezvous, were soon able to silence the guns of the enemy, but they were not able to drive them from their fort, where they remained silent and sullen after their ammunition was exhausted.

Seeing that the women of the Nez Perces and Flatheads were gathering up sticks to set fire to their breastwork of logs, an old chief proclaimed in a loud voice from within, the startling intelligence that there were four hundred lodges of his people close at hand, who would soon be there to avenge their deaths, should the whites choose to reduce them to ashes. This harangue, delivered in the usual high-flown style of Indian oratory, either was not clearly understood, or was wrongly interpreted, and the impression got abroad that an attack was being made on the great encampment. This intelligence occasioned a diversion, and a division of forces ; for while a small party was left to watch the fort, the rest galloped in hot haste to the rescue of the main camp. When they arrived, they found it had been a false alarm, but it was too late to return that night, and the several camps remained where they were until the next day.

Meantime the trappers left to guard the fort remained stationed within the wood all night, firmly believing they had their enemy "corraled," as the horsemen of the plains would say. On the return, in the morning, of their comrades from the main camp, they advanced cautiously up to the breastwork of logs, and behold! not a buffalo skin nor red blanket was to be seen! Through the crevices among the logs was seen an empty fort. On making this discovery there was much chagrin among the white trappers, and much lamentation among the Indian allies, who had abandoned the burning of the fort expressly to save for themselves the fine blankets and other goods of their hereditary foes.

From the reluctance displayed by the trappers, in the beginning of the battle, to engage with the Indians while under cover of the woods, it must not be inferred that they were lacking in courage. They were too well informed in Indian modes of warfare to venture recklessly into the den of death, which a savage ambush was quite sure to be. The very result which attended the impetuosity of their leaders, in the death of Sinclair and the wounding of Captain Sublette, proved them not over cautious.

On entering the fort, the dead bodies of ten Blackfeet were found, besides others dead outside the fort, and over thirty horses, some of which were recognized as those stolen from Sublette's night camp on the other side of the mountains, besides those abandoned by Fitzpatrick. Doubtless the rascals had followed his trail to Pierre's

Hole, not thinking, however, to come upon so large a camp as they found at last. The savage garrison which had so cunningly contrived to elude the guard set upon them, carried off some of their wounded, and, perhaps, also some of their dead ; for they acknowledged afterwards a much larger loss than appeared at the time. Besides Sinclair, there were five other white men killed, one half-breed, and seven Nez Perces. About the same number of whites and their Indian allies were wounded.

An instance of female devotion is recorded by Bonneville's historian as having occurred at this battle. On the morning following it, as the whites were exploring the thickets about the fort, they discovered a Blackfoot woman leaning silent and motionless against a tree. According to Mr. Irving, whose fine feeling for the sex would incline him to put faith in this bit of romance, " their surprise at her lingering here alone, to fall into the hands of her enemies, was dispelled when they saw the corpse of a warrior at her feet. Either she was so lost in grief as not to perceive their approach, or a proud spirit kept her silent and motionless. The Indians set up a yell on discovering her, and before the trappers could interfere, her mangled body fell upon the corpse which she had refused to abandon." This version is true in the main incidents, but untrue in the sentiment. The woman's leg had been broken by a ball, and she was unable to move from the spot where she leaned. When the trappers approached her, she stretched out her hands supplicatingly, crying out in a wailing voice, " kill me! kill me! O white men, kill me!"—but this the trappers had no disposition to do. While she was entreating them, and they refusing, a ball from some vengeful Nez Perce or Flathead put an end to her sufferings.

Still remembering the threats of the Blackfoot chief,

that four hundred lodges of his brethren were advancing on the valley, all the companies returned to rendezvous, and remained for several days, to see whether an attack should take place. But if there had ever been any such intention on the part of the Blackfoot nation, the timely lesson bestowed on their advance guard had warned them to quit the neighborhood of the whites.

Captain Sublette's wound was dressed by Mr. Wyeth's physician, and although it hindered his departure for St. Louis for some time, it did not prevent his making his usual journey later in the season. It was as well, perhaps, that he did not set out earlier, for of a party of seven who started for St. Louis a few days after the battle, three were killed in Jackson's Hole, where they fell in with the four hundred warriors with whom the Blackfoot chief threatened the whites at the battle of Pierre's Hole. From the story of the four survivors who escaped and returned to camp, there could no longer be any doubt that the big village of the Blackfeet had actually been upon the trail of Capt. Sublette, expecting an easy victory when they should overtake him. How they were disappointed by the reception met with by the advance camp, has already been related.

CHAPTER VII.

1832. ON the 23d of July, Milton Sublette's brigade and the company of Mr. Wyeth again set out for the southwest, and met no more serious interruptions while they traveled in company. On the head-waters of the Humboldt River they separated, Wyeth proceeding north to the Columbia, and Sublette continuing on into a country hitherto untraversed by American trappers.

It was the custom of a camp on the move to depend chiefly on the men employed as hunters to supply them with game, the sole support of the mountaineers. When this failed, the stock on hand was soon exhausted, and the men reduced to famine. This was what happened to Sublette's company in the country where they now found themselves, between the Owyhee and Humboldt Rivers. Owing to the arid and barren nature of these plains, the largest game to be found was the beaver, whose flesh proved to be poisonous, from the creature having eaten of the wild parsnip in the absence of its favorite food. The men were made ill by eating of beaver flesh, and the horses were greatly reduced from the scarcity of grass and the entire absence of the cotton-wood.

In this plight Sublette found himself, and finally resolved to turn north, in the hope of coming upon some better and more hospitable country. The sufferings of the men now became terrible, both from hunger and thirst. In the effort to appease the former, everything was eaten that could be eaten, and many things at which the well-fed man would sicken with disgust. "I have," says Joe Meek, "held my hands in an ant-hill until they were covered with the ants, then greedily licked them off. I have taken the soles off my moccasins, crisped them in the fire, and eaten them. In our extremity, the large black crickets which are found in this country were considered game. We used to take a kettle of hot water, catch the crickets and throw them in, and when they stopped kicking, eat them. That was not what we called *cant tickup ko hanch*, (good meat, my friend), but it kept us alive."

Equally abhorrent expedients were resorted to in order to quench thirst, some of which would not bear mention. In this condition, and exposed to the burning suns and the dry air of the desert, the men now so nearly exhausted began to prey upon their almost equally exhausted animals. At night when they made their camp, by mutual consent a mule was bled, and a soup made from its blood. About a pint was usually taken, when two or three would mess together upon this reviving, but scanty and not very palatable dish. But this mode of subsistence could not be long depended on, as the poor mules could ill afford to lose blood in their famishing state; nor could the men afford to lose their mules where there was a chance of life: therefore hungry as they were, the men were cautious in this matter; and it generally caused a quarrel when a man's mule was selected for bleeding by the others.

A few times a mule had been sacrificed to obtain meat; and in this case the poorest one was always selected, so as to economise the chances for life for the whole band. In this extremity, after four days of almost total abstinence and several weeks of famine, the company reached the Snake River, about fifty miles above the fishing falls, where it boils and dashes over the rocks, forming very strong rapids. Here the company camped, rejoiced at the sight of the pure mountain water, but still in want of food. During the march a horse's back had become sore from some cause; probably, his rider thought, because the saddle did not set well; and, although that particular animal was selected to be sacrificed on the morrow, as one that could best be spared, he set about taking the stuffing out of his saddle and re-arranging the padding. While engaged in this considerate labor, he uttered a cry of delight and held up to view a large brass pin, which had accidentally got into the stuffing, when the saddle was made, and had been the cause of all the mischief to his horse.

The same thought struck all who saw the pin: it was soon converted into a fish-hook, a line was spun from horse-hair, and in a short time there were trout enough caught to furnish them a hearty and a most delicious repast. "In the morning," says Meek, "we went on our way rejoicing;" each man with the "five fishes" tied to his saddle, if without any "loaves." This was the end of their severest suffering, as they had now reached a country where absolute starvation was not the normal condition of the inhabitants; and which was growing more and more bountiful, as they neared the Rocky Mountains, where they at length joined camp, not having made a very profitable expedition.

It may seem incredible to the reader that any country so poor as that in which our trappers starved could have native inhabitants. Yet such was the fact; and the people who lived in and who still inhabit this barren waste, were called *Diggers*, from their mode of obtaining their food—a few edible roots growing in low grounds, or marshy places. When these fail them they subsist as did our trappers, by hunting crickets and field mice.

Nothing can be more abject than the appearance of the Digger Indian, in the fall, as he roams about, without food and without weapons, save perhaps a bow and arrows, with his eyes fixed upon the ground, looking for crickets! So despicable is he, that he has neither enemies nor friends; and the neighboring tribes do not condescend to notice his existence, unless indeed he should come in their way, when they would not think it more than a mirthful act to put an end to his miserable existence. And so it must be confessed the trappers regarded him. When Sublette's party first struck the Humboldt, Wyeth's being still with them, Joe Meek one day shot a Digger who was prowling about a stream where his traps were set.

"Why did you shoot him?" asked Wyeth.

"To keep him from stealing traps."

"Had he stolen any?"

"No: but he *looked as if he was going to!*"

This recklessness of life very properly distressed the just minded New Englander. Yet it was hard for the trappers to draw lines of distinction so nice as his. If a tribe was not known to be friendly, it was a rule of necessity to consider it unfriendly. The abjectness and cowardice of the Diggers was the fruit of their own helpless condition. That they had the savage instinct, held in check only by circumstances, was demonstrated about the same time that Meek shot one, by his being pursued by four of them when out trapping alone, and only escaping at last by the assistance of one of his comrades who came to the rescue. They could not fight, like the Crows and Blackfeet, but they could steal and murder, when they had a safe opportunity.

It would be an interesting study, no doubt, to the philanthropist, to ascertain in how great a degree the habits, manners, and morals of a people are governed by their resources, especially by the quality and quantity of their diet. But when diet and climate are both taken into consideration, the result is striking.

The character of the Blackfeet who inhabited the good hunting grounds on the eastern side of the Rocky Mountains, is already pretty well given. They were tall, sinewy, well-made fellows; good horsemen, and good fighters, though inclined to marauding and murdering. They dressed comfortably and even handsomely, as dress goes amongst savages, and altogether were more to be feared than despised.

The Crows resembled the Blackfeet, whose enemies they were, in all the before-mentioned traits, but were if possible, even more predatory in their habits. Unlike the Blackfeet, however, they were not the enemies of *all* mankind; and even were disposed to cultivate some friendliness with the white traders and trappers, in order, as they acknowledged, to strengthen their own hands against the Blackfeet. They too inhabited a good country, full of game, and had horses in abundance. These were the mountain tribes.

Comparing these with the coast tribes, there was a striking difference. The natives of the Columbia were not a tall and robust people, like those east of the Rocky Mountains, who lived by hunting. Their height rarely exceeded five feet six inches; their forms were good, rather inclining to fatness, their faces round, features coarse, but complexion light, and their eyes large and intelligent. The custom of flattening their heads in infancy gave them a grotesque and unnatural appearance, otherwise they could not be called ill-looking. On the first advent of white men among them, they were accustomed to go entirely naked, except in winter, when a panther skin, or a mantle of other skins sewed together, served to protect them from the cold: or if the weather was rainy, as it generally was in that milder climate, a long mantle of rush mats, like the toga of the ancient Romans, took the place of that made of skins. To this was added a conical hat, woven of fibrous roots, and gaily painted.

For defensive armor they were provided with a tunic of elkskin double, descending to the ankles, with holes in it for the arms, and quite impenetrable to arrows. A helmet of similar material covered the head, rendering them like Achilles, invulnerable except in the heels. In this secure dress they went to battle in their canoes, notice being first given to the enemy of the intended attack. Their battles might therefore be termed compound duels, in which each party observed great punctiliousness and decorum. Painted and armor-encased, the warriors in two flotillas of canoes were rowed to the battle ground by their women, when the battle raged furiously for some time; not, however, doing any great harm to either side. If any one chanced to be killed, that side considered itself beaten, and retired from the conflict to mourn over and bury the estimable and departed brave. If the case was a stubborn one, requiring several days fighting, the opponents encamped near each other, keeping up a confusion of cries, taunts, menaces, and raillery, during the whole night; after which they resumed the conflict, and continued it until one was beaten. If a village was to be attacked, notice being received, the women and children were removed; and if the village was beaten they made presents to their conquerors. Such were the decorous habits of the warriors of the lower Columbia.

These were the people who lived almost exclusively by fishing, and whose climate was a mild and moist one. Fishing, in which both sexes engaged about equally, was an important accomplishment, since it was by fish they lived in this world; and by being good fishermen that they had hopes of the next one. The houses in which they lived, instead of being lodges made of buffalo skins, were of a large size and very well constructed, being made out of cedar planks. An excavation was first made in the earth two or three feet deep, probably to secure greater warmth in winter. A double row of cedar posts was then planted firmly all round the excavation, and between these the planks were laid, or, sometimes cedar bark, so overlapped as to exclude the rain and wind. The ridge-pole of the roof was supported on a row of taller posts, passing through the centre of the building, and notched to receive it. The rafters were then covered with planks or bark, fastened down with ropes made of the fibre of the cedar bark. A house made in this manner, and often a hundred feet long by thirty or forty wide, accommodated several families, who each had their separate entrance and fire-place; the entrance being by a low oval-shaped door, and a flight of steps.

The canoes of these people were each cut out of a single log of cedar; and were often thirty feet long and five wide at midships. They were gaily painted, and their shape was handsome, with a very long bow so constructed as to cut the surf in landing with the greatest ease, or the more readily to go through a rough sea. The oars were about five feet long, and bent in the shape of a crescent; which shape enabled them to draw them edgewise through the water with little or no noise—this noiselessness being an important quality in hunting the sea otter, which is always caught sleeping on the rocks.

The single instrument which sufficed to build canoes and houses was the chisel; generally being a piece of old iron obtained from some vessel and fixed in a wooden handle. A stone mallet aided them in using the chisel; and with this simple "kit" of tools they contrived to manufacture plates, bowls, carved oars, and many ornamental things.

Like the men of all savage nations, they made slaves of
their captives, and their women.   The dress of the latter
consisted merely of a short petticoat, manufactured from
the fibre of the cedar bark, previously soaked and prepared.   This material was worked into a fringe, attached
to a girdle, and only long enough to reach the middle of
the thigh.   When the season required it, they added a
mantle of skins.   Their bodies were anointed with fish-oil,
and sometimes painted with red ochre in imitation of the
men.   For ornaments they wore strings of glass beads,
and also of a white shell found on the northern coast, called
haiqua.   Such were the *Chinooks,* who lived upon the
coast.

Farther up the river, on the eastern side of the Cascade
range of mountains, a people lived, the same, yet different
from the Chinooks.   They resembled them in form, features, and manner of getting a living.   But they were
more warlike and more enterprising; they even had some
notions of commerce, being traders between the coast
Indians and those to the east of them.   They too were
great fishermen, but used the net instead of fishing in
boats.   Great scaffoldings were erected every year at the
narrows of the Columbia, known as the Dalles, where, as
the salmon passed up the river in the spring, in incredible
numbers, they were caught and dried.   After drying, the
fish were then pounded fine between two stones, pressed
tightly into packages or bales of about a hundred pounds,
covered with matting, and corded up for transportation.
The bales were then placed in storehouses built to receive
them, where they awaited customers.

By and by there came from the coast other Indians,
with different varieties of fish, to exchange for the salmon
in the Wish-ram warehouses.   And by and by there came
from the plains to the eastward, others who had horses,

camas-root, bear-grass, fur robes, and whatever constituted the wealth of the mountains and plains, to exchange for the rich and nutritious salmon of the Columbia. These Wish-ram Indians were sharp traders, and usually made something by their exchanges; so that they grew rich and insolent, and it was dangerous for the unwary stranger to pass their way. Of all the tribes of the Columbia, they perpetrated the most outrages upon their neighbors, the passing traveler, and the stranger within their gates.

Still farther to the east, on the great grassy plains, watered by beautiful streams, coming down from the mountains, lived the Cayuses, Yakimas, Nez Perces, Wallah-Wallahs, and Flatheads; as different in their appearance and habits as their different modes of living would naturally make them. Instead of having many canoes, they had many horses; and in place of drawing the fishing net, or trolling lazily along with hook and line, or spearing fish from a canoe, they rode pell-mell to the chase, or sallied out to battle with the hostile Blackfeet, whose country lay between them and the good hunting-grounds, where the great herds of buffalo were. Being Nimrods by nature, they were dressed in complete suits of skins, instead of going naked, like their brethren in the lower country. Being wandering and pastoral in their habits, they lived in lodges, which could be planted every night and raised every morning.

Their women, too, were good riders, and comfortably clad in dressed skins, kept white with chalk. So wealthy were some of the chiefs that they could count their fifteen hundred head of horses grazing on their grassy uplands. Horse-racing was their delight, and betting on them their besetting vice. For bridles they used horse-hair cords, attached around the animal's mouth. This was sufficient

9

to check him, and by laying a hand on this side or that of the horse's neck, the rider could wheel him in either direction. The simple and easy-fitting saddle was a stuffed deer-skin, with stirrups of wood, resembling in shape those used by the Mexicans, and covered with deer-skin sewed on wet, so as to tighten in drying. The saddles of the women were furnished with a pair of deer's antlers for the pommel.

In many things their customs and accoutrements resembled those of the Mexicans, from whom, no doubt, they were borrowed. Like the Mexican, they threw the lasso to catch the wild horse. Their horses, too, were of Mexican stock, and many of them bore the brand of that country, having been obtained in some of their not infrequent journeys into California and New Mexico.

As all the wild horses of America are said to have sprung from a small band, turned loose upon the plains by Cortez, it would be interesting to know at what time they came to be used by the northern Indians, or whether the horse and the Indian did not emigrate together. If the horse came to the Indian, great must have been the change effected by the advent of this new element in the savage's life. It is impossible to conceive, however, that the Indian ever could have lived on these immense plains, barren of everything but wild grass, without his horse. With him he does well enough, for he not only "lives on horseback," by which means he can quickly reach a country abounding in game, but he literally lives on horse-flesh, when other game is scarce.

Curious as the fact may seem, the Indians at the mouth of the Columbia and those of New Mexico speak languages similar in construction to that of the Aztecs; and from this fact, and the others before mentioned, it may be very fairly inferred that difference of circumstances and localities have made of the different tribes what they are.

As to the Indian's moral nature, that is pretty much alike everywhere; and with some rare exceptions, the rarest of which is, perhaps, the Flathead and Nez Perces nations, all are cruel, thieving, and treacherous. The Indian gospel is literally the "gospel of blood"; an "eye for an eye, and a tooth for a tooth." Vengeance is as much a commandment to him as any part of the decalogue is to the Christian. But we have digressed far from our narrative; and as it will be necessary to refer to the subject of the moral code of savages further on in our narrative, we leave it for the present.

After the incident of the pin and the fishes, Sublette's party kept on to the north, coursing along up Payette's River to Payette Lake, where he camped, and the men went out trapping. A party of four, consisting of Meek, Antoine Godin, Louis Leaugar, and Small, proceeded to the north as far as the Salmon river and beyond, to the head of one of its tributaries, where the present city of Florence is located. While camped in this region, three of the men went out one day to look for their horses, which had strayed away, or been stolen by the Indians. During their absence, Meek, who remained in camp, had killed a fine fat deer, and was cooking a portion of it, when he saw a band of about a hundred Indians approaching, and so near were they that flight was almost certainly useless; yet as a hundred against one was very great odds, and running away from them would not increase their number, while it gave him something to do in his own defence, he took to his heels and ran as only a mountain-man can run. Instead, however, of pursuing him, the practical-minded braves set about finishing his cooking for him, and soon had the whole deer roasting before the fire.

This procedure provoked the gastronomic ire of our trapper, and after watching them for some time from his

hiding-place, he determined to return and share the feast.
On reaching camp again, and introducing himself to his
not over-scrupulous visitors, he found they were from the
Nez Perces tribe inhabiting that region, who, having been
so rude as to devour his stock of provisions, invited him
to accompany them to their village, not a great way off,
where they would make some return for his involuntary
hospitality.   This he did, and there found his three comrades and all their horses.   While still visiting at the Nez
Perces village, they were joined by the remaining portion
of Sublette's command, when the whole company started
south again.   Passing Payette's lake to the east, traversing
the Boise Basin, going to the head-waters of that river,
thence to the Malade, thence to Godin's river, and finally
to the forks of the Salmon, where they found the main
camp.   Captain Bonneville, of whose three years wanderings in the wilderness Mr. Irving has given a full and interesting account, was encamped in the same neighborhood, and had built there a small fort or trading-house,
and finally wintered in the neighborhood.

An exchange of men now took place, and Meek went
east of the mountains under Fitzpatrick and Bridger.
When these famous leaders had first set out for the summer hunt, after the battle of Pierre's Hole, their course
had been to the head-waters of the Missouri, to the Yellowstone lake, and the forks of the Missouri, some of the
best beaver grounds known to them.   But finding their
steps dogged by the American Fur Company, and not
wishing to be made use of as pilots by their rivals, they
had flitted about for a time like an Arab camp, in the endeavor to blind them, and finally returned to the west side
of the mountains, where Meek fell in with them.

Exasperated by the perseverance of the American
Company, they had come to the determination of leading

them a march which should tire them of the practice of keeping at their heels. They therefore planned an expedition, from which they expected no other profit than that of shaking off their rivals. Taking no pains to conceal their expedition, they rather held out the bait to the American Company, who, unsuspicious of their purpose, took it readily enough. They led them along across the mountains, and on to the head-waters of the Missouri. Here, packing up their traps, they tarried not for beaver, nor even tried to avoid the Blackfeet, but pushed right ahead, into the very heart of their country, keeping away from any part of it where beaver might be found, and going away on beyond, to the elevated plains, quite destitute of that small but desirable game, but followed through it by their rivals.

However justifiable on the part of trade this movement of the Rocky Mountain Company might have been, it was a cruel device as concerned the inexperienced leaders of the other company, one of whom lost his life in consequence. Not knowing of their danger, they only discovered their situation in the midst of Blackfeet, after discovering the ruse that had been played upon them. They then halted, and being determined to find beaver, divided their forces and set out in opposite directions for that purpose. Unhappily, Major Vanderburg took the worst possible direction for a small party to take, and had not traveled far when his scouts came upon the still smoking camp-fires of a band of Indians who were returning from a buffalo hunt. From the "signs" left behind them, the scout judged that they had become aware of the near neighborhood of white men, and from their having stolen off, he judged that they were only gone for others of their nation, or to prepare for war.

But Vanderburg, with the fool-hardiness of one not

"up to Blackfeet," determined to ascertain for himself
what there was to fear; and taking with him half a score
of his followers, put himself upon their trail, galloping
hard after them, until, in his rashness, he found himself
being led through a dark and deep defile, rendered darker
and gloomier by overhanging trees. In the midst of this
dismal place, just where an ambush might have been expected, he was attacked by a horde of savages, who
rushed upon his little party with whoops and frantic gestures, intended not only to appal the riders, but to frighten
their horses, and thus make surer their bloody butchery.
It was but the work of a few minutes to consummate their
demoniac purpose. Vanderburg's horse was shot down
at once, falling on his rider, whom the Indians quickly
dispatched. One or two of the men were instantly toma-
hawked, and the others wounded while making their escape to camp. The remainder of Vanderburg's company,
on learning the fate of their leader, whose place there
was no one to fill, immediately raised camp and fled with
all haste to the encampment of the Pends Oreille Indians
for assistance. Here they waited, while those Indians, a
friendly tribe, made an effort to recover the body of their
unfortunate leader; but the remains were never recovered,
probably having first been fiendishly mutilated, and then
left to the wolves.

Fitzpatrick and Bridger, finding they were no longer
pursued by their rivals, as the season advanced began to
retrace their steps toward the good trapping grounds.
Being used to Indian wiles and Blackfeet maraudings and
ambushes, they traveled in close columns, and never
camped or turned out their horses to feed, without the
greatest caution. Morning and evening scouts were sent
out to beat up every thicket or ravine that seemed to
offer concealment to a foe, and the horizon was searched

in every direction for signs of an Indian attack. The complete safety of the camp being settled almost beyond a peradventure, the horses were turned loose, though never left unguarded.

It was not likely, however, that the camp should pass through the Blackfoot country without any encounters with that nation. When it had reached the head-waters of the Missouri, on the return march, a party of trappers, including Meek, discovered a small band of Indians in a bend of the lake, and thinking the opportunity for sport a good one, commenced firing on them. The Indians, who were without guns, took to the lake for refuge, while the trappers entertained themselves with the rare amusement of keeping them in the water, by shooting at them occasionally. But it chanced that these were only a few stragglers from the main Blackfoot camp, which soon came up and put an end to the sport by putting the trappers to flight in their turn. The trappers fled to camp, the Indians pursuing, until the latter discovered that they had been led almost into the large camp of the whites. This occasioned a halt, the Blackfeet not caring to engage with superior numbers.

In the pause which ensued, one of the chiefs came out into the open space, bearing the peace-pipe, and Bridger also advanced to meet him, but carrying his gun across the pommel of his saddle. He was accompanied by a young Blackfoot woman, wife of a Mexican in his service, as interpreter. The chief extended his hand in token of amity; but at that moment Bridger saw a movement of the chiefs, which he took to mean treachery, and cocked his rifle. But the lock had no sooner clicked than the chief, a large and powerful man, seized the gun and turned the muzzle downward, when the contents were discharged into the earth. With another dexterous movement he wrested it from Bridger's hand, and struck him with it, felling him to the ground.   In an instant all was confusion.   The noise of whoops, yells, of fire-arms, and of running hither and thither, gathered like a tempest. At the first burst of this demoniac blast, the horse of the interpreter became frightened, and, by a sudden move-ment, unhorsed her, wheeling and running back to camp. In the melee which now ensued, the woman was carried off by the Blackfeet, and Bridger was wounded twice in the back with arrows.   A chance medley fight now ensued, continuing until night put a period to the contest.   So well matched were the opposing forces, that each fought with caution firing from the cover of thickets and from behind rocks, neither side doing much execution.   The loss on the part of the Blackfeet was nine warriors, and on that of the whites, three men and six horses.

As for the young Blackfoot woman, whose people re-tained her a prisoner, her lamentations and struggles to escape and return to her husband and child so wrought upon the young Mexican, who was the pained witness of her grief, that he took the babe in his arms, and galloped with it into the heart of the Blackfoot camp, to place it in the arms of the distracted mother.   This daring act, which all who witnessed believed would cause his death, so excited the admiration of the Blackfoot chief, that he gave him permission to return, unharmed, to his own camp.   Encouraged by this clemency, Loretta begged to have his wife restored to him, relating how he had res-cued her, a prisoner, from the Crows, who would certainly have tortured her to death.   The wife added her entreat-ies to his, but the chief sternly bade him depart, and as sternly reminded the Blackfoot girl that she belonged to his tribe, and could not go with his enemies.   Loretta was therefore compelled to abandon his wife and child, and return to camp.

It is, however, gratifying to know that so true an instance of affection in savage life was finally rewarded; and that when the two rival fur companies united, as they did in the following year, Loretta was permitted to go to the American Company's fort on the Missouri, in the Blackfoot country, where he was employed as interpreter, assisted by his Blackfoot wife.

Such were some of the incidents that signalized this campaign in the wilderness, where two equally persistent rivals were trying to outwit one another. Subsequently, when several years of rivalry had somewhat exhausted both, the Rocky Mountain and American companies consolidated, using all their strategy thereafter against the Hudson's Bay Company, and any new rival that chanced to enter their hunting grounds.

After the fight above described, the Blackfeet drew off in the night, showing no disposition to try their skill next day against such experienced Indian fighters as Bridger's brigade had shown themselves. The company continued in the Missouri country, trapping and taking many beaver, until it reached the Beaver Head Valley, on the headwaters of the Jefferson fork of the Missouri. Here the lateness of the season compelled a return to winter-quarters, and by Christmas all the wanderers were gathered into camp at the forks of the Snake River.

1833. In the latter part of January it became necessary to move to the junction of the Portneuf to subsist the animals. The main body of the camp had gone on in advance, while some few, with pack horses, or women with children, were scattered along the trail. Meek, with five others, had been left behind to gather up some horses that had strayed. When about a half day's journey from camp, he overtook *Umentucken*, the Mountain Lamb, now the wife of Milton Sublette, with her child, on horseback. The weather was terribly cold, and seeming to grow colder. The naked plains afforded no shelter from the piercing winds, and the air fairly glittered with frost. Poor Umentucken was freezing, but more troubled about her babe than herself. The camp was far ahead, with all the extra blankets, and the prospect was imminent that they would perish. Our gallant trapper had thought himself very cold until this moment, but what were his sufferings compared to those of the Mountain Lamb and her little Lambkin? Without an instant's hesitation, he divested himself of his blanket capote, which he wrapped round the mother and child, and urged her to hasten to camp. For himself, he could not hasten, as he had the horses in charge, but all that fearful afternoon rode naked above the waist, exposed to the wind, and the fine, dry, icy hail, which filled the air as with diamond needles, to pierce the skin; and, probably, to the fact that the hail *was* so stinging, was owing the fact that his blood did not congeal.

"O what a day was that!" said Meek to the writer; "why, the air war thick with fine, sharp hail, and the sun shining, too! not one sun only, but three suns—there were *three* suns! And when night came on, the northern lights blazed up the sky! It was the most beautiful sight I ever saw. That is the country for northern lights!"

When some surprise was expressed that he should have been obliged to expose his naked skin to the weather, in order to save Umentucken—"In the mountains," he answered, "we do not have many garments. Buckskin breeches, a blanket capote, and a beaver skin cap makes up our rig."

" You do not need a laundress, then ?   But with such clothing how could you keep free of vermin ? "

" We didn't always do that.   Do you want to know how we got rid of lice in the mountains ?   We just took off our clothes and laid them on an ant-hill, and you ought to see how the ants would carry off the lice ! "

But to return to our hero, frozen, or nearly so.   When he reached camp at night, so desperate was his condition that the men had to roll him and rub him in the snow for some time before allowing him to approach the fire.   But Umentucken was saved, and he became heroic in her eyes. Whether it was the glory acquired by the gallant act just recorded, or whether our hero had now arrived at an age when the tender passion has strongest sway, the writer is unprepared to affirm : for your mountain-man is shy of revealing his past gallantries ; but from this time on, there are evidences of considerable susceptibility to the charms of the dusky beauties of the mountains and the plains.

The cold of this winter was very severe, insomuch that men and mules were frozen to death.   " The frost," says Meek, " used to hang from the roofs of our lodges in the morning, on first waking, in skeins two feet long, and our blankets and whiskers were white with it.   But we trap- pers laid still, and called the camp-keepers to make a fire, and in our close lodges it was soon warm enough.

" The Indians suffered very much.   Fuel war scarce on the Snake River, and but little fire could be afforded— just sufficient for the children and their mothers to get warm by, for the fire was fed only with buffalo fat torn in strips, which blazed up quickly and did not last long. Many a time I have stood off, looking at the fire, but not venturing to approach, when a chief would say, ' Are you cold, my friend ? come to the fire '—so kind are these Nez Perces and Flatheads."

The cold was not the only enemy in camp that winter, but famine threatened them. The buffalo had been early driven east of the mountains, and other game was scarce. Sometimes a party of hunters were absent for days, even weeks, without finding more game than would subsist themselves. As the trappers were all hunters in the winter, it frequently happened that Meek and one or more of his associates went on a hunt in company, for the benefit of the camp, which was very hungry at times.

On one of these hunting expeditions that winter, the party consisting of Meek, Hawkins, Doughty, and Antoine Claymore, they had been out nearly a fortnight without killing anything of consequence, and had clambered up the side of the mountains on the frozen snow, in hopes of finding some mountain sheep. As they traveled along under a projecting ledge of rocks, they came to a place where there were the impressions in the snow of enormous grizzly bear feet. Close by was an opening in the rocks, revealing a cavern, and to this the tracks in the snow conducted. Evidently the creature had come out of its winter den, and made just one circuit back again. At these signs of game the hunters hesitated—certain it was there, but doubtful how to obtain it.

At length Doughty proposed to get up on the rocks above the mouth of the cavern and shoot the bear as he came out, if somebody would go in and dislodge him.

" I'm your man," answered Meek.

" And I too," said Claymore.

" I'll be —— if we are not as brave as you are," said Hawkins, as he prepared to follow.

On entering the cave, which was sixteen or twenty feet square, and high enough to stand erect in, instead of one, three bears were discovered. They were standing, the largest one in the middle, with their eyes staring at the

entrance, but quite quiet, greeting the hunters only with
a low growl. Finding that there was a bear apiece to be
disposed of, the hunters kept close to the wall, and out of
the stream of light from the entrance, while they advanced a little way, cautiously, towards their game, which,
however, seemed to take no notice of them. After ma-
neuvering a few minutes to get nearer, Meek finally struck
the large bear on the head with his wiping-stick, when it
immediately moved off and ran out of the cave. As it
came out, Doughty shot, but only wounded it, and it
came rushing back, snorting, and running around in a
circle, till the well directed shots from all three killed it
on the spot. Two more bears now remained to be disposed of.

The successful shot put Hawkins in high spirits. He
began to hallo and laugh, dancing around, and with the
others striking the next largest bear to make him run out,
which he soon did, and was shot by Doughty. By this
time their guns were reloaded, the men growing more
and more elated, and Hawkins declaring they were "all
Daniels in the lions' den, and no mistake." This, and
similar expressions, he constantly vociferated, while they
drove out the third and smallest bear. As it reached the
cave's mouth, three simultaneous shots put an end to the
last one, when Hawkins' excitement knew no bounds.
"Daniel was a humbug," said he. "Daniel in the lions'
den! Of course it was winter, and the lions were sucking
their paws! Tell me no more of Daniel's exploits. We
are as good Daniels as he ever dared to be. Hurrah for
these Daniels!" With these expressions, and playing
many antics by way of rejoicing, the delighted Hawkins
finally danced himself out of his "lion's den," and set to
work with the others to prepare for a return to camp.

Sleds were soon constructed out of the branches of the

mountain willow, and on these light vehicles the fortunate find of bear meat was soon conveyed to the hungry camp in the plain below. And ever after this singular exploit of the party, Hawkins continued to aver, in language more strong than elegant, that the Scripture Daniel was a humbug compared to himself, and Meek, and Claymore.

CHAPTER VIII.

1833. In the spring the camp was visited by a party of twenty Blackfeet, who drove off most of the horses; and among the stolen ones, Bridger's favorite race-horse, Grohean, a Camanche steed of great speed and endurance. To retake the horses, and if possible punish the thieves, a company of the gamest trappers, thirty in number, including Meek, and Kit Carson, who not long before had joined the Rocky Mountain Company, was dispatched on their trail. They had not traveled long before they came up with the Blackfeet, but the horses were nowhere to be seen, having been secreted, after the manner of these thieves, in some defile of the mountains, until the skirmish was over which they knew well enough to anticipate. Accordingly when the trappers came up, the wily savages were prepared for them. Their numbers were inferior to that of the whites; accordingly they assumed an innocent and peace-desiring air, while their head man advanced with the inevitable peace-pipe, to have a "talk." But as their talk was a tissue of lies, the trappers soon lost patience, and a quarrel quickly arose. The Indians betook themselves to the defences which were selected beforehand, and a fight began, which without giving to either party the victory of arms, ended in the killing of two or three of the Blackfeet, and the wounding very severely of Kit Carson. The firing ceased with nightfall; and when morning came, as usual the Blackfeet were gone, and the trappers returned to camp without their horses.

The lost animals were soon replaced by purchase from the Nez Perces, and the company divided up into brigades, some destined for the country east of the mountains, and others for the south and west. In this year Meek rose a grade above the hired trapper, and became one of the order denominated skin trappers. These, like the hired trappers, depend upon the company to furnish them an outfit; but do not receive regular wages, as do the others. They trap for themselves, only agreeing to sell their beaver to the company which furnishes the outfit, and to no other. In this capacity, our Joe, and a few associates, hunted this spring, in the Snake River and Salt Lake countries; returning as usual to the annual rendezvous, which was appointed this summer to meet on Green River. Here were the Rocky Mountain and American Companies; the St. Louis Company, under Capt. Wm. Sublette and his friend Campbell; the usual camp of Indian allies; and, a few miles distant, that of Captain Bonneville. In addition to all these, was a small company belonging to Capt. Stuart, an Englishman, of noble family, who was traveling in the far west only to gratify his own love of wild adventure, and admiration of all that is grand and magnificent in nature. With him was an artist named Miller, and several servants; but he usually traveled in company with one or another of the fur companies; thus enjoying their protection, and at the same time gaining a knowledge of the habits of mountain life.

The rendezvous, at this time, furnished him a striking example of some of the ways of mountain-men, least to their honorable fame; and we fear we must confess that our friend Joe Meek, who had been gathering laurels as a valiant hunter and trapper during the three or four years of his apprenticeship, was also becoming fitted, by frequent practice, to graduate in some of the vices of camp life, especially the one of conviviality during rendezvous. Had he not given his permission, we should not perhaps have said what he says of himself, that he was at such times often very "powerful drunk."

During the indulgence of these excesses, while at this rendezvous, there occurred one of those incidents of wilderness life which make the blood creep with horror. Twelve of the men were bitten by a mad wolf, which hung about the camp for two or three nights. Two of these were seized with madness in camp, sometime afterwards, and ran off into the mountains, where they perished. One was attacked by the paroxysm while on a hunt; when, throwing himself off his horse, he struggled and foamed at the mouth, gnashing his teeth, and barking like a wolf. Yet he retained consciousness enough to warn away his companions, who hastened in search of assistance; but when they returned he was nowhere to be found. It was thought that he was seen a day or two afterwards, but no one could come up with him, and of course, he too, perished. Another died on his journey to St. Louis; and several died at different times within the next two years.

At the time, however, immediately following the visit of the wolf to camp, Captain Stuart was admonishing Meek on the folly of his ways, telling him that the wolf might easily have bitten him, he was so drunk.

"It would have killed him,—sure, if it hadn't *cured* him!" said Meek,—alluding to the belief that alcohol is a remedy for the poison of hydrophobia.

When sobriety returned, and work was once more to be resumed, Meek returned with three or four associates to the Salt Lake country, to trap on the numerous streams that flow down from the mountains to the east of Salt Lake. He had not been long in this region when he fell in on Bear River with a company of Bonneville's men, one hun-

10

dred and eighteen in number, under Jo Walker, who had been sent to explore the Great Salt Lake, and the adjacent country; to make charts, keep a journal, and, in short, make a thorough discovery of all that region. Great expectations were cherished by the Captain concerning this favorite expedition, which were, however, utterly blighted, as his historian has recorded. The disappointment and loss which Bonneville suffered from it, gave a tinge of prejudice to his delineations of the trapper's character. It was true that they did not explore Salt Lake; and that they made a long and expensive journey, collecting but few peltries. It is true also, that they caroused in true mountain style, while among the Californians: but that the expedition was unprofitable was due chiefly to the difficulties attending the exploration of a new country, a large portion of which was desert and mountain.

But let us not anticipate. When Meek and his companions fell in with Jo Walker and his company, they resolved to accompany the expedition; for it was "a feather in a man's cap," and made his services doubly valuable to have become acquainted with a new country, and fitted himself for a pilot.

On leaving Bear River, where the hunters took the precaution to lay in a store of dried meat, the company passed down on the west side of Salt Lake, and found themselves in the Salt Lake desert, where their store, insufficiently large, soon became reduced to almost nothing. Here was experienced again the sufferings to which Meek had once before been subjected in the Digger country, which, in fact, bounded this desert on the northwest. "There was," says Bonneville, "neither tree, nor herbage, nor spring, nor pool, nor running stream; ᴉ thing but parched wastes of sand, where horse and rider were in danger of perishing." Many an emigrant has since confirmed the truth of this account.

It could not be expected that men would continue on in such a country, in that direction which offered no change for the better. Discerning at last a snowy range to the northwest, they traveled in that direction; pinched with famine, and with tongues swollen out of their mouths with thirst. They came at last to a small stream, into which both men and animals plunged to quench their raging thirst.

The instinct of a mule on these desert journeys is something wonderful. We have heard it related by others besides the mountain-men, that they will detect the neighborhood of water long before their riders have discovered a sign; and setting up a gallop, when before they could hardly walk, will dash into the water up to their necks, drinking in the life-saving moisture through every pore of the skin, while they prudently refrain from swallowing much of it. If one of a company has been off on a hunt for water, and on finding it has let his mule drink, when he returns to camp, the other animals will gather about it, and snuff its breath, and even its body, betraying the liveliest interest and envy. It is easy to imagine that in the case of Jo Walker's company, not only the animals but the men were eager to steep themselves in the reviving waters of the first stream which they found on the border of this weary desert.

It proved to be a tributary of Mary's or Ogden's River, along which the company pursued their way, trapping as they went, and living upon the flesh of the beaver. They had now entered upon the same country inhabited by Digger Indians, in which Milton Sublette's brigade had so nearly perished with famine the previous year. It was unexplored, and the natives were as curious about the movements of their white visitors, as Indians always are on the first appearance of civilized men.

They hung about the camps, offering no offences by day, but contriving to do a great deal of thieving during the night-time. Each day, for several days, their numbers increased, until the army which dogged the trappers by day, and filched from them at night, numbered nearly a thousand. They had no guns; but carried clubs, and some bows and arrows. The trappers at length became uneasy at this accumulation of force, even though they had no fire-arms, for was it not this very style of people, armed with clubs, that attacked Smith's party on the Umpqua, and killed all but four?

"We must kill a lot of them, boys," said Jo Walker. "It will never do to let that crowd get into camp." Accordingly, as the Indians crowded round at a ford of Mary's River, always a favorite time of attack with the savages, Walker gave the order to fire, and the whole company poured a volley into the jostling crowd. The effect was terrible. Seventy-five Diggers bit the dust; while the others, seized with terror and horror at this new and instantaneous mode of death, fled howling away, the trappers pursuing them until satisfied that they were too much frightened to return. This seemed to Captain Bonneville, when he came to hear of it, like an unnecessary and ferocious act. But Bonneville was not an experienced Indian fighter. His views of their character were much governed by his knowledge of the Flatheads and Nez Perces; and also by the immunity from harm he enjoyed among the Shoshonies on the Snake River, where the Hudson's Bay Company had brought them into subjection, and where even two men might travel in safety at the time of his residence in that country.

Walker's company continued on down to the main or Humboldt River, trapping as they went, both for the furs, and for something to eat; and expecting to find that the river whose course they were following through these barren plains, would lead them to some more important river, or to some large lake or inland sea. This was a country entirely unknown, even to the adventurous traders and trappers of the fur companies, who avoided it because it was out of the buffalo range; and because the borders of it, along which they sometimes skirted, were found to be wanting in water-courses in which beaver might be looked for. Walker's company therefore, now determined to prosecute their explorations until they came to some new and profitable beaver grounds.

But after a long march through an inhospitable country they came at last to where the Humboldt sinks itself in a great swampy lake, in the midst of deserts of sage-brush. Here was the end of their great expectations. To the west of them, however, and not far off, rose the lofty summits of the Sierra Nevada range, some of whose peaks were covered with eternal snows. Since they had already made an unprofitable business of their expedition, and failed in its principal aim, that of exploring Salt Lake, they resolved upon crossing the mountains into California, and seeking new fields of adventure on the western side of the Nevada mountains.

Accordingly, although it was already late in the autumn, the party pushed on toward the west, until they came to Pyramid Lake, another of those swampy lakes which are frequently met with near the eastern base of these Sierras. Into this flowed a stream similar to the Humboldt, which came from the south, and, they believed, had its rise in the mountains. As it was important to find a good pass, they took their course along this stream, which they named Trucker's River, and continued along it to its head-waters in the Sierras.

And now began the arduous labor of crossing an unknown range of lofty mountains. Mountaineers as they were, they found it a difficult undertaking, and one attended with considerable peril. For a period of more than three weeks they were struggling with these dangers; hunting paths for their mules and horses, traveling around canyons thousands of feet deep; sometimes sinking in new fallen snow; always hungry, and often in peril from starvation. Sometimes they scrambled up almost smooth declivities of granite, that offered no foothold save the occasional seams in the rock; at others they traveled through pine forests made nearly impassable by snow; and at other times on a ridge which wind and sun made bare for them. All around rose rocky peaks and pinnacles fretted by ages of denudation to very spears and needles of a burnt looking, red colored rock. Below, were spread out immense fields, or rather oceans, of granite that seemed once to have been a molten sea, whose waves were suddenly congealed. From the fissures between these billows grew stunted pines, which had found a scanty soil far down in the crevices of the rock for their hardy roots. Following the course of any stream flowing in the right direction for their purpose, they came not infrequently to some small fertile valley, set in amidst the rocks like a cup, and often containing in its depth a bright little lake. These are the oases in the mountain deserts. But the lateness of the season made it necessary to avoid the high valleys on account of the snow, which in winter accumulates to a depth of twenty feet.

Great was the exultation of the mountaineers when they emerged from the toils and dangers, safe into the bright and sunny plains of California; having explored almost the identical route since fixed upon for the Union Pacific Railroad.

They proceeded down the Sacramento valley, toward

the coast, after recruiting their horses on the ripe wild oats, and the freshly springing grass which the December rains had started into life, and themselves on the plentiful game of the foot-hills. Something of the stimulus of the Californian climate seemed to be imparted to the ever buoyant blood of these hardy and danger-despising men. They were mad with delight on finding themselves, after crossing the stern Sierras, in a land of sunshine and plenty; a beautiful land of verdant hills and tawny plains; of streams winding between rows of alder and willow, and valleys dotted with picturesque groves of the evergreen oak. Instead of the wild blasts which they were used to encounter in December, they experienced here only those dainty and wooing airs which poets have ascribed to spring, but which seldom come even with the last May days in an eastern climate.

In the San José valley they encountered a party of one hundred soldiers, which the Spanish government at Monterey had sent out to take a party of Indians accused of stealing cattle. The soldiers were native Californians, descendants of the mixed blood of Spain and Mexico, a wild, jaunty looking set of fellows, who at first were inclined to take Walker's party for a band of cattle thieves, and to march them off to Monterey. But the Rocky Mountain trapper was not likely to be taken prisoner by any such brigade as the dashing *cabelleros* of Monterey.

After astonishing them with a series of whoops and yells, and trying to astonish them with feats of horsemanship, they began to discover that when it came to the latter accomplishment, even mountain-men could learn something from a native Californian. In this latter frame of mind they consented to be conducted to Monterey as prisoners or not, just as the Spanish government should hereafter be pleased to decree; and they had confidence in themselves that they should be able to bend that high and mighty authority to their own purposes thereafter.

Nor were they mistaken in their calculations. Their fearless, free and easy style, united to their complete furnishing of arms, their numbers, and their superior ability to stand up under the demoralizing effect of the favorite *aguadiente*, soon so far influenced the soldiery at least, that the trappers were allowed perfect freedom under the very eyes of the jealous Spanish government, and were treated with all hospitality.

The month which the trappers spent at Monterey was their "red letter day" for a long time after. The habits of the Californians accorded with their own, with just difference enough to furnish them with novelties and excitements such as gave a zest to their intercourse. The Californian, and the mountain-men, were alike centaurs. Horses were their necessity, and their delight; and the plains swarmed with them, as also with wild cattle, descendants of those imported by the Jesuit Fathers in the early days of the Missions. These horses and cattle were placed at the will and pleasure of the trappers. They feasted on one, and bestrode the other as it suited them. They attended bull-fights, ran races, threw the lasso, and played monte, with a relish that delighted the inhabitants of Monterey.

The partial civilization of the Californians accorded with every feeling to which the mountain-men could be brought to confess. To them the refinements of cities would have been oppressive. The adobe houses of Monterey were not so restraining in their elegance as to trouble the sensations of men used to the heavens for a roof in summer, and a skin lodge for shelter in winter. Some fruits and vegetables, articles not tasted for years, they obtained at the missions, where the priests received them

BRANDING CATTLE.

courteously and hospitably, as they had done Jedediah Smith and his company, five years before, when on their long and disastrous journey they found themselves almost destitute of the necessaries of life, upon their arrival in California. There was something too, in the dress of the people, both men and women, which agreed with, while differing from, the dress of the mountaineers and their now absent Indian dulcineas.

The men wore garments of many colors, consisting of blue velveteen breeches and jacket, the jacket having a scarlet collar and cuffs, and the breeches being open at the knee to display the stocking of white. Beneath these were displayed high buskins made of deer skin, fringed down the outside of the ankle, and laced with a cord and tassels. On the head was worn a broad brimmed *sombrero;* and over the shoulders the jaunty Mexican *sarape.* When they rode, the Californians wore enormous spurs, fastened on by jingling chains. Their saddles were so shaped that it was difficult to dislodge the rider, being high before and behind; and the indispensable lasso hung coiled from the pommel. Their stirrups were of wood, broad on the bottom, with a guard of leather that protected the fancy buskin of the horseman from injury. Thus accoutred, and mounted on a wild horse, the Californian was a suitable comrade, in appearance, at least, for the buckskin clad trapper, with his high beaver-skin cap, his gay scarf, and moccasins, and profusion of arms.

The dress of the women was a gown of gaudy calico or silk, and a bright colored shawl, which served for mantilla and bonnet together. They were well formed, with languishing eyes and soft voices; and doubtless appeared charming in the eyes of our band of trappers, with whom they associated freely at fandangoes, bull-fights, or bear-baitings. In such company, what wonder that Bonneville's men lingered for a whole month! What wonder that the California expedition was a favorite theme by camp-fires, for a long time subsequent?

1834. In February the trappers bethought themselves of returning to the mountains. The route fixed upon was one which should take them through Southern California, and New Mexico, along the course of all the principal rivers. Crossing the coast mountains, into the valley of the San Joaquin, they followed its windings until they came to its rise in the Lulare Lake. Thence turning in a southeasterly course, they came to the Colorado, at the Mohave villages, where they traded with the natives, whom they found friendly. Keeping on down the Colorado, to the mouth of the Gila, they turned back from that river, and ascended the Colorado once more, to Williams' Fork, and up the latter stream to some distance, when they fell in with a company of sixty men under Frapp and Jervais, two of the partners in the Rocky Mountain Company. The meeting was joyful on all sides; but particularly so between Meek and some of his old comrades, with whom he had fought Indians and grizzly bears, or set beaver traps on some lonely stream in the Blackfoot country. A lively exchange of questions and answers took place, while gaiety and good feeling reigned.

Frapp had been out quite as long as the Monterey party. It was seldom that the brigade which traversed the southern country, on the Colorado, and its large tributaries, returned to winter quarters; for in the region where they trapped winter was unknown, and the journey to the northern country a long and hazardous one. But the reunited trappers had each their own experiences to relate.

The two companies united made a party nearly two hundred strong. Keeping with Frapp, they crossed over from

Williams' Fork to the Colorado Chiquito river, at the Moquis village, where some of the men disgraced themselves far more than did Jo Walker's party at the crossing of Mary's River. For the Moquis were a half-civilized nation, who had houses and gardens, and conducted themselves kindly, or at the worst peaceably, toward properly behaved strangers. These trappers, instead of approaching them with offers of purchase, lawlessly entered their gardens, rifling them of whatever fruit or melons were ripe, and not hesitating to destroy that which was not ripe. To this, as might be expected, the Moquises objected; and were shot down for so doing. In this truly infamous affair fifteen or twenty of them were killed.

"I didn't belong to that crowd," says Joe Meek, "I sat on the fence and saw it, though. It was a shameful thing."

From the Moquis village, the joint companies crossed the country in a northeasterly direction, crossing several branches of the Colorado at their head-waters, which course finally brought them to the head-waters of the Rio Grande. The journey from the mouth of the Gila, though long, extended over a country comparatively safe. Either farther to the south or east, the caravan would have been in danger of a raid from the most dangerous tribes on the continent.

CHAPTER IX.

1834.   But Joe Meek was not destined to return to the
Rocky Mountains without having had an Indian fight.   If
adventures did not come in his way he was the man to put
himself in the way of adventures.

While the camp was on its way from the neighborhood
of Grande River to the New Park, Meek, Kit Carson,
and Mitchell, with three Delaware Indians, named Tom
Hill, Manhead, and Jonas, went on a hunt across to the
east of Grande River, in the country lying between the
Arkansas and Cimarron, where numerous small branches
of these rivers head together, or within a small extent of
country.

They were about one hundred and fifty miles from camp,
and traveling across the open plain between the streams,
one beautiful May morning, when about five miles off they
descried a large band of Indians mounted, and galloping
toward them.   As they were in the Camanche country,
they knew what to expect if they allowed themselves
to be taken prisoners.   They gave but a moment to the
observation of their foes, but that one moment revealed
a spirited scene.   Fully two hundred Camanches, their
warriors in front, large and well formed men, mounted on
fleet and powerful horses, armed with spears and battle
axes, racing like the wind over the prairie, their feather
head-dresses bending to the breeze, that swept past them
in the race with double force; all distinctly seen in the

THE MULE FORT.

clear air of the prairie, and giving the beholder a thrill of fear mingled with admiration.

The first moment given to this spectacle, the second one was employed to devise some means of escape. To run was useless. The swift Camanche steeds would soon overtake them; and then their horrible doom was fixed. No covert was at hand, neither thicket nor ravine, as in the mountains there might have been. Carson and Meek exchanged two or three sentences. At last, "we must kill our mules!" said they.

That seems a strange devise to the uninitiated reader, who no doubt believes that in such a case their mules must be their salvation. And so they were intended to be. In this plight a dead mule was far more useful than a live one. To the ground sprang every man; and placing their mules, seven in number, in a ring, they in an instant cut their throats with their hunting knives, and held on to the bridles until each animal fell dead in its appointed place. Then hastily scooping up what earth they could with knives, they made themselves a fort—a hole to stand in for each man, and a dead mule for a breastwork.

In less than half an hour the Camanches charged on them; the medicine-man in advance shouting, gesticulating, and making a desperate clatter with a rattle which he carried and shook violently. The yelling, the whooping, the rattling, the force of the charge were appalling. But the little garrison in the mule fort did not waver. The Camanche horses did. They could not be made to charge upon the bloody carcasses of the mules, nor near enough for their riders to throw a spear into the fort.

This was what the trappers had relied upon. They were cool and determined, while terribly excited and wrought up by their situation. It was agreed that no more than three should fire at a time, the other three reserving their fire while the empty guns could be reloaded. They were to pick their men, and kill one at every shot.

They acted up to their regulations. At the charge the Camanche horses recoiled and could not be urged upon the fort of slaughtered mules. The three whites fired first, and the medicine-man and two other Camanches fell. When a medicine-man is killed, the others retire to hold a council and appoint another, for without their "medicine" they could not expect success in battle. This was time gained. The warriors retired, while their women came up and carried off the dead.

After devoting a little time to bewailing the departed, another chief was appointed to the head place, and another furious charge was made with the same results as before. Three more warriors bit the dust; while the spears of their brethren, attached to long hair ropes by which they could be withdrawn, fell short of reaching the men in the fort. Again and again the Camanches made a fruitless charge, losing, as often as they repeated it, three warriors, either dead or wounded. Three times that day the head chief or medicine-man was killed; and when that happened, the heroes in the fort got a little time to breathe. While the warriors held a council, the women took care of the wounded and slain.

As the women approached the fort to carry off the fallen warriors, they mocked and reviled the little band of trappers, calling them "women," for fighting in a fort, and resorting to the usual Indian ridicule and gasconade. Occasionally, also, a warrior raced at full speed past the fort apparently to take observations. Thus the battle continued through the entire day.

It was terrible work for the trappers. The burning sun of the plains shone on them, scorching them to faintness. Their faces were begrimed with powder and dust; their throats parched, and tongues swollen with thirst, and their whole frames aching from their cramped positions, as well as the excitement and fatigue of the battle. But they dared not relax their vigilance for a moment. They were fighting for their lives, and they meant to win.

At length the sun set on that bloody and wearisome day. Forty-two Camanches were killed, and several more wounded, for the charge had been repeated fifteen or twenty times. The Indians drew off at nightfall to mourn over their dead, and hold a council. Probably they had lost faith in their medicines, or believed that the trappers possessed one far greater than any of theirs. Under the friendly cover of the night, the six heroes who had fought successfully more than a hundred Camanches, took each his blanket and his gun, and bidding a brief adieu to dead mules and beaver packs, set out to return to camp.

When a mountain-man had a journey to perform on foot, to travel express, or to escape from an enemy, he fell into what is called a dog trot, and ran in that manner, sometimes, all day. On the present occasion, the six, escaping for life, ran all night, and found no water for seventy-five mile. When they did at last come to a clear running stream, their thankfulness was equal to their necessity, "for," says Meek, "thirst is the greatest suffering I ever experienced. It is far worse than hunger or pain."

Having rested and refreshed themselves at the stream, they kept on without much delay until they reached camp in that beautiful valley of the Rocky Mountains called the New, or the South Park.

While they remained in the South Park, Mr. Guthrie, one of the Rocky Mountain Company's traders, was killed by lightning. A number of persons were collected in the lodge of the Booshway, Frapp, to avoid the rising tempest, when Guthrie, who was leaning against the lodge pole, was struck by a flash of the electric current, and fell dead instantly. Frapp rushed out of the lodge, partly bewildered himself by the shock, and under the impression that Guthrie had been shot. Frapp was a German, and spoke English somewhat imperfectly. In the excitement of the moment he shouted out, "Py ——, who did shoot Guttery!"

" — a' ——, I expect: He's a firing into camp;" drawled out Hawkins, whose ready wit was very disregardful of sacred names and subjects.

The mountaineers were familiar with the most awful aspects of nature; and if their familiarity had not bred contempt, it had at least hardened them to those solemn impressions which other men would have felt under their influence.

From New Park, Meek traveled north with the main camp, passing first to the Old Park; thence to the Little Snake, a branch of Bear River; thence to Pilot Butte; and finally to Green River to rendezvous; having traveled in the past year about three thousand miles, on horseback, through new and often dangerous countries. It is easy to believe that the Monterey expedition was the popular theme in camp during rendezvous. It had been difficult to get volunteers for Bonneville's Salt Lake Exploration: but such was the wild adventure to which it led, that volunteering for a trip to Monterey would have been exceedingly popular immediately thereafter.

On Bear River, Bonneville's men fell in with their commander, Captain Bonneville, whose disappointment and indignation at the failure of his plans was exceedingly great. In this indignation there was considerable justice; yet much of his disappointment was owing to causes which a more experienced trader would have avoided. The only conclusion which can be arrived at by an impartial observer of the events of 1832–35, is, that none but certain men of long experience and liberal means, could succeed in the business of the fur-trade. There were too many chances of loss; too many wild elements to be mingled in amity; and too powerful opposition from the old established companies. Captain Bonneville's experience was no different from Mr. Wyeth's. In both cases there was much effort, outlay, and loss. Nor was their failure owing to any action of the Hudson's Bay Company, different from, or more tyrannical, than the action of the American companies, as has frequently been represented. It was the American companies in the Rocky Mountains that drove both Bonneville and Wyeth out of the field. Their inexperience could not cope with the thorough knowledge of the business, and the country, which their older rivals possessed. Raw recruits were no match, in trapping or fighting, for old mountaineers: and those veterans who had served long under certain leaders could not be inveigled from their service except upon the most extravagant offers; and these extravagant wages, which if one paid, the other must, would not allow a profit to either of the rivals.

"How much does your company pay you?" asked Bonneville of Meek, to whom he was complaining of the conduct of his men on the Monterey expedition.

"Fifteen hundred dollars," answered Meek.

"Yes: and I will give it to you," said Bonneville with bitterness.

It was quite true. Such was the competition aroused by the Captain's efforts to secure good men and pilots, that rather than lose them to a rival company, the Rocky Mountain Company paid a few of their best men the wages above named.

11

CHAPTER X.

1834. THE gossip at rendezvous was this year of an unusually exciting character. Of the brigades which left for different parts of the country the previous summer, the Monterey travelers were not the only ones who had met with adventures. Fitzpatrick, who had led a party into the Crow country that autumn, had met with a characteristic reception from that nation of cunning vagabonds.

Being with his party on Lougue River, in the early part of September, he discovered that he was being dogged by a considerable band of Crows, and endeavored to elude their spying; but all to no purpose. The Crow chief kept in his neighborhood, and finally expressed a desire to bring his camp alongside that of Fitzpatrick, pretending to the most friendly and honorable sentiments toward his white neighbors. But not feeling any confidence in Crow friendship, Fitzpatrick declined, and moved camp a few miles away. Not, however, wishing to offend the dignity of the apparently friendly chief, he took a small escort, and went to pay a visit to his Crow neighbors, that they might see that he was not afraid to trust them. Alas, vain subterfuge!

While he was exchanging civilities with the Crow chief, a party of the young braves stole out of camp, and taking advantage of the leader's absence, made an attack on his camp, so sudden and successful that not a horse, nor anything else which they could make booty of was left.

Even Captain Stuart, who was traveling with Fitzpatrick, and who was an active officer, was powerless to resist the attack, and had to consent to see the camp rifled of everything valuable.

In the meantime Fitzpatrick, after concluding his visit in the most amicable manner, was returning to camp, when he was met by the exultant braves, who added insult to injury by robbing him of his horse, gun, and nearly all his clothes, leaving him to return to his party in a deplorable condition, to the great amusement of the trappers, and his own chagrin.

However, the next day a talk was held with the head chief of the Crows, to whom Fitzpatrick represented the infamy of such treacherous conduct in a very strong light. In answer to this reproof, the chief disowned all knowledge of the affair; saying that he could not always control the conduct of the young men, who would be a little wild now and then, in spite of the best Crow precepts: but that he would do what he could to have the property restored. Accordingly, after more talk, and much eloquence on the part of Fitzpatrick, the chief part of the plunder was returned to him, including the horses and rifles of the men, together with a little ammunition, and a few beaver traps.

Fitzpatrick understood the meaning of this apparent fairness, and hastened to get out of the Crow country before another raid by the mischievous young braves, at a time when their chief was not "honor bound," should deprive him of the recovered property. That his conjecture was well founded, was proven by the numerous petty thefts which were committed, and by the loss of several horses and mules, before he could remove them beyond the limits of the Crow territory.

While the trappers exchanged accounts of their indi-

vidual experiences, the leaders had more important matters to gossip over.   The rivalry between the several fur
companies was now at its climax.   Through the energy
and ability of Captain Sublette of the St. Louis Company,
and the experience and industry of the Rocky Mountain
Company, which Captain Sublette still continued to control in a measure, the power still remained with them.
The American Company had never been able to cope with
them in the Rocky Mountains; and the St. Louis Company were already invading their territory on the Missouri
River, by carrying goods up that river in boats, to trade
with the Indians under the very walls of the American
Company's forts.

    In August of the previous year, when Mr. Nathaniel
Wyeth had started on his return to the states, he was accompanied as far as the mouth of the Yellowstone by
Milton Sublette; and had engaged with that gentleman
to furnish him with goods the following year, as he believed he could do, cheaper than the St. Louis Company,
who purchased their goods in St. Louis at a great advance
on Boston prices.   But Milton Sublette fell in with his
brother the Captain, at the mouth of the Yellowstone,
with a keel-boat loaded with merchandise; and while
Wyeth pursued his way eastward to purchase the Indian
goods which were intended to supply the wants of the
fur-traders in the Rocky Mountains, at a profit to him, and
an advantage to them, the Captain was persuading his
brother not to encourage any interlopers in the Indian
trade; but to continue to buy goods from himself, as formerly.   So potent were his arguments, that Milton yielded
to them, in spite of his engagement with Wyeth.   Thus
during the autumn of 1833, while Bonneville was being
wronged and robbed, as he afterwards became convinced,
by his men under Walker, and anticipated in the hunting-

ground selected for himself, in the Crow country, by Fitz-patrick, as he had previously been in the Snake country by Milton Sublette, Wyeth was proceeding to Boston in good faith, to execute what proved to be a fool's errand. Bonneville also had gone on another, when after the trap-ping season was over he left his camp to winter on the Snake River, and started with a small escort to visit the Columbia, and select a spot for a trading-post on the lower portion of that river. On arriving at Wallah-Wallah, af-ter a hard journey over the Blue Mountains in the winter, the agent at that post had refused to supply him with pro-visions to prosecute his journey, and given him to under-stand that the Hudson's Bay Company might be polite and hospitable to Captain Bonneville as the gentleman, but that it was against their regulations to encourage the advent of other traders who would interfere with their business, and unsettle the minds of the Indians in that region.

This reply so annoyed the Captain, that he refused the well meant advice of Mr. Pambrun that he should not un-dertake to recross the Blue Mountains in March snows, but travel under the escort of Mr. Payette, one of the Hud-son's Bay Company's leaders, who was about starting for the Nez Perce country by a safer if more circuitous route. He therefore set out to return by the route he came, and only arrived at camp in May, 1834, after many dan-gers and difficulties. From the Portneuf River, he then proceeded with his camp to explore the Little Snake River, and Snake Lake; and it was while so doing that he fell in with his men just returned from Monterey.

Such was the relative position of the several fur com-panies in the Rocky Mountains in 1834; and it was of such matters that the leaders talked in the lodge of the Booshways, at rendezvous. In the meantime Wyeth ar-

rived in the mountains with his goods, as he had contracted with Milton Sublette in the previous year. But
on his heels came Captain Sublette, also with goods, and
the Rocky Mountain Company violated their contract with
Wyeth, and purchased of their old leader.

Thus was Wyeth left, with his goods on his hands, in a
country where it was impossible to sell them, and useless
to undertake an opposition to the already established fur-
traders and trappers. His indignation was great, and certainly was just. In his interview with the Rocky Mountain Company, in reply to their excuses for, and vindica-
tion of their conduct, his answer was:

"Gentlemen, I will roll a stone into your garden that
you will never be able to get out."

And he kept his promise; for that same autumn he
moved on to the Snake River, and built Fort Hall, storing
his goods therein. The next year he sold out goods and
fort to the Hudson's Bay Company; and the stone was in
the garden of the Rocky Mountain Fur Company that
they were never able to dislodge. When Wyeth had built
his fort and left it in charge of an agent, he dispatched a
party of trappers to hunt in the Big Blackfoot country,
under Joseph Gale, who had previously been in the service of the Rocky Mountain Company, and of whom we
shall learn more hereafter, while he set out for the Columbia to meet his vessel, and establish a salmon fishery.
The fate of that enterprise has already been recorded.

As for Bonneville, he made one more effort to reach the
lower Columbia; failing, however, a second time, for the
same reason as before—he could not subsist himself and
company in a country where even every Indian refused to
sell to him either furs or provisions. After being reduced
to horse-flesh, and finding no encouragement that his condition would be improved farther down the river, he

turned back once more from about Wallah-Wallah, and returned to the mountains, and from there to the east in the following year. A company of his trappers, however, continued to hunt for him east of the mountains for two or three years longer.

The rivalry between the Rocky Mountain and American Companies was this year diminished by their mutually agreeing to confine themselves to certain parts of the country, which treaty continued for two years, when they united in one company. They were then, with the exception of a few lone traders, the only competitors of the Hudson's Bay Company, for the fur-trade of the West.

CHAPTER XI.

1834. THE Rocky Mountain Company now confined themselves to the country lying east of the mountains, and upon the head-waters and tributaries of the Missouri, a country very productive in furs, and furnishing abundance of game. But it was also the most dangerous of all the northern fur-hunting territory, as it was the home of those two nations of desperadoes, the Crows and Blackfeet. During the two years in which the company may have been said almost to reside there, desperate encounters and hair-breadth escapes were incidents of daily occurrence to some of the numerous trapping parties.

The camp had reached the Blackfoot country in the autumn of this year, and the trappers were out in all directions, hunting beaver in the numerous small streams that flow into the Missouri. On a small branch of the Gallatin Fork, some of the trappers fell in with a party of Wyeth's men, under Joseph Gale. When their neighborhood became known to the Rocky Mountain camp, Meek and a party of sixteen of his associates immediately resolved to pay them a visit, and inquire into their experience since leaving rendezvous. These visits between different camps are usually seasons of great interest and general ·rejoicing. But glad as Gale and his men were to meet with old friends, when the first burst of hearty greeting was over, they had but a sorry experience to relate. They had been out a long time. The Blackfeet had used them badly — several men had been killed.

Their guns were out of order, their ammunition all but exhausted; they were destitute, or nearly so, of traps, blankets, knives, everything. They were what the Indian and the mountain-man call "very poor."

Half the night was spent in recounting all that had passed in both companies since the fall hunt began. Little sympathy did Wyeth's men receive for their forlorn condition, for sympathy is repudiated by your true mountaineer for himself, nor will he furnish it to others. The absurd and humorous, or the daring and reckless, side of a story is the only one which is dwelt upon in narrating his adventures. The laugh which is raised at his expense when he has a tale of woes to communicate, is a better tonic to his dejected spirits than the gentlest pity would be. Thus lashed into courage again, he is ready to declare that all his troubles were only so much pastime.

It was this sort of cheer which the trapping party conveyed to Wyeth's men on this visit, and it was gratefully received, as being of the true kind.

In the morning the party set out to return to camp, Meek and Liggit starting in advance of the others. They had not proceeded far when they were fired on by a large band of Blackfeet, who came upon them quite suddenly, and thinking these two trappers easy game, set up a yell and dashed at them. As Meek and Liggit turned back and ran to Gale's camp, the Indians in full chase charged on them, and rushed pell-mell into the midst of camp, almost before they had time to discover that they had surprised so large a party of whites. So sudden was their advent, that they had almost taken the camp before the whites could recover from the confusion of the charge.

It was but a momentary shock, however. In another instant the roar of twenty guns reverberated from the mountains that rose high on either side of camp. The

Blackfeet were taken in a snare ; but they rallied and fell back beyond the grove in which the camp was situated, setting on fire the dry grass as they went. The fire quickly spread to the grove, and shot up the pine trees in splendid columns of flame, that seemed to lick the face of heaven. The Indians kept close behind the fire, shooting into camp whenever they could approach near enough, the trappers replying by frequent volleys. The yells of the savages, the noise of the flames roaring in the trees, the bellowing of the guns, whose echoes rolled among the hills, and the excitement of a battle for life, made the scene one long to be remembered with distinctness.

Both sides fought with desperation. The Blackfoot blood was up—the trapper blood no less. Gale's men, from having no ammunition, nor guns that were in order, could do little more than take charge of the horses, which they led out into the bottom land to escape the fire, fight the flames, and look after the camp goods. The few whose guns were available, showed the game spirit, and the fight became interesting as an exhibition of what mountain white men could do in a contest of one to ten, with the crack warriors of the red race. It was, at any time, a game party, consisting of Meek, Carson, Hawkins, Gale, Liggit, Rider, Robinson, Anderson, Russel, Larison, Ward, Parmaley, Wade, Michael Head, and a few others whose names have been forgotten.

The trappers being driven out of the grove by the fire, were forced to take to the open ground. The Indians, following the fire, had the advantage of the shelter afforded by the trees, and their shots made havoc among the horses, most of which were killed because they could not be taken. As for the trappers, they used the horses for defence, making rifle-pits behind them, when no other covert could be found. In this manner the battle was sustained until three o'clock in the afternoon, without loss of life to the whites, though several men were wounded.

At three in the afternoon, the Blackfoot chief ordered a retreat, calling out to the trappers that they would fight no more. Though their loss had been heavy, they still greatly outnumbered the whites; nor would the condition of the arms and the small amount of ammunition left permit the trappers to pursue them. The Indians were severely beaten, and no longer in a condition to fight, all of which was highly satisfactory to the victors. The only regret was, that Bridger's camp, which had become aware during the day that a battle was going on in the neighborhood, did not arrive early enough to exterminate the whole band. As it was, the big camp only came up in time to assist in taking care of the wounded. The destruction of their horses put an end to the independent existence of Gale's brigade, which joined itself and its fortunes to Bridger's command for the remainder of the year. Had it not been for the fortunate visit of the trappers to Gale's camp, without doubt every man in it would have perished at the hands of the Blackfeet: a piece of bad fortune not unaccordant with that which seemed to pursue the enterprises set on foot by the active but unlucky New England trader.

Not long after this battle with the Blackfeet, Meek and a trapper named Crow, with two Shawnees, went over into the Crow Country to trap on Pryor's River, a branch of the Yellowstone. On coming to the pass in the mountains between the Gallatin Fork of the Missouri and the great bend in the Yellowstone, called Pryor's Gap, Meek rode forward, with the mad-cap spirit strong in him, to " have a little fun with the boys," and advancing a short distance into the pass, wheeled suddenly, and came racing back, whooping and yelling, to make his comrades think

he had discovered Indians.   And lo! as if his yells had
invoked them from the rocks and trees, a war party suddenly emerged from the pass, on the heels of the jester,
and what had been sport speedily became earnest, as the
trappers turned their horses' heads and made off in the
direction of camp.   They had a fine race of it, and heard
other yells and war-whoops besides their own; but they
contrived to elude their pursuers, returning safe to camp.

This freak of Meek's was, after all, a fortunate inspiration, for had the four trappers entered the pass and come
upon the war party of Crows, they would never have escaped alive.

A few days after, the same party set out again, and
succeeded in reaching Pryor's River unmolested, and setting their traps.   They remained some time in this neighborhood trapping, but the season had become pretty well
advanced, and they were thinking of returning to camp
for the winter.   The Shawnees set out in one direction
to take up their traps, Meek and Crow in another.   The
stream where their traps were set was bordered by thickets of willow, wild cherry, and plum trees, and the bank
was about ten feet above the water at this season of the
year.

Meek had his traps set in the stream about midway between two thickets.   As he approached the river he observed with the quick eye of an experienced mountain-
man, certain signs which gave him little satisfaction.   The
buffalo were moving off as if disturbed; a bear ran suddenly out of its covert among the willows.

" I told Crow," said Meek, " that I didn't like to go in
there.   He laughed at me, and called me a coward.   'All
the same,' I said; I had no fancy for the place just then
—I didn't like the indications.   But he kept jeering me,
and at last I got mad and started in.   Just as I got to my

traps, I discovered that two red devils war a watching me
from the shelter of the thicket to my left, about two rods
off. When they saw that they war discovered they raised
their guns and fired. I turned my horse's head at the
same instant, and one ball passed through his neck, under
the neck bone, and the other through his withers, just
forward of my saddle.

"Seeing that they had not hit me, one of them ran up
with a spear to spear me. My horse war rearing and pitch-
ing from the pain of his wounds, so that I could with difficulty govern him; but I had my gun laid across my arm,
and when I fired I killed the rascal with the spear. Up
to that moment I had supposed that them two war all I
had to deal with. But as I got my horse turned round,
with my arm raised to fire at the other red devil, I encountered the main party, forty-nine of them, who war in the
bed of the stream, and had been covered by the bank.
They fired a volley at me. Eleven balls passed through
my blanket, under my arm, which war raised. I thought
it time to run, and run I did. Crow war about two hundred yards off. So quick had all this happened, that he
had not stirred from the spot whar I left him. When I
came up to him I called out that I must get on behind
him, for my horse war sick and staggering.

"'Try him again,' said Crow, who war as anxious to be
off as I war. I did try him agin, and sure enough, he got
up a gallop, and away we went, the Blackfeet after us.
But being mounted, we had the advantage, and soon dis-
tanced them. Before we had run a mile, I had to dismount
and breathe my horse. We war in a narrow pass whar it
war impossible to hide, so when the Indians came up with
us, as they did, while I war dismounted we took sure aim
and killed the two foremost ones. Before the others could
get close enough to fire we war off agin. It didn't take

much urging to make my horse go then, for the yells of them Blackfeet spurred him on.

"When we had run another mile I dismounted agin, for fear that my horse would give out, and agin we war overtaken. Them Blackfeet are powerful runners:—no better than us mountain-men, though. This time we served them just as we did before. We picked off two of the foremost, and then went on, the rest whooping after us. We war overtaken a third time in the same manner; and the third time two Blackfeet fell dead in advance. At this, they took the hint. Six warriors already gone for two white scalps and two horses; they didn't know how many more would go in the same way. And I reckon they had run about all they wanted to, anyway."

It is only necessary to add that Meek and Crow arrived safely at camp; and that the Shawnees came in after a day or two all right. Soon after the whole command under Bridger moved on to the Yellowstone, and went into winter camp in the great bend of that river, where buffalo were plenty, and cotton-wood was in abundance.

1835. Towards spring, however, the game had nearly all disappeared from the neighborhood of the camp; and the hunters were forced to follow the buffalo in their migration eastward. On one of these expeditions a party of six trappers, including Meek, and a man named Rose, made their camp on Clarke's fork of the Yellowstone. The first night in camp Rose had a dream with which he was very much impressed. He dreamed of shaking hands with a large white bear, which insisted on taking his right hand for that friendly ceremony. He had not given it very willingly, for he knew too much about bears in general to desire to be on very intimate terms with them.

Seeing that the dream troubled Rose, who was superstitiously inclined, Meek resorted to that "certain medicine

for minds diseased" which was in use in the mountains, and
added to the distress of Rose his interpretation, in the
spirit of ridicule, telling him that he was an adept in the
matter of dreams, and that unless he, Rose, was very mind-
ful of himself that day, he would shake hands with Beel-
zebub before he slept again.

With this comforting assurance, Rose set out with the
remainder of the party to hunt buffalo. They had pro
ceeded about three miles from camp, Rose riding in advance, when they suddenly encountered a company of
Blackfeet, nine in number, spies from a war, party of one
hundred and fifty, that was prowling and marauding
through the country on the lookout for small parties from
the camp of Bridger. The Blackfeet fired on the party
as it came up, from their place of concealment, a ball striking Rose's right arm, and breaking it at the elbow. This
caused his gun to fall, and an Indian sprang forward and
raised it up quickly, aiming it at Meek. The ball passed
through his cap without doing any other harm. By this
time the trappers were made aware of an ambuscade; but
how numerous the enemy was they could not determine.
However, as the rest, who were well mounted, turned to
fly, Meek, who was riding an old mule that had to be beaten
over the head to make it go, seeing that he was going to
be left behind, called out lustily, "hold on, boys! There's
not many of them. Let's stop and fight 'em;" at the
same time pounding the mule over the head, but without
effect. The Indians saw the predicament, and ran up to
seize the mule by the bridle, but the moment the mule got
wind of the savages, away he went, racing like a thorough-
bred, jumping impediments, and running right over a ravine, which was fortunately filled with snow. This movement brought Meek out ahead.

The other men then began to call out to Meek to stop

and fight. "Run for your lives, boys," roared Meek back at them, "there's ten thousand of them; they'll kill every one of you!"

The mule had got his head, and there was no more stopping him than there had been starting him. On he went in the direction of the Yellowstone, while the others made for Clarke's Fork. On arriving at the former river, Meek found that some of the pack horses had followed him, and others the rest of the party. This had divided the Indians, three or four of whom were on his trail. Springing off his mule, he threw his blankets down on the ice, and by moving them alternately soon crossed the mule over to the opposite side, just in time to avoid a bullet that came whistling after him. As the Indians could not follow, he pursued his way to camp in safety, arriving late that evening. The main party were already in and expecting him. Soon after, the buffalo hunters returned to the big camp, minus some pack horses, but with a good story to tell, at the expense of Meek, and which he enjoys telling of himself to this day.

CHAPTER XII.

1835. OWING to the high rate of pay which Meek was now able to command, he began to think of imitating the example of that distinguished order, the free trappers, to which he now belonged, and setting up a lodge to himself as a family man. The writer of this veracious history has never been able to obtain a full and particular account of our hero's earliest love adventures. This is a subject on which, in common with most mountain-men, he observes a becoming reticence. But of one thing we feel quite well assured: that from the time when the young Shoshonie beauty assisted in the rescue of himself and Sublette from the execution of the death sentence at the hands of her people, Meek had always cherished a rather more than friendly regard for the "Mountain Lamb."

But Sublette, with wealth and power, and the privileges of a Booshway, had hastened to secure her for himself; and Meek had to look and long from afar off, until, in the year of which we are writing, Milton Sublette was forced to leave the mountains and repair to an eastern city for surgical aid; having received a very troublesome wound in the leg, which was only cured at last by amputation.

Whether it was the act of a gay Lothario, or whether the law of divorce is even more easy in the mountains than in Indiana, we have always judiciously refrained from inquiring; but this we do know, upon the word of Meek himself, no sooner was Milton's back turned, than his friend

12

so insinuated himself into the good graces of his *Isabel*, as Sublette was wont to name the lovely Umentucken, that she consented to join her fortunes to those of the handsome young trapper without even the ceremony of serving a notice on her former lord.   As their season of bliss only extended over one brief year, this chapter shall be entirely devoted to recording such facts as have been imparted to us concerning this free trapper's wife.

" She was the most beautiful Indian woman I ever saw," says Meek: "and when she was mounted on her dapple gray horse, which cost me three hundred dollars, she made a fine show.   She wore a skirt of beautiful blue broadcloth, and a bodice and leggins of scarlet cloth, of the very finest make.   Her hair was braided and fell over her shoulders, a scarlet silk handkerchief, tied on hood fashion, covered her head; and the finest embroidered moccasins her feet.   She rode like all the Indian women, astride, and carried on one side of the saddle the toma- hawk for war, and on the other the pipe of peace.

" The name of her horse was " All Fours."   His accou- trements were as fine as his rider's.   The saddle, crupper, and bust girths cost one hundred and fifty dollars; the bridle fifty dollars; and the musk-a-moots fifty dollars more. All these articles were ornamented with fine cut glass beads, porcupine quills, and hawk's bells, that tinkled at every step. Her blankets were of scarlet and blue, and of the finest quality.   Such was the outfit of the trapper's wife, *Umen- tucken, Tukutey Undenwatsy*, the Lamb of the Mountains."

Although Umentucken was beautiful, and had a name signifying gentleness, she was not without a will and a spirit of her own, when the occasion demanded it.   While the camp was on the Yellowstone River, in the summer of 1835, a party of women left it to go in search of berries, which were often dried and stored for winter use by the

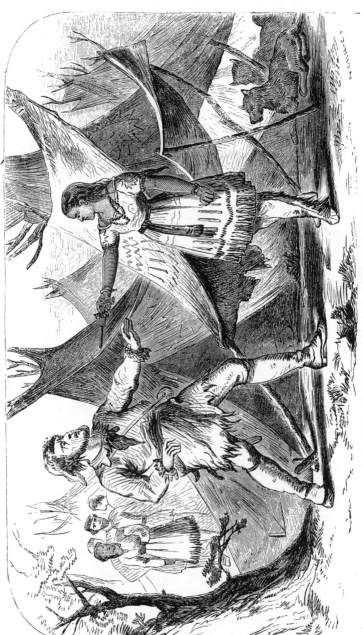

THE FREE TRAPPER'S INDIAN WIFE.

Indian women. Umentucken accompanied this party, which was attacked by a band of Blackfeet, some of the squaws being taken prisoners. But Umentucken saved herself by flight, and by swimming the Yellowstone while a hundred guns were leveled on her, the bullets whistling about her ears.

At another time she distinguished herself in camp by a quarrel with one of the trappers, in which she came off with flying colors. The trapper was a big, bullying Irishman named O'Fallen, who had purchased two prisoners from the Snake Indians, to be kept in a state of slavery, after the manner of the savages. The prisoners were Utes, or Utahs, who soon contrived to escape. O'Fallen, imagining that Umentucken had liberated them, threatened to whip her, and armed himself with a horsewhip for that purpose. On hearing of these threats Umentucken repaired to her lodge, and also armed herself, but with a pistol. When O'Fallen approached, the whole camp looking on to see the event, Umentucken slipped out at the back of the lodge and coming around confronted him before he could enter.

"Coward!" she cried. "You would whip the wife of Meek. He is not here to defend me; not here to kill you. But I shall do that for myself," and with that she presented the pistol to his head. O'Fallen taken by surprise, and having every reason to believe she would keep her word, and kill him on the spot, was obliged not only to apologize, but to beg to have his life spared. This Umentucken consented to do on condition of his sufficiently humbling himself, which he did in a very shame-faced manner; and a shout then went up from the whole camp—"hurrah for the Mountain Lamb!" for nothing more delights a mountaineer than a show of pluck, especially in an unlooked for quarter.

The Indian wives of the trappers were often in great peril, as well as their lords. Whenever it was convenient they followed them on their long marches through dangerous countries. But if the trapper was only going out for a few days, or if the march before him was more than usually dangerous, the wife remained with the main camp.

During this year of which we are writing, a considerable party had been out on Powder River hunting buffalo, taking their wives along with them. When on the return, just before reaching camp, Umentucken was missed from the cavalcade. She had fallen behind, and been taken prisoner by a party of twelve Crow Indians. As soon as she was missed, a volunteer party mounted their buffalo horses in such haste that they waited not for saddle or bridle, but snatched only a halter, and started back in pursuit. They had not run a very long distance when they discovered poor Umentucken in the midst of her jubilant captors, who were delighting their eyes with gazing at her fine feathers, and promising themselves very soon to pluck the gay bird, and appropriate her trinkets to their own use.

Their delight was premature. Swift on their heels came an avenging, as well as a saving spirit. Meek, at the head of his six comrades, no sooner espied the drooping form of the Lamb, than he urged his horse to the top of its speed. The horse was a spirited creature, that seeing something wrong in all these hasty maneuvers, took fright and adding terror to good will, ran with the speed of madness right in amongst the startled Crows, who doubtless regarded as a great "medicine" so fearless a warrior. It was now too late to be prudent, and Meek began the battle by yelling and firing, taking care to hit his Indian. The other trappers, emulating the bold example of their leader, dashed into the melee and a chance medley fight was carried on, in which Umentucken escaped, and another

Crow bit the dust. Finding that they were getting the worst of the fight, the Indians at length took to flight, and the trappers returned to camp rejoicing, and complimenting Meek on his gallantry in attacking the Crows single-handed.

"I took their compliments quite naturally," says Meek, "nor did I think it war worth while to explain to them that I couldn't hold my horse."

The Indians are lordly and tyrannical in their treatment of women, thinking it no shame to beat them cruelly; even taking the liberty of striking other women than those belonging to their own families. While the camp was traveling through the Crow country in the spring of 1836, a party of that nation paid a visit to Bridger, bringing skins to trade for blankets and ammunition. The bargaining went on quite pleasantly for some time; but one of the braves who was promenading about camp inspecting whatever came in his way, chanced to strike Umentucken with a whip he carried in his hand, by way of displaying his superiority to squaws in general, and trappers' wives in particular. It was an unlucky blow for the brave, for in another instant he rolled on the ground, shot dead by a bullet from Meek's gun.

At this rash act the camp was in confusion. Yells from the Crows, who took the act as a signal for war; hasty questions, and cries of command arming and shooting. It was some time before the case could be explained or understood. The Crows had two or three of their party shot; the whites also lost a man. After the unpremeditated fight was over, and the Crows departed not thoroughly satisfied with the explanation, Bridger went round to Meek's lodge.

"Well, you raised a hell of a row in camp;" said the commander, rolling out his deep bass voice in the slow

monotonous tones which mountain men very quickly acquire from the Indians.

"Very sorry, Bridger; but couldn't help it. No devil
of an Indian shall strike Meek's wife."

"But you got a man killed."

"Sorry for the man ; couldn't help it, though, Bridger."

And in truth it was too late to mend the matter. Fearing, however, that the Crows would attempt to avenge
themselves for the losses they had sustained, Bridger hurried his camp forward, and got out of their neighborhood
as quickly as possible.

So much for the female element in the camp of the
Rocky Mountain trapper. Woman, it is said, has held the
apple of discord, from mother Eve to Umentucken, and
in consonance with this theory, Bridger, doubtless, considered the latter as the primal cause of the unfortunate
"row in camp," rather than the brutality of the Crow, or
the imprudence of Meek.

But Umentucken's career was nearly run. In the following summer she met her death by a Bannack arrow;
dying like a warrior, although living she was only a woman.

CHAPTER XIII.

1835. The rendezvous of the Rocky Mountain Company seldom took place without combining with its many wild elements, some other more civilized and refined. Artists, botanists, travelers, and hunters, from the busy world outside the wilderness, frequently claimed the companionship, if not the hospitality of the fur companies, in their wanderings over prairies and among mountains. Up to the year 1835, these visitors had been of the classes just named; men traveling either for the love of adventure, to prosecute discoveries in science, or to add to art the treasure of new scenes and subjects.

But in this year there appeared at rendezvous two gentlemen, who had accompanied the St. Louis Company in its outward trip to the mountains, whose object was not the procurement of pleasure, or the improvement of science. They had come to found missions among the Indians; the Rev. Samuel Parker and Rev. Dr. Marcus Whitman; the first a scholarly and fastidious man, and the other possessing all the boldness, energy, and contempt of fastidiousness, which would have made him as good a mountain leader, as he was an energetic servant of the American Board of Foreign Missions.

The cause which had brought these gentlemen to the wilderness was a little incident connected with the fur trade. Four Flathead Indians, in the year 1832, having heard enough of the Christian religion, from the few devout men connected with the fur companies, to desire to know more, performed a winter journey to St. Louis, and there made inquiry about the white man's religion. This incident, which to any one acquainted with Indian character, would appear a very natural one, when it became known to Christian churches in the United States, excited a very lively interest, and seemed to call upon them like a voice out of heaven, to fly to the rescue of perishing heathen souls. The Methodist Church was the first to respond. When Wyeth returned to the mountains in 1834, four missionaries accompanied him, destined for the valley of the Wallamet River in Oregon. In the following year, the Presbyterian Church sent out its agents, the two gentlemen above mentioned; one of whom, Dr. Whitman, subsequently located near Fort Walla-Walla.

The account given by Capt. Bonneville of the Flatheads and Nez Perces, as he found them in 1832, before missionary labor had been among them, throws some light on the incident of the journey to St. Louis, which so touched the Christian heart in the United States. After relating his surprise at finding that the Nez Perces observed certain sacred days, he continues: "A few days afterwards, four of them signified that they were about to hunt. 'What!' exclaimed the captain, 'without guns or arrows; and with only one old spear? What do you expect to kill?' They smiled among themselves, but made no answer. Preparatory to the chase, they performed some religious rights, and offered up to the Great Spirit a few short prayers for safety and success; then having received the blessing of their wives, they leaped upon their horses and departed, leaving the whole party of Christian spectators amazed and rebuked by this lesson of faith and dependence on a supreme and benevolent Being. Accustomed as I had heretofore been to find the wretched Indian rev-eling in blood, and stained by every vice which can degrade human nature, I could scarcely realize the scene which I had witnessed. Wonder at such unaffected tenderness and piety, where it was least to have been sought, contended in all our bosoms with shame and confusion, at receiving such pure and wholesome instructions from creatures so far below us in all the arts and comforts of life.

" Simply to call these people religious," continued Bonneville, " would convey but a faint idea of the deep hue of piety and devotion which pervades their whole conduct. Their honesty is immaculate, and their purity of purpose, and their observance of the rites of their religion, are most uniform and remarkable. They are certainly more like a nation of saints than a horde of savages."

This was a very enthusiastic view to take of the Nez Perce character, which appeared all the brighter to the Captain, by contrast with the savage life which he had witnessed in other places, and even by contrast with the conduct of the white trappers. But the Nez Perces and Flatheads were, intellectually and morally, an exception to all the Indian tribes west of the Missouri River. Lewis and Clarke found them different from any others ; the fur-traders and the missionaries found them different; and they remain at this day an honorable example, for probity and piety, to both savage and civilized peoples.

To account for this superiority is indeed difficult. The only clue to the cause is in the following statement of Bonneville's. " It would appear," he says, " that they had imbibed some notions of the Christian faith from Catholic missionaries and traders who had been among them. They even had a rude calender of the fasts and festivals of the Romish Church, and some traces of its ceremonials. These have become blended with their own wild rites, and present a strange medley, civilized and barbarous."

Finding that these people among whom he was thrown exhibited such remarkable traits of character, Captain Bonneville exerted himself to make them acquainted with the history and spirit of Christianity. To these explanations they listened with great eagerness. "Many a time," he says, "was my little lodge thronged, or rather piled with hearers, for they lay on the ground, one leaning over the other, until there was no further room, all listening with greedy ears to the wonders which the Great Spirit had revealed to the white man. No other subject gave them half the satisfaction, or commanded half the attention; and but few scenes of my life remain so freshly on my memory, or are so pleasurably recalled to my contemplation, as these hours of intercourse with a distant and benighted race in the midst of the desert."

It was the interest awakened by these discourses of Captain Bonneville, and possibly by Smith, and other traders who happened to fall in with the Nez Perces and Flatheads, that stimulated those four Flatheads to undertake the journey to St. Louis in search of information; and this it was which resulted in the establishment of missions, both in western Oregon, and among the tribes inhabiting the country between the two great branches of the Columbia.

The trait of Indian character which Bonneville, in his pleased surprise at the apparent piety of the Nez Perces and Flatheads, failed to observe, and which the missionaries themselves for a long time remained oblivious to, was the material nature of their religious views. The Indian judges of all things by the material results. If he is possessed of a good natural intelligence and powers of observation, he soon discovers that the God of the Indian is but a feeble deity; for does he not permit the Indian to be defeated in war; to starve, and to freeze? Do not the Indian medicine men often fail to save life, to win battles, to curse their enemies? The Indian's God, he argues, must be a good deal of a humbug. He sees the white men faring much better. They have guns, ammunition, blankets, knives, everything in plenty; and they are successful in war; are skillful in a thousand things the Indian knows nothing of. To be so blest implies a very wise and powerful Deity. To gain all these things they are eager to learn about the white man's God; are willing to do whatever is necessary to please and propitiate Him. Hence their attentiveness to the white man's discourse about his religion. Naturally enough they were struck with wonder at the doctrine of peace and good will; a doctrine so different from the law of blood by which the Indian, in his natural state, lives. Yet if it is good for the white men, it must be good for him; at all events he is anxious to try it.

That is the course of reasoning by which an Indian is led to inquire into Christianity. It is a desire to better his physical, rather than his spiritual condition; for of the latter he has but a very faint conception. He was accustomed to desire a material Heaven, such a world beyond the grave, as he could only imagine from his earthly experience. Heaven was happiness, and happiness was plenty; therefore the most a good Indian could desire was to go where there should forevermore be plenty.

Such was the Indian's view of religion, and it could be no other. Until the wants of the body have been supplied by civilization, the wants of the soul do not develop themselves: and until then the savage is not prepared to understand Christianity. This is the law of Nature and of God. Primeval man was a savage; and it was little

by little, through thousands of years, that Christ was revealed.   Every child born, even now, is a savage, and has
to be taught civilization year after year, until he arrives
at the possibility of comprehending spiritual religion.   So
every full grown barbarian is a child in moral development; and to expect him to comprehend those mysteries
over which the world has agonized for centuries, is to
commit the gravest error.   Into this error fell all the missionaries who came to the wilds that lay beyond the Rocky
Mountains.   They undertook to teach religion first, and
more simple matters afterward—building their edifice like
the Irishman's chimney, by holding up the top brick, and
putting the others under it.   Failure was the result of
such a process, as the record of the Oregon Missions sufficiently proves.

The reader will pardon this digression—made necessary
by the part which one of the gentlemen present at this
year's rendezvous, was destined to take in the history
which we are writing.   Shortly after the arrival of Messrs.
Parker and Whitman, rendezvous broke up.   A party, to
which Meek was attached, moved in the direction of the
Snake River head-waters, the missionaries accompanying
them, and after making two camps, came on Saturday eve
to Jackson's Little Hole, a small mountain valley near the
larger one commonly known as Jackson's Hole.

On the following day religious services were held in the
Rocky Mountain Camp.   A scene more unusual could
hardly have transpired than that of a company of trappers listening to the preaching of the Word of God.
Very little pious reverence marked the countenances of
that wild and motley congregation.   Curiosity, incredulity,
sarcasm, or a mocking levity, were more plainly perceptible in the expression of the men's faces, than either devotion or the longing expectancy of men habitually deprived

of what they once highly valued. The Indians alone showed by their eager listening that they desired to become acquainted with the mystery of the "Unknown God."

The Rev. Samuel Parker preached, and the men were as politely attentive as it was in their reckless natures to be, until, in the midst of the discourse, a band of buffalo appeared in the valley, when the congregation incontinently broke up, without staying for a benediction, and every man made haste after his horse, gun, and rope, leaving Mr. Parker to discourse to vacant ground.

The run was both exciting and successful. About twenty fine buffaloes were killed, and the choice pieces brought to camp, cooked and eaten, amidst the merriment, mixed with something coarser, of the hunters. On this noisy rejoicing Mr. Parker looked with a sober aspect: and following the dictates of his religious feeling, he rebuked the sabbath-breakers quite severely. Better for his influence among the men, if he had not done so, or had not eaten so heartily of the tender-loin afterwards, a circumstance which his irreverent critics did not fail to remark, to his prejudice; and upon the principle that the "partaker is as bad as the thief," they set down his lecture on sabbath-breaking as nothing better than pious humbug.

Dr. Marcus Whitman was another style of man. Whatever he thought of the wild ways of the mountain-men he discreetly kept to himself, preferring to teach by example rather than precept; and showing no fastidious contempt for any sort of rough duty he might be called upon to perform. So aptly indeed had he turned his hand to all manner of camp service on the journey to the mountains, that this abrogation of clerical dignity had become a source of solicitude, not to say disapproval and displeasure on the part of his colleague; and it was agreed be-

tween them that the Doctor should return to the states
with the St. Louis Company, to procure recruits for the
promising field of labor which they saw before them,
while Mr. Parker continued his journey to the Columbia
to decide upon the location of the missionary stations.
The difference of character of the two men was clearly
illustrated by the results of this understanding.   Parker
went to Vancouver, where he was hospitably entertained,
and where he could inquire into the workings of the missionary system as pursued by the Methodist missionaries.
His investigations not proving the labor to his taste, he
sailed the following summer for the Sandwich Islands, and
thence to New York; leaving only a brief note for Doctor
Whitman, when he, with indefatigable exertions, arrived
that season among the Nez Perces with a missionary company, eager for the work which they hoped to make as
great as they believed it to be good.

CHAPTER XIV.

FROM the mountains about the head-waters of the Snake River, Meek returned, with Bridger's brigade to the Yellowstone country, where he fell into the hands of the Crows. The story as he relates it, is as follows:

"I war trapping on the Rocky Fork of the Yellowstone. I had been out from camp five days; and war solitary and alone, when I war discovered by a war party of Crows. They had the prairie, and I war forced to run for the Creek bottom; but the beaver had throwed the water out and made dams, so that my mule mired down. While I war struggling in the marsh, the Indians came after me, with tremendous yells; firing a random shot now and then, as they closed in on me.

"When they war within about two rods of me, I brought old *Sally*, that is my gun, to my face, ready to fire, and then die; for I knew it war death this time, unless Providence interfered to save me: and I didn't think Providence would do it. But the head chief, when he saw the warlike looks of *Sally*, called out to me to put down my gun, and I should live.

"Well, I liked to live,—being then in the prime of life; and though it hurt me powerful, I resolved to part with *Sally*. I laid her down. As I did so, the chief picked her up, and one of the braves sprang at me with a spear, and would have run me through, but the chief knocked him down with the butt of my gun. Then they led me forth to the high plain on the south side of the stream. There

they called a halt, and I was given in charge of three women, while the warriors formed a ring to smoke and consult. This gave me an opportunity to count them: they
numbered one hundred and eighty-seven men, nine boys,
and three women.

"After a smoke of three long hours, the chief, who war
named 'The Bold,' called me in the ring, and said:

"'I have known the whites for a long time, and I know
them to be great liars, deserving death; but if *you* will
tell the truth, you shall live.'

"Then I thought to myself, they will fetch the truth
out of me, if thar is any in me. But his highness continued:

"'Tell me whar are the whites you belong to; and what
is your captain's name.'

"I said 'Bridger is my captain's name; or, in the Crow
tongue, *Casapy*,' the 'Blanket chief.' At this answer the
chief seemed lost in thought. At last he asked me—

"'How many men has he?'

"I thought about telling the truth and living; but I
said 'forty,' which war a tremendous lie; for thar war
two hundred and forty. At this answer The Bold laughed:

"'We will make them poor,' said he; 'and you shall
live, but they shall die.'

"I thought to myself, 'hardly;' but I said nothing. He
then asked me whar I war to meet the camp, and I told
him:—and then how many days before the camp would
be thar; which I answered truly, for I wanted them to
find the camp.

"It war now late in the afternoon, and thar war a great
bustle, getting ready for the march to meet Bridger. Two
big Indians mounted my mule, but the women made me
pack moccasins. The spies started first, and after awhile
the main party. Seventy warriors traveled ahead of me:

I war placed with the women and boys; and after us the balance of the braves. As we traveled along, the women would prod me with sticks, and laugh, and say 'Masta Sheela,' (which means white man,) 'Masta sheela very poor now.' The fair sex war very much amused.

"We traveled that way till midnight, the two big bucks riding my mule, and I packing moccasins. Then we camped; the Indians in a ring, with me in the centre, to keep me safe. I didn't sleep very well that night. I'd a heap rather been in some other place.

"The next morning we started on in the same order as before: and the squaws making fun of me all day; but I kept mighty quiet. When we stopped to cook that evening, I war set to work, and war head cook, and head waiter too. The third and the fourth day it war the same. I felt pretty bad when we struck camp on the last day: for I knew we must be coming near to Bridger, and that if any thing should go wrong, my life would pay the forfeit.

"On the afternoon of the fourth day, the spies, who war in advance, looking out from a high hill, made a sign to the main party. In a moment all sat down. Directly they got another sign, and then they got up and moved on. I war as well up in Indian signs as they war; and I knew they had discovered white men. What war worse, I knew they would soon discover that I had been lying to them. All I had to do then war to trust to luck. Soon we came to the top of the hill, which overlooked the Yellowstone, from which I could see the plains below extending as far as the eye could reach, and about three miles off, the camp of my friends. My heart beat double quick about that time; and I once in a while put my hand to my head, to feel if my scalp war thar.

"While I war watching our camp, I discovered that the horse guard had seen us, for I knew the sign he would

13

make if he discovered Indians. I thought the camp a splendid sight that evening. It made a powerful show to me, who did not expect ever to see it after that day. And it *war* a fine sight any how, from the hill whar I stood. About two hundred and fifty men, and women and children in great numbers, and about a thousand horses and mules. Then the beautiful plain, and the sinking sun; and the herds of buffalo that could not be numbered; and the cedar hills, covered with elk,—I never saw so fine a sight as all that looked to me then!

"When I turned my eyes on that savage Crow band, and saw the chief standing with his hand on his mouth, lost in amazement; and beheld the warriors' tomahawks and spears glittering in the sun, my heart war very little. Directly the chief turned to me with a horrible scowl. Said he:

"'I promised that you should live if you told the truth; but you have told me a great lie.'

"Then the warriors gathered around, with their tomahawks in their hands; but I war showing off very brave, and kept my eyes fixed on the horse-guard who war approaching the hill to drive in the horses. This drew the attention of the chief, and the warriors too. Seeing that the guard war within about two hundred yards of us, the chief turned to me and ordered me to tell him to come up. I pretended to do what he said; but instead of that I howled out to him to stay off, or he would be killed; and to tell Bridger to try to treat with them, and get me away.

"As quick as he could he ran to camp, and in a few minutes Bridger appeared, on his large white horse. He came up to within three hundred yards of us, and called out to me, asking who the Indians war. I answered

'Crows.'   He then told me to say to the chief he wished him to send one of his sub-chiefs to smoke with him.

"All this time my heart beat terribly hard.   I don't know now why they didn't kill me at once; but the head chief seemed overcome with surprise.   When I repeated to him what Bridger said, he reflected a moment, and then ordered the second chief, called Little-Gun, to go and smoke with Bridger.   But they kept on preparing for war; getting on their paint and feathers, arranging their scalp locks, selecting their arrows, and getting their ammunition ready.

"While this war going on, Little-Gun had approached to within about a hundred yards of Bridger; when, according to the Crow laws of war, each war forced to strip himself, and proceed the remaining distance in a state of nudity, and kiss and embrace.   While this interesting ceremony war being performed, five of Bridger's men had followed him, keeping in a ravine until they got within shooting distance, when they showed themselves, and cut off the return of Little-Gun, thus making a prisoner of him.

"If you think my heart did not jump up when I saw that, you think wrong.   I knew it war kill or cure, now. Every Indian snatched a weapon, and fierce threats war howled against me.   But all at once about a hundred of our trappers appeared on the scene.   At the same time Bridger called to me, to tell me to propose to the chief to exchange me for Little-Gun.   I explained to The Bold what Bridger wanted to do, and he sullenly consented: for, he said, he could not afford to give a chief for one white dog's scalp.   I war then allowed to go towards my camp, and Little-Gun towards his; and the rescue I hardly hoped for war accomplished.

"In the evening the chief, with forty of his braves, visited Bridger and made a treaty of three months. They said they war formerly at war with the whites; but that they desired to be friendly with them now, so that together they might fight the Blackfeet, who war everybody's enemies. As for me, they returned me my mule, gun, and beaver packs, and said my name should be *Shiam Shaspusia*, for I could out-lie the Crows."

In December, Bridger's command went into winter quarters in the bend of the Yellowstone. Buffalo, elk, and bear were in great abundance, all that fall and winter. Before they went to camp, Meek, Kit Carson, Hawkins, and Doughty were trapping together on the Yellowstone, about sixty miles below. They had made their temporary camp in the ruins of an old fort, the walls of which were about six feet high. One evening, after coming in from setting their traps, they discovered three large grizzly bears in the river bottom, not more than half a mile off, and Hawkins went out to shoot one. He was successful in killing one at the first shot, when the other two, taking fright, ran towards the fort. As they came near enough to show that they were likely to invade camp, Meek and Carson, not caring to have a bear fight, clambered up a cotton-wood tree close by, at the same time advising Doughty to do the same. But Doughty was tired, and lazy besides, and concluded to take his chances where he was; so he rolled himself in his blanket and laid quite still. The bears, on making the fort, reared up on their hind legs and looked in as if meditating taking it for a defence.

The sight of Doughty lying rolled in his blanket, and the monster grizzlys inspecting the fort, caused the two trappers who were safely perched in the cotton-wood to make merry at Doughty's expense; saying all the mirth-provoking things they could, and then advising him not to laugh, for fear the bears should seize him. Poor Doughty, agonizing between suppressed laughter and growing fear, contrived to lie still however, while the bears gazed upward at the speakers in wonder, and alternately at the suspicious looking bundle inside the fort. Not being able to make out the meaning of either, they gave at last a grunt of dissatisfaction, and ran off into a thicket to consult over these strange appearances; leaving the trappers to enjoy the incident as a very good joke. For a long time after, Doughty was reminded how close to the ground he laid, when the grizzlys paid their compliments to him. Such were the every-day incidents from which the mountain-men contrived to derive their rude jests, and laughter-provoking reminiscences.

A few days after this incident, while the same party were trapping a few miles farther down the river, on their way to camp, they fell in with some Delaware Indians, who said they had discovered signs of Blackfeet, and wanted to borrow some horses to decoy them. To this the trappers very willingly agreed, and they were furnished with two horses. The Delawares then went to the spot where signs had been discovered, and tying the horses, laid flat down on the ground near them, concealed by the grass or willows. They had not long to wait before a Blackfoot was seen stealthily advancing through the thicket, confident in the belief that he should gain a couple of horses while their supposed owners were busy with their traps.

But just as he laid his hand on the bridle of the first one, crack went the rifles of the Delawares, and there was one less Blackfoot thief on the scent after trappers. As soon as they could, after this, the party mounted and rode to camp, not stopping by the way, lest the main body of Blackfeet should discover the deed and seek for vengeance.

Truly indeed, was the Blackfoot the Ishmael of the wilderness, whose hand was against every man, and every man's hand against him.

The Rocky Mountain Company passed the first part of the winter in peace and plenty in the Yellowstone camp, unannoyed either by enemies or rivals. Hunting buffalo, feeding their horses, playing games, and telling stories, occupied the entire leisure of these months of repose. Not only did the mountain-men recount their own adventures, but when these were exhausted, those whose memories served them rehearsed the tales they had read in their youth. Robinson Crusoe and the Arabian Nights Entertainment, were read over again by the light of memory; and even Bunyan's Pilgrim's Progress was made to recite like a sensation novel, and was quite as well enjoyed.

1836. In January, however, this repose was broken in upon by a visit from the Blackfeet. As their visitations were never of a friendly character, so then they were not bent upon pacific rites and ceremonies, such as all the rest of the world find pleasure in, but came in full battle array to try their fortunes in war against the big camp of the whites. They had evidently made great preparation. Their warriors numbered eleven hundred, got up in the top of the Blackfoot fashions, and armed with all manner of savage and some civilized weapons. But Bridger was prepared for them, although their numbers were so overwhelming. He built a fort, had the animals corraled, and put himself on the defensive in a prompt and thorough manner. This made the Blackfeet cautious; they too built forts of cotton-wood in the shape of lodges, ten men to each fort, and carried on a skirmishing fight for two days, when finding there was nothing to be gained, they departed, neither side having sustained much loss; the whites losing only two men by this grand Blackfoot army.

Soon after this attack Bridger broke camp, and traveled up the Yellowstone, through the Crow country.   It was while on this march that Umentucken was struck by a Crow, and Meek put the whole camp in peril, by shooting him.   They passed on to the Big Horn and Little Horn rivers, down through the Wind River valley and through the South Pass to Green River.

While in that country, there occurred the fight with the Bannacks in which Umentucken was killed.   A small party of Nez Perces had lost their horses by the thieving of the Bannacks.   They came into camp and complained to the whites, who promised them their protection, should they be able to recover their horses.   Accordingly the Nez Perces started after the thieves, and by dogging their camp, succeeded in re-capturing their horses and getting back to Bridger's camp with them.   In order to divert the vengeance of the Bannacks from themselves, they presented their horses to the whites, and a very fine one to Bridger.

All went well for a time.   The Bannacks went on their way to hunt buffalo; but they treasured up their wrath against the supposed white thieves who had stolen the horses which they had come by so honestly.   On their return from the hunt, having learned by spies that the horses were in the camp of the whites, they prepared for war. Early one morning they made their appearance mounted and armed, and making a dash at the camp, rode through it with the usual yells and frantic gestures.   The attack was entirely unexpected.   Bridger stood in front of his lodge, holding his horse by a lasso, and the head chief rode over it, jerking it out of his hand.   At this unprecedented insult to his master, a negro named Jim, cook to the Booshways, seized a rifle and shot the chief dead.   At the same time, an arrow shot at random struck Umentucken in the breast, and the joys and sorrows of the Mountain Lamb were over forevermore.

The killing of a head chief always throws an Indian war party into confusion, and negro Jim was greatly elated at this signal feat of his. The trappers, who were as much surprised at the suddenness of the assault as it is in the mountain-man's nature to be, quickly recovered themselves. In a few moments the men were mounted and in motion, and the disordered Bannacks were obliged to fly towards their village, Bridger's company pursuing them.

All the rest of that day the trappers fought the Bannacks, driving them out of their village and plundering it, and forcing them to take refuge on an island in the river. Even there they were not safe, the guns of the mountain-men picking them off, from their stations on the river banks. Umentucken was well avenged that day.

All night the Indians remained on the island, where sounds of wailing were heard continually; and when morning came one of their old women appeared bearing the pipe of peace. "You have killed all our warriors," she said; "do you now want to kill the women? If you wish to smoke with women, I have the pipe."

Not caring either to fight or to smoke with so feeble a representative of the Bannacks, the trappers withdrew. But it was the last war party that nation ever sent against the mountain-men; though in later times they have by their atrocities avenged the losses of that day.

While awaiting, in the Green River valley, the arrival of the St. Louis Company, the Rocky Mountain and North American companies united; after which Captain Sublette and his brother returned no more to the mountains. The new firm was known only as the American Fur Company, the other having dropped its title altogether. The object of their consolidation was by combining their capital and experience to strengthen their hands against the Hudson's Bay Company, which now had an establishment at Fort Hall, on the Snake River. By this new arrangement, Bridger and Fontenelle commanded; and Dripps was to be the traveling partner who was to go to St. Louis for goods.

After the conclusion of this agreement, Dripps, with the restlessness of the true mountain-man, decided to set out, with a small party of equally restless trappers, always eager to volunteer for any undertaking promising either danger or diversion, to look for the St. Louis Company which was presumed to be somewhere between the Black Hills and Green River. According to this determination Dripps, Meek, Carson, Newell, a Flathead chief named Victor, and one or two others, set out on the search for the expected company.

It happened, however, that a war party of a hundred Crows were out on the trail before them, looking perhaps for the same party, and the trappers had not made more than one or two camps before they discovered signs which satisfied them of the neighborhood of an enemy. At their next camp on the Sandy, Meek and Carson, with the caution and vigilance peculiar to them, kept their saddles on their horses, and the horses tied to themselves by a long rope, so that on the least unusual motion of the animals they should be readily informed of the disturbance. Their precaution was not lost. Just after midnight had given place to the first faint kindling of dawn, their ears were stunned by the simultaneous discharge of a hundred guns, and the usual furious din of the war-whoop and yell. A stampede immediately took place of all the horses excepting those of Meek and Carson. "Every man for himself and God for us all," is the motto of the mountain-man in case of an Indian attack; nor did our trappers forget it on this occasion. Quickly mounting, they put their horses to their speed, which was not checked until they had left the Sandy far behind them. Continuing on in the direction of the proposed meeting with the St. Louis Company, they made their first camp on the Sweetwater, where they fell in with Victor, the Flathead chief, who had made his way on foot to this place. One or two others came into camp that night, and the following day this portion of the party traveled on in company until within about five miles of Independence Rock, when they were once more charged on by the Indians, who surrounded them in such a manner that they were obliged to turn back to escape.

Again Meek and Carson made off, leaving their dismounted comrades to their own best devices. Finding that with so many Indians on the trail, and only two horses, there was little hope of being able to accomplish their journey, these two lucky ones made all haste back to camp. On Horse Creek, a few hours travel from rendezvous, they came up with Newell, who after losing his horse had fled in the direction of the main camp, but becoming bewildered had been roaming about until he was quite tired out, and on the point of giving up. But as if the Creek where he was found meant to justify itself for having so inharmonious a name, one of their own horses, which had escaped from the Crows was found quietly grazing on its banks, and the worn out fugitive at once remounted. Strange as it may appear, not one of the party was killed, the others returning to camp two days later than Meek and Carson, the worse for their expedition only by the loss of their horses, and rather an unusually fatigued and forlorn aspect.

CHAPTER XV.

1836. WHILE the resident partners of the consolidated company waited at the rendezvous for the arrival of the supply trains from St. Louis, word came by a messenger sent forward, that the American Company under Fitzpatrick, had reached Independence Rock, and was pressing forward. The messenger also brought the intelligence that two other parties were traveling in company with the fur company; that of Captain Stuart, who had been to New Orleans to winter, and that of Doctor Whitman, one of the missionaries who had visited the mountains the year previous. In this latter party, it was asserted, there were two white ladies.

This exhilarating news immediately inspired some of the trappers, foremost among whom was Meek, with a desire to be the first to meet and greet the on-coming caravan; and especially to salute the two white women who were bold enough to invade a mountain camp. In a very short time Meek, with half-a-dozen comrades, and ten or a dozen Nez Perces, were mounted and away, on their self-imposed errand of welcome; the trappers because they were "spoiling" for a fresh excitement; and the Nez Perces because the missionaries were bringing them information concerning the powerful and beneficent Deity of the white men. These latter also were charged with a letter to Doctor Whitman from his former associate, Mr. Parker.

On the Sweetwater about two days' travel from camp

the caravan of the advancing company was discovered, and the trappers prepared to give them a characteristic greeting. To prevent mistakes in recognizing them, a white flag was hoisted on one of their guns, and the word was given to start. Then over the brow of a hill they made their appearance, riding with that mad speed only an Indian or a trapper can ride, yelling, whooping, dashing forward with frantic and threatening gestures; their dress, noises, and motions, all so completely savage that the white men could not have been distinguished from the red.

The first effect of their onset was what they probably intended. The uninitiated travelers, including the missionaries, believing they were about to be attacked by Indians, prepared for defence, nor could be persuaded that the preparation was unnecessary until the guide pointed out to them the white flag in advance. At the assurance that the flag betokened friends, apprehension was changed to curiosity and intense interest. Every movement of the wild brigade became fascinating. On they came, riding faster and faster, yelling louder and louder, and gesticulating more and more madly, until, as they met and passed the caravan, they discharged their guns in one volley over the heads of the company, as a last finishing *feu de joie;* and suddenly wheeling rode back to the front as wildly as they had come. Nor could this first brief display content the crazy cavalcade. After reaching the front, they rode back and forth, and around and around the caravan, which had returned their salute, showing off their feats of horsemanship, and the knowing tricks of their horses together; hardly stopping to exchange questions and answers, but seeming really intoxicated with delight at the meeting. What strange emotions filled the breasts of the lady missionaries, when they beheld among whom their lot was cast, may now be faintly outlined by a vivid imagination, but have never been, perhaps never could be put into words.

The caravan on leaving the settlements had consisted of nineteen laden carts, each drawn by two mules driven tandem, and one light wagon, belonging to the American Company; two wagons with two mules to each, belonging to Capt. Stuart; and one light two-horse wagon, and one four-horse freight wagon, belonging to the missionaries. However, all the wagons had been left behind at Fort Laramie, except those of the missionaries, and one of Capt. Stuart's; so that the three that remained in the train when it reached the Sweetwater were alone in the enjoyment of the Nez Perces' curiosity concerning them; a curiosity which they divided between them and the domesticated cows and calves belonging to the missionaries: another proof, as they considered it, of the superior power of the white man's God, who could give to the whites the ability to tame wild animals to their uses.

But it was towards the two missionary ladies, Mrs. Whitman and Mrs. Spalding, that the chief interest was directed; an interest that was founded in the Indian mind upon wonder, admiration, and awe; and in the minds of the trappers upon the powerful recollections awakened by seeing in their midst two refined Christian women, with the complexion and dress of their own mothers and sisters. United to this startling effect of memory, was respect for the religious devotion which had inspired them to undertake the long and dangerous journey to the Rocky Mountains, and also a sentiment of pity for what they knew only too well yet remained to be encountered by those delicate women in the prosecution of their duty.

Mrs. Whitman, who was in fine health, rode the greater part of the journey on horseback. She was a large, stately, fair-skinned woman, with blue eyes and light auburn, almost golden hair. Her manners were at once dignified and gracious. She was, both by nature and education a lady; and had a lady's appreciation of all that was courteous and refined; yet not without an element of romance and heroism in her disposition strong enough to have impelled her to undertake a missionary's life in the wilderness.

Mrs. Spalding was a different type of woman. Talented, and refined in her nature, she was less pleasing in exterior, and less attached to that which was superficially pleasing in others. But an indifference to outside appearances was in her case only a sign of her absorption in the work she had taken in hand. She possessed the true missionary spirit, and the talent to make it useful in an eminent degree; never thinking of herself, or the impression she made upon others; yet withal very firm and capable of command. Her health, which was always rather delicate, had suffered much from the fatigue of the journey, and the constant diet of fresh meat, and meat only, so that she was compelled at last to abandon horseback exercise, and to keep almost entirely to the light wagon of the missionaries.

As might be expected, the trappers turned from the contemplation of the pale, dark-haired occupant of the wagon, with all her humility and gentleness, to observe and admire the more striking figure, and more affably attractive manners of Mrs. Whitman. Meek, who never lost an opportunity to see and be seen, was seen riding alongside Mrs. Whitman, answering her curious inquiries, and entertaining her with stories of Blackfeet battles, and encounters with grizzly bears. Poor lady! could she have looked into the future about which she was then so curious, she would have turned back appalled, and have fled with fran-

tic fear to the home of her grieving parents. How could
she then behold in the gay and boastful mountaineer,
whose peculiarities of dress and speech so much diverted
her, the very messenger who was to bear to the home of
her girlhood the sickening tale of her bloody sacrifice to
savage superstition and revenge? Yet so had fate decreed it.

When the trappers and Nez Perces had slaked their thirst
for excitement by a few hours' travel in company with the
Fur Company's and Missionary's caravan, they gave at
length a parting display of horsemanship, and dashed off
on the return trail to carry to camp the earliest news. It
was on their arrival in camp that the Nez Perce and Flathead village, which had its encampment at the rendezvous
ground on Green River, began to make preparations for
the reception of the missionaries. It was then that Indian
finery was in requisition! Then the Indian women combed
and braided their long black hair, tying the plaits with
gay-colored ribbons, and the Indian braves tied anew
their streaming scalp-locks, sticking them full of flaunting
eagle's plumes, and not despising a bit of ribbon either.
Paint was in demand both for the rider and his horse. Gay
blankets, red and blue, buckskin fringed shirts, worked
with beads and porcupine quills, and handsomely embroidered moccasins, were eagerly sought after. Guns were
cleaned and burnished, and drums and fifes put in tune.

After a day of toilsome preparation all was ready for
the grand reception in the camp of the Nez Perces. Word
was at length given that the caravan was in sight. There
was a rush for horses, and in a few moments the Indians
were mounted and in line, ready to charge on the advancing caravan. When the command of the chiefs was given
to start, a simultaneous chorus of yells and whoops burst
forth, accompanied by the deafening din of the war-drum,

the discharge of fire-arms, and the clatter of the whole cavalcade, which was at once in a mad gallop toward the on-coming train. Nor did the yelling, whooping, drumming, and firing cease until within a few yards of the train.

All this demoniac hub-bub was highly complimentary toward those for whom it was intended; but an unfortunate ignorance of Indian customs caused the missionaries to fail in appreciating the honor intended them. Instead of trying to reciprocate the noise by an attempt at imitating it, the missionary camp was alarmed at the first burst and at once began to drive in their cattle and prepare for an attack. As the missionary party was in the rear of the train they succeeded in getting together their loose stock before the Nez Perces had an opportunity of making themselves known, so that the leaders of the Fur Company, and Captain Stuart, had the pleasure of a hearty laugh at their expense, for the fright they had received.

A general shaking of hands followed the abatement of the first surprise, the Indian women saluting Mrs. Whitman and Mrs. Spalding with a kiss, and the missionaries were escorted to their camping ground near the Nez Perce encampment. Here the whole village again formed in line, and a more formal introduction of the missionaries took place, after which they were permitted to go into camp.

When the intention of the Indians became known, Dr. Whitman, who was the leader of the missionary party, was boyishly delighted with the reception which had been given him. His frank, hearty, hopeful nature augured much good from the enthusiasm of the Indians. If his estimation of the native virtues of the savages was much too high, he suffered with those whom he caused to suffer for his belief, in the years which followed. Peace to the ashes of a good man! And honor to his associates, whose hearts were in the cause they had undertaken of Christianizing the Indians.   Two of them still live—one of whom, Mr. Spalding, has conscientiously labored and deeply suffered for the faith.   Mr. Gray, who was an unmarried man, returned the following year to the States, for a wife, and settled for a time among the Indians, but finally abandoned the missionary service, and removed to the Wallamet valley.   These five persons constituted the entire force of teachers who could be induced at that time to devote their lives to the instruction of the savages in the neighborhood of the Rocky Mountains.

The trappers, and gentlemen of the Fur Company, and Captain Stuart, had been passive but interested spectators of the scene between the Indians and the missionaries. When the excitement had somewhat subsided, and the various camps had become settled in their places, the tents of the white ladies were beseiged with visitors, both civilized and savage.   These ladies, who were making an endeavor to acquire a knowledge of the Nez Perce tongue in order to commence their instructions in the language of the natives, could have made very little progress, had their purpose been less strong than it was.   Mrs. Spalding perhaps succeeded better than Mrs. Whitman in the difficult study of the Indian dialect.   She seemed to attract the natives about her by the ease and kindness of her manner, especially the native women, who, seeing she was an invalid, clung to her rather than to her more lofty and self-asserting associate.

On the contrary, the leaders of the American Fur Company, Captain Wyeth and Captain Stuart, paid Mrs. Whitman the most marked and courteous attentions.   She shone the bright particular star of that Rocky Mountain encampment, softening the hearts and the manners of all who came within her womanly influence.   Not a gentleman

14

among them but felt her silent command upon him to be his better self while she remained in his vicinity; not a trapper or camp-keeper but respected the presence of womanhood and piety. But while the leaders paid court to her, the bashful trappers contented themselves with promenading before her tent. Should they succeed in catching her eye, they never failed to touch their beaver-skin caps in their most studiously graceful manner, though that should prove so dubious as to bring a mischievous smile to the blue eyes of the observant lady.

But our friend Joe Meek did not belong by nature to the bashful brigade. He was not content with disporting himself in his best trapper's toggery in front of a lady's tent. He became a not infrequent visitor, and amused Mrs. Whitman with the best of his mountain adventures, related in his soft, slow, yet smooth and firm utterance, and with many a merry twinkle of his mirthful dark eyes. In more serious moments he spoke to her of the future, and of his determination, sometime, to "settle down." When she inquired if he had fixed upon any spot which in his imagination he could regard as "home" he replied that he could not content himself to return to civilized life, but thought that when he gave up "bar fighting and In-jun fighting" he should go down to the Wallamet valley and see what sort of life he could make of it there. How he lived up to this determination will be seen hereafter.

The missionaries remained at the rendezvous long enough to recruit their own strength and that of their stock, and to restore to something like health the invalid Mrs. Spald-ing, who, on changing her diet to dried meat, which the resident partners were able to supply her, commenced rap-idly to improve. Letters were written and given to Capt. Wyeth to carry home to the States. The Captain had completed his sale of Fort Hall and the goods it contained to the Hudson's Bay Company only a short time previous, and was now about to abandon the effort to establish any enterprise either on the Columbia or in the Rocky Mountains. He had, however, executed his threat of the year previous, and punished the bad faith of the Rocky Mountain Company by placing them in direct competition with the Hudson's Bay Company.

The missionaries now prepared for their journey to the Columbia River. According to the advice of the mountain-men the heaviest wagon was left at the rendezvous, together with every heavy article that could be dispensed with. But Dr. Whitman refused to leave the light wagon, although assured he would never be able to get it to the Columbia, nor even to the Snake River. The good Doctor had an immense fund of determination when there was an object to be gained or a principle involved. The only persons who did not oppose wagon transportation were the Indians. They sympathised with his determination, and gave him their assistance. The evidences of a different and higher civilization than they had ever seen were held in great reverence by them. The wagons, the domestic cattle, especially the cows and calves, were always objects of great interest with them. Therefore they freely gave their assistance, and a sufficient number remained behind to help the Doctor, while the main party of both missionaries and Indians, having bidden the Fur Company and others farewell, proceeded to join the camp of two Hudson's Bay traders a few miles on their way.

The two traders, whose camp they now joined, were named McLeod and McKay. The latter, Thomas McKay, was the half-breed son of that unfortunate McKay in Mr. Astor's service, who perished on board the *Tonquin*, as related in Irving's ASTORIA. He was one of the bravest and most skillful partisans in the employ of the Hudson's

Bay Company. McLeod had met the missionaries at the American rendezvous and invited them to travel in his company; an offer which they were glad to accept, as it secured them ample protection and other more trifling benefits, besides some society other than the Indians.

By dint of great perseverance, Doctor Whitman contrived to keep up with the camp day after day, though often coming in very late and very weary, until the party arrived at Fort Hall. At the fort the baggage was again reduced as much as possible; and Doctor Whitman was compelled by the desertion of his teamster to take off two wheels of his wagon and transform it into a cart which could be more easily propelled in difficult places. With this he proceeded as far as the Boise River where the Hudson's Bay Company had a small fort or trading-post; but here again he was so strongly urged to relinquish the idea of taking his wagon to the Columbia, that after much discussion he consented to leave it at Fort Boise until some future time when unencumbered by goods or passengers he might return for it.

Arrived at the crossing of the Snake River, Mrs. Whitman and Mrs. Spalding were treated to a new mode of ferriage, which even in their varied experience they had never before met with. This new ferry was nothing more or less than a raft made of bundles of bulrushes woven together by grass ropes. Upon this frail flat-boat the passengers were obliged to stretch themselves at length while an Indian swam across and drew it after him by a rope. As the waters of the Snake River are rapid and often "dancing mad," it is easy to conjecture that the ladies were ill at ease on their bulrush ferry.

On went the party from the Snake River through the Grand Ronde to the Blue Mountains. The crossing here was somewhat difficult but accomplished in safety. The descent from the Blue Mountains on the west side gave the missionaries their first view of the country they had come to possess, and to civilize and Christianize. That view was beautiful and grand—as goodly a prospect as longing eyes ever beheld this side of Canaan. Before them lay a country spread out like a map, with the windings of its rivers marked by fringes of trees, and its boundaries fixed by mountain ranges above which towered the snowy peaks of Mt. Hood, Mt. Adams, and Mt. Rainier. Far away could be traced the course of the Columbia; and over all the magnificent scene glowed the red rays of sunset, tinging the distant blue of the mountains until they seemed shrouded in a veil of violet mist. It were not strange that with the recep-

DESCENDING THE BLUE MOUNTAINS.

tion given them by the Indians, and with this bird's-eye view of their adopted country, the hearts of the missionaries beat high with hope.

The descent from the Blue Mountains brought the party out on the Umatilla River, where they camped, Mr. McLeod parting company with them at this place to hasten forward to Fort Walla-Walla, and prepare for their reception. After two more days of slow and toilsome travel with cattle whose feet were cut and sore from the sharp rocks of the mountains, the company arrived safely at Walla-Walla fort, on the third of September. Here they found Mr. McLeod, and Mr. Panbram who had charge of that post.

Mr. Panbram received the missionary party with every token of respect, and of pleasure at seeing ladies among them. The kindest attentions were lavished upon them from the first moment of their arrival, when the ladies were lifted from their horses, to the time of their departure; the apartments belonging to the fort being assigned to them, and all that the place afforded of comfortable living placed at their disposal. Here, for the first time in several months, they enjoyed the luxury of bread—a favor for which the suffering Mrs. Spalding was especially grateful.

At Walla-Walla the missionaries were informed that they were expected to visit Vancouver, the head-quarters of the Hudson's Bay Company on the Lower Columbia. After resting for two days, it was determined to make this visit before selecting places for mission work among the Indians. Accordingly the party embarked in the company's boats, for the voyage down the Columbia, which occupied six days, owing to strong head winds which were encountered at a point on the Lower Columbia, called Cape Horn. They arrived safely on the eleventh of September, at Vancouver, where they were again received with the warmest hospitality by the Governor, Dr. John McLaughlin, and his associates. The change from the privations of wilderness life to the luxuries of Fort Vancouver was very great indeed, and two weeks passed rap-

idly away in the enjoyment of refined society, and all
the other elegancies of the highest civilization.

At the end of two weeks, Dr. Whitman, Mr. Spalding,
and Mr. Gray returned to the Upper Columbia, leaving
the ladies at Fort Vancouver while they determined upon
their several locations in the Indian country.   After an
absence of several weeks they returned, having made their
selections, and on the third day of November the ladies
once more embarked to ascend the Columbia, to take up
their residence in Indian wigwams while their husbands
prepared rude dwellings by the assistance of the natives.
The spot fixed upon by Dr. Whitman for his mission was
on the Walla-Walla River about thirty miles from the fort
of that name.   It was called *Waiïlatpu;* and the tribe
chosen for his pupils were the Cayuses, a hardy, active,
intelligent race, rich in horses and pasture lands.

Mr. Spalding selected a home on the Clearwater River,
among the Nez Perces, of whom we already know so
much.   His mission was called *Lapwai*.   Mr. Gray went
among the Flatheads, an equally friendly tribe ; and here
we shall leave the missionaries, to return to the Rocky
Mountains and the life of the hunter and trapper.   At a
future date we shall fall in once more with these devoted
people and learn what success attended their efforts to
Christianize the Indians.

CHAPTER XVI.

1836. THE company of men who went north this year under Bridger and Fontenelle, numbered nearly three hundred.   Rendezvous with all its varied excitements being over, this important brigade commenced its march. According to custom, the trappers commenced business on the head-waters of various rivers, following them down as the early frosts of the mountains forced them to do, until finally they wintered in the plains, at the most favored spots they could find in which to subsist themselves and animals.

From Green River, Meek proceeded with Bridger's command to Lewis River, Salt River, and other tributaries of the Snake, and camped with them in Pierre's Hole, that favorite mountain valley which every year was visited by the different fur companies.

Pierre's Hole, notwithstanding its beauties, had some repulsive features, or rather perhaps *one* repulsive feature, which was, its great numbers of rattlesnakes. Meek relates that being once caught in a very violent thunder storm, he dismounted, and holding his horse, a fine one, by the bridle, himself took shelter under a narrow shelf of rock projecting from a precipitous bluff.   Directly he observed an enormous rattlesnake hastening close by him to its den in the mountain.   Congratulating himself on his snakeship's haste to get out of the storm and his vicinity, he had only time to have one rejoicing thought when two or three others followed the trail of the first one. They were seeking the same rocky den, of whose proximity Meek now felt uncomfortably assured. Before these were out of sight, there came instead of twos and threes, tens and twenties, and then hundreds, and finally Meek believes thousands, the ground being literally alive with them. Not daring to stir after he discovered the nature of his situation, he was obliged to remain and endure the disgusting and frightful scene, while he exerted himself to keep his horse quiet, lest the reptiles should attack him. By and by, when there were no more to come, but all were safe in their holes in the rock, Meek hastily mounted and galloped in the face of the tempest in preference to remaining longer in so unpleasant a neighborhood.

There was an old Frenchman among the trappers who used to charm rattlesnakes, and handling them freely, place them in his bosom, or allow them to wind about his arms, several at a time, their flat heads extending in all directions, and their bodies waving in the air, in the most snaky and nerve-shaking manner, to the infinite disgust of all the camp, and of Hawkins and Meek in particular. Hawkins often became so nervous that he threatened to shoot the Frenchman on the instant, if he did not desist; and great was the dislike he entertained for what he termed the " —— infernal old wizard."

It was often the case in the mountains and on the plains that the camp was troubled with rattlesnakes, so that each man on laying down to sleep found it necessary to encircle his bed with a hair rope, thus effectually fencing out the reptiles, which are too fastidious and sensitive of touch to crawl over a hair rope. But for this precaution, the trapper must often have shared his blanket couch with this foe to the " seed of the woman," who being asleep would have neglected to " crush his head," receiving instead the serpent's fang in "his heel," if not in some nobler portion of his body.

There is a common belief abroad that the prairie dog harbors the rattlesnake, and the owl also, in his subterranean house, in a more or less friendly manner. Meek, however, who has had many opportunities of observing the habits of these three ill-assorted denizens of a common abode, gives it as his opinion that the prairie dog consents to the invasion of his premises alone through his inability to prevent it. As these prairie dog villages are always found on the naked prairies, where there is neither rocky den for the rattlesnake, nor shade for the blinking eyes of the owl, these two idle and impudent foreigners, availing themselves of the labors of the industrious little animal which builds itself a cool shelter from the sun, and a safe one from the storm, whenever their own necessities drive them to seek refuge from either sun or storm, enter uninvited and take possession. It is probable also, that so far from being a welcome guest, the rattlesnake occasionally gorges himself with a young prairie-dog, when other game is not conveniently nigh, or that the owl lies in wait at the door of its borrowed-without-leave domicile, and succeeds in nabbing a careless field-mouse more easily than it could catch the same game by seeking it as an honest owl should do. The owl and the rattlesnake are like the Sioux when they go on a visit to the Omahas—the visit being always timed so as to be identical in date with that of the Government Agents who are distributing food and clothing. They are very good friends for the nonce, the poor Omahas not daring to be otherwise for fear of the ready vengeance on the next summer's buffalo hunt; therefore they conceal their grimaces and let the Sioux eat them up; and when summer comes get massacred on their buffalo hunt, all the same.

But to return to our brigade. About the last of October Bridger's company moved down on to the Yellowstone by a circuitous route through the North Pass, now known as Hell Gate Pass, to Judith River, Mussel Shell River, Cross Creeks of the Yellowstone, Three Forks of Missouri, Missouri Lake, Beaver Head country, Big Horn River, and thence east again, and north again to the wintering ground in the great bend of the Yellowstone.

The company had not proceeded far in the Blackfeet country, between Hell Gate Pass and the Yellowstone, before they were attacked by the Blackfeet. On arriving at the Yellowstone they discovered a considerable encampment of the enemy on an island or bar in the river, and proceeded to open hostilities before the Indians should have discovered them. Making little forts of sticks or bushes, each man advanced cautiously to the bank overlooking the island, pushing his leafy fort before him as he crept silently nearer, until a position was reached whence firing could commence with effect. The first intimation the luckless savages had of the neighborhood of the whites was a volley of shots discharged into their camp, killing several of their number. But as this was their own mode of attack, no reflections were likely to be wasted upon the unfairness of the assault; quickly springing to their arms the firing was returned, and for several hours was kept up on both sides. At night the Indians stole off, having lost nearly thirty killed; nor did the trappers escape quite unhurt, three being killed and a few others wounded.

Since men were of such value to the fur companies, it would seem strange that they should deliberately enter upon an Indian fight before being attacked. But unfortunate as these encounters really were, they knew of no other policy to be pursued. They, (the American Companies,) were not resident, with a long acquaintance, and settled policy, such as rendered the Hudson's Bay Company so secure amongst the savages. They knew that among these unfriendly Indians, not to attack was to be attacked, and consequently little time was ever given for an Indian to discover his vicinity to a trapper. The trapper's shot informed him of that, and afterwards the race was to the swift, and the battle to the strong. Besides this acknowledged necessity for fighting whenever and wherever Indians were met with in the Blackfeet and Crow countries, almost every trapper had some private injury to avenge—some theft, or wound, or imprisonment, or at the very least, some terrible fright sustained at the hands of the universal foe. Therefore there was no reluctance to shoot into an Indian camp, provided the position of the man shooting was a safe one, or more defensible than that of the man shot at. Add to this that there was no law in the mountains, only license, it is easy to conjecture that might would have prevailed over right with far less incentive to the exercise of savage practices than actually did exist. Many a trapper undoubtedly shot his Indian "for the fun of it," feeling that it was much better to do so than run the risk of being shot at for no better reason. Of this class of reasoners, it must be admitted, Meek was one. Indian-fighting, like bear-fighting, had come to be a sort of pastime, in which he was proud to be known as highly accomplished. Having so many opportunities for the display of game qualities in encounters with these two by-no-means-to-be despised foes of the trapper, it was not often that they quarreled among themselves after the grand frolic of the rendezvous was over.

It happened, however, during this autumn, that while the main camp was in the valley of the Yellowstone, a party of eight trappers, including Meek and a comrade named Stanberry, were trapping together on the Mussel

THE BEAR IN CAMP.

Shell, when the question as to which was the bravest man got started between them, and at length, in the heat of controversy, assumed such importance that it was agreed to settle the matter on the following day according to the Virginia code of honor, *i. e.*, by fighting a duel, and shooting at each other with guns, which hitherto had only done execution on bears and Indians.

But some listening spirit of the woods determined to avert the danger from these two equally brave trappers, and save their ammunition for its legitimate use, by giving them occasion to prove their courage almost on the instant. While sitting around the camp-fire discussing the coming event of the duel at thirty paces, a huge bear, already wounded by a shot from the gun of their hunter who was out looking for game, came running furiously into camp, giving each man there a challenge to fight or fly.

"Now," spoke up one of the men quickly, "let Meek and Stanberry prove which is bravest, by fighting the bear!" "Agreed," cried the two as quickly, and both sprang with guns and wiping-sticks in hand, charging upon the infuriated beast as it reached the spot where they were awaiting it. Stanberry was a small man, and Meek a large one. Perhaps it was owing to this difference of stature that Meek was first to reach the bear as it advanced. Running up with reckless bravado Meek struck the creature two or three times over the head with his wiping-stick before aiming to fire, which however he did so quickly and so surely that the beast fell dead at his feet. This act settled the vexed question. Nobody was disposed to dispute the point of courage with a man who would stop to strike a grizzly before shooting him: therefore Meek was proclaimed by the common voice to be "cock of the walk" in that camp. The pipe of peace was solemnly smoked by himself and Stanberry, and the tomahawk buried never more to be resurrected between them, while a fat supper of bear meat celebrated the compact of everlasting amity.

It was not an unfrequent occurrence for a grizzly bear to be run into camp by the hunters, in the Yellowstone country where this creature abounded. An amusing incident occurred not long after that just related, when the whole camp was at the Cross Creeks of the Yellowstone, on the south side of that river. The hunters were out, and had come upon two or three bears in a thicket. As these animals sometimes will do, they started off in a great fright, running toward camp, the hunters after them, yelling, frightening them still more. A runaway bear, like a runaway horse, appears not to see where it is going, but keeps right on its course no matter what dangers lie in advance. So one of these animals having got headed for the middle of the encampment, saw nothing of what lay in its way, but ran on and on, apparently taking note of nothing but the yells in pursuit. So sudden and unexpected was the charge which he made upon camp, that the Indian women, who were sitting on the ground engaged in some ornamental work, had no time to escape out of the way. One of them was thrown down and run over, and another was struck with such violence that she was thrown twenty feet from the spot where she was hastily attempting to rise. Other objects in camp were upset and thrown out of the way, but without causing so much merriment as the mishaps of the two women who were so rudely treated by the monster.

It was also while the camp was at the Cross Creeks of the Yellowstone that Meek had one of his best fought battles with a grizzly bear. He was out with two companions, one Gardiner, and Mark Head, a Shawnee Indian. Seeing a very large bear digging roots in the creek bottom, Meek proposed to attack it, if the others would hold his horse ready to mount if he failed to kill the creature. This being agreed to he advanced to within about forty paces of his game, when he raised his gun and attempted to fire, but the cap bursting he only roused the beast, which turned on him with a terrific noise between a snarl and a growl, showing some fearful looking teeth. Meek turned to run for his horse, at the same time trying to put a cap on his gun; but when he had almost reached his comrades, their horses and his own took fright at the bear now close on his heels, and ran, leaving him alone with the now fully infuriated beast. Just at the moment he succeeded in getting a cap on his gun, the teeth of the bear closed on his blanket capote which was belted around the waist, the suddenness and force of the seizure turning him around, as the skirt of his capote yielded to the strain and tore off at the belt. Being now nearly face to face

SATISFIED WITH BEAR FIGHTING.

with his foe, the intrepid trapper thrust his gun into the

creature's mouth and attempted again to fire, but the gun being double triggered and not set, it failed to go off. Perceiving the difficulty he managed to set the triggers with the gun still in the bear's mouth, yet no sooner was this done than the bear succeeded in knocking it out, and firing as it slipped out, it hit her too low down to inflict a fatal wound and only served to irritate her still farther.

In this desperate situation when Meek's brain was rapidly working on the problem of live Meek or live bear, two fresh actors appeared on the scene in the persons of two cubs, who seeing their mother in difficulty seemed desirous of doing something to assist her. Their appearance seemed to excite the bear to new exertions, for she made one desperate blow at Meek's empty gun with which he was defending himself, and knocked it out of his hands, and far down the bank or sloping hillside where the struggle was now going on. Then being partially blinded by rage, she seized one of her cubs and began to box it about in a most unmotherly fashion. This diversion gave Meek a chance to draw his knife from the scabbard, with which he endeavored to stab the bear behind the ear: but she was too quick for him, and with a blow struck it out of his hand, as she had the gun, nearly severing his forefinger.

At this critical juncture the second cub interfered, and got a boxing from the old bear, as the first one had done. This too, gave Meek time to make a movement, and loosening his tomahawk from his belt, he made one tremendous effort, taking deadly aim, and struck her just behind the ear, the tomahawk sinking into the brain, and his powerful antagonist lay dead before him. When the blow was struck he stood with his back against a little bluff of rock, beyond which it was impossible to retreat. It was his last chance, and his usual good fortune stood by him.

When the struggle was over the weary victor mounted the rock behind him and looked down upon his enemy slain; and " came to the conclusion that he was satisfied with bar-fighting."

But renown had sought him out even here, alone with his lifeless antagonist. Capt. Stuart with his artist, Mr. Miller, chanced upon this very spot, while yet the conqueror contemplated his slain enemy, and taking possession at once of the bear, whose skin was afterward preserved and stuffed, made a portrait of the "satisfied" slayer. A picture was subsequently painted by Miller of this scene, and was copied in wax for a museum in St. Louis, where it probably remains to this day, a monument of Meek's best bear fight. As for Meek's runaway horse and runaway comrades, they returned to the scene of action too late to be of the least service, except to furnish our hero with transportation to camp, which, considering the weight of his newly gathered laurels, was no light service after all.

In November Bridger's camp arrived at the Bighorn River, expecting to winter; but finding the buffalo all gone, were obliged to cross the mountains lying between the Bighorn and Powder rivers to reach the buffalo country on the latter stream. The snow having already fallen quite deep on these mountains the crossing was attended with great difficulty; and many horses and mules were lost by sinking in the snow, or falling down precipices made slippery by the melting and freezing of the snow on the narrow ridges and rocky benches along which they were forced to travel.

About Christmas all the company went into winter-quarters on Powder River, in the neighborhood of a company of Bonneville's men, left under the command of Antoine Montero, who had established a trading-post and fort at

15

this place, hoping, no doubt, that here they should be comparatively safe from the injurious competition of the older companies.   The appearance of three hundred men, who had the winter before them in which to do mischief, was therefore as unpleasant as it was unexpected; and the result proved that even Montero, who was Bonneville's experienced trader, could not hold his own against so numerous and expert a band of marauders as Bridger's men, assisted by the Crows, proved themselves to be; for by the return of spring Montero had very little remaining of the property belonging to the fort, nor anything to show for it.   This mischievous war upon Bonneville was prompted partly by the usual desire to cripple a rival trader, which the leaders encouraged in their men; but in some individual instances far more by the desire for revenge upon Bonneville personally, on account of his censures passed upon the members of the Monterey expedition, and on the ways of mountain-men generally.

About the first of January, Fontenelle, with four men, and Captain Stuart's party, left camp to go to St. Louis for supplies.   At Fort Laramie Fontenelle committed suicide, in a fit of *mania a potu*, and his men returned to camp with the news.

CHAPTER XVII.

1837. THE fate of Fontenelle should have served as a warning to his associates and fellows. 'Should have done,' however, are often idle words, and as sad as they are idle; they match the poets 'might have been,' in their regretful impotency. Perhaps there never was a winter camp in the mountains more thoroughly demoralized than that of Bridger during the months of January and February. Added to the whites, who were reckless enough, were a considerable party of Delaware and Shawnee Indians, excellent allies, and skillful hunters and trappers, but having the Indian's love of strong drink. "Times were pretty good in the mountains," according to the mountain-man's notion of good times; that is to say, beaver was plenty, camp large, and alcohol abundant, if dear. Under these favorable circumstance much alcohol was consumed, and its influence was felt in the manners not only of the trappers, white and red, but also upon the neighboring Indians.

The Crows, who had for two years been on terms of a sort of semi-amity with the whites, found it to their interest to conciliate so powerful an enemy as the American Fur Company was now become, and made frequent visits to the camp, on which occasion they usually succeeded in obtaining a taste of the fire-water of which they were inordinately fond. Occasionally a trader was permitted to sell liquor to the whole village, when a scene took place whose peculiar horrors were wholly indescribable, from the inability of language to convey an adequate idea of its hellish degradation. When a trader sold alcohol to a village it was understood both by himself and the Indians what was to follow. And to secure the trader against injury a certain number of warriors were selected out of the village to act as a police force, and to guard the trader during the 'drunk' from the insane passions of his customers. To the police not a drop was to be given.

This being arranged, and the village disarmed, the carousal began. Every individual, man, woman, and child, was permitted to become intoxicated. Every form of drunkenness, from the simple stupid to the silly, the heroic, the insane, the beastly, the murderous, displayed itself. The scenes which were then enacted beggared description, as they shocked the senses of even the hard-drinking, license-loving trappers who witnessed them. That they did not "point a moral" for these men, is the strangest part of the whole transaction.

When everybody, police excepted, was drunk as drunk could be, the trader began to dilute his alcohol with water, until finally his keg contained water only, slightly flavored by the washings of the keg, and as they continued to drink of it without detecting its weak quality, they finally drank themselves sober, and were able at last to sum up the cost of their intoxication. This was generally nothing less than the whole property of the village, added to which were not a few personal injuries, and usually a few murders. The village now being poor, the Indians were correspondingly humble ; and were forced to begin a system of reprisal by stealing and making war, a course for which the traders were prepared, and which they avoided by leaving that neighborhood. Such were some of the sins and sorrows for which the American fur companies were

answerable, and which detracted seriously from the respect that the courage, and other good qualities of the
mountain-men freely commanded.

By the first of March these scenes of wrong and riot
were over, for that season at least, and camp commenced
moving back toward the Blackfoot country. After recrossing the mountains, passing the Bighorn, Clarke's, and
Rosebud rivers, they came upon a Blackfoot village on
the Yellowstone, which as usual they attacked, and a battle ensued, in which Manhead, captain of the Delawares
was killed, another Delaware named Tom Hill succeeding
him in command. The fight did not result in any great
loss or gain to either party. The camp of Bridger fought
its way past the village, which was what they must do, in
order to proceed.

Meek, however, was not quite satisfied with the punishment the Blackfeet had received for the killing of Manhead, who had been in the fight with him when the Camanches attacked them on the plains. Desirous of doing
something on his own account, he induced a comrade
named LeBlas, to accompany him to the village, after night
had closed over the scene of the late contest. Stealing
into the village with a noiselessness equal to that of one
of Fennimore Cooper's Indian scouts, these two daring
trappers crept so near that they could look into the lodges,
and see the Indians at their favorite game of *Hand*. In-
ferring from this that the savages did not feel their losses
very severely, they determined to leave some sign of their
visit, and wound their enemy in his most sensitive part,
the horse. Accordingly they cut the halters of a number
of the animals, fastened in the customary manner to a
stake, and succeeded in getting off with nine of them,
which property they proceeded to appropriate to their
own use.

As the spring and summer advanced, Bridger's brigade advanced into the mountains, passing the Cross Creek of the Yellowstone, Twenty-five-Yard River, Cherry River, and coming on to the head-waters of the Missouri spent the early part of the summer in that locality. Between Gallatin and Madison forks the camp struck the great trail of the Blackfeet. Meek and Mark Head had fallen four or five days behind camp, and being on this trail felt a good deal of uneasiness. This feeling was not lessened by seeing, on coming to Madison Fork, the skeletons of two men tied to or suspended from trees, the flesh eaten off their bones. Concluding discretion to be the safest part of valor in this country, they concealed themselves by day and traveled by night, until camp was finally reached near Henry's Lake. On this march they forded a flooded river, on the back of the same mule, their traps placed on the other, and escaped from pursuit of a dozen yelling savages, who gazed after them in astonishment; "taking their mule," said Mark Head," to be a beaver, and themselves great medicine men. "That," said Meek, "is what I call 'cooning' a river."

From this point Meek set out with a party of thirty or forty trappers to travel up the river to head-waters, accompanied by the famous Indian painter Stanley, whose party was met with, this spring, traveling among the mountains. The party of trappers were a day or two ahead of the main camp when they found themselves following close after the big Blackfoot village which had recently passed over the trail, as could be seen by the usual signs; and also by the dead bodies strewn along the trail, victims of that horrible scourge, the small pox. The village was evidently fleeing to the mountains, hoping to rid itself of the plague in their colder and more salubrious air.

Not long after coming upon these evidences of prox-

THE TRAPPER'S LAST SHOT.

imity to an enemy, a party of a hundred and fifty of their warriors were discovered encamped in a defile or narrow bottom enclosed by high bluffs, through which the trappers would have to pass. Seeing that in order to pass this war party, and the village, which was about half a mile in advance, there would have to be some fighting done, the trappers resolved to begin the battle at once by attacking their enemy, who was as yet ignorant of their neighborhood. In pursuance of this determination, Meek, Newell, Mansfield, and Le Blas, commenced hostilities. Leaving their horses in camp, they crawled along on the edge of the overhanging bluff until opposite to the encampment of Blackfeet, firing on them from the shelter of some bushes which grew among the rocks. But the Blackfeet, though ignorant of the number of their enemy, were not to be dislodged so easily, and after an hour or two of random shooting, contrived to scale the bluff at a point higher up, and to get upon a ridge of ground still higher than that occupied by the four trappers. This movement dislodged the latter, and they hastily retreated through the bushes and returned to camp.

The next day, the main camp having come up, the fight was renewed. While the greater body of the company, with the pack-horses, were passing along the high bluff overhanging them, the party of the day before, and forty or fifty others, undertook to drive the Indians out of the bottom, and by keeping them engaged allow the train to pass in safety. The trappers rode to the fight on this occasion, and charged the Blackfeet furiously, they having joined the village a little farther on. A general skirmish now took place. Meek, who was mounted on a fine horse, was in the thickest of the fight. He had at one time a side to side race with an Indian who strung his bow so hard that the arrow dropped, just as Meek, who had loaded his gun running, was ready to fire, and the Indian dropped after his arrow.

Newell too had a desperate conflict with a half-dead warrior, who having fallen from a wound, he thought dead and was trying to scalp. Springing from his horse he seized the Indian's long thick hair in one hand, and with his knife held in the other made a pass at the scalp, when the savage roused up knife in hand, and a struggle took place in which it was for a time doubtful which of the combatants would part with the coveted scalp-lock. Newell might have been glad to resign the trophy, and leave the fallen warrior his tuft of hair, but his fingers were in some way caught by some gun-screws with which the savage had ornamented his *coiffure*, and would not part company. In this dilemma there was no other alternative but fight. The miserable savage was dragged a rod or two in the struggle, and finally dispatched.

Mansfield also got into such close quarters, surrounded by the enemy, that he gave himself up for lost, and called out to his comrades: "Tell old Gabe, (Bridger,) that old Cotton (his own sobriquet) is gone." He lived, however, to deliver his own farewell message, for at this critical juncture the trappers were re-inforced, and relieved. Still the fight went on, the trappers gradually working their way to the upper end of the enclosed part of the valley, past the point of danger.

Just before getting clear of this entanglement Meek became the subject of another picture, by Stanley, who was viewing the battle from the heights above the valley. The picture which is well known as "The Trapper's Last Shot," represents him as he turned upon his horse, a fine and spirited animal, to discharge his last shot at an Indian pursuing, while in the bottom, at a little distance away, other Indians are seen skulking in the tall reedy grass.

The last shot having been discharged with fatal effect, our trapper, so persistently lionized by painters, put his horse to his utmost speed and soon after overtook the camp, which had now passed the strait of danger. But the Blackfeet were still unsatisfied with the result of the contest. They followed after, reinforced from the village, and attacked the camp. In the fight which followed a Blackfoot woman's horse was shot down, and Meek tried to take her prisoner: but two or three of her people com-

"AND THEREBY HANGS A TAIL."

ing to the rescue, engaged his attention; and the woman was saved by seizing hold of the tail of her husband's horse, which setting off at a run, carried her out of danger.

The Blackfeet found the camp of Bridger too strong for them. They were severely beaten and compelled to retire to their village, leaving Bridger free to move on. The following day the camp reached the village of Little-Robe, a chief of the Peagans, who held a talk with Bridger, complaining that his nation were all perishing from the small-pox which had been given to them by the whites. Bridger was able to explain to Little-Robe his error; inasmuch as although the disease might have originated among the whites, it was communicated to the Blackfeet by Jim Beckwith, a negro, and principal chief of their enemies the Crows.   This unscrupulous wretch had caused two infected articles to be taken from a Mackinaw boat, up from St. Louis, and disposed of to the Blackfeet— whence the horrible scourge under which they were suffering.

This matter being explained, Little-Robe consented to trade horses and skins; and the two camps parted amicably.   The next day after this friendly talk, Bridger being encamped on the trail in advance of the Blackfeet, an Indian came riding into camp, with his wife and daughter, pack-horse and lodge-pole, and all his worldly goods, unaware until he got there of the snare into which he had fallen.   The French trappers, generally, decreed to kill the man and take possession of the woman.   But Meek, Kit Carson, and others of the American trappers of the better sort, interfered to prevent this truly savage act. Meek took the woman's horse by the head, Carson the man's, the daughter following, and led them out of camp. Few of the Frenchmen cared to interrupt either of these two men, and they were suffered to depart in peace. When at a safe distance, Meek stopped, and demanded as some return for having saved the man's life, a present of tobacco, a luxury which, from the Indian's pipe, he suspected him to possess.   About enough for two chews was the result of this demand, complied with rather grudgingly, the Indian vieing with the trapper in his devotion to the weed.   Just at this time, owing to the death of

Fontenelle, and a consequent delay in receiving supplies, tobacco was scarce among the mountaineers.

Bridger's brigade of trappers met with no other serious interruptions on their summer's march. They proceeded to Henry's Lake, and crossing the Rocky Mountains, traveled through the Pine Woods, always a favorite region, to Lewis' Lake on Lewis' Fork of the Snake River; and finally up the Grovant Fork, recrossing the mountains to Wind River, where the rendezvous for this year was appointed.

Here, once more, the camp was visited by a last years' acquaintance. This was none other than Mr. Gray, of the Flathead Mission, who was returning to the States on business connected with the missionary enterprise, and to provide himself with a helpmeet for life,—a co-laborer and sufferer in the contemplated toil of teaching savages the rudiments of a religion difficult even to the comprehension of an old civilization.

Mr. Gray was accompanied by two young men (whites) who wished to return to the States, and also by a son of one of the Flathead chiefs. Two other Flathead Indians, and one Iroquois and one Snake Indian, were induced to accompany Mr. Gray. The undertaking was not without danger, and so the leaders of the Fur Company assured him. But Mr. Gray was inclined to make light of the danger, having traveled with entire safety when under the protection of the Fur Companies the year before. He proceeded without interruption until he reached Ash Hollow, in the neighborhood of Fort Laramie, when his party was attacked by a large band of Sioux, and compelled to accept battle. The five Indians, with the whites, fought bravely, killing fifteen of the Sioux, before a parley was obtained by the intervention of a French trader who chanced to be among the Sioux. When Mr. Gray was able to hold a 'talk' with the attacking party he was assured that his life and that of his two white associates would be spared, but that they wanted to kill the strange Indians and take their fine horses. It is not at all probable that Mr. Gray consented to this sacrifice; though he has been accused of doing so.

No doubt the Sioux took advantage of some hesitation on his part, and rushed upon his Indian allies in an unguarded moment. However that may be, his allies were killed and he was allowed to escape, after giving up the property belonging to them, and a portion of his own.

This affair was the occasion of much ill-feeling toward Mr. Gray, when, in the following year, he returned to the mountains with the tale of massacre of his friends and his own escape. The mountain-men, although they used their influence to restrain the vengeful feelings of the Flathead tribe, whispered amongst themselves that Gray had preferred his own life to that of his friends. The old Flathead chief too, who had lost a son by the massacre, was hardly able to check his impulsive desire for revenge; for he held Mr. Gray responsible for his son's life. Nothing more serious, however, grew out of this unhappy tragedy than a disaffection among the tribe toward Mr. Gray, which made his labors useless, and finally determined him to remove to the Wallamet Valley.

There were no outsiders besides Gray's party at the rendezvous of this year, except Captain Stuart, and he was almost as good a mountaineer as any. This doughty English traveler had the bad fortune together with that experienced leader Fitzpatrick, of being robbed by the Crows in the course of the fall hunt, in the Crow country. These expert horse thieves had succeeded in stealing nearly all the horses belonging to the joint camp, and had so disabled the company that it could not proceed. In this emergency, Newell, who had long been a sub-trader and was wise in Indian arts and wiles, was sent to hold a talk with the thieves. The talk was held, according to custom, in the the Medicine lodge, and the usual amount of smoking, of long silences, and grave looks, had to be participated in, before the subject on hand could be considered. Then the chiefs complained as usual of wrongs at the hands of the white men; of their fear of small-pox, from which some of their tribe had suffered; of friends killed in battle with the whites, and all the list of ills that Crow flesh is heir to at the will of their white enemies. The women too had their complaints to proffer, and the number of widows and orphans in the tribe was pathetically set forth. The chiefs also made a strong point of this latter complaint; and on it the wily Newell hung his hopes of recovering the stolen property.

"It is true," said he to the chiefs, "that you have sustained heavy losses. But that is not the fault of the Blanket chief (Bridger.) If your young men have been killed, they were killed when attempting to rob or kill our Captain's men. If you have lost horses, your young men have stolen five to our one. If you are poor in skins and other property, it is because you sold it all for drink which did you no good. Neither is Bridger to blame that you have had the small-pox. Your own chief, in trying to kill your enemies the Blackfeet, brought that disease into the country.

"But it is true that you have many widows and orphans to support, and that is bad. I pity the orphans, and will help you to support them, if you will restore to my captain the property stolen from his camp. Otherwise Bridger will bring more horses, and plenty of ammunition, and there will be more widows and orphans among the Crows than ever before."

This was a kind of logic easy to understand and quick to convince among savages. The bribe, backed by a threat, settled the question of the restoration of the horses, which were returned without further delay, and a present of blankets and trinkets was given, ostensibly to the bereaved women, really to the covetous chiefs.

CHAPTER XVIII.

1837. THE decline of the business of hunting furs began to be quite obvious about this time. Besides the
American and St. Louis Companies, and the Hudson's Bay
Company, there were numerous lone traders with whom
the ground was divided. The autumn of this year was
spent by the American Company, as formerly, in trapping
beaver on the streams issuing from the eastern side of the
Rocky Mountains. When the cold weather finally drove
the Fur Company to the plains, they went into winter
quarters once more in the neighborhood of the Crows on
Powder River. Here were re-enacted the wild scenes of
the previous winter, both trappers and Indians being
given up to excesses.

On the return of spring, Bridger again led his brigade
all through the Yellowstone country, to the streams on
the north side of the Missouri, to the head-waters of that
river; and finally rendezvoused on the north fork of the
Yellowstone, near Yellowstone Lake. Though the amount
of furs taken on the spring hunt was considerable, it was
by no means equal to former years. The fact was becoming apparent that the beaver was being rapidly exterminated.

However there was beaver enough in camp to furnish
the means for the usual profligacy. Horse-racing, betting,
gambling, drinking, were freely indulged in. In the
midst of this " fun," there appeared at the rendezvous Mr.

Gray, now accompanied by Mrs. Gray and six other mission-ary ladies and gentlemen.   Here also were two gentlemen from the Methodist mission on the Wallamet, who were returning to the States.   Captain Stuart was still traveling with the Fur Company, and was also present with his party; besides which a Hudson's Bay trader named Ema-tinger was encamped near by.   As if actuated to extra-ordinary displays by the unusual number of visitors, espe-cially the four ladies, both trappers and Indians conducted themselves like the mad-caps they were.   The Shawnees and Delawares danced their great war-dance before the tents of the missionaries; and Joe Meek, not to be out-done, arrayed himself in a suit of armor belonging to Cap-tain Stuart and strutted about the encampment; then mounting his horse played the part of an ancient knight, with a good deal of *eclat*.

Meek had not abstained from the alcohol kettle, but had offered it and partaken of it rather more freely than usual; so that when rendezvous was broken up, the St. Louis Company gone to the Popo Agie, and the American Com-pany going to Wind River, he found that his wife, a Nez Perce who had succeeded Umentucken in his affections, had taken offence, or a fit of homesickness, which was synonymous, and departed with the party of Ematinger and the missionaries, intending to visit her people at Walla-Walla.   This desertion wounded Meek's feelings; for he prided himself on his courtesy to the sex, and did not like to think that he had not behaved handsomely. All the more was he vexed with himself because his spouse had carried with her a pretty and sprightly baby-daugh-ter, of whom the father was fond and proud, and who had been christened Helen Mar, after one of the heroines of Miss Porter's *Scottish Chiefs*—a book much admired in the mountains, as it has been elsewhere.

Therefore at the first camp of the American Company, Meek resolved to turn his back on the company, and go after the mother and daughter. Obtaining a fresh kettle of alcohol, to keep up his spirits, he left camp, returning toward the scene of the late rendezvous. But in the effort to keep up his spirits he had drank too much alcohol, and the result was that on the next morning he found himself alone on the Wind River Mountain, with his horses and pack mules, and very sick indeed. Taking a little more alcohol to brace up his nerves, he started on again, passing around the mountain on to the Sweetwater; thence to the Sandy, and thence across a country without water for seventy-five miles, to Green River, where the camp of Ematinger was overtaken.

The heat was excessive; and the absence of water made the journey across the arid plain between Sandy and Green Rivers one of great suffering to the traveler and his animals; and the more so as the frequent references to the alcohol kettle only increased the thirst-fever instead of allaying it. But Meek was not alone in suffering. About half way across the scorching plain he discovered a solitary woman's figure standing in the trail, and two riding horses near her, whose drooping heads expressed their dejection. On coming up with this strange group, Meek found the woman to be one of the missionary ladies, a Mrs. Smith, and that her husband was lying on the ground, dying, as the poor sufferer believed himself, for water.

Mrs. Smith made a weeping appeal to Meek for water for her dying husband; and truly the poor woman's situation was a pitiable one. Behind camp, with no protection from the perils of the desert and wilderness—only a terrible care instead—the necessity of trying to save her husband's life. As no water was to be had, alcohol was

16

offered to the famishing man, who, however, could not be aroused from his stupor of wretchedness. Seeing that death really awaited the unlucky missionary unless something could be done to cause him to exert himself, Meek commenced at once, and with unction, to abuse the man for his unmanliness. His style, though not very refined, was certainly very vigorous.

"You're a —— pretty fellow to be lying on the ground here, lolling your tongue out of your mouth, and trying to die. Die, if you want to, you're of no account and will never be missed. Here's your wife, who you are keeping standing here in the hot sun; why don't *she* die? She's got more pluck than a white-livered chap like you. But I'm not going to leave her waiting here for you to die. Thar's a band of Indians behind on the trail, and I've been riding like — to keep out of their way. If you want to stay here and be scalped, you can stay; Mrs. Smith is going with me. Come, madam," continued Meek, leading up her horse, "let me help you to mount, for we must get out of this cursed country as fast as possible."

Poor Mrs. Smith did not wish to leave her husband; nor did she relish the notion of staying to be scalped. Despair tugged at her heart-strings. She would have sunk to the ground in a passion of tears, but Meek was too much in earnest to permit precious time to be thus wasted. "Get on your horse," said he rather roughly. "You can't save your husband by staying here, crying. It is better that one should die than two; and he seems to be a worthless dog anyway. Let the Indians have him."

Almost lifting her upon the horse, Meek tore the distracted woman away from her husband, who had yet strength enough to gasp out an entreaty not to be left.

"You can follow us if you choose," said the apparently merciless trapper, "or you can stay where you are. Mrs. Smith can find plenty of better men than you. Come, madam!" and he gave the horse a stroke with his riding-whip which started him into a rapid pace.

The unhappy wife, whose conscience reproached her for leaving her husband to die alone, looked back, and saw him raising his head to gaze after them. Her grief broke out afresh, and she would have gone back even then to remain with him: but Meek was firm, and again started up her horse. Before they were quite out of sight, Meek turned in his saddle, and beheld the dying man sitting up. "Hurrah;" said he: "he's all right. He will overtake us in a little while:" and as he predicted, in little over an hour Smith came riding up, not more than half dead by this time. The party got into camp on Green River, about eleven o'clock that night, and Mrs. Smith having told the story of her adventures with the unknown trapper who had so nearly kidnaped her, the laugh and the cheer went round among the company. "That's Meek," said Ematinger, "you may rely on that. He's just the one to kidnap a woman in that way." When Mrs. Smith fully realized the service rendered, she was abundantly grateful, and profuse were the thanks which our trapper received, even from the much-abused husband, who was now thoroughly alive again. Meek failed to persuade his wife to return with him. She was homesick for her people, and would go to them. But instead of turning back, he kept on with Ematinger's camp as far as Fort Hall, which post was then in charge of Courtenay Walker.

While the camp was at Soda Springs, Meek observed the missionary ladies baking bread in a tin reflector before a fire. Bread was a luxury unknown to the mountain-man,—and as a sudden recollection of his boyhood, and the days of bread-and-butter came over him, his mouth began to water. Almost against his will he continued to hang round the missionary camp, thinking about the bread. At length one of the Nez Perces, named James, whom the missionary had taught to sing, at their request struck up a hymn, which he sang in a very creditable manner. As a reward of his pious proficiency, one of the ladies gave James a biscuit. A bright thought struck our longing hero's brain. " Go back," said he to James, " and sing another hymn ; and when the ladies give you another biscuit, bring it to me." And in this manner, he obtained a taste of the coveted luxury, bread—of which, during nine years in the mountains he had not eaten.

At Fort Hall, Meek parted company with the missionaries, and with his wife and child. As the little black-eyed daughter took her departure in company with this new element in savage life,—the missionary society,—her father could have had no premonition of the fate to which the admixture of the savage and the religious elements was step by step consigning her.

After remaining a few days at the fort, Meek, who found some of his old comrades at this place, went trapping with them up the Portneuf, and soon made up a pack of one hundred and fifty beaver-skins. These, on returning to the fort, he delivered to Jo. Walker, one of the American Company's traders at that time, and took Walker's receipt for them. He then, with Mansfield and Wilkins, set out about the first of September for the Flathead country, where Wilkins had a wife. In their company was an old Flathead woman, who wished to return to her people, and took this opportunity.

The weather was still extremely warm. It had been a season of great drought, and the streams were nearly all entirely dried up. The first night out, the horses, eight in number, strayed off in search of water, and were lost. Now commenced a day of fearful sufferings. No water had been found since leaving the fort. The loss of the horses made it necessary for the company to separate to look for them; Mansfield and Wilkins going in one direction, Meek and the old Flathead woman in another. The little coolness and moisture which night had imparted to the atmosphere was quickly dissipated by the unchecked rays of the pitiless sun shining on a dry and barren plain, with not a vestige of verdure anywhere in sight. On and on went the old Flathead woman, keeping always in the advance, and on and on followed Meek, anxiously scanning the horizon for a chance sight of the horses. Higher and higher mounted the sun, the temperature increasing in intensity until the great plain palpitated with radiated heat, and the horizon flickered almost like a flame where the burning heavens met the burning earth. Meek had been drinking a good deal of rum at the fort, which circumstance did not lessen the terrible consuming thirst that was torturing him.

Noon came, and passed, and still the heat and the suffering increased, the fever and craving of hunger being now added to that of thirst. On and on, through the whole of that long scorching afternoon, trotted the old Flathead woman in the peculiar traveling gait of the Indian and the mountaineer, Meek following at a little distance, and going mad, as he thought, for a little water. And mad he probably was, as famine sometimes makes its victims. When night at last closed in, he laid down to die, as the missionary Smith had done before. But he did not remember Smith: he only thought of water, and heard it running, and fancied the old woman was lapping it like a wolf. Then he rose to follow her and find it; it was always just ahead, and the woman was howling to him to show him the trail.

Thus the night passed, and in the cool of the early morning he experienced a little relief. He was really following his guide, who as on the day before was trotting on ahead. Then the thought possessed him to overtake and kill her, hoping from her shriveled body to obtain a morsel of food, and drop of moisture. But his strength was failing, and his guide so far ahead that he gave up the thought as involving too great exertion, continuing to follow her in a helpless and hopeless kind of way.

At last! There was no mistake this time: he heard running water, and the old woman *was* lapping it like a wolf. With a shriek of joy he ran and fell on his face in the water, which was not more than one foot in depth, nor the stream more than fifteen feet wide. But it had a white pebbly bottom; and the water was clear, if not very cool. It was something to thank God for, which the none too religious trapper acknowledged by a fervent "Thank God!"

For a long time he lay in the water, swallowing it, and by thrusting his finger down his throat vomiting it up again, to prevent surfeit, his whole body taking in the welcome moisture at all its million pores. The fever abated, a feeling of health returned, and the late perishing man was restored to life and comparative happiness. The stream proved to be Godin's Fork, and here Meek and his faithful old guide rested until evening, in the shade of some willows, where their good fortune was completed by the appearance of Mansfield and Wilkins with the horses. The following morning the men found and killed a fat buffalo cow, whereby all their wants were supplied, and good feeling restored in the little camp.

From Godin's Fork they crossed over to Salmon River,

and presently struck the Nez Perce trail which leads from
that river over into the Beaver-head country, on the
Beaver-head or Jefferson Fork of the Missouri, where
there was a Flathead and Nez Perce village, on or about
the present site of Virginia City, in Montana.

Not stopping long here, Meek and his companions went
on to the Madison Fork with the Indian village, and to
the shores of Missouri Lake, joining in the fall hunt for
buffalo.

CHAPTER XIX.

"Tell me all about a buffalo hunt," said the writer to Joe Meek, as we sat at a window overlooking the Columbia River, where it has a beautiful stretch of broad waters and curving wooded shores, and talking about mountain life, "tell me how you used to hunt buffalo."

"Waal, there is a good deal of sport in runnin' buffalo. When the camp discovered a band, then every man that wanted to run, made haste to catch his buffalo horse. We sometimes went out thirty or forty strong; sometimes two or three, and at other times a large party started on the hunt; the more the merrier. We alway had great bantering about our horses, each man, according to his own account, having the best one.

"When we first start we ride slow, so as not to alarm the buffalo. The nearer we come to the band the greater our excitement. The horses seem to feel it too, and are worrying to be off. When we come so near that the band starts, then the word is given, our horses' mettle is up, and away we go!

"Thar may be ten thousand in a band. Directly we crowd them so close that nothing can be seen but dust, nor anything heard but the roar of their trampling and bellowing. The hunter now keeps close on their heels to escape being blinded by the dust, which does not rise as high as a man on horseback, for thirty yards behind the animals. As soon as we are close enough the firing begins,

A BUFFALO HUNT.

and the band is on the run; and a herd of buffalo can run about as fast as a good race-horse.   How they *do* thunder along!   They give us a pretty sharp race.   Take care! Down goes a rider, and away goes his horse with the band. Do you think we stopped to look after the fallen man? Not we.   We rather thought that war fun, and if he got killed, why, 'he war unlucky, that war all.   Plenty more men: couldn't bother about him.'

"Thar's a fat cow ahead.   I force my way through the band to come up with her.   The buffalo crowd around so that I have to put my foot on them, now on one side, now the other, to keep them off my horse.   It is lively work, I can tell you.   A man has to look sharp not to be run down by the band pressing him on; buffalo and horse at the top of their speed.

"Look out; thar's a ravine ahead, as you can see by the plunge which the band makes.   Hold up! or somebody goes to the d—l now.   If the band is large it fills the ravine full to the brim, and the hindmost of the herd pass over on top of the foremost.   It requires horseman-ship not to be carried over without our own consent; but then we mountain-men are *all* good horsemen.   Over the ravine we go; but we do it our own way.

"We keep up the chase for about four miles, selecting our game as we run, and killing a number of fat cows to each man; some more and some less.   When our horses are tired we slacken up, and turn back.   We meet the camp-keepers with pack-horses.   They soon butcher, pack up the meat, and we all return to camp, whar we laugh at each other's mishaps, and eat fat meat: and this constitutes the glory of mountain life."

"But you were going to tell me about the buffalo hunt at Missouri Lake?"

"Thar isn't much to tell.   It war pretty much like other

buffalo hunts. Thar war a lot of us trappers happened to be at a Nez Perce and Flathead village in the fall of '38, when they war agoin' to kill winter meat; and as their hunt lay in the direction we war going, we joined in. The old Nez Perce chief, *Kow-e-so-te* had command of the village, and we trappers had to obey him, too.

"We started off slow; nobody war allowed to go ahead of camp. In this manner we caused the buffalo to move on before us, but not to be alarmed. We war eight or ten days traveling from the Beaver-head to Missouri Lake, and by the time we got thar, the whole plain around the lake war crowded with buffalo, and it war a splendid sight!

"In the morning the old chief harangued the men of his village, and ordered us all to get ready for the surround. About nine o'clock every man war mounted, and we began to move.

"That war a sight to make a man's blood warm! A thousand men, all trained hunters, on horseback, carrying their guns, and with their horses painted in the height of Indians' fashion. We advanced until within about half a mile of the herd; then the chief ordered us to deploy to the right and left, until the wings of the column extended a long way, and advance again.

"By this time the buffalo war all moving, and we had come to within a hundred yards of them. *Kow-e-so-te* then gave us the word, and away we went, pell-mell. Heavens, what a charge! What a rushing and roaring—men shooting, buffalo bellowing and trampling until the earth shook under them!

"It war the work of half an hour to slay two thousand or may be three thousand animals. When the work was over, we took a view of the field. Here and there and everywhere, laid the slain buffalo. Occasionally a horse with a broken leg war seen; or a man with a broken arm; or maybe he had fared worse, and had a broken head.

"Now came out the women of the village to help us butcher and pack up the meat. It war a big job; but we war not long about it. By night the camp war full of meat, and everybody merry. Bridger's camp, which war passing that way, traded with the village for fifteen hundred buffalo tongues—the tongue being reckoned a choice part of the animal. And that's the way we helped the Nez Perces hunt buffalo."

"But when you were hunting for your own subsistence in camp, you sometimes went out in small parties?"

"Oh yes, it war the same thing on a smaller scale. One time Kit Carson and myself, and a little Frenchman, named Marteau, went to run buffalo on Powder River. When we came in sight of the band it war agreed that Kit and the Frenchman should do the running, and I should stay with the pack animals. The weather war very cold and I didn't like my part of the duty much.

"The Frenchman's horse couldn't run; so I lent him mine. Kit rode his own; not a good buffalo horse either. In running, my horse fell with the Frenchman, and nearly killed him. Kit, who couldn't make his horse catch, jumped off, and caught mine, and tried it again. This time he came up with the band, and killed four fat cows.

"When I came up with the pack-animals, I asked Kit how he came by my horse. He explained, and wanted to know if I had seen anything of Marteau: said my horse had fallen with him, and he thought killed him. 'You go over the other side of yon hill, and see,' said Kit.

"What'll I do with him if he is dead?" said I.

"Can't you pack him to camp?"

"Pack — " said I; "I should rather pack a load of meat."

"Waal," said Kit, "I'll butcher, if you'll go over and see, anyhow."

"So I went over, and found the dead man leaning his head on his hand, and groaning; for he war pretty bad hurt. I got him on his horse, though, after a while, and took him back to whar Kit war at work. We soon finished the butchering job, and started back to camp with our wounded Frenchman, and three loads of fat meat."

"You were not very compassionate toward each other, in the mountains?"

"That war not our business. We had no time for such things. Besides, live men war what we wanted; dead ones war of no account."

CHAPTER XX.

1838. From Missouri Lake, Meek started alone for the Gallatin Fork of the Missouri, trapping in a mountain basin called Gardiner's Hole. Beaver were plenty here, but it was getting late in the season, and the weather was cold in the mountains. On his return, in another basin called the Burnt Hole, he found a buffalo skull; and knowing that Bridger's camp would soon pass that way, wrote on it the number of beaver he had taken, and also his intention to go to Fort Hall to sell them.

In a few days the camp passing found the skull, which grinned its threat at the angry Booshways, as the chuckling trapper had calculated that it would. To prevent its execution runners were sent after him, who, however, failed to find him, and nothing was known of the supposed renegade for some time. But as Bridger passed through Pierre's Hole, on his way to Green river to winter, he was surprised at Meek's appearance in camp. He was soon invited to the lodge of the Booshways, and called to account for his supposed apostasy.

Meek, for a time, would neither deny nor confess, but put on his free trapper airs, and laughed in the face of the Booshways. Bridger, who half suspected some trick, took the matter lightly, but Dripps was very much annoyed, and made some threats, at which Meek only laughed the more. Finally the certificate from their own trader, Jo Walker, was produced, the new pack of furs surrendered, and Dripps' wrath turned into smiles of approval.

Here again Meek parted company with the main camp, and went on an expedition with seven other trappers, under John Larison, to the Salmon River: but found the cold very severe on this journey, and the grass scarce and poor, so that the company lost most of their horses.

On arriving at the Nez Perce village in the Forks of the Salmon, Meek found the old chief *Kow-e-so-te* full of the story of the missionaries and their religion, and anxious to hear preaching. Reports were continually arriving by the Indians, of the wonderful things which were being taught by Mr. and Mrs. Spalding at Lapwai, on the Clearwater, and at Waiilatpu, on the Walla-Walla River. It was now nearly two years since these missions had been founded, and the number of converts among the Nez Perces and Flatheads was already considerable.

Here was an opening for a theological student, such as Joe Meek was! After some little assumption of modesty, Meek intimated that he thought himself capable of giving instruction on religious subjects; and being pressed by the chief, finally consented to preach to *Kow-e-so-te's* people. Taking care first to hold a private council with his associates, and binding them not to betray him, Meek preached his first sermon that evening, going regularly through with the ordinary services of a "meeting."

These services were repeated whenever the Indians seemed to desire it, until Christmas. Then, the village being about to start upon a hunt, the preacher took occasion to intimate to the chief that a wife would be an agreeable present. To this, however, *Kow-e-so-te* demurred, saying that Spalding's religion did not permit men to have two wives: that the Nez Perces had many of them given up their wives on this account; and that therefore, since Meek already had one wife among the Nez Perces, he could not have another without being false to the religion he professed.

To this perfectly clear argument Meek replied, that among white men, if a man's wife left him without his consent, as his had done, he could procure a divorce, and take another wife. Besides, he could tell him how the Bible related many stories of its best men having several wives. But *Kow-e-so-te* was not easily convinced. He could not see how, if the Bible approved of polygamy, Spalding should insist on the Indians putting away all but one of their wives. "However," says Meek, "after about two weeks' explanation of the doings of Solomon and David, I succeeded in getting the chief to give me a young girl, whom I called Virginia;—my present wife, and the mother of seven children."

After accompanying the Indians on their hunt to the Beaver-head country, where they found plenty of buffalo, Meek remained with the Nez Perce village until about the first of March, when he again intimated to the chief that it was the custom of white men to pay their preachers. Accordingly the people were notified, and the winter's salary began to arrive. It amounted altogether to thirteen horses, and many packs of beaver, beside sheep-skins and buffalo-robes; so that he "considered that with his young wife, he had made a pretty good winter's work of it."

In March he set out trapping again, in company with one of his comrades named Allen, a man to whom he was much attached. They traveled along up and down the Salmon, to Godin's River, Henry's Fork of the Snake, to Pierre's Fork, and Lewis' Fork, and the Muddy, and finally set their traps on a little stream that runs out of the pass which leads to Pierre's Hole.

Leaving their camp one morning to take up their traps, they were discovered and attacked by a party of Blackfeet just as they came near the trapping ground. The only refuge at hand was a thicket of willows on the opposite side of the creek, and towards this the trappers directed their flight. Meek, who was in advance, succeeded in gaining the thicket without being seen; but Allen stumbled and fell in crossing the stream, and wet his gun. He quickly recovered his footing and crossed over; but the Blackfeet had seen him enter the thicket, and came up to within a short distance, yet not approaching too near the place where they knew he was concealed. Unfortunately, Allen, in his anxiety to be ready for defense, commenced snapping caps on his gun to dry it. The quick ears of the savages caught the sound, and understood the meaning of it. Knowing him to be defenceless, they plunged into the thicket after him, shooting him almost immediately, and dragging him out still breathing to a small prairie about two rods away.

And now commenced a scene which Meek was compelled to witness, and which he declares nearly made him insane through sympathy, fear, horror, and suspense as to his own fate. Those devils incarnate deliberately cut up their still palpitating victim into a hundred pieces, each taking a piece; accompanying the horrible and inhuman butchery with every conceivable gesture of contempt for the victim, and of hellish delight in their own acts.

Meek, who was only concealed by the small patch of willows, and a pit in the sand hastily scooped out with his knife until it was deep enough to lie in, was in a state of the most fearful excitement. All day long he had to endure the horrors of his position. Every moment seemed an hour, every hour a day, until when night came, and the Indians left the place, he was in a high state of fever.

About nine o'clock that night he ventured to creep to the edge of the little prairie, where he lay and listened a long time, without hearing anything but the squirrels running over the dry leaves; but which he constantly feared was the stealthy approach of the enemy. At last, however, he summoned courage to crawl out on to the open ground, and gradually to work his way to a wooded bluff not far distant. The next day he found two of his horses, and with these set out alone for Green River, where the American Company was to rendezvous. After twenty-six days of solitary and cautious travel he reached the appointed place in safety, having suffered fearfully from the recollection of the tragic scene he had witnessed in the death of his friend, and also from solitude and want of food.

The rendezvous of this year was at Bonneville's old fort on Green River, and was the last one held in the mountains by the American Fur Company. Beaver was growing scarce, and competition was strong. On the disbanding of the company, some went to Santa Fe, some to California, others to the Lower Columbia, and a few remained in the mountains trapping, and selling their furs to the Hudson's Bay Company at Fort Hall. As to the leaders, some of them continued for a few years longer to trade with the Indians, and others returned to the States, to lose their fortunes more easily far than they made them.

Of the men who remained in the mountains trapping, that year, Meek was one. Leaving his wife at Fort Hall, he set out in company with a Shawnee, named Big Jim, to take beaver on Salt River, a tributary of the Snake. The two trappers had each his riding and his pack horse, and at night generally picketed them all; but one night Big Jim allowed one of his to remain loose to graze. This horse, after eating for some hours, came back and

17

laid down behind the other horses, and every now and
then raised up his head; which slight movement at length
aroused Big Jim's attention, and his suspicions also.

"My friend," said he in a whisper to Meek, "Indian
steal our horses."

"Jump up and shoot," was the brief answer.

Jim shot, and ran out to see the result. Directly he
came back saying: "My friend, I shoot my horse; break
him neck;" and Big Jim became disconsolate over what
his white comrade considered a very good joke.

The hunt was short and not very remunerative in furs.
Meek soon returned to Fort Hall; and when he did so,
found his new wife had left that post in company with a
party under Newell, to go to Fort Crockett, on Green
River,—Newell's wife being a sister of Virginia's,—on
learning which he started on again alone, to join that party.
On Bear River, he fell in with a portion of that Quixotic
band, under Farnham, which was looking for paradise and
perfection, something on the Fourier plan, somewhere in
this western wilderness. They had already made the discovery in crossing the continent, that perfect disinterest-
edness was lacking among themselves; and that the
nearer they got to their western paradise the farther off it
seemed in their own minds.

Continuing his journey alone, soon after parting from
Farnham, he lost the hammer of his gun, which accident
deprived him of the means of subsisting himself, and he
had no dried meat, nor provisions of any kind. The
weather, too, was very cold, increasing the necessity for
food to support animal heat. However, the deprivation
of food was one of the accidents to which mountain-men
were constantly liable, and one from which he had often
suffered severely; therefore he pushed on, without feeling
any unusual alarm, and had arrived within fifteen miles

of the fort before he yielded to the feeling of exhaustion, and laid down beside the trail to rest. Whether he would ever have finished the journey alone he could not tell; but fortunately for him, he was discovered by Jo Walker, and Gordon, another acquaintance, who chanced to pass that way toward the fort.

Meek answered their hail, and inquired if they had any-thing to eat. Walker replied in the affirmative, and get-ting down from his horse, produced some dried buffalo meat which he gave to the famishing trapper. But seeing the ravenous manner in which he began to eat, Walker inquired how long it had been since he had eaten any-thing.

"Five days since I had a bite."

"Then, my man, you can't have any more just now," said Walker, seizing the meat in alarm lest Meek should kill himself.

"It was hard to see that meat packed away again," says Meek in relating his sufferings, "I told Walker that if my gun had a hammer I'd shoot and eat him. But he talked very kindly, and helped me on my horse, and we all went on to the Fort."

At Fort Crockett were Newell and his party, the remain-der of Farnham's party, a trading party under St. Clair, who owned the fort, Kit Carson, and a number of Meek's former associates, including Craig and Wilkins. Most of these men, Othello-like, had lost their occupation since the dis-banding of the American Fur Company, and were much at a loss concerning the future. It was agreed between Newell and Meek to take what beaver they had to Fort Hall, to trade for goods, and return to Fort Crockett, where they would commence business on their own account with the Indians.

Accordingly they set out, with one other man belonging

to Farnham's former adherents.   They traveled to Henry's
Fork, to Black Fork, where Fort Bridger now is, to Bear
River, to Soda Springs, and finally to Fort Hall, suffering
much from cold, and finding very little to eat by the way.
At Fort Hall, which was still in charge of Courtenay
Walker, Meek and Newell remained a week, when, having
purchased their goods and horses to pack them, they once
more set out on the long, cold journey to Fort Crockett.
They had fifteen horses to take care of and only one assistant, a Snake Indian called Al.   The return proved an
arduous and difficult undertaking.   The cold was very severe; they had not been able to lay in a sufficient stock of
provisions at Fort Hall, and game there was none, on the
route.   By the time they arrived at Ham's Fork the only
atom of food they had left was a small piece of bacon which
they had been carefully saving to eat with any poor meat
they might chance to find.

The next morning after camping on Ham's Fork was
stormy and cold, the snow filling the air; yet Snake Al,
with a promptitude by no means characteristic of him, rose
early and went out to look after the horses.

"By that same token," said Meek to Newell, "Al has
eaten the bacon."   And so it proved, on investigation.
Al's uneasy conscience having acted as a goad to stir him
up to begin his duties in season.   On finding his conjecture confirmed, Meek declared his intention, should no
game be found before next day night, of killing and eating Al, to get back the stolen bacon.   But Providence
interfered to save Al's bacon.   On the following afternoon
the little party fell in with another still smaller but better
supplied party of travelers, comprising a Frenchman and
his wife.   These had plenty of fat antelope meat, which
they freely parted with to the needy ones, whom also they
accompanied to Fort Crockett.

It was now Christmas; and the festivities which took place at the Fort were attended with a good deal of rum drinking, in which Meek, according to his custom, joined, and as a considerable portion of their stock in trade consisted of this article, it may fairly be presumed that the home consumption of these two "lone traders" amounted to the larger half of what they had with so much trouble transported from Fort Hall. In fact, "times were bad enough" among the men so suddenly thrown upon their own resources among the mountains, at a time when that little creature, which had made mountain life tolerable, or possible, was fast being exterminated.

To make matters more serious, some of the worst of the now unemployed trappers had taken to a life of thieving and mischief which made enemies of the friendly Indians, and was likely to prevent the better disposed from enjoying security among any of the tribes. A party of these renegades, under a man named Thompson, went over to Snake River to steal horses from the Nez Perces. Not succeeding in this, they robbed the Snake Indians of about forty animals, and ran them off to the Uintee, the Indians following and complaining to the whites at Fort Crockett that their people had been robbed by white trappers, and demanding restitution.

According to Indian law, when one of a tribe offends, the whole tribe is responsible. Therefore if whites stole their horses they might take vengeance on any whites they met, unless the property was restored. In compliance with this well understood requisition of Indian law, a party was made up at Fort Crockett to go and retake the horses, and restore them to their rightful owners. This party consisted of Meek, Craig, Newell, Carson, and twenty-five others, under the command of Jo Walker.

The horses were found on an island in Green River, the

robbers having domiciled themselves in an old fort at the mouth of the Uintee. In order to avoid having a fight with the renegades, whose white blood the trappers were not anxious to spill, Walker made an effort to get the horses off the island undiscovered. But while horses and men were crossing the river on the ice, the ice sinking with them until the water was knee-deep, the robbers discovered the escape of their booty, and charging on the trappers tried to recover the horses. In this effort they were not successful; while Walker made a masterly flank movement and getting in Thompson's rear, ran the horses into the fort, where he stationed his men, and succeeded in keeping the robbers on the outside. Thompson then commenced giving the horses away to a village of Utes in the neighborhood of the fort, on condition that they should assist in retaking them. On his side, Walker threatened the Utes with dire vengeance if they dared interfere. The Utes who had a wholesome fear not only of the trappers, but of their foes the Snakes, declined to enter into the quarrel. After a day of strategy, and of threats alternated with arguments, strengthened by a warlike display, the trappers marched out of the fort before the faces of the discomfitted thieves, taking their booty with them, which was duly restored to the Snakes on their return to Fort Crockett, and peace secured once more with that people.

Still times continued bad. The men not knowing what else to do, went out in small parties in all directions seeking adventures, which generally were not far to find. On one of these excursions Meek went with a party down the canyon of Green River, on the ice. For nearly a hundred miles they traveled down this awful canyon without finding but one place where they could have come out; and left it at last at the mouth of the Uintee.

This passed the time until March. Then the company of Newell and Meek was joined by Antoine Rubideau, who had brought goods from Sante Fe to trade with the Indians. Setting out in company, they traded along up Green River to the mouth of Ham's fork, and camped. The snow was still deep in the mountains, and the trappers found great sport in running antelope. On one occasion a large herd, numbering several hundreds, were run on to the ice, on Green River, where they were crowded into an air hole, and large numbers slaughtered only for the cruel sport which they afforded.

But killing antelope needlessly was not by any means the worst of amusements practiced in Rubideau's camp. That foolish trader occupied himself so often and so long in playing *Hand*, (an Indian game,) that before he parted with his new associates he had gambled away his goods, his horses, and even his wife; so that he returned to Santa Fe much poorer than nothing—since he was in debt.

On the departure of Rubideau, Meek went to Fort Hall, and remained in that neighborhood, trapping and trading for the Hudson's Bay Company, until about the last of June, when he started for the old rendezvous places of the American Companies, hoping to find some divisions of them at least, on the familiar camping ground. But his journey was in vain. Neither on Green River or Wind River, where for ten years he had been accustomed to meet the leaders and their men, his old comrades in danger, did he find a wandering brigade even. The glory of the American companies was departed, and he found himself solitary among his long familiar haunts.

With many melancholy reflections, the man of twenty-eight years of age recalled how, a mere boy, he had fallen half unawares into the kind of life he had ever since led amongst the mountains, with only other men equally the victims of circumstance, and the degraded savages, for his companions. The best that could be made of it, such life had been and must be constantly deteriorating to the minds and souls of himself and his associates. Away from all laws, and refined habits of living; away from the society of religious, modest, and accomplished women; always surrounded by savage scenes, and forced to cultivate a taste for barbarous things—what had this life made of him? what was he to do with himself in the future?

Sick of trapping and hunting, with brief intervals of carousing, he felt himself to be. And then, even if he were not, the trade was no longer profitable enough to support him. What could he do? where could he go? He remembered his talk with Mrs. Whitman, that fair, tall, courteous, and dignified lady who had stirred in him longings to return to the civilized life of his native state. But he felt unfit for the society of such as she. Would he ever, could he ever attain to it now? He had promised her he might go over into Oregon and settle down. But could he settle down? Should he not starve at trying to do what other men, mechanics and farmers, do? And as to learning, he had none of it; there was no hope then of "living by his wits," as some men did—missionaries and artists and school teachers, some of whom he had met at the rendezvous. Heigho! to be checkmated in life at twenty-eight, that would never do.

At Fort Hall, on his return, he met two more missionaries and their wives going to Oregon, but these four did not affect him pleasantly; he had no mind to go with them. Instead, he set out on what proved to be his last trapping expedition, with a Frenchman, named Mattileau.

They visited the old trapping grounds on Pierre's Fork, Lewis' Lake, Jackson's River, Jackson's Hole, Lewis River and Salt River: but beaver were scarce; and it was with a feeling of relief that, on returning by way of Bear River, Meek heard from a Frenchman whom he met there, that he was wanted at Fort Hall, by his friend Newell, who had something to propose to him.

CHAPTER XXI.

1840. When Meek arrived at Fort Hall, where Newell
was awaiting him, he found that the latter had there the
two wagons which Dr. Whitman had left at the points on
the journey where further transportation by their means
had been pronounced impossible. The Doctor's idea of
finding a passable wagon-road over the lava plains and
the heavily timbered mountains lying between Fort Hall
and the Columbia River, seemed to Newell not so wild a
one as it was generally pronounced to be in the mountains. At all events, he was prepared to undertake the
journey. The wagons were put in traveling order, and
horses and mules purchased for the expedition.

"Come," said Newell to Meek, "we are done with this
life in the mountains—done with wading in beaver-dams,
and freezing or starving alternately—done with Indian
trading and Indian fighting. The fur trade is dead in the
Rocky Mountains, and it is no place for us now, if ever it
was. We are young yet, and have life before us. We
cannot waste it here ; we cannot or will not return to the
States. Let us go down to the Wallamet and take farms.
There is already quite a settlement there made by the
Methodist Mission and the Hudson's Bay Company's retired servants.

"I have had some talk with the Americans who have
gone down there, and the talk is that the country is going
to be settled up by our people, and that the Hudson's

Bay Company are not going to rule this country much longer. What do you say, Meek? Shall we turn American settlers?"

"I'll go where you do, Newell. What suits you suits me."

"I thought you'd say so, and that's why I sent for you, Meek. In my way of thinking, a white man is a little better than a Canadian Frenchman. I'll be —— if I'll hang 'round a post of the Hudson's Bay Company. So you'll go?"

"I reckon I will! What have you got for me to do? _I_ haven't got anything to begin with but a wife and baby!"

"Well, you can drive one of the wagons, and take your family and traps along. Nicholas will drive the other, and I'll play leader, and look after the train. Craig will go also, so we shall be quite a party, with what strays we shall be sure to pick up."

Thus it was settled. Thus Oregon began to receive her first real emigrants, who were neither fur-traders nor missionaries, but true frontiersmen — border-men. The training which the mountain-men had received in the service of the fur companies admirably fitted them to be, what afterwards they became, a valuable and indispensable element in the society of that country in whose peculiar history they played an important part. But we must not anticipate their acts before we have witnessed their gradual transformation from lawless rangers of the wilderness, to law-abiding and even law-making and law-executing citizens of an isolated territory.

In order to understand the condition of things in the Wallamet Valley, or Lower Columbia country, it will be necessary to revert to the earliest history of that territory, as sketched in the first chapter of this book. A history

of the fur companies is a history of Oregon up to the
year 1834, so far as the occupation of the country was
concerned.   But its political history was begun long before—from the time (May 11th, 1792) when the captain
of a New England coasting and fur-trading vessel entered
the great " River of the West," which nations had been
looking for for a hundred years.   At the very time when
the inquisitive Yankee was heading his little vessel through
the white line of breakers at the mouth of the long-sought
river, a British exploring expedition was scanning the
shore between it and the Straits of Fuca, having wisely
declared its scientific opinion that there was no such river
on that coast.   Vancouver, the chief of that expedition,
so assured the Yankee trader, whose views did not agree
with his own : and, Yankee-like, the trader turned back
to satisfy himself.

A bold and lucky man was Captain Gray of the ship
Columbia.   No explorer he—only an adventurous and,
withal, a prudent trader, with an eye to the main chance;
emulous, too, perhaps, of a little glory!   It is impossible
to conceive how he could have done this thing calmly.
We think his stout heart must have shivered somewhat,
both with anticipation and dread, as he ran for the " opening," and plunged into the frightful tumult—straight
through the proper channel, thank God! and sailed out
on to the bosom of that beautiful bay, twenty-five miles
by six, which the great river forms at its mouth.

We trust the morning was fine : for then Captain Gray
must have beheld a sight which a discoverer should remember for a lifetime.   This magnificent bay, surrounded
by lofty hills, clad thick with noble forests of fir, and
fretted along its margin with spurs of the highlands, forming other smaller bays and coves, into which ran streams
whose valleys were hidden among the hills.   From beyond

the farthest point, whose dark ridge jutted across this inland sea, flowed down the deep, broad river, whose course and origin was still a magnificent mystery, but which indicated by its volume that it drained a mighty region of probable great fertility and natural wealth. Perhaps Captain Gray did not fully realize the importance of his discovery. If the day was fine, with a blue sky, and the purple shadows lying in among the hills, with smooth water before him and the foamy breakers behind — *if* he felt what his discovery was, in point of importance, to the world, he was a proud and happy man, and enjoyed the reward of his daring.

The only testimony on that head is the simple entry on his log-book, telling us that he had named the river " *Columbia's River*," — with an apostrophe, that tiny point intimating much. This was one ground of the American claim, though Vancouver, after Gray had reported his success to him, sent a lieutenant to explore the river, and then claimed the discovery for England ! The next claim of the United States upon the Oregon territory was by virtue of the Florida treaty and the Louisiana purchase. These, and the general one of natural boundaries, England contested also. Hence the treaty of joint occupancy for a term of ten years, renewable, unless one of the parties to it gave a twelve-month's notice of intention to withdraw. Meantime this question of territorial claims hung over the national head like the sword suspended by a hair, which statesmen delight in referring to. We did not dare to say Oregon was ours, because we were afraid England would make war on us; and England did not dare say Oregon was hers, for the same reason. Therefore "joint-occupancy" was the polite word with which statesmen glossed over the fact that Great Britain actually possessed the country through the monopoly of the Hudson's Bay Company. That company had a good thing so long as the government of Great Britain prevented any outbreak, by simply renewing the treaty every ten years. Their manner of doing business was such as to prevent any less powerful corporation from interfering with them, while individual enterprise was sure to be crushed at the start.

Meanwhile the Yankee nation, some members of which at one time had vessels trading on the northwest coast, became uneasy at this state of affairs. Since the war of 1812 and the failure of Astor's expedition, their vessels had been driven off that coast, or had been fain to content themselves with picking up cargoes of hides and tallow from the Indian missions in California. It was not in Yankee nature to stand this foreign monopoly. As if they had not land enough on the eastern side of the Rocky Mountains, they began to expatiate on the beauties and excellencies of the country which lay beyond.

As early as 1817, even before the obnoxious Convention, a Bostonian school teacher, named Hall J. Kelly, had conceived the idea of colonizing the Oregon territory. He labored to impress others with the views which he held, and formed many emigration schemes, besides memorializing Congress on the subject, as well as the legislature of his own State. Finally, in 1831, he succeeded in getting the Legislature of Massachusetts to pass an act incorporating the "*American Society for Encouraging the Settlement of the Oregon Territory*," and a large number of persons became members. But the fur companies, American as well as British, steadily discouraged all efforts which were directed towards the settlement of the coveted territory, so that nothing was accomplished by the above named society ; and at length, in 1832, Kelly sent out two young men only, for the country west of the

Rocky Mountains. On arriving at Fort Vancouver they found the same difficulties in their way which prevented Wyeth and Bonneville from succeeding. In truth, their case was worse, for there was nothing for them to do, and if there had been, they would not have been permitted to do it, except in the service of the Hudson's Bay Company. For the first winter, one of them, a Mr. Ball, was employed as teacher of the half-breed children at the Fort. The following spring, Ball and his companion, Tibbits, began farming. This, however, proving unprofitable business in a country where there was no market, Ball returned to the States, and Tibbits remained to teach the school at Fort Vancouver. In the meantime, Kelly was trying to organize an expedition to proceed by sea. This also failed to be successful, through the inaction of the general government and the antagonism of the fur companies. Persisting in his plan of colonizing Oregon and opening commerce on the west coast, Kelly went to Mexico and endeavored to open a trade between that country and Oregon. But the Mexican revenue officers remorselessly robbed him of a large share of the goods he was taking to Oregon, so that by the time he arrived at Fort Vancouver there was little or nothing left of his stock in trade, while he was broken down in health and spirits. Like Wyeth, he returned home without having been able to realize any one of his many schemes of profit.

Such was the experience of all who in that early day attempted to oppose themselves to the Hudson's Bay Company. For this reason all these adventurers execrated its influence, and denounced everything British. The truth was, however, that the case would have been just the same had it been an American company which occupied the Columbia River, so far as their fortunes

were concerned. Any company, to succeed in that far
off wilderness country, must have done just as the English company did do. To enter into competition among
the Indians was to ruin the trade for all concerned, to induce misunderstandings with the savages, and finally to
devastate, instead of settling up, the country. This the
Hudson's Bay Company understood, and they would
rather lose money by trying to keep other traders out,
than to make it for a little while by competing with
them.

But "man proposes and God disposes." In 1834, the
Methodist Episcopal Board of Missions sent out four missionaries to labor among the Indians. These were two
preachers, the Rev. Messrs. Jason and Daniel Lee, and
two lay members, Cyrus Shepard and P. L. Edwards.
These gentlemen were liberally furnished with all the
necessaries and comforts of life by the Board, in addition
to which they received the kindest attentions and consideration from the officers of the Hudson's Bay Company at
Vancouver. Their vessel, the *May Dacre*, Captain Lambert, had arrived safely in the river with the mission
goods. The gentlemen at Vancouver encouraged their
enterprise, and advised them to settle in the Wallamet
valley, the most fertile tract of country west of the Rocky
Mountains. Being missionaries, nothing was to be feared
from them in the way of trade. The Wallamet valley
was a good country for the mission—at the same time it
was south of the Columbia River. This latter consideration was not an unimportant one with the Hudson's Bay
Company, it being understood among those in the confidence of the British government, that in case the Oregon
territory had to be divided with the United States, the
Columbia River would probably be made the northern
boundary of the American possessions. The missionaries

being content to settle south of the Columbia, all went well.

These three points were what the Hudson's Bay Company must insist upon, so far as, under the terms of the treaty, they could do : first, that the Americans occupying the country jointly with them, should not attempt to trade with the Indians; secondly, that they should confine themselves to agricultural pursuits and missionary labor ; and thirdly, that the settlers should keep to the south side of the Columbia. Not that the servants of the Hudson's Bay Company confined themselves to the north side of this probable boundary ; on the contrary, the retired servants of that company had begun to settle in the Wallamet valley in 1831.

We have said that the political history of Oregon began near the close of the last century. As early as the winter of 1820–21, the first proposition was made in Congress for the occupation and settlement of the Columbia River.

"It * was made by Dr. Floyd, a representative from Virginia, a man of ability, and strongly imbued with western feelings, from a long residence in Kentucky. It required both energy and courage to embrace a subject which seemed likely to bring more ridicule than credit to its advocate. He took up the idea from some essays of Mr. Benton's, which had been published the year previous. He had also made the acquaintance of Mr. Russell Farnham and Mr. Ramsey Crooks, who had been in the employment of Astor in founding the colony at Astoria. He resolved to bring forward the question of occupation, and did so. He moved for a select committee to consider and report upon the subject. The committee was granted by the House, more through courtesy to a respected member, than with any view to business results. It was a committee of three, himself chairman according to a parliamentary rule, and Thomas Metcalf of Kentucky, and Thomas V. Swearingen of Virginia, both, like himself, ardent men, and strong in western feeling. They reported a bill within six days after the committee was raised, " to authorize the occupation of the Columbia River, and to regulate trade and intercourse with the Indian tribes thereon." In their report they represented the advantages of the fur trade, the Asiatic trade, and the preservation of our own territory. Nothing

---

* From *Benton's Thirty Years in Congress.*

further was done at that session, but enough had been said to awaken public attention, and the facts set forth in the report made a lodgement in the public mind."

At a subsequent session, both Floyd and Benton pursued the subject with ardor, and the latter dwelt strongly on the danger of a contest with Great Britain, to whom had been granted joint occupancy, and who had already taken possession ; and reminded the Government " that a vigorous effort of policy, and perhaps of arms, might be necessary to break her hold." Unauthorized or individual occupation was intimated as a consequence of government neglect, and what has since taken place was foreshadowed in the following sentence : " Mere adventurers may enter upon it, as Æneus entered upon the Tiber, and as our forefathers came upon the Potomac, the Delaware, and the Hudson, and renew the phenomenon of individuals laying the foundations of future empire." He predicted the intercourse with China and Japan which has since followed, and prophesied that the overflowing population of those countries would seek our Pacific shores.

Mr. Benton said, when the subject of the joint occupation treaty was before the House in 1825 :—

" The claim of Great Britain is nothing but a naked pretension, founded on the double prospect of benefitting herself and injuring the United States. The fur-trader, Sir Alexander McKenzie, is at the bottom of this policy. Failing in his attempt to explore the Columbia River in 1793, he nevertheless urged upon the British government the advantages of taking it to herself, and of expelling the Americans from the whole region west of the Rocky Mountains. He recommended that the Hudson's Bay and Northwest companies should be united, and they have been united. He proposed to extend the fur trade to the Pacific Ocean, and it has been so extended. He proposed that a chain of trading posts should be formed through the continent, from sea to sea, and it has been formed. He recommended that no boundary line should be formed which did not give the Columbia River to the British, and the British Ministry declare that none other shall be formed. He proposed to obtain the command of the fur trade from latitude 45° North, and they have it, even to the Mandan villages and the neighborhood of Council Bluffs. He recommended the expulsion of the American traders from the whole region west of the Rocky Mountains, and they are expelled from it."

In addition to the influence of the fur companies, political considerations also governed Great Britain in acquiring possession of the Northwest coast, and the command of the Pacific Ocean.

In a Pacific Railroad speech which Mr. Benton made at Brunswick, Mo., thirty years later, there occurs this paragraph:

"I caught the idea (of a Pacific Railroad) from Mr. Jefferson, who in his message to Congress proposing the expedition of Lewis and Clarke, presented the commercial communication as the leading object, and the one which gave Congress the Constitutional jurisdiction in the case; and the extension of geographical science as the incident to the pursuit of that main object. That was before we acquired Oregon, or set up any claim to territory on the Pacific Ocean."

From these extracts it will appear that while the fur Companies were contending for the occupation of the Orégon territory, and had finally parceled it off as we have already seen,—the American companies keeping in and about the Rocky Mountains, and the Hudson's Bay Company excluding them from the country west of the Blue Mountains, while that which laid between had been contested ground,—two governments were equally active and studious in their efforts to substantiate their claims.

But it was not, after all, either the fur companies or the general government which directed the entering wedge in the settlement of the much-talked-of claims. It was the missionary settlements which effected this.

There was nothing in the character of the Christian Missionary's labor which the Hudson's Bay Company could possibly object to without a palpable violation of the

THE MISSIONARY
WEDGE.

Convention of 1818. Therefore, although the Methodist mission in the Wallamet Valley received a large accession to its numbers in 1837, they were as kindly welcomed as had been those of 1834; and also those Presbyterian missionaries of 1836, who had settled in the "upper country."

Not an immigrant entered Oregon in that day who did not proceed at once to Vancouver: nor was there one, in any way deserving, who did not meet with the most liberal and hospitable treatment. Neither was this hospitality a trifling benefit; to the weary traveler just arrived from a long and most fatiguing journey, it was extremely welcome and refreshing. At Vancouver was the only society, and the only luxurious living to be enjoyed on the whole Northwest coast.

At the head of the first was Dr. John McLaughlin, already mentioned as the Chief Factor, and Deputy Governor of the Hudson's Bay Company in Oregon, and all the Northwest. He was of Scotch origin, and Canadian birth, a gentleman bred, with a character of the highest integrity, to which were united justice and humanity. His position as head of the Hudson's Bay Company's affairs, was no enviable one during that period of Oregon history which followed the advent of Americans in the Wallamet Valley. Himself a British subject, and a representative of that powerful corporation which bent the British Government to its will, he was bound to execute its commands when they did not conflict too strongly with his consciousness of right and justice. And while he was willing and anxious to do his duty towards the company he served, circumstances arose, and occasions grew out of those circumstances which tried his loyalty, integrity, and humanity, to the utmost. One course, however, he steadily pursued, which was that of a beneficent friend toward all who deserved his friendship, and many who did not, in all private and personal matters. Hence of the many who went to Vancouver, all were kindly received; and every man of any intelligence or position among the Americans was most hospitably treated, not only by himself but by all the factors, traders, and clerks of the establishment. It often happened in the early days of Oregon that some of the most prominent Americans were not decently clad, through their inability to procure clothing suitable to their position. But the seat of honor at the Chief Factor's table was reserved with as much punctiliousness for these ragged pioneers, as if they had come clad in beautiful raiment. Nor were finger bowls and napkins withheld from the use of soiled and blackened pioneer fingers. Wine, and good cheer, and cultivated conversation, were freely offered and enjoyed. There was nothing in the line of his duty which prevented Dr. McLaughlin from exercising private hospitality and gentlemanly courtesy toward the Americans. A man of religious feeling himself, he respected the motive which was presumed to actuate the missionaries. To be sure, he had been educated in the Roman Catholic doctrines; but yet he was not unwilling that the Protestants should entertain and disseminate their own religious views. As a representative of the Hudson's Bay Company he had one duty to execute: as a Christian gentleman, another. That these separate duties sometimes conflicted will appear in the course of this narrative. So far, however, as encouraging the missionaries in their undertakings was concerned, he did not hold them to be conflicting; not, at all events, until they undeceived him, by entering upon secular enterprises.

As has been stated, the Methodist mission settlement was reinforced in 1837, by the arrival of about twenty persons, among whom were several ladies, and a few children. These, like those preceding them, were first entertained at Fort Vancouver before proceeding to the mission, which was between fifty and sixty miles up the Wallamet, in the heart of that delightful valley.   These persons came by a sailing vessel around Cape Horn, bringing with them supplies for the mission.

In the two following years there were about a dozen missionary arrivals overland, all of whom tarried a short time at the American Company's rendezvous, as before related.   These were some of them designed for the upper country, but most of them soon settled in the Wallamet valley.

During these years, between 1834 and 1840, there had drifted into the valley various persons from California, the Rocky Mountains, and from the vessels which sometimes appeared in the Columbia; until at the time when Newell and Meek resolved to quit the mountains, the American settlers numbered nearly one hundred, men, women, and children.   Of these, about thirty belonged to the missions; the remainder were mountain-men, sailors, and adventurers.   The mountain-men, most of them, had native wives. Besides the Americans there were sixty Canadian Frenchmen, who had been retired upon farms by the Hudson's Bay Company; and who would probably have occupied these farms so long as the H. B. Company should have continued to do business in Oregon.

With the American mountain-men it was, however, different.   It was the fact of the mission having been established there, with all the means and appliances of a settlement independent of the H. B. Company, which induced them to remain and settle also upon farms. They looked to the Mission to become to them, what Fort Vancouver was to the Canadians, a supply station; an expectation which was only half fulfilled, as will be seen hereafter.

The Missionaries themselves had been compelled to depend upon Fort Vancouver for many things, and among others for cattle, and milch cows. It was a matter of serious complaint among the American settlers that the H. B. Company would sell none of their stock. Lend it they would; *sell* it they would not. This effort on the part of the company to retain a monopoly in so important an element of civilized comfort as oxen, beef-cattle, and milch cows, created much ill feeling for a time, as it cramped the means of productive labor excessively.

But in 1837 there appeared in the Columbia river the U. S. Brig *Loriot*, Captain Slocum, on an errand of observation. Upon learning from the settlers that no cattle could be procured in Oregon, Captain Slocum encouraged a plan which was then on foot, of sending to California for a supply of Spanish stock. To further this enterprise he contributed fifteen dollars, and offered a free passage to such persons as wished to go to California on this errand. The way being thus opened, a meeting of the settlers was held, and shares taken in what was called the "California Cattle Company." Whatever may have been the feelings of the H. B. Company, they offered no direct opposition: on the contrary, Dr. Mc Laughlin took several shares in the Cattle Company, on his own account. The expedition was headed by Mr. P. L. Edwards of the Methodist mission, and Mr. Ewing Young of the American settlement. Young was of the same class as the mountain-men, and had in fact been a trader at Taos in New Mexico; after which he had led a hunting and trapping party through California; and had accompanied Kelly in his journey to Oregon in 1835. He was just the man to conduct an expedition such as this one; though the Mission thought it necessary to send Mr. Edwards along to look out for the funds of the company. The expedition set sail in January, and returned by land in the autumn, with several hundred head of cattle; having met with some loss of stock, by an attack from the Rogue River Indians, or Shastas,—the same tribe who attacked Smith's party in 1829. The cattle were then divided up among the settlers according to the shares previously taken; those who went to California receiving pay for their services out of the herd. This importation of cattle placed the American colony, for such it now really was, on a more independent footing, besides furnishing a means for the rapid acquisition of wealth.

The distribution of settlers was as follows: the mission proper, about fifty-two miles above the mouth of the Wallamet; the Canadian settlement ten or twelve miles below the mission, and Wallamet Falls, or as it afterwards was called, Oregon City. At this latter place Dr. McLaughlin, as early as 1829, had begun the erection of a mill, and had continued to make improvements from time to time, up to 1840, when some members of the Mission applied to him for permission to erect a building for mission purposes upon the land claimed and improved by the Doctor. This request was granted, together with another for the use of some timbers already squared for building, which had been intended for the mill. At the same time that Dr. McLaughlin made these generous concessions to the mission gentlemen, he notified them that he intended to claim the land already improved by him, so soon as the boundary line was drawn by a proper survey.

CHAPTER XXII.

WHEN it was settled that Newell and Meek were to go to the Wallamet, they lost no time in dallying, but packed the wagons with whatever they possessed in the way of worldly goods, topped them with their Nez Perce wives and half-breed children, and started for Walla-Walla, accompanied by Craig, another mountain-man, and either followed or accompanied by several others. Meek drove a five-in-hand team of four horses and one mule. Nicholas drove the other team of four horses, and Newell, who owned the train, was mounted as leader.

The journey was no easy one, extending as it did over immense plains of lava, round impassable canyons, over rapid unbridged rivers, and over mountains hitherto believed to be only passable for pack trains. The honor which has heretofore been accorded to the Presbyterian missionaries solely, of opening a wagon road from the Rocky Mountains to the Columbia River, should in justice be divided with these two mountaineers, who accomplished the most difficult part of this difficult journey.

Arrived at Fort Boise, a post of the Hudson's Bay Company, the little caravan stopped for a few days to rest and recruit their animals. With the usual courtesy of that Company, Mr. Payette, the trader in charge, offered Newell quarters in the fort, as leader of his party. To Meek and Craig who were encamped outside, he sent a piece of sturgeon with his compliments, which our incipient Ore-

gonians sent back again with *their* compliments. No
Hudson's Bay distinctions of rank for them! No, indeed!
The moment that an American commenced to think of
himself as a settler on the most remote corner of American soil, that moment, as if by instinct, he began to defend
and support his republicanism.

After a few days' rest, the party went on, encountering,
as might be expected, much difficulty and toil, but arriving
safely after a reasonable time at the Columbia River, at
the junction of the Umatilla. Here the wagons and stock
were crossed over, and the party proceeded directly to
Dr. Whitman's mission at Waiilatpu. Dr. Whitman gave
them a friendly reception; killing for them, if not the fat-
ted calf, the fattest hog he had; telling Meek at the same
time that " fat pork was good for preachers," referring to
Meek's missionary labors among the Nez Perces.

During the three years since the commencement of the
mission at Waiilatpu considerable advancement had been
made in the progress of civilization among the Cayuses.
Quite a number of Indian children were domesticated with
Mrs. Whitman, who were rapidly acquiring a knowledge
of housekeeping, sewing, reading, and writing, and farm
labor. With Mrs. Whitman, for whom Meek still entertained great admiration and respect, he resolved to leave
his little girl, Helen Mar; the fruit of his connexion with
the Nez Perce woman who persisted in abandoning him in
the mountains, as already related. Having thus made
provision for the proper instruction of his daughter, and
conferred with the Doctor on the condition of the American settlers in Oregon—the Doctor being an ardent
American—Meek and his associates started once more for
the Wallamet.

At Walla-Walla Newell decided to leave the wagons,
the weather having become so rainy and disagreeable as

to make it doubtful about getting them over the Cascade Mountains that fall. Accordingly the goods were transferred to pack-horses for the remainder of the journey. In the following year, however, one of the wagons was brought down by Newell, and taken to the plains on the Tualatin River, being the first vehicle of the kind in the Wallamet Valley.

On arriving at the Dalles of the Columbia, our mountain men found that a mission had been established at that place for the conversion of those inconscionable thieves, the Wish-ram Indians, renowned in Indian history for their acquisitiveness. This mission was under the charge of Daniel Lee and a Mr. Perkins, and was an offshoot of the Methodist Mission in the Wallamet Valley. These gentlemen having found the benighted condition of the Indians to exceed their powers of enlightment in any ordinary way, were having recourse to extraordinary efforts, and were carrying on what is commonly termed a *revival;* though what piety there was in the hearts of these savages to be revived, it would be difficult to determine. However, they doubtless hoped so to wrestle with God themselves, as to compel a blessing upon their labors.

The Indians indeed were not averse to prayer. They could pray willingly and sincerely enough when they could hope for a speedy and actual material answer to their prayers. And it was for that, and that only, that they importuned the Christian's God. Finding that their prayers were not answered according to their desire, it at length became difficult to persuade them to pray at all. Sometimes, it is true, they succeeded in deluding the missionaries with the belief that they were really converted, for a time. One of these most hopeful converts at the Dalles mission, being in want of a shirt and capote, volunteered to "pray for a whole year," if Mr. Lee would furnish him with these truly desirable articles.

It is no wonder that with such hopeless material to work
upon the Dalles missionaries withdrew from them a portion
of their zeal, and bestowed it, where it was quite as much
needed, upon any "stray mountain-man" who chanced to
be entertained "within their gates." Newell's party,
among others, received the well-meant, but not always
well-received or appreciated attentions of these gentlemen.
The American mountaineer was not likely to be suddenly
surprised into praying in earnest; and he generally had
too much real reverence to be found making a jest in the
form of a mocking prayer.

Not so scrupulous, however, was Jandreau, a lively
French Canadian, who was traveling in company with the
Americans. On being repeatedly importuned to pray,
with that tireless zeal which distinguishes the Methodist
preacher above all others, Jandreau appeared suddenly to
be smitten with a consciousness of his guilt, and kneeling
in the midst of the 'meeting,' began with clasped hands
and upturned eyes to pour forth a perfect torrent of words.
With wonderful dramatic power he appeared to confess,
to supplicate, to agonize, in idiomatic French. His tears
and ejaculations touched the hearts of the missionaries,
and filled them with gladness. They too ejaculated and
wept, with frequently uttered "Amens" and "hallelujahs,"
until the scene became highly dramatic and exciting. In
the midst of this grand tableau, when the enthusiasm was
at its height, Jandreau suddenly ceased and rose to his feet,
while an irrepressible outburst of laughter from his associates aroused the astonished missionaries to a partial comprehension of the fact that they had been made the subjects
of a practical joke, though they never knew to exactly
how great an extent.

The mischievous Frenchman had only recited with truly
artistic power, and with such variations as the situation

suggested, one of the most wonderful and effective tales from the *Arabian Nights Entertainment*, with which he was wont to delight and amuse his comrades beside the winter camp-fire!

But Jandreau was called to account when he arrived at Vancouver. Dr. McLaughlin had heard the story from some of the party, and resolved to punish the man's irreverence, at the same time that he gave himself a bit of amusement. Sending for the Rev. Father Blanchet, who was then resident at Vancouver, he informed him of the circumstance, and together they arranged Jandreau's punishment. He was ordered to appear in their united presence, and make a true statement of the affair. Jandreau confessed that he had done what he was accused of doing—made a mock of prayer, and told a tale instead of offering a supplication. He was then ordered by the Rev. Father to rehearse the scene exactly as it occurred, in order that he might judge of the amount of his guilt, and apportion him his punishment.

Trembling and abashed, poor Jandreau fell upon his knees and began the recital with much trepidation. But as he proceeded he warmed with the subject, his dramatic instinct asserted itself, tears streamed, and voice and eyes supplicated, until this second representation threatened to outdo the first. With outward gravity and inward mirth his two solemn judges listened to the close, and when Jandreau rose quite exhausted from his knees, Father Blanchet hastily dismissed him with an admonition and a light penance. As the door of Dr. McLaughlin's office closed behind him, not only the Doctor, but Father Blanchet indulged in a burst of long restrained laughter at the comical absurdities of this impious Frenchman.

To return to our immigrants. On leaving the Dalles they proceeded on down the south side of the river as far as practicable, or opposite to the Wind Mountain. At this point the Indians assisted to cross them over to the north side, when they again made their way along the river as far as *Tea Prairie* above Vancouver. The weather was execrable, with a pouring rain, and sky of dismal gray; December being already far advanced. Our travelers were not in the best of humors: indeed a saint-like amiability is seldom found in conjunction with rain, mud, fatigue, and an empty stomach. Some ill-natured suspicions were uttered to the effect that the Indians who were assisting to cross the party at this point, had stolen some ropes that were missing.

Upon this dishonorable insinuation the Indian heart was fired, and a fight became imminent. This undesirable climax to emigrant woes was however averted by an attack upon the indignant natives with firebrands, when they prudently retired, leaving the travelers to pursue their way in peace. It was on Sunday that the weary, dirty, hungry little procession arrived at a place on the Wallamet River where the present town of Milwaukie is situated, and found here two missionaries, the Rev. Messrs. Waller and Beers, who were preaching to the Indians.

Meek immediately applied to Mr. Waller for some provisions, and received for answer that it was "Sunday." Mr. Waller, however, on being assured that it was no more agreeable starving on Sunday than a week-day, finally allowed the immigrants to have a peck of small potatoes. But as a party of several persons could not long subsist on so short allowance, and as there did not seem to be any encouragement to expect more from the missionaries, there was no course left to be pursued but to make an appeal to Fort Vancouver.

To Fort Vancouver then, Newell went the next day, and returned on the following one with some dried salmon, tea, sugar, and sea-bread.   It was not quite what the mountain-men could have wished, this dependence on the Hudson's Bay Company for food, and did not quite agree with what they had said when their hearts were big in the mountains.   Being patriotic on a full stomach is easy compared to being the same thing on an empty one; a truth which became more and more apparent as the winter progressed, and the new settlers found that if they would eat they must ask food of some person or persons outside of the Methodist Mission.   And outside of that there was in all the country only the Hudson's Bay Company, and a few mountain-men like themselves, who had brought nothing into the country, and could get nothing out of it at present.

There was but short time in which to consider what was to be done.   Newell and Meek went to Wallamet Falls, the day after Newell's return from Vancouver, and there met an old comrade, Doughty, who was looking for a place to locate.   The three made their camp together on the west side of the river, on a hill overlooking the Falls.   While in camp they were joined by two other Rocky Mountain men, Wilkins and Ebbarts, who were also looking for a place to settle in.   There were now six of the Rocky Mountain men together; and they resolved to push out into the plains to the west of them, and see what could be done in the matter of selecting homes.

As for our hero, we fear we cannot say much of him here which would serve to render him heroic in criticising Yankee eyes.   He was a mountain-man, and *that only*. He had neither book learning, nor a trade, nor any knowledge of the simplest affairs appertaining to the ordinary ways of getting a living.   He had only his strong hands, and a heart naturally stout and light.

His friend Newell had the advantage of him in several

particulars. He had rather more book-knowledge, more business experience, and also more means. With these advantages he became a sort of "Booshway" among his old comrades, who consented to follow his lead in the important movement about to be made, and settle in the Tualatin Plains should he decide to do so.

Accordingly camp was raised, and the party proceeded to the Plains, where they arrived on Christmas, and went into camp again. The hardships of mountain life were light compared to the hardships of this winter. For in the mountains, when the individual's resources were exhausted, there was always the Company to go to, which was practically inexhaustible. Should it be necessary, the Company was always willing to become the creditor of a good mountain-man. And the debtor gave himself no uneasiness, because he knew that if he lived he could discharge his indebtedness. But everything was different now. There was no way of paying debts, even if there had been a company willing to give them credit, which there was not, at least among Americans. Hard times they had seen in the mountains; harder times they were likely to see in the valley; indeed were already experiencing.

Instead of fat buffalo meat, antelope, and mountain mutton, which made the plenty of a camp on Powder River, our carniverous hunters were reduced to eating daily a little boiled wheat. In this extremity, Meek went on an expedition of discovery across the highlands that border the Lower Wallamet, and found on Wappatoo (now Sauvis) Island, a Mr. and Mrs. Baldra living, who were in the service of the Hudson's Bay Company, and drew rations from them. With great kindness they divided the provisions on hand, furnishing him with dried salmon and sea-bread, to which he added ducks and swans procured from the Indians. Poor and scanty as was the supply thus obtained, it was, after boiled wheat, comparative luxury while it lasted.

1841. The winter proved a very disagreeable one. Considerable snow fell early, and went off with heavy rains, flooding the whole country. The little camp on the Tualatin Plains had no defence from the weather better than Indian lodges, and one small cabin built by Doughty on a former visit to the Plains ; for Doughty had been one of the first of the mountain-men to come to the Wallamet on the breaking up of the fur companies. Indian lodges, or no lodges at all, were what the men were used to ; but in the dryer climate of the Rocky Mountains it had not seemed such a miserable life, as it now did, where, for months together, the ground was saturated with rain, while the air was constantly charged with vapor.

As for going anywhere, or doing anything, either were equally impossible. No roads, the streams all swollen and out of banks, the rains incessant, there was nothing for them but to remain in camp and wait for the return of spring. When at last the rainy season was over, and the sun shining once more, most of the mountain-men in the Tualatin Plains camp took land-claims and set to work improving them. Of those who began farming that spring, were Newell, Doughty, Wilkins, and Walker. These obtained seed-wheat from the Hudson's Bay Company, also such farming implements as they must have, and even oxen to draw the plow through the strong prairie sod. The wheat was to be returned to the company—the cattle also ; and the farming implements paid for whenever the debtor became able. This was certainly liberal conduct on the part of a company generally understood to be opposed to American settlement.

19

CHAPTER XXIII.

We find, according to their own account, that about 1838–9, "Jason Lee was lecturing in New England, on the Oregon Missions, and creating considerable zeal for the cause. As the result of his labors before the Board and elsewhere, $40,000 were collected for missionary purposes, and thirty-six additional assistants, viz: five missionaries, one physician, six mechanics, four farmers, one steward, four female teachers, with millers and others, were sent out to strengthen the mission, besides a saw mill, grist mill, agricultural and mechanical tools. This last reinforcement arrived in 1840, some months earlier than the mountain-men. A new mission was projected about ten miles above the old one, on the present site of Salem, the capital of Oregon.

Here the mills were to be erected, a new school building put up, and other substantial improvements carried on. There was no poverty among the members of the mission; on the contrary, according to Commodore Wilkes, there was wastefulness and reprehensible neglect of the agricultural and mechanical tools so generously furnished by the Board at home, who believed the mission to be doing a good work. So far, however, from benefitting the Indians, they were an actual injury to them. The sudden and absolute change of habits which the Indian students were compelled to make did not agree with them. The first breaking up of the ground for making

farms caused malaria, and induced much sickness among
them.   Many had died, and many others had gone back
to their former habits.   Much vice and disease also prevailed among the natives, which had been introduced by
deserting sailors and other profligate adventurers.   The
Indians could not be made to comprehend the spiritual
meaning of religion, and seeing among the whites themselves so frequent violations of what was represented to
be their belief, they ceased to regard their teachings,
until their moral condition became worse in their half-
civilized condition than it had been in their savage state.
The mission school had degenerated to such a mere pre-
tense of a school that in 1841, when Wilkes visited the
mission, he was not permitted to see it.

Hence, at the time when other settlers began to gather
into Oregon, the Methodist Mission was such by courtesy
only, and not in fact; and of this the Hudson's Bay Company and the mountain-men were perfectly aware.   This
was a colony, an American colony, stolen in under the
very nose of the Hudson's Bay Company, claiming their
friendship and their services on account of their holy calling.   And if the home Board was deceived, what mat-
tered it? "they builded better than they knew:" they
furnished the means by which an American colony established itself on Oregon soil, and being once established,
it could not be dislodged.

It is no part of the writer's design to say that the event
which happened was foreseen.   It was the logical result
of unforeseen circumstances.   A few religious enthusiasts
had undertaken what they could not perform—the Christianizing of a low order of savages.   They found themselves in a distant and beautiful country, where it was
easier to remain than to return.   Homes were growing
up around them; children were born here; it was a mild

and salubrious climate : why should they desire to quit it ? As for the mission property, had it not been intended to benefit them ? why should they relinquish it ? Let the future take care of itself.

All this is not so very difficult to understand. What was ill-looking and hard to be comprehended was the reluctance with which they ever assisted any other American settlers. It would seem natural that, in their isolated situation, surrounded by Indians, and subject most completely to the will of the anti-American Hudson's Bay Company, they should ardently desire an influx of their own countrymen, even at a considerable expense to themselves; for they were exceeding jealous of the British influence, and of the designs of the British government. Already had they memorialized Congress that they had "settled themselves in said Territory, under the belief that it was a part of the public domain of said States, (United States,) and that they might rely upon the government thereof for the blessings of free institutions and the protection of its arms."

They had also intimated that they had reason not only to fear the Indians, but "also others that would do them harm," meaning the Hudson's Bay Company. In this early memorial they set forth, in glowing colors, the natural advantages and abundant resources of the Territory, and warned the Government of the intention of the English to claim that portion of it, at least, which laid north of the Columbia River, and closed by respectfully asking for the "civil institutions of the American Republic."

In the main the memorial was correct enough, as the Government was aware. It was, however, ungenerous and *ungrateful* toward the Hudson's Bay Company, or its representative, Dr. McLaughlin, who certainly had done nothing but good to themselves and their country-

men. Unless, indeed, they considered it evil for him to
be faithful to the interests of the Company, and the British Government, as they meant to be to the interests of
their own.

It was truly an unenviable position which Dr. McLaughlin held during those years of waiting for the settlement
of the boundary question. Even in his own particular
place and private domain he was not left at peace. For
at Vancouver there were two parties, the Patriots or
British, and the Philosophers or Liberals.* Of the latter
was Dr. McLaughlin, "who held that American principles
of legislation, in commercial and civil matters, were, generally speaking, just and humane; and from which even
British legislation derived some useful hints." It required,
what Dr. McLaughlin was, a man of unusual force of
character and goodness of heart, to preserve the peace in
Oregon as he did do.

Had he been what he was continually suspected and
accused of being, the enemy of American settlement and
settlers, it would have been an easy matter enough to have
got rid of them altogether. Instead of entertaining, helping, and succoring them on all occasions, if he had simply
let them quite alone they must have perished. No small
community like the Methodist Mission could have sustained
itself in Oregon without a government, without arms,
without a market, and surrounded as they were by twenty
thousand savages. It was Fort Vancouver which kept the
Indians quiet. It was the Hudson's Bay Company who
settled all difficulties with the savages, and who furnished
means of communication, transportation, and protection
at the same time. With unblushing selfishness the missionaries never ceased to accept and even solicit every benefit

* *Oregon Territory, By John Dunn* of the H. B. C.

the Company could bestow, at the same time they continually uttered their suspicions and charges against the Company's principal agent, who continued with wonderful
magnanimity to load them with his favors.

It was not altogether because Dr. McLaughlin was a
representative of the British influence in the country, that
the missionaries persisted in misconstruing his every action.
Quite as strong a reason was his sectarian belief. A
Roman Catholic was, in those days of religious prejudice,
something totally abhorrent in Protestant estimation. The
Oregon missionaries, neither Methodist nor Presbyterian,
could ever quite rid themselves of the notion that Dr.
McLaughlin was in some secret and mysterious manner
implicated in a design to overthrow Protestantism in Oregon, and by a sort of second St. Bartholomew's Eve, to
exterminate every man, woman, and child who professed
it. What especially confirmed their suspicions was the
fact that after the Protestant missionaries had been sometime settled in the country, the Doctor invited some priests
of his own church to do the same; having one stationed at
Vancouver, and another over the Canadian settlement at
Champoeg. Then, as might be expected, others followed,
and settled among the Indians in the Upper country.
That the multitude of doctrines afterwards created distrust
in the minds of the savages, there can be no doubt; but
then, could they not see that the Protestants differed
among themselves, and that the Catholics did not?

Besides the mission party, which was inimical to the
British influence, and even to the name of anything British,
there was also the American party, which was made up of
everybody American outside of the Mission. The mountain-men were antagonistic from long habit, from the custom of making war upon the Hudson's Bay Company,
which the leaders of the American Fur Companies incul-

cated during years of rivalry in the mountains. As for the few other adventurers then in Oregon, most of them had some personal quarrel with the H. B. Company's agents, or simply joined the American party from a sentiment of patriotism.

In the case of Ewing Young, for example: When he first came into the country from California, he was accompanied by Mr. Kelly, whose history has already been given. Besides Kelly, there were a number of sailors, deserters from vessels, and not having a very reputable appearance. This party traveled in company with the Hudson's Bay trading party through the most dangerous part of the country, accompanying them to Vancouver.

It so happened that the trader from California brought a letter to Dr. McLaughlin from the Spanish governor of California, warning him against Kelly and Young, saying that they had stolen horses. On this information, Dr. McLaughlin refused to have anything to do with Young and his associates, except Kelly, who being ill, was placed in a house at the fort, and nursed and fed through the winter, and finally sent to the Sandwich Islands in one of the Company's vessels.

In revenge for the slight put upon him by Dr. McLaughlin, Young and one of his associates, in the following year, started the erection of a distillery, with the intention of selling liquor to the Indians. But upon this movement the missionaries took alarm, and offered to pay Young the full value of his outlay if he would give up the business and undertake something else. To this Young and his partner consented on being properly petitioned by nearly all the white settlers in the country outside of the Hudson's Bay Company.

Shortly after this the Cattle Company was formed, and the mission gave Young something to do, by sending him to California for cattle, and as he received cattle for payment, and stock was immensely high in Oregon, he soon became a man of wealth and standing. The mission made much of him, because he was as it were, a brand snatched from the burning, and a good hater of the Hudson's Bay Company besides. In truth Mr. Young became a historical character by dying in the summer of 1841, and thereby causing to be held the first Primary Meeting of the People of Oregon. Having died possessed of considerable wealth, and no heirs appearing to claim it on the spot, his friends, after first prudently burying him, adjourned from the grave to the shade of a tree, and took prompt measures to "call a public meeting for the purpose of appointing officers for the government of the community, and *particularly to provide for the proper disposition of the estate of Ewing Young.*" The legend runs, that the state, that is to say the Mission, divided the property affectionately among themselves, and that afterwards there appeared a claimant who succeeded in regaining a portion; but that is neither here nor there in this narrative.

It is the writer's opinion that earthly perfection is far to seek and hard to find; and that it does not reside in Fur Companies' forts, nor mission establishments. One thing, however, the mind persists in asking itself: Would there not have been more unity among all the American settlers, more respect for religion, and more universal benevolence in Oregon, had the prominent men of the mission party shown themselves less selfish and grasping? No wonder that when the superior benevolence of the Hudson's Bay Company put to shame their avarice, many accounted for the superior kindness of Dr. McLaughlin by calling it *Jesuitical.* A little more of the same Jesuitical spirit would have softened and brightened the character of those missionaries to the future historian of Oregon.

Yet be it not said that they did no good in their day and generation.   If they were not all consistent Christian teachers, a few were.   If as a class or party they proved themselves selfish and illiberal, they were yet as a class advocates of good morals, and good order, of industry, education, and free institutions.

It will be readily understood that there could be little sympathy between the missionaries and the mountain-men, for while one party prayed a great deal and very conspicuously, the other never prayed at all, but on the contrary rather inclined to make a jest of sacred matters, and pious observances.   Then too, the mission party were well-to-do, and continually increasing their worldly goods by sharp bargains and general acquisitiveness, while the mountain-men were poor, prodigal, and not always industrious.   In short, the aristocracy of American Oregon was the Methodist mission, an aristocracy second only to that of the Hudson's Bay Company, while the mountain-men, with big, rebellious hearts, were compelled, at the same time that they refused, to accept the position thrust upon them.

CHAPTER XXIV.

1841. WHEN spring opened, Meek assisted Newell in
breaking the ground for wheat.   This done, it became necessary to look out for some immediately paying employment.   But paying occupations were hard to find in that
new country.   At last, like everybody else, Meek found
himself, if not "hanging about," at least frequently visiting Vancouver.   Poor as he was, and unpromising as
looked the future, he was the same light-hearted, reckless,
and fearless Joe Meek that he had been in the mountains:
as jaunty and jolly a ragged mountaineer as ever was seen
at the Fort.   Especially he delighted in recounting his Indian fights, because the Company, and Dr. McLaughlin in
particular, disapproved the American Company's conduct
with the Indians.

When the Doctor chanced to overhear Meek's stories,
as he sometimes did, he would say "Mr. Joe, Mr. Joe,—(a
habit the Doctor had of speaking rapidly, and repeating
his words,)—Mr. Joe, Mr. Joe, you must leave off killing
Indians, and go to work."

"I can't work," Meek would answer in his impressively
slow and smooth utterance, at the same time giving his
shoulders a slight shrug, and looking the Doctor pleasantly
in the face.

During the summer, however, the United States Exploring Squadron, under Commodore Wilkes, entered the Columbia River, and proceeded to explore the country in
several directions; and it was now that Meek found an

employment suited to him; being engaged by Wilkes as pilot and servant while on his several tours through the country.

On the arrival of three vessels of the squadron at Vancouver, and the first ceremonious visit of Dr. McLaughlin and his associates to Commodore Wilkes on board, there was considerable display, the men in the yards, saluting, and all the honors due to the representative of a friendly foreign power. After dinner, while the guests were walking on deck engaged in conversation, the talk turned upon the loss of the *Peacock*, one of the vessels belonging to the U. S. squadron, which was wrecked on the bar at the mouth of the Columbia. The English gentlemen were polite enough to be expressing their regrets at the loss to the United States, when Meek, who had picked up a little history in spite of his life spent in the mountains, laughingly interrupted with:

"No loss at all, gentlemen. Uncle Sam can get another Peacock the way he got that one."

Wilkes, who probably regretted the allusion, as not being consonant with the spirit of hospitality, passed over the interruption in silence. But when the gentlemen from Vancouver had taken leave he turned to Meek with a meaning twinkle in his eyes:

"Meek," said he, "go down to my cabin and you'll find there something good to eat, and some first-rate brandy." Of course Meek went.

While Wilkes was exploring in the Cowelitz Valley, with Meek and a Hudson's Bay man named Forrest, as guides, he one day laid down in his tent to sleep, leaving his chronometer watch lying on the camp-table beside him. Forrest, happening to observe that it did not agree with his own, which he believed to be correct, very kindly, as he supposed, regulated it to agree with his. On awakening and taking up his watch, a puzzled expression came over Wilkes' face for a moment, as he discovered the change in the time; then one of anger and disappointment, as what had occurred flashed over his mind; followed by some rather strong expressions of indignation. Forrest was penitent when he perceived the mischief done by his meddling, but that would not restore the chronometer to the true time: and this accident proved a serious annoyance and hindrance during the remainder of the expedition.

After exploring the Cowelitz Valley, Wilkes dispatched a party under Lieutenant Emmons, to proceed up the Wallamet Valley, thence south along the old trail of the Hudson's Bay Company, to California. Meek was employed to pilot this party, which had reached the head of the valley, when it became necessary to send for some papers in the possession of the Commodore; and he returned to Astoria upon this duty. On joining Emmons again he found that some of his men had become disaffected toward him; especially Jandreau, the same Frenchman who prayed so dramatically at the Dalles.

Jandreau confided to Meek that he hated Emmons, and intended to kill him. The next morning when Lieut. E. was examining the arms of the party, he fired off Jandreau's gun, which being purposely overcharged, flew back and inflicted some injuries upon the Lieutenant.

"What do you mean by loading a gun like that?" inquired Emmons, in a rage.

"I meant it to kill two Injuns;—one before, and one behind;" answered Jandreau.

As might be conjectured Jandreau was made to fire his own gun after that.

The expedition had not proceeded much farther when it again became necessary to send an express to Vancouver, and Meek was ordered upon this duty. Here he found that Wilkes had purchased a small vessel which he named the *Oregon*, with which he was about to leave the country. As there was no further use for his services our quondam trapper was again thrown out of employment. In this exigency, finding it necessary to make some provision for the winter, he became a gleaner of wheat in the fields of his more provident neighbors, by which means a sufficient supply was secured to keep himself and his small family in food until another spring.

When winter set in, Meek paid a visit to the new mission. He had been there once before, in the spring, to buy an axe. Think, O reader, of traveling fifty or more miles, on horseback, or in a small boat, to procure so simple and necessary an article of civilized life as an axe! But none of the every-day conveniencies of living grow spontaneously in the wilderness—more's the pity:—else life in the wilderness would be thought more delightful far than life in the most luxurious of cities; inasmuch as Nature is more satisfying than art.

Meek's errand to the mission on this occasion was to find whether he could get a cow, and credit at the same time: for the prospect of living for another winter on boiled wheat was not a cheerful one. He had not succeeded, and was returning, when at Champoeg he met a Mr. Whitcom, superintendent of the mission farm. A conversation took place wherein Meek's desire for a cow became known. The missionaries never lost an opportunity of proposing prayers, and Mr. Whitcom thought this a good one. After showing much interest in the condition of Meek's soul, it was proposed that he should pray.

"*I* can't pray: that's your business, not mine," said Meek pleasantly.

"It is every man's business to pray for himself," answered Whitcom.

"Very well; some other time will do for that. What I want now is a cow."

"How can you expect to get what you want, if you wont ask for it?" inquired Whitcom.

"I reckon I have asked you; and I don't see nary cow yet."

"You must ask God, my friend: but in the first place you must pray to be forgiven for your sins."

"I'll tell you what I'll do. If you will furnish the cow, I'll agree to pray for half an hour, right here on the spot."

"Down on your knees then."

"You'll furnish the cow?"

"Yes," said Whitcom, fairly cornered.

Down on his knees dropped the merry reprobate, and prayed out his half hour, with how much earnestness only himself and God knew.

But the result was what he had come for, a cow; for Whitcom was as good as his word, and sent him home rejoicing. And thus, with what he had earned from Wilkes, his gleaned wheat, and his cow, he contrived to get through another winter.

The summer had not been altogether wasted either, in other respects. He had seen nearly the whole of Western Oregon; had acquired not only an understanding of its geography, but had learned to appreciate it, and its consequence in a national point of view. He had found it lovely, genial, and productive above any country he had ever seen, excepting that portion of California which he had once visited;—in some respects superior even to that. He had begun to comprehend the political position of Oregon more thoroughly than before; he thought he knew what was good and what was bad about the Hudson's Bay Company's influence, and the mission influence;—in short he had been learning to be an American citizen, instead of a mountain ranger—an individual instead of a fraction of a company.

The events which he had been a witness to, and the associations he had enjoyed, had been doing much to educate in him unbiased views of Oregon affairs. The great event of that summer, in Oregon, had been the presence of the American Squadron in Oregon waters. It was understood by the Americans to be significant on the part of the Government, of some action which it was about to take in regard to the treaty of joint occupancy. So also it was understood by the Hudson's Bay Company. The Americans were naturally anxious to find Commodore Wilkes favorably impressed with the country and its natural wealth. They were also very desirous that he should sympathize with their desire to have the United States extend its government over them.

As has been elsewhere stated, the death of Ewing Young, which occurred early in this year, furnished the pretext for the first primary meeting in Oregon. Following up the idea of a form of laws, the mission party consulted with the United States officers on the propriety of establishing a civil code for the government of the colony, and were disappointed, and not a little hurt, at finding that they did not see the necessity for it.

" A committee of five," says Wilkes, " principally lay-members of the mission, waited upon me to consult and ask advice relative to the establishment of laws, etc. After hearing attentively all their arguments and reasons for this change, I could see none sufficiently strong to induce this step. No crime appears yet to have been committed, and the persons and property of settlers are secure. Their principal reasons appear to me to be, that it would give them more importance in the eyes of others at a distance, and induce settlers to flock in, thereby raising the value of their farms and stock. I could not view the subject in such a light, and differed with them entirely as to the necessity or policy of adopting the change."

Commodore Wilkes knew, and everybody knew, that the British interest already felt itself threatened by the presence of the exploring expedition. So sensitive was Wilkes on this subject, that he preferred camping outside the Fort to accepting its hospitalities. He felt that for the Americans to follow it up immediately with any attempt at an independent government, would, or might be, to precipitate upon the Government the necessity of action for which it was not yet prepared, or to provoke an enmity by no means desirable in their present weak condition.

Another difficulty was also submitted to Commodore Wilkes. A party of eight young men from the States, who had, like other adventurers, drifted into Oregon from the mountains and California, had determined to return to their homes, because, as they said, there were no young white women in that country to marry, and they were unwilling to remain without female society, or to take native wives. Not being able to recross the continent, they had determined to build a vessel and to go by sea, at least so far as the Bay of San Francisco, where they might fall in with a trading vessel going home. Not one of them knew anything about navigation, though one of them was a ship-carpenter, but they trusted they should be able to sail their little craft, which they had named the *Star of Oregon*, safely to some port where assistance could reach them. What they wanted of the Commodore was a sea-letter, and that he should intercede with Dr. McLaughlin, who, through some misunderstanding, had refused them any further supplies. On receiving advice from Wilkes that they should explain to Dr. McLaughlin whatever seemed wrong to him, they did so, and obtained the necessary ropes, sails, provisions, etc., for their vessel, and finally made a safe voyage to San Francisco, where they sold their vessel for a good price, and took passage home by some larger one. Such were some of the examples of successful daring which the early history of Oregon furnished.

During this summer, also, a trading vessel—the *Thomas Perkins*, from Boston, *Varney*, master,—entered the Columbia with a cargo of Indian goods and liquor. To prevent the liquor being sold to the Indians, Dr. McLaughlin bought up the whole cargo, storing the liquor at Vancouver, where it remained for several years untasted. Had that liquor got among the Indians, it is most probable that the American colony would have been destroyed, or driven into Fort Vancouver for protection.

Perhaps the most important personal event which distinguished this year in Meek's history, was the celebration, according to the rites of the Christian church, of his marriage with the Nez Perce woman who had already borne him two children, and who still lives, the mother of a family of seven.

20

CHAPTER XXV.

1842. By the opening of another spring, Meek had so far overcome his distaste for farm labor as to put in a field of wheat for himself, with Doughty, and to make some arrangements about his future subsistence. This done, he was ready, as usual, for anything in the way of adventure which might turn up. This was, however, a very quiet summer in the little colony. Important events were brooding, but as yet results were not perceptible, except to the mind of a prophet. The Hudson's Bay Company, conformably to British policy, were at work to turn the balance of power in Oregon in favor of British occupation, and, unknown even to the colonists, the United States Government was taking what measures it could to shift the balance in its own favor. Very little was said about the subject of government claims among the colonists, but a feeling of suspense oppressed all parties.

The work of putting in wheat and improving of farms had just begun to slacken a little, when there was an arrival in the Columbia River of a vessel from Boston—the *Chenamus*, Captain Couch. The *Chenamus* brought a cargo of goods, which were placed in store at Wallamet Falls, to be sold to the settlers, being the first successful attempt at trade ever made in Oregon, outside of the Hudson's Bay and Methodist Mission stores.

When the Fourth of July came, the *Chenamus* was

lying in the Wallamet, below the Falls, near where the present city of Portland stands. Meek, who was always first to be at any spot where noise, bustle, or excitement might be anticipated, and whose fine humor and fund of anecdote made him always welcome, had borrowed a boat from Capt. Couch's clerk, at the Falls, and gone down to the vessel early in the morning, before the salute for the Glorious Fourth was fired. There he remained all day, enjoying a patriotic swagger, and an occasional glass of something good to drink. Other visitors came aboard during the day, which was duly celebrated to the satisfaction of all.

Towards evening, a party from the Mission, wishing to return to the Falls, took possession of Meek's borrowed boat to go off with. Now was a good opportunity to show the value of free institutions. Meek, like other mountain-men, felt the distance which the missionaries placed between him and themselves, on the score of their moral and social superiority, and resented the freedom with which they appropriated what he had with some trouble secured to himself. Intercepting the party when more than half of them were seated in the boat, he informed them that they were trespassing upon a piece of property which for the present belonged to him, and for which he had a very urgent need. Vexed by the delay, and by having to relinquish the boat to a man who, according to their view of the case, could not "read his title clear," to anything either on earth or in heaven, the missionaries expostulated somewhat warmly, but Meek insisted, and so compelled them to wait for some better opportunity of leaving the ship. Then loading the boat with what was much more to the purpose—a good supply of provisions, Meek proceeded to drink the Captain's health in a very ostentatious manner, and take his leave.

This slight encounter is related only to illustrate the sort of feeling which made the missionaries and those Americans usually denominated as "settlers," two parties instead of one.

The summer passed away, the harvest was gathered, and in September there was a fresh excitement in the Valley. Dr. White, a member of the mission, who came out in 1840, quarreled with the superintendent of the mission, Mr. Lee, and returned to the States in 1841, now re-appeared in Oregon as the bearer of glad tidings. It appeared that Dr. White, after settling his affairs with the Board at home, had given such information to the Government concerning Oregon affairs, as had induced the Executive to commission him Indian Agent, with certain not very clearly defined powers. What these powers were, did not at first so much interest the community, as that he had any at all; for the fact of his holding any commission from the United States indicated to them that the Government was about to take a step in their behalf, which their eager imaginations willingly construed into a settlement of the boundary question, the erection of a territorial government in Oregon, and the complete discomfiture of the Hudson's Bay Company.

In addition to the pleasure which Dr. White's commission gave, he was able to furnish another and equally good promise for the future, in the shape of a printed copy of a bill, then before the Senate, proposing to donate 640 acres of land to every white male inhabitant, half that quantity to a wife, and one-fourth to every child under eighteen years of age. That these liberal offers were contained in Mr. Linn's bill was well understood to be a bid for settlers, nor did the colonists doubt that it would induce emigration.

To crown their satisfaction, over a hundred immigrants

had accompanied Dr. White on his return, each with a copy of Mr. Linn's bill in their hands, as it were to show their title to the country. These immigrants had left their wagons at Fort Hall, having been overtaken by heavy storms, and concluded their journey on horseback, traveling from the Dalles of the Columbia to the Wallamet Falls, by a trail over the Cascade mountains and around the base of Mt. Hood, thus avoiding Fort Vancouver entirely.

To receive the new comers properly, required some considerable exertion on the part of the colony, which was hardly prepared in matter of tenements and provisions for such an influx of population. However, being the first invoice, they were made very welcome, and the more so, that there were among them a number of intelligent professional gentlemen, with their families, and that, for the most part, all were in independent circumstances.

The only thing that dampened the ardor of the colonists was, that Dr. White affirmed that his authority among them amounted to that of governor of the colony. Now, in the first place, they had not any government, therefore could not have any governor. True, there had been certain persons elected to fill certain offices, on the occasion before referred to, of the death of Young. But there had been no occasion for the exercise of their various functions, and the whole matter was of doubtful substantiality. Besides, if they were to have a governor, which they persisted they did not need, they would have desired to signify their preference. After considerable controversy, Dr. White was finally obliged to be satisfied with his Indian agency, and Oregon got on as before, without a governor.

As might be anticipated, the Hudson's Bay Company were not well pleased with the turn affairs seemed taking.

They, on their own part, were watching the action of their own and the United States government, and had their colonization schemes beside, as well as the Americans. Sir George Simpson, governor of the Hudson's Bay Company, had induced about one hundred and fifty of the French Canadian and Scotch settlers of the Red River settlement to come down into Oregon and locate on the North side of the Columbia. Their arrival happened rather later than that of the American immigrants, and was in no way satisfactory, since most of them disliked the portion of country assigned to them, that being the gravelly region around Puget Sound, and finally settled in the Wallamet Valley.

In the meantime, however, Dr. Whitman, of the Waiilatpu Mission, in the upper country, was so fearful of the intentions of the British government that he set out for Washington late in the autumn of 1842, to put the Secretary of State on his guard concerning the boundary question, and to pray that it might be settled conformably with the wishes of the Americans in Oregon. On his arrival he found that the treaty known as the "Ashburton Treaty" had been confirmed in the preceding summer, and that it avoided all reference to the Oregon boundary, by simply fixing upon a line for our frontier, extending from the Atlantic coast to the Lake of the Woods, or less than half-way across the continent. He, however, conferred with Mr. Webster on the subject, representing to him the folly of being persuaded to "swap off the Oregon territory for a cod-fishery," and probably was able to enlighten him on the value of said territory.

It was in March, 1843, that Dr. Whitman arrived at Washington. On reaching the Missouri frontier he had found that a large number of persons held themselves in readiness to emigrate, on the strength of Mr. Linn's bill, should it pass. To these he spoke encouragingly, advising them to go without delay, as such a bill would certainly be passed. Hastening over his business at Washington, he returned to the frontier early, joining the emigration, to whom he proved a most useful friend, and indefatigable guide and assistant. Such was the struggle for the possession of the Oregon Territory.

There was one feature, however, of this otherwise rather entertaining race for possession, which was becoming quite alarming. In all this strife about claiming the country, the Indian claim had not been considered. It has been already mentioned that the attempt to civilize or Christianize the Indians of western Oregon was practically an entire failure. But they were not naturally of a warlike disposition, and had been so long under the control of the Hudson's Bay Company that there was comparatively little to apprehend from them, even though they felt some discontent at the incoming immigration.

But with the Indians of the upper Columbia it was different; especially so with the tribes among whom the Presbyterian missionaries were settled—the Walla-Wallas, Cayuses, and Nez Perces, three brave and powerful nations, much united by intermarriages. The impression which these people had first made on the missionaries was very favorable, their evident intelligence, inquisitiveness, and desire for religious teachings seeming to promise a good reward of missionary labor. Dr. Whitman and his associates had been diligent in their efforts to civilize and Christianize them—to induce the men to leave off their migratory habits and learn agriculture, and the women to learn spinning, sewing, cooking, and all the most essential arts of domestic life. At the first, the novelty of these new pursuits engaged their interest, as it also excited their hope of gain. But the task of keeping them to their work with sufficient steadiness, was very great. They required, like children, to be bribed with promises of more or less immediate reward of their exertions, nor would they relinquish the fulfilment of a promise, even though they had failed to perform the conditions on which the promise became binding.

By-and-by they made the discovery that neither the missionaries could, nor the white man's God did, confer upon them what they desired—the enjoyment of all the blessings of the white men—and that if they wished to enjoy these blessings, they must labor to obtain them. This discovery was very discouraging, inasmuch as the Indian nature is decidedly averse to steady labor, and they could perceive that very little was to be expected from any progress which could be achieved in one generation. As for the Christian faith, they understood about as much of its true spirit as savages, with the law of blood written in their hearts, could be expected to understand. They looked for nothing more nor less than the literal fulfilment of the Bible promises—nothing less would content them; and as to the forms of their new religion, they liked them well enough—liked singing and praying, and certain orderly observances, the chiefs leading in these as in other matters. So much interest did they discover at first, that their teachers were deceived as to the actual extent of the good they were doing.

As time went on, however, there began to be cause for mutual dissatisfaction. The Indians became aware that no matter how many concessions their teachers made to them, they were still the inferiors of the whites, and that they must ever remain so. But the thought which produced the deepest chagrin was, that they had got these white people settled amongst them by their own invitation and aid, and that now it was evident they were not

to be benefited as had been hoped, as the whites were
turning their attention to benefiting themselves.

As early as 1839, Mr. Smith, an associate of Mr. Spalding in the country of the Nez Perces, was forbidden by
the high chief of the Nez Perces to cultivate the ground.
He had been permitted to build, but was assured that if he
broke the soil for the purpose of farming it, the ground
so broken should serve to bury him in.   Still Smith went
on in the spring to prepare for ploughing, and the chief
seeing him ready to begin, inquired if he recollected that
he had been forbidden.   Yet persisting in his undertaking,
several of the Indians came to him and taking him by the
shoulder asked him again "if he did not know that the hole
he should make in the earth would be made to serve for
his grave."   Upon which third warning Smith left off, and
quitted the country.   Other missionaries also left for the
Wallamet Valley.

In 1842 there were three mission stations in the upper
country; that of Dr. Whitman at Waiilatpu on the Walla-
Walla River, that of Mr. Spalding on the Clearwater River,
called Lapwai, and another on the Spokane River, called
Cimakain.   These missions were from one hundred and
twenty to three hundred miles distant from each other,
and numbered altogether only about one dozen whites of
both sexes.   At each of these stations there was a small
body of land under cultivation, a few cattle and hogs, a
flouring and saw mill, and blacksmith shop, and such improvements as the needs of the mission demanded.   The
Indians also cultivated, under the direction of their teachers, some little patches of ground, generally but a small
garden spot, and the fact that they did even so much was
very creditable to those who labored to instruct them.
There was no want of ardor or industry in the Presbyterian

mission; on the contrary they applied themselves conscientiously to the work they had undertaken.

But this conscientious discharge of duty did not give them immunity from outrage. Both Mr. Spalding and Dr. Whitman had been rudely handled by the Indians, had been struck and spat upon, and had nose and ears pulled. Even the delicate and devoted Mrs. Spalding had been grossly insulted. Later the Cayuses had assailed Dr. Whitman in his house with war-clubs, and broken down doors of communication between the private apartments and the public sitting room. Explanations and promises generally followed these acts of outrage, yet it would seem that the missionaries should have been warned.

The station at Waiilatpu being near fort Walla-Walla was much resorted to by visitors and travelers. Dr. Whitman, who looked upon the country as belonging to the United States, and who was actively opposed to British influence from patriotic motives, had frequent and long conversations with his visitors not only on the subject of the American claim, but upon the natural advantages of the country, the fertility of its soil, and kindred topics, much of which the Indians, who were always about the mission, were able to understand, and from which they gathered that the Americans intended to possess the country which they considered as their own. They had seen that year by year, for a long time, some Americans had passed through their country and gone down to settle in the Walla-met Valley. They had had a fresh alarm in the recent emigration which had accompanied Dr. White from the States. But most conclusive of all was the fact of Dr. Whitman's visit to Washington, and his avowed intention of bringing back with him a large party of settlers to hold the country against the English.

Taking advantage of Dr. Whitman's absence, the Cayuses had frightened Mrs. Whitman from her home to the Methodist mission at the Dalles, by breaking into her bed-chamber at night, with an infamous design from which she barely escaped, and by subsequently burning down the mill and destroying a considerable quantity of grain. About the same time the Nez Perces at the Lapwai mission were very insolent, and had threatened Mr. Spalding's life; all of which, one would say, was but a poor return for the care and instruction bestowed upon them during six years of patient effort on the part of their teachers.   Poor as it was, the Indians did not see it in that light, but only thought of the danger which threatened them, in the possible loss of their country.

The uneasiness among the Indians had so much increased since Dr. Whitman's departure, that it became necessary, in November, for the newly arrived Indian agent to make a journey to the upper country to inquire into the cause of the disturbances, and if possible to adjust the difficulties.   In order the better to succeed in this, Dr. White obtained the services of Thomas McKay of the Hudson's Bay Company—a son of that ill-fated McKay who perished on board the *Tonquin* in 1811, and whose mother, a half-breed woman, was afterwards married to Dr. McLaughlin.

Both by his Indian blood, his long service in the Hudson's Bay Company, and the natural urbanity of his disposition, Mr. McKay was a man of note among the Indians; understanding their peculiarities better, and having more influence over them than almost any trader in the whole country.   Half a dozen well armed men, and two interpreters, were the only escort which, according to McKay, was thought necessary.   With this small party the agent proceeded to the mission station at Waiilatpu, where some gentlemen of the mission were staying, Mrs. Whitman being absent at the Dalles. After taking note of the injury done to the mission property here, the party continued on to the Lapwai mission, where they had sent word for the chiefs of the disaffected tribes to meet them.

Then took place the customary exchange of "talks" which always characterize the Indian council. The Indians were grave and dignified; they heard the addresses of the agent and his friends, and received the compliments paid to their advancement in the arts and in letters, with the utmost decorum. They professed themselves desirous of peace, and appeared satisfied with the promises made by the agent concerning what the Great Father of the United States intended doing for them.

As has been stated in another place, the Hudson's Bay Company had done all it could to destroy chieftainships among the tribes, in order to prevent coalitions among them. Dr. White restored it among the Nez Perces, by counseling them to elect one high chief, and to have besides a chief to every village, in all about a dozen, to assist him in the administration of the laws. A code of laws for their government was then proposed and agreed to, which made hanging the punishment for murder or for burning a dwelling house. Theft was punishable by double payment, and by whipping. Misdemeanors generally were left to the discretion of the chiefs, the penalties being in most cases fines, and in some cases whipping.

The naturally good character of the Nez Perces, and the presence and sanction of two of the Hudson's Bay Company, McKay, and McKinley of Walla-Walla, made it comparatively easy for Dr. White to arrange a peace with the Indians at Lapwai. On returning to

Waiilatpu, however, few of the chiefs were found to be assembled, while many of them held aloof, and nothing satisfactory was concluded. Under these circumstances. Dr. White left an appointment to meet them in April, of the next year, for the purpose of holding a council. He then returned to the Wallamet, to watch the course of events in the colony.

CHAPTER XXVI.

1842–3. The plot thickened that winter, in the little drama being enacted west of the Rocky Mountains.   As much as Dr. McLaughlin had felt it to be his duty towards his country and the company he served, to do what he could to secure their interests, he had also always acknowledged the claims of humanity, hospitality, and social good feeling.   So much, in fact, did his nature lean towards the social virtue of brotherly love, that he became sometimes the object of criticism bordering on censure, to his associates, who on their side were as patriotic as the Americans on theirs.

But so rapidly portentous events seemed hurrying on at this particular juncture, that the good Doctor was led to doubt almost that he had done the best thing in extending the hand of fellowship so freely to the political enemies of Great Britain.   His critics might with some justice accuse him of encouraging American settlement in Oregon, and of giving just that touch required, to shift the balance of power into the hands of the United States.   Such a suspicion against him would be bad enough in the eyes of his superiors; but the pain it would occasion him could hardly be exceeded by that occasioned by the denial to such a suspicion given by the settlers themselves.

In a memorial to the Congress of the United States they had petitioned for the protection of Government upon the express ground that they apprehended harm, not only from the Indians, but from the Hudson's Bay Company; which apprehension was a direct insinuation or accusation against Dr. McLaughlin. Naturally of a temper as irritable as his heart was warm and generous, these attacks upon his honor and humanity by the very individuals whom he had ever shown himself willing to serve, annoyed him excessively, and occasioned him to say that to those individuals who had signed the obnoxious memorial he would never more show favor. As might be expected, this pardonable show of indignation was made to stand for a threat against the welfare of the whole colony.

To add to the confusion, the subject of a form of government continued to be agitated in the colony. So far as legal forms were necessary to the welfare of the Hudson's Bay Company, they had in their charter certain privileges of arrest and punishment sufficient for the preservation of good order among their employes; hence had no need for any thing further in the way of laws. Why then should they be desirous of joining any foreign organization, or of subscribing to the laws made by a people who owed allegiance to a rival government, and thereby strengthening their hands against their own government? Such was the logical reasoning of the Canadian settlers on the Wallamet, who at that time rather out-numbered the Americans.

On the other hand, it was equally logical for the Americans to fear that a code of laws intended only to apply to a portion of the population, would prove of little service, and might be provocative of frequent difficulties; inasmuch as any criminal might take refuge under the flag of the Hudson's Bay Company, and escape by that Company's denial of jurisdiction.

In this interval of doubt, the colony managed to get along very well without any laws. But the subject was

not allowed to rest.   Some truly long-headed politicians
had hit upon an expedient to unite the population, Canadian and American, upon one common ground of interest.

The forests which clad the mountains and foot-hills in
perpetual verdure, and the thickets which skirted the numerous streams flowing into the Wallamet, all abounded
in wild animals, whose depredations upon the domestic
cattle, lately introduced into the country, were a serious
drawback to their natural increase.   Not a settler, owning
cattle or hogs, but had been robbed more or less frequently by the wolves, bears, and panthers, which prowled
unhindered in the vicinity of their herds.

This was a ground of common interest to all settlers of
whatever allegiance.   Accordingly, a notice was issued
that a meeting would be held at a certain time and place,
to consider the best means of preventing the destruction
of stock in the country, and all persons interested were
invited to attend.   This meeting was held on the 2d of
February, 1843, and was well attended by both classes of
colonists.   It served, however, only as a preliminary step
to the regular "Wolf Association" meeting which took
place a month later.   At the meeting, on the 4th of March,
there was a full attendance, and the utmost harmony prevailed, notwithstanding there was a well-defined suspicion
in the minds of the Canadians, that they were going to be
called upon to furnish protection to something more than
the cattle and hogs of the settlers.

After the proper parliamentary forms, and the choosing
of the necessary officers for the Association, the meeting
proceeded to fix the rate of bounty for each animal killed
by any one out of the Association, viz: $3.00 for a large
wolf; $1.50 for a lynx; $2.00 for a bear; and $5.00 for
a panther.   The money to pay these bounties was to be
raised by subscription, and handed over to the treasurer

for disbursement; the currency being drafts on Fort Vancouver, the Mission, and the Milling Company; besides wheat and other commodities.

This business being arranged, the real object of the meeting was announced in this wise:

"*Resolved*,—That a committee be appointed to take into consideration the propriety of taking measures for the civil and military protection of this colony."

A committee of twelve were then selected, and the meeting adjourned. But in that committee there was a most subtle mingling of all the elements—missionaries, mountain-men, and Canadians—an attempt by an offer of the honors, to fuse into one all the several divisions of political sentiment in Oregon.

That the Canadians were prepared for something of this kind was probable from several circumstances. In the first place, the subject of government, in several forms, had been openly discussed that winter. The immigration, of the previous autumn had added much to the social resources of the colony, both in numbers, and in variety of ideas. The colony was not so much a missionary institution as formerly, simply because there had been an influx of other than missionary brains; and there were people now in Oregon, who, after studying the position of affairs, were able to see the merits and demerits of the various propositions brought up. Even in the Debating Society, which was maintained by the most able men of the colony and of the Hudson's Bay Company, at the Wallamet Falls, the subject of a provisional form of government was freely and fully discussed;—some parties favoring the adoption of a simple code of such laws as were needful to regulate society in that isolated country, temporarily, until the United States should recognize and adopt them into the Union. Others wished for an independent form of gov-

21

ernment, acknowledging no allegiance to any other, either then or later. A few still argued for no change in the then existing state of things, feeling that no necessity had yet arisen for manufacturing governments.

Of the independent government party Dr. McLaughlin was believed to be. Even some of the mission party favored a separate government, if, after waiting a term of four years, the United States had set up no claim to their allegiance. But the greater number of the people, not Canadians, and the mountain-men especially, were for a provisional government to last as long as in the course of events it was needed, after which its powers were to revert to the United States.

In view of all this talk, the Canadians were prepared with an address which was to express their view of the case, and would have presented it at the meeting of the Wolf Association, had not that meeting been so thoroughly "wolfish" in its action as almost to disarm suspicion, and quite prevent any reference to the main topic of thought in all minds. The address was therefore reserved for a more appropriate occasion, which was not long in coming.

On the 2d day of May, 1843, the committee appointed March 4th to "take into consideration the propriety of taking measures for the civil and military protection of the colony," met at Champoeg, the Canadian settlement, and presented to the people their ultimatum in favor of organizing a provisional government.

On a motion being made that the report of the committee should be accepted, it was put to vote, and lost. All was now confusion, various expressions of disappointment or gratification being mingled in one tempest of sound.

When the confusion had somewhat subsided, Mr. G. W. LeBreton made a motion that the meeting should divide; those who were in favor of an organization taking their positions on the right hand; and those opposed to it on the left, marching into file. The proposition carried; and Joe Meek, who, in all this historical reminiscence we have almost lost sight of—though he had not lost sight of events—stepped to the front, with a characteristic air of the free-born American in his gait and gestures:—

"Who's for a divide! All in favor of the Report, and an Organization, follow me!"—then marched at the head of his column, which speedily fell into line, as did also the opposite party.

On counting, fifty-two were found to be on the right hand side, and fifty on the left,—so evenly were the two parties balanced at that time. When the result was made known, once more Meek's voice rang out—

"Three cheers for our side!"

It did not need a second invitation; but loud and long the shout went up for FREEDOM; and loudest and longest were heard the voices of the American "mountain-men." Thus the die was cast which made Oregon ultimately a member of the Federal Union.

The Canadians were somewhat alarmed at the demonstrations they had witnessed, and withdrew from the meeting soon after the last vote was taken, not, however, without presenting the address, which had been previously prepared; and which is given here, both as a curiosity of literature, and a comprehensive bit of Oregon history.

ADDRESS

OF THE CANADIAN CITIZENS OF OREGON TO THE MEETING AT CHAMPOEG.

MARCH 4th, 1843.

We, the Canadian citizens of the Willamette, considering, with interest and reflection, the subject which unites the people at the present meeting, present to the American citizens, and particularly to the gentlemen who called said meeting, the unanimous expression of our sentiments of cordiality, desire of union and inexhaustible peace between all the people, in view of our duty and the interest of the new colony, and declare :—

1st.   That we wish for laws, or regulations, for the welfare of our persons, and the security of our property and labors.

2d.   That we do not intend to rebel against the measures of that kind taken last year, by a party of the people;—although we do not approve of certain regulations, nor certain modes of laws;—let those magistrates finish their time.

3d.   That we will not address a new petition to the Government of the United States, because we have our reasons, till the line be decided, and the frontiers of the states are fixed.

4th.   That we are opposed to the regulations anticipated, and exposed to consequences for the quantity, direction, &c., of lands, and whatsoever expense for the same lands, because we have no direct guarantee from the government to come, and, perhaps, to-morrow, all those measures may be broken.

5th.   That we do not wish a provisional mode of government, too self-interested, and full of degrees, useless to our power, and overloading the colony instead of improving it; besides, men of laws and science are too scarce, and have too much to do in such a new country.

6th.   That we wish either the mode of senate or council, to judge the difficulties, punish the crimes, (except capital penalties,) and make the regulations suitable to the people.

7th.   That the same council be elected, and composed of members from all parts of the country, and should act in body, on the plan of civilized countries in parliament, or as a jury, and to be represented, for example, by the president of said council, and another member, as judge of peace, in each county, allowing the principle of recalling to the whole senate.

8th.   That the members should be influenced to interest themselves to their own welfare, and that of the public, by the love of doing good, rather than by the hope of gain, in order to take off from the esteem of the people all suspicions of interest in the persons of their representatives.

9th.   That they must avoid every law loading, and inexpedient to the people, especially to the new arrivals.   Unnecessary taxes, and whatever records are of that kind, we do not want them.

10th.   That the militia is useless at present, and rather a danger of bad suspicion to the Indians, and a delay for the necessary labors, in the same time it is a load; we do not want it, either, at present.

11th.   That we consider the country free, at present to all nations, till government shall have decided; open to every individual wishing to settle, without any distinction of origin, and without asking him anything, either to become an English, Spanish, or American citizen.

12th.   So we, English subjects, proclaim to be free, as well as those who came from France, California, United States, or even natives of this country; and we desire unison with all the respectable citizens who wish to settle in this country; or, we ask to be recognized as free amongst ourselves, to make such regulations as appear suitable to our wants, save the general interest of having justice from all strangers who might injure us, and that our reasonable customs and pretensions be respected.

13th. That we are willing to submit to any lawful government, when it comes.

14th. That we do not forget that we must make laws only for necessary circumstances. The more laws there are, the more opportunities for roguery, for those who make a practice of it, and, perhaps, the more alterations there will be some day.

15th. That we do not forget in a trial, that before all fraud on fulfilling of some points of law, the ordinary proofs of the certainty of the fact ought to be duly weighed, so that justice may be done, and no shame given for fraud.

16th. In a new country, the more men employed and paid by the public, the less remains for industry.

17th. That no one can be more desirous than we are for the prosperity, ameliorations, and general peace of the country, and especially for the guarantee of our rights and liberties; and such is the wish we make for all those who are, or may become, our fellow-countrymen, &c., for long years of peace.

[Then follow our names and persons.]

The business of the meeting was concluded by the election of a Supreme Judge, with probate powers, a clerk of the court, a sheriff, four magistrates, four constables, a treasurer, a mayor, and a captain,—the two latter officers being instructed to form companies of mounted riflemen. In addition to these officers, a legislative committee was chosen, consisting of nine members, who were to report to the people at a public meeting to be held at Champoeg on the 5th of July following. Of the legislative committee, two were mountain-men, with whose names the reader is familiar—Newell and Doughty. Among the other appointments, was Meek, to the office of sheriff; a position for which his personal qualities of courage and good humor admirably fitted him in the then existing state of society.

And thus was formed the Provisional Government of Oregon—a country without a governor, or any magisterial head; and without a treasury, or means to pay its legislative committee, except by subscription, and at the rate of $1.25 per day in orders on some of the few business firms west of the Rocky Mountains. On the 4th of

July the people met at Champoeg to celebrate the day, and camped on the ground, to be in readiness for the meeting of the 5th. At this meeting the reports of the various committees of the legislature were approved by the people, Dr. McLaughlin voting with the others.

At this meeting the Judiciary Committee recommended that the executive power should be vested in a *committee of three persons*, elected by qualified voters at the annual election, who should have power to grant pardons and reprieve for offences against the laws of the territory; to call out the military force of the territory to repel invasion or suppress insurrection, to take care that the laws were faithfully executed, and to recommend such laws as they may consider necessary, to the representatives of the people, for their action: two members of this committee to constitute a quorum to transact business.

Among the most notable of the acts of the first Oregon legislature, was one which regarded a militia law, ordering the territorial militia to be formed into one battalion consisting of three companies of mounted riflemen; and another regarding marriage, which permitted "All male persons, of the age of sixteen and upwards, and all females of the age of fourteen and upwards" to engage in marriage, provided the sanction of the parents could be obtained. Unfortunately for the good of Oregon there were too many parents, who, looking forward to the passage of the Donation Act, and being desirous of gaining possession through their children of large bodies of land, were only too eager to see their children married and assuming the responsibilities of parentage, before their own childhood was fairly passed.

As for the laws generally adopted, they were those of Iowa and New York mixed, and made suitable to the condition of the colony.

The result of success in the matter of effecting an organization was not altogether unalloyed happiness. The Indians in the upper country were again in a tumult, and freely expressed their dread of the coming immigration, then on its way, under the leadership of Dr. Whitman. They were not ignorant of what had taken place in the Wallamet Valley; neither, upon reflection, did they look upon the visit of the Indian agent in the previous autumn as a promise of good, but regarded it rather as a token of the encroachments of the whites. So far as the Nez Perces were concerned, they had kept the laws given them at that time, partly through the natural prudence of their dispositions, and partly through the wise counsels of their head chief, Ellis, who, having been educated at the Red River settlement of the Hudson's Bay Company, was prepared to use a reasonable discretion in controling the bad passions of his people.

But the Cayuses and Walla-Wallas, the allies and relatives of the Nez Perces, were in a different frame of mind, having more immediate cause for alarm, from the fact that their own teacher, Dr. Whitman, was bringing upon them the curse they dreaded. In a state of mind totally unsettled and rebellious, they waited for the promised visit of Dr. White in the spring.

Such were the reports which had reached the Wallamet from the upper country of the turbulence of the Indians, that it was regarded as a dangerous movement for the agent to go among them. However, he resolved to undertake it, and accompanied by only one gentleman from the mission, Mr. Hines, and their servants, set out for the infected district. Before reaching Vancouver they were met by a letter from Dr. McLaughlin, advising them not to proceed, and informing them that, from intelligence lately received, there was really much to apprehend. He also informed them that the Indians had expressed their determination not to make war upon the Hudson's Bay Company, but only upon the Americans; and gave it as his opinion that the best way to end the disturbance was to remain quietly at home.

Not agreeing with Dr. McLaughlin in respect to the best manner of soothing the Indians, Dr. White and Mr. Hines proceeded to the fort, where they wished to obtain supplies of goods, provisions, powder, and balls for the expedition. This visit to the fort, under the circumstances, was one of those frequent acts, half cringing and half audacious, which the sensitive historian rather flinches from recording, as reflecting upon the honor and dignity of Americans. In explanation we shall quote Mr. Hines' own words:

" Called on Dr. McLaughlin for goods, provisions, powder, balls, &c., for our accommodation on our voyage up the Columbia; and although he was greatly suprised that, under the circumstances, we should think of going among those excited Indians, yet he ordered his clerks to let us have whatever we wanted. However, we found it rather squally at the fort, not so much on account of our going among the Indians of the interior, as in consequence of a certain memorial having been sent to the United States Congress, *implicating the conduct of Dr. McLaughlin and the Hudson's Bay Company*, and bearing the signatures of seventy Americans. I inquired of the Doctor if he had refused to grant supplies to those Americans who had signed that document; he replied that he had not, but that the authors of the memorial need expect no more favors from him. *Not being one of the authors, but merely a signer of the petition, I did not come under the ban of the company, consequently I obtained my outfit for the expedition, though at first there were strong indications that I would be refused.*"

To the honor of Dr. McLaughlin be it said, that however great the provocation, he never avenged his injuries upon the American settlers, by refusing to aid them in their times of want or peril.

Arrived at the Dalles, the Indian agent tarried only long enough to inquire into the working of the system of laws which he had persuaded them to accept on his previous visit. The report which the Indians had to give was both melancholy and amusing. According to Mr. Hines' Journal of the expedition:

"The chiefs had found much difficulty in enforcing the laws; in punishing delinquents, some of the Indians resisting even to the point of the knife. The chiefs who were appointed through the influence of Dr. White, were desirous that these regulations should continue, evidently because they placed the people under their absolute control, and gave them the power to regulate all their intercourse with the whites, and with the other Indian tribes. But the other influential men, who were not in office, desired to know of Dr. White, of what benefit this whipping system was going to be to them. They said they were willing it should continue, provided they were to receive blankets, shirts, and pants, as a reward for being whipped. They had been whipped a good many times, and they had got nothing for it, and it had done them no good. If this state of things was to continue it was all good for nothing, and they would throw it all away. In reply they were told by the Doctor that we could not be detained to settle any of their difficulties now, that we were going farther into the interior, and were in a very great hurry, and that when we returned he would endeavor to make all straight. But he wished them to understand that they need not expect pay for being flogged, when they deserved it. They laughed heartily at the idea, and dispersed, giving us an opportunity to make arrangements for the continuance of our journey."

On leaving the Dalles, Dr. White proceeded as rapidly as possible, now with horses instead of boats, to the station at Waiilatpu, where Mrs. Whitman and a Mr. Giger of the mission were awaiting them with anxious expectation. Dr. White found quite as much uneasiness as he had anticipated, and learned incidentally why he had been counseled at Fort Vancouver not to attempt going among the Indians. It appeared on investigation that a mischievous half-breed, named Dorio, son of the same Madame Dorio who figures as a heroine in Irving's *Astoria*, being well informed in Indian sentiments, and influential as an interpreter among them, had wickedly inflamed the passions of the Indians by representing to them that it was useless making farms and building houses, as in a short time the whites would overrun their land, and destroy everything, besides killing them.

This evil counsel so well agreed with what they had seen and heard, and had reason to apprehend, that much excitement was the result. The warriors among the Cayuses were eager to go to war at once, and exterminate all the white settlements on the Wallamet and elsewhere. But the old men counseled patience and caution, advising a consultation with the Hudson's Bay Company, who had always been their friends. They remembered the answer they had received, when on the first breaking out of their fear of the Americans they had gone to Fort Walla-Walla, to ask McKinley's opinion of the expediency of driving the missionaries away from their lands. "You are braves," said McKinley, "and there are many of you. It would be easy to kill two men and two women, and a few little children. Go quickly and do it, if you wish; but remember if you do so, that I will have you punished." For that time the subject was dropped.

But now that their fears were thoroughly aroused, the Cayuses resolved to send a messenger to Dr. McLaughlin at Vancouver to inquire what had better be done in view of their difficulties, and to take observations in the lower country, for the Indians were well aware that the whites had not been at peace among themselves, and that Fort Vancouver had been strengthened in its defences, and had had a government vessel lying before it the previous winter. Seeing that there seemed more unity between the Hudson's Bay Company and the Americans, a new fear entered into their minds lest they might combine against them.

Full of such feelings, a Walla-Walla chief, called Yellow-Serpent, made a journey to Vancouver and opened his heart to Dr. McLaughlin. In answer to his inquiries the Doctor assured him that there was nothing to apprehend from any class of whites; that he could not believe the

Americans had any warlike designs toward them, and that if they should make war on them, they would not be joined by the Hudson's Bay men. Comforted by the assurances of the great white chief, Yellow-Serpent returned, and reported to his people, and for a time they were quiet, and worked at their little plantations, as taught them by Dr. Whitman.

As we have seen it was but a brief lull in the rising tempest. The wicked Dorio still continued to poison their minds, and to stir up all the native suspiciousness and jealousy of the Indian character. Thus it happened that on Dr. White's arrival they were full of mutiny, as difficult of approach as in the preceding autumn. However, Dr. White, with Mr. Hines, Mrs. Whitman and Mr. Giger, made many friendly advances, and a meeting was finally appointed to take place after the agent had first made a visit to the Nez Perces.

The Nez Perces were found to have remembered their promises, and to have continued to profit by the instructions of their teachers. They received the agent in a cordial manner, entertaining him and his friends with a rehearsal of a late battle with the Blackfeet in which they had been victorious. Arrangements were then made for Mr. Spalding, Ellis, and several hundreds of men, women and children to visit Waiilatpu in company with the Doctor, as the Cayuses would agree to nothing without first consulting with the chief of the Nez Perces.

Nor were they all inclined to receive the agent hospitably, even in company with Ellis. The reception was conducted in the usual style of Indian welcome, by first exhibiting their warlike accomplishments in a sham battle, so well fought and life-like in its representation that even Ellis was almost persuaded some real fighting would follow. The excitement was finally allayed by Mr. Spalding proposing to adjourn to the house of worship for evening prayers, after which the people scattered to their lodges to await the meeting of the next day.

On the following morning the chiefs came together at Dr. Whitman's, and Dr. White addressed them. He assured them that if they feared war on the part of the whites, they were quite mistaken; that the Great Father of the whites had not sent him among them for that purpose, but to come to some understanding about their future intercourse. He promised them that if they would lay aside their former practices, as they had been instructed by the missionaries to do, leave off feuds among themselves, and cultivate the land, they might become a great and happy people. He counseled unity between the chiefs, and consideration and kindness towards the people, and also counseled the people to obey the chiefs, and love and pray for them.

The subject of the laws was then brought forward, and the young men were exhorted to accept and keep them, that when they became chiefs their people might obey them. The laws were then read both in English and Nez Perce, when the Walla-Walla chief, Yellow-Serpent, arose and said:

"I have a message to you. Where are these laws from? Are they from God, or from the earth? I would you might say they were from God. But I think they are from the earth, because, what I know of white men, they do not honor these laws." A short speech, and to the point.

When it was explained to him that in all civilized countries men were bound to honor the laws, he replied that he was "glad to learn that it was so, because many of his people had been angry with him when he had whipped them for crime, and had told him that God would send him to hell for it, and he was glad to know that it was not displeasing to God."

Other chiefs then spoke in turn, one favoring the adoption of the laws, another rejecting, and giving as a reason that the chief in favor was a Catholic; to which Doctor White replied that religious belief had nothing to do with the making or keeping of laws. And after this an old chief, who had seen Lewis and Clarke when they were in the country, spoke of the treaty made with them; adding that " ever since that time people had been coming along and promising to do them good; but that they had all passed by and left no blessing behind them. That the Hudson's Bay Company had persuaded them to keep good friends with them, and to let the Americans alone. But if the Americans designed to do good to them, why did they not bring goods with them to leave with their people. They were fools to listen to the promises of the Americans; they only would talk, while the Hudson's Bay Company gave presents." In reply to which begging speech the Doctor reminded them that his business with them was that neither of missionary or trader.

After a day spent in listening to and answering speeches the meeting adjourned. In the evening the Nez Perce chief, Ellis, and his associate Sawyer, held a talk with Dr. White in which they demanded a salary, as chiefs; and thought that they were already entitled to enough to make them wealthy. So avaricious is the Indian in all his feelings and pursuits.

On the day following the speeches were resumed, the laws finally accepted, and the Catholic chief Tan-i-tan was elected to the office of head chief, but resigned it the next day in favor of his brother Five-Crows, because, as he said, his religion differed from that of most of his nation, and Five-Crows would be more agreeable to them.

His decision proved his wisdom as well as his generosity; for the people declared themselves delighted with the change, though they had nothing against Tan-i-tan.

At the conclusion of each day the Indians had been feasted with fat beef and pork, obtained from the mission; and on the last day a grand feast was spread, to which Dr. White's party were invited, and at which, contrary to Indian custom, the women were permitted to appear and partake; Dr. White having made this a special request, and furnished them with new dresses for the occasion. After this happy conclusion of business in the Indian country, Dr. White appointed his leave-taking for the next morning. Mrs. Whitman, who had been an anxious and interested spectator of events, notwithstanding the amicable termination of the agent's efforts, thought it prudent to return with his party to the lower country until the time approached for her husband's return. Better for both had they never returned to Waiilatpu. Many were the warnings which those missionaries had, and disregarded. Many times had the Indians said to them "we do not wish to go to war, but if the Americans come to take away our lands, and reduce us to a state of vassalage, we will fight so long as we have a drop of blood." Yet no one more than Dr. Whitman, did everything in his power to encourage the settlement of the country. He was an enthusiast in the cause of the American occupation of Oregon; and like many another, in all the great questions of time, his enthusiasm won for him only the crown of a martyr.

Dr. White remained some time at the Dalles, on his return, endeavoring to bring the Indians into a cheerful subjection to the laws that had been given them. The success of the Doctor's labors may be pretty correctly estimated from events which will hereafter be related.

CHAPTER XXVII.

THE immigration into Oregon of the year 1843, was the first since Newell and Meek, who had brought wagons through to the Columbia River; and in all numbered nearly nine hundred men, women, and children. These immigrants were mostly from Missouri and other border States. They had been assisted on their long and perilous journey by Dr. Whitman, whose knowledge of the route, and the requirements of the undertaking, made him an invaluable counselor, as he was an untiring friend of the immigrants.

At the Dalles of the Columbia the wagons were abandoned; it being too late in the season, and the wants of the immigrants too pressing, to admit of an effort being made to cut out a wagon road through the heavy timber of the Cascade mountains. Already a trail had been made over them and around the base of Mount Hood, by which cattle could be driven from the Dalles to the settlements on the Wallamet; and by this route the cattle belonging to the train, amounting to thirteen hundred, were passed over into the valley.

But for the people, especially the women and children, active and efficient help was demanded. There was something truly touching and pitiable in the appearance of these hundreds of worn-out, ragged, sun-burnt, dusty, emaciated, yet indomitable pioneers, who, after a journey of nearly two thousand miles, and of several months duration, over fertile plains, barren deserts, and rugged mountains, stood at last beside the grand and beautiful river of their hopes, exhausted by the toils of their pilgrimage, dejected and yet rejoicing.

Much they would have liked to rest, even here; but their poverty admitted of no delay. The friends to whom they were going, and from whom they must exact and receive a temporary hospitality, were still separated from them a weary and dangerous way. They delayed as little as possible, yet the fall rains came upon them, and snow fell in the mountains, so as seriously to impede the labor of driving the cattle, and hunger and sickness began to affright them.

In this unhappy situation they might have remained a long time, had there been no better dependence than the American settlers already in the valley, with the Methodist Mission at their head; for from them it does not appear that aid came, nor that any provision had been made by them to assist the expected immigrants. As usual in these crises, it was the Hudson's Bay Company who came to the rescue, and, by the offer of boats, made it possible for those families to reach the Wallamet. Not only were the Hudson's Bay Company's boats all required, but canoes and rafts were called into requisition to transport passengers and goods. No one, never having made the voyage of the Columbia from above the Dalles to Vancouver, could have an adequate idea of the perils of the passage, as it was performed in those days, by small boats and the flat-bottomed "Mackinaw" boats of the Hudson's Bay Company. The Canadian "voyageurs," who handled a boat as a good rider governs a horse, were not always able to make the passage without accident: how, then, could the clumsy landsmen, who were more used to the feel of a plow handle than an oar, be expected to do so?

Numerous have been the victims suddenly clutched from life by the grasp of the whirlpools, or dashed to death among the fearful rapids of the beautiful, but wild and pitiless, Columbia.

The immigration of 1843 did not escape without loss and bereavement. Three brothers from Missouri, by the name of Applegate, with their families, were descending the river together, when, by the striking of a boat on a rock in the rapids, a number of passengers, mostly children of these gentlemen, were precipitated into the frightful current. The brothers each had a son in this boat, one of whom was lost, another injured for life, and the third escaped as by a miracle. This last boy was only ten years of age, yet such was the presence of mind and courage displayed in saving his own and a companion's life, that the miracle of his escape might be said to be his own. Being a good swimmer, he kept himself valiantly above the surface, while being tossed about for nearly two miles. Succeeding at last in grasping a feather bed which was floating near him, he might have passed the remaining rapids without serious danger, had he not been seized, as it were, by the feet, and drawn down, down, into a seething, turning, roaring abyss of water, where he was held, whirling about, and dancing up and down, striking now and then upon the rocks, until death seemed not only imminent but certain. After enduring this violent whirling and dashing for what seemed a hopelessly long period of time, he was suddenly vomited forth by the whirlpool once more upon the surface of the rapids, and, notwithstanding the bruises he had received, was able, by great exertion, to throw himself near, and seize upon a ledge of rocks. To this he clung with desperation, until, by dint of much effort, he finally drew himself out of the water, and stretched himself on the narrow shelf, where,

22

for a moment, he swooned away. But on opening his eyes, he beheld, struggling in the foaming flood, a young man who had been a passenger in the wrecked boat with himself, and who, though older, was not so good a swimmer. Calling to him with all his might, to make his voice heard above the roar of the rapids, he at last gained his attention, and encouraged him to try to reach the ledge of rocks, where he would assist him to climb up ; and the almost impossible feat was really accomplished by their united efforts. This done, young Applegate sank again into momentary unconsciousness, while poor exhausted Nature recruited her forces.

But, although they were saved from immediate destruction, death still stared them in the face. That side of the river on which they had found lodgment, was bounded by precipitous mountains, coming directly down to the water. They could neither ascend nor skirt along them, for foot-hold there was none. On the other side was level ground, but to reach it they must pass through the rapids —an alternative that looked like an assurance of destruction.

In this extremity, it was the boy who resolved to risk his life to save it. Seeing that a broken ledge of rock extended nearly across the river from a point within his reach, but only coming to the surface here and there, and of course very slippery, he nevertheless determined to attempt to cross on foot, amidst the roaring rapids. Starting alone to make the experiment, he actually made the crossing in safety, amid the thundering roar and dizzying rush of waters—not only made it once, but returned to assure his companion of its practicability. The young man, however, had not the courage to undertake it, until he had repeatedly been urged to do so, and at last only by being pursuaded to go before, while his younger comrade fol-

WRECKED IN THE RAPIDS.

lowed after, not to lose sight of him, (for it was impossible to turn around,) and directed him where to place his steps. In this manner that which appears incredible was accomplished, and the two arrived in safety on the opposite side, where they were ultimately discovered by their distressed relatives, who had believed them to be lost. Such was the battle which young Applegate had with the rocks, that the flesh was torn from the palms of his hands, and his whole body bruised and lacerated.

So it was with sorrow, after all, that the immigrants arrived in the valley. Nor were their trials over when they had arrived. The worst feature about this long and exhausting journey was, that it could not be accomplished so as to allow time for recruiting the strength of the travelers, and providing them with shelter before the rainy season set in. Either the new arrivals must camp out in the weather until a log house was thrown up, or they must, if they were invited, crowd into the small cabins of the settlers until there was scarce standing room, and thus live for months in an atmosphere which would have bred pestilence in any other less healthful climate.

Not only was the question of domiciles a trying one, but that of food still more so. Some, who had families of boys to help in the rough labor of building, soon became settled in houses of their own, more or less comfortable; nor was anything very commodious required for the frontiers-men from Missouri; but in the matter of something to eat, the more boys there were in the family, the more hopeless the situation. They had scarcely managed to bring with them provisions for their summer's journey — it was not possible to bring more. In the colony was food, but they had no money—few of them had much, at least; they had not goods to exchange; labor was not in demand: in short, the first winter in

Oregon was, to nearly all the new colonists, a time of trial, if not of actual suffering. Many families now occupying positions of eminence on the Pacific coast, knew what it was, in those early days, to feel the pangs of hunger, and to want for a sufficient covering for their nakedness.

Two anecdotes of this kind come to the writer's memory, as related by the parties themselves: the Indians, who are everywhere a begging race, were in the habit of visiting the houses of the settlers and demanding food. On one occasion, one of them came to the house of a now prominent citizen of Oregon, as usual petitioning for something to eat. The lady of the house, and mother of several young children, replied that she had nothing to give. Not liking to believe her, the Indian persisted in his demand, when the lady pointed to her little children and said, "Go away; I have nothing—not even for those." The savage turned on his heel and strode quickly away, as the lady thought, offended. In a short time he reappeared with a sack of dried venison, which he laid at her feet. " Take that," he said, " and give the *tenas tillicum* (little children) something to eat." From that day, as long as he lived, that humane savage was a " friend of the family.

The other anecdote concerns a gentleman who was chief justice of Oregon under the provisional government, afterwards governor of California, and at present a banker in San Francisco. He lived, at the time spoken of, on the Tualatin Plains, and was a neighbor of Joe Meek. Not having a house to go into at first, he was permitted to settle his family in the district school-house, with the understanding that on certain days of the month he was to allow religious services to be held in the building. In this he assented. Meeting day came, and the family put on their best apparel to make themselves tidy in the eyes of their neighbors. Only one difficulty was hard to get over: Mr. —— had only one shoe, the other foot was bare. But he considered the matter for some time, and then resolved that he might take a sheltered position behind the teacher's desk, where his deficiency would be hidden, and when the house filled up, as it would do very rapidly, he could not be expected to stir for want of space. However, that happened to the ambitious young lawyer which often does happen to the "best laid schemes of mice and men"—his went "all aglee." In the midst of the services, the speaker needed a cup of water, and requested Mr. —— to furnish it. There was no refusing so reasonable a request. Out before all the congregation, walked the abashed and blushing pioneer, with his ill-matched feet exposed to view. This mortifying exposure was not without an agreeable result; for next day he received a present of a pair of moccasins, and was enabled thereafter to appear with feet that bore a brotherly resemblance to each other.

About this time, the same gentleman, who was, as has been said, a neighbor of Meek's, was going to Wallamet Falls with a wagon, and Meek was going along. "Take something to eat," said he to Meek, "for I have nothing;" and Meek promised that he would.

Accordingly when it came time to camp for the night, Meek was requested to produce his lunch basket. Going to the wagon, Meek unfolded an immense pumpkin, and brought it to the fire.

"What!" exclaimed Mr. ——, "is that all we have for supper?"

"Roast pumpkin is not so bad," said Meek, laughing back at him; "I've had worse fare in the mountains. It's buffalo tongue compared to ants or moccasin soles."

And so with much merriment they proceeded to cut up their pumpkin and roast it, finding it as Meek had said— " not so bad " when there was no better.

These anecdotes illustrate what a volume could only describe—the perils and privations endured by the colonists in Oregon. If we add that there were only two flouring mills in the Wallamet Valley, and these two not convenient for most of the settlers, both belonging to the mission, and that to get a few bushels of wheat ground involved the taking of a journey of from four to six days, for many, and that, too, over half-broken roads, destitute of bridges, it will be seen how difficult it was to obtain the commonest comforts of life. As for such luxuries as groceries and clothing, they had to wait for better times. Lucky was the man who, "by hook or by crook," got hold of an order on the Hudson's Bay Company, the Methodist Mission, or the Milling Company at the Falls. Were he thus fortunate, he had much ado to decide how to make it go farthest, and obtain the most. Not far would it go, at the best, for fifty per cent. profit on all sales was what was demanded and obtained. Perhaps the holder of a ten dollar draft made out his list of necessaries, and presented himself at the store, expecting to get them. He wanted some unbleached cotton, to be dyed to make dresses for the children; he would buy a pair of calf-skin shoes if he could afford them; and—yes—he would indulge in the luxury of a little—a very little— sugar, just for that once!

Arrived at the store after a long, jolting journey, in the farm wagon which had crossed the continent the year before, he makes his inquiries: " Cotton goods ?" " No ; just out." " Shoes ?" " Got one pair, rather small— wouldn't fit you." " What have you got in the way of goods ?" " Got a lot of silk handkerchiefs and twelve dozen straw hats." "Any pins?" "No; a few knitting needles." "Any yarn?" "Yes, there's a pretty good lot of yarn, but don't you want some sugar? the last ship that was in left a quantity of sugar." So the holder of the draft exchanges it for some yarn and a few nails, and takes the balance in sugar: fairly compelled to be luxurious in one article, for the reason that others were not to be had till some other ship came in.

No mails reached the colony, and no letters left it, except such as were carried by private hand, or were sent once a year in the Hudson's Bay Company's express to Canada, and thence to the States. Newspapers arrived in the same manner, or by vessel from the Sandwich Islands. Notwithstanding all these drawbacks, education was encouraged even from the very beginning; a library was started, and literary societies formed, and this all the more, perhaps, that the colony was so isolated and dependent on itself for intellectual pleasures. Such was the state of the colony when the Indian Agent returned from the upper country, when the Provisional Government was formed, and when the emigration arrived at the close of 1843.

The spring of 1844 saw the colony in a state of some excitement on account of an attempt to introduce the manufacture of ardent spirits. This dangerous article had always been carefully excluded from the country, first by the Hudson's Bay Company, and secondly by the Methodist Mission; and since the time when Ewing Young had been induced to relinquish its manufacture, no serious effort had been made to introduce it.

It does not appear from the Oregon archives, that any law against its manufacture existed at that time: it had probably been overlooked in the proceedings of the legislative committee of the previous summer; neither was there yet any executive head to the Provisional Government, the election not having taken place. In this dilemma the people found themselves in the month of February, when one James Conner had been discovered to be erecting a distillery at the Falls of the Wallamet.

Now when Dr. White had so speedily returned from the States, whither he had as speedily gone, after a few months residence in Oregon, and a quarrel with the mission to which he was surgeon—with a commission from the United States which he wished to construe as conferring on him the authority of governor of the colony, his pretentions were regarded as insufferable, and he was given to understand that he would do well to confine himself to his duties as Indian agent. There was a great deal that was absurd about the whole matter, and the United States had as little right to appoint an Indian agent as a governor—neither being consistent with the terms of the treaty of joint occupation. But it was not that question which the settlers regarded; they were willing enough to acknowledge the authority of the United States to do anything; and were constantly petitioning the government to do those things which threatened to involve the country in war; in which case they would doubtless have been immediately exterminated; for it only required a hint to the Indians that the " King George men " and the "Bostons" were at war, to bring them down upon the settlers in one fell swoop.

What the colonists, and especially the mission, did not like about the matter, was Dr. White himself. They would have been glad enough to have had a governor appointed; but there were other men in and out of the mission, more pleasing to them than the Doctor for governor; and perhaps the most pleasing man of all to each one, was himself. But as they could not all be governors, it was decided at the meeting in the previous July that a trinity of governors would answer their purpose, and divide the honors.

It happened, however, that an occasion for the exercise of executive power had occurred before the election of the executive committee, and now what was to be done? It was a case too, which required absolute power, for there was no law on the subject of distilleries. After some deliberation it was decided to allow the Indian agent temporary power, and several letters were addressed to him, informing him of the calamity which threatened the community at the Falls. "Now, we believe that if there is anything which calls your attention in your official capacity, or anything in which you would be most cordially supported by the good sense and prompt action of the better part of community, it is the present case. We do not wish to dictate, but we hope for the best, begging pardon for intrusions." So read the closing paragraph of one of the letters.

Perhaps this humble petition touched the Doctor's heart; perhaps he saw in the circumstance a possible means of acquiring influence; at all events he hastened to the Falls, a distance of fifty miles, and entered at once upon the discharge of the executive duties thus thrust upon him in the hour of danger. Calling upon Meek, who had entered upon his duties as sheriff the previous summer, he gave him his orders. Writ in hand, Meek proceeded to the distillery, frightened the poor sinner into quiet submission with a display of his mountain manners; made a bugle of the worm, and blew it, to announce to the Doctor his complete success; after which he tumbled the distillery apparatus into the river, and retired. Connor was put under three hundred dollar bonds, and so the case ended.

But there were other occasions on which the Doctor's

authority was put in requisition. It happened that a vessel from Australia had been in the river, and left one Madam Cooper, who was said to have brought with her a barrel of whisky. Her cabin stood on the east bank of the Wallamet, opposite the present city ot Portland. Not thinking it necessary to send the sheriff to deal with a woman, the Doctor went in person, accompanied by a couple of men. Entering the cabin the Doctor remarked blandly, "you have a barrel of whisky, I believe."

Not knowing but her visitor's intention was to purchase, and not having previously resided in a strictly temperance community, Madam Cooper replied frankly that she had, and pointed to the barrel in question.

The Doctor then stepped forward, and placing his foot on it, said: "In the name of the United States, I levy execution on it!"

At this unexpected declaration, the English woman stared wildly one moment, then recovering herself quickly, seized the poker from the chimney corner, and raising it over the Doctor's head, exclaimed—"In the name of Great Britain, Ireland, and Scotland, I levy execution on you!"

But when the stick descended, the Doctor was not there. He had backed out at the cabin door ; nor did he afterwards attempt to interfere with a subject of the crown of Great Britain

On the following day, however, the story having got afloat at the Falls, Meek and a young man highly esteemed at the mission, by the name of Le Breton, set out to pay their respects to Madam Cooper. Upon entering the cabin, the two callers cast their eyes about until they rested on the whisky barrel.

"Have *you* come to levy on my whisky?" inquired the now suspicious Madam.

"Yes," said Meek, "I have come to levy on it; but as I am not quite so high in authority as Doctor White, I don't intend to levy on the whole of it at once. I think about a quart of it will do me."

Comprehending by the twinkle in Meek's eye that she had now a customer more to her mind, Madam Cooper made haste to set before her visitors a bottle and tin cup, upon which invitation they proceded to levy frequently upon the contents of the bottle; and we fear that the length of time spent there, and the amount of whisky drank must have strongly reminded Meek of past rendez-vous times in the mountains; nor can we doubt that he entertained Le Breton and Madam Cooper with many reminiscences of those times. However that may be, this was not the last visit of Meek to Madam Cooper's, nor his last levy on her whisky.

The sheriff, despite his natural antagonism to what is usually denominated the better portion of the community," or putting it more correctly, despite their antagonism to *him*, on account of his mountain ways and Indian wife, was becoming a man of note amongst them. They might denominate him amongst themselves as "old Joe Meek" at thirty-four years of age, because he cared nothing whatever for their pious prejudices, and broke through their solemn prohibitions as if they had been ropes of sand; yet when courage and firmness were required to get them out of a difficulty, they appealed deferentially enough to "Mr. Meek."

Shortly after his election as sheriff he had been called upon to serve a writ upon a desperate character, for an attempt to kill. Many persons, however, fearing the result of trying to enforce the law upon desperadoes, in the then defenceless condition of the colony, advised him to wait for the immigration to come in before attempting the arrest. But Meek preferred to do his duty then, and went with the writ to arrest him. The man resisted, making an attack on the sheriff with a carpenter's axe; but Meek coolly presented a pistol, assuring the culprit of the use-lessness of such demonstrations, and soon brought him to terms of compliance. Such coolness, united with a fine physique, and a mountain-man's reputation for reckless courage, made it very desirable that Meek should con-tinue to hold the office of sheriff during that stage of the colony's development.

CHAPTER XXVIII.

1844. As has before been mentioned, the Indians of the Wallamet valley were by no means so formidable as those of the upper country: yet considering their numbers and the condition of the settlers, they were quite formidable enough to occasion considerable alarm when any one of them, or any number of them betrayed the savage passions by which they were temporarily overcome. Considerable excitement had prevailed among the more scattered settlers, ever since the reports of the disaffection among the up-country tribes had reached them; and Dr. White had been importuned to throw up a strong fortification in the most central part of the colony, and to procure arms for their defence, at the expense of the United States.

This excitement had somewhat subsided when an event occurred which for a time renewed it: a house was plundered and some horses stolen from the neighborhood of the Falls. An Indian from the Dalles, named Cockstock, was at the bottom of the mischief, and had been committing or instigating others to commit depredations upon the settlers, for a year previous, because he had been, as he fancied, badly treated in a matter between himself and a negro in the colony, in which the latter had taken an unfair advantage of him in a bargain.

To crown his injuries Dr. White had caused a relative of his to be flogged by the Dalles chief, for entering the house of the Methodist missionary at that place, and tying him, with the purpose of flogging him. (It was a poor law, he thought, that would not work both ways.)

In revenge for this insult Cockstock came to the Doctor's house in the Wallamet, threatening to shoot him at sight, but not finding him at home, contented himself for that time, by smashing all the windows in the dwelling and office of the Doctor, and nearly frightening to death a young man on the premises.

When on the Doctor's return in the evening, the extent of the outrage became known, a party set out in pursuit of Cockstock and his band, but failed to overtake them, and the settlers remained in ignorance concerning the identity of the marauders. About a month later, however, a party of Klamath and Molalla Indians from the south of Oregon, numbering fifteen, came riding into the settlement, armed and painted in true Indian war-style. They made their way to the lodge of a Calapooya chief in the neighborhood—the Calapooyas being the Indians native to the valley. Dr. White fearing these mischievous visitors might infect the mind of the Calapooya chief, sent a message to him, to bring his friends to call upon him in the morning, as he had something good to say to them.

This they did, when Dr. White explained the laws of the Nez Perces to them, and told them how much it would be to their advantage to adopt such laws. He gave the Calapooya chief a fine fat ox to feast his friends with, well knowing that an Indian's humor depends much on the state of his stomach, whether shrunken or distended. After the feast there was some more talk about the laws, in the midst of which the Indian Cockstock made his appearance, armed, and sullen in his demeanor. But as Dr. White did not know him for the perpetrator of the outrage on his premises, he took no notice of him more than of the others. The Molallas and Klamaths finally agreed to receive the laws; departing in high good humor, singing and shouting. So little may one know of the savage heart from the savage professions! Some of these Indians were boiling over with secret wrath at the weakness of their brethren in consenting to laws of the Agent's dictation; and while they were crossing a stream, fell upon and massacred them without mercy, Cockstock taking an active part in the murder.

The whites were naturally much excited by the villianous and horrible affray, and were for taking and hanging the murderers. The Agent, however, was more cautious, and learning that there had been feuds among these Indians long unsettled, decided not to interfere.

In February, 1844, fresh outrages on settlers having been committed so that some were leaving their claims and coming to stop at the Falls through fear, Dr. White was petitioned to take the case in hand. He accordingly raised a party of ten men, who had nearly all suffered some loss or outrage at Cockstock's hands, and set out in search of him, but did not succeed in finding him. His next step was to offer a reward of a hundred dollars for his arrest, meaning to send him to the upper country to be tried and punished by the Cayuses and Nez Perces, the Doctor prudently desiring to have them bear the odium, and suffer the punishment, should any follow, of executing justice on the Indian desperado. Not so had the fates ordained.

About a week after the reward was offered, Cockstock came riding into the settlement at the Falls, at mid-day, accompanied by five other Indians, all well armed, and frightfully painted. Going from house to house on their horses, they exhibited their pistols, and by look and gesture seemed to defy the settlers, who, however, kept quiet through prudential motives. Not succeeding in provoking the whites to commence the fray, Cockstock finally retired to an Indian village on the other side of the river, where he labored to get up an insurrection, and procure the burning of the settlement houses.

Meantime the people at the Falls were thoroughly alarmed, and bent upon the capture of this desperate savage. When, after an absence of a few hours, they saw him recrossing the river with his party, a crowd of persons ran down to the landing, some with offers of large reward to any person who would attempt to take him, while others, more courageous, were determined upon earning it. No definite plan of capture or concert of action was decided on, but all was confusion and doubt. In this frame of mind a collision was sure to take place; both the whites and Indians firing at the moment of landing. Mr. LeBreton, the young man mentioned in the previous chapter, after firing ineffectually, rushed unarmed upon Cockstock, whose pistol was also empty, but who still had his knife. In the struggle both fell to the ground, when a mulatto man, who had wrongs of his own to avenge, ran up and struck Cockstock a blow on the head with the butt of his gun which dispatched him at once.

Thus the colony was rid of a scourge, yet not without loss which counterbalanced the gain. Young LeBreton besides having his arm shattered by a ball, was wounded by a poisoned arrow, which occasioned his death; and Mr. Rogers, another esteemed citizen, died from the same cause; while a third was seriously injured by a slight wound from a poisoned arrow. As for the five friends of Cockstock, they escaped to the bluffs overlooking the settlement, and commenced firing down upon the people. But fire-arms were mustered sufficient to dislodge them, and thus the affair ended; except that the Agent had some trouble to settle it with the Dalles Indians, who came down in a body to demand payment for the loss of their brother. After much talk and explanation, a present to the widow of the dead Indian was made to smooth over the difficulty.

Meek, who at the time of the collision was rafting timber for Dr. McLaughlin's mill at the Falls, as might have been expected was appealed to in the melee by citizens who knew less about Indian fighting.

A prominent citizen and merchant, who probably seldom spoke *of* him as Mr. Meek, came running to him in great affright:—"Mr. Meek! Mr. Meek! Mr. Meek!—I want to send my wife down to Vancouver. Can you assist me? Do you think the Indians will take the town?"

" It 'pears like half-a-dozen Injuns might do it," retorted Meek, going on with his work.

"What do you think we had better do, Mr. Meek?— What do you advise?"

"I think *you'd* better RUN."

In all difficulties between the Indians and settlers, Meek usually refrained from taking sides—especially from taking sides against the Indians. For Indian slayer as he had once been when a ranger of the mountains, he had too much compassion for the poor wretches in the Wallamet Valley, as well as too much knowledge of the savage nature, to like to make unnecessary war upon them. Had he been sent to take Cockstock, very probably he would have done it with little uproar; for he had sufficient influence among the Calapooyas to have enlisted them in the undertaking. But this was the Agent's business and he let him manage it; for Meek and the Doctor were not in love with one another; one was solemnly audacious, the other mischievously so. Of the latter sort of audacity,

23

here is an example.   Meek wanted a horse to ride out to
the Plains where his family were, and not knowing how
else to obtain it, helped himself to one belonging to Dr.
White; which presumption greatly incensed the Doctor,
and caused him to threaten various punishments, hanging
among the rest.   But the Indians overhearing him replied,
" *Wake nika cumtux*—You dare not.—You no put rope
round Meek's neck.   He *tyee* (chief)—no hang him."

Upon which the Doctor thought better of it, and having
vented his solemn audacity, received smiling audacity with
apparent good humor when he came to restore the borrowed horse.

While Indian affairs occupied so much of the attention
of the colony, other topics of interest were not overlooked,
and colonial politics were as jealously guarded as ever by
the American party.   The unique form of government hit
upon by the genius of the American people, which consisted of a legislative committe who might frame laws for
the people to vote upon at the ensuing election, and an
executive committee, equally under the control of the people, promised to prove a success.   However, that passion
by which " the angels fell," did not sleep in Oregon more
than in other portions of the globe, and there were those
in the legislative committee for 1844, and in the executive
committee also, who were revolving in their minds the question of an independent government; that is, a government
owning no allegiance either to the United States or Great
Britain, but which should lay the foundations of empire on
the Pacific coast.

The first message of the executive committee recommended the vesting of the executive power in a single
individual, the appointment of several judges, and a general amendment of the organization with a view to increasing its strength.   It was also decided this year to increase
the legislative committee, so that it should number no less

than thirteen, nor more than sixty members.   An assessor was appointed as a preliminary measure to imposing taxes: an act passed to exclude slavery from Oregon, and also an act to prevent the manufacture or sale of intoxicating drinks.   On the two latter acts the people were generally very well agreed, seeing that temperance was necessary to the preservation of the colony; and the majority favoring the exclusion of negroes from Oregon.   That there should have been so general a sentiment against the introduction of blacks seems rather remarkable, when it is remembered that a large proportion of the settlers were from the border slave states.   Perhaps, having experienced the disadvantages of being " poor whites " in a slave-holding community, and being without the means of procuring slaves, they resolved to prevent any future influx of slave-holders, who should reduce them to the condition of " poor whites " in the country of their adoption.   So fearful were they that the negro element might be introduced into their social and political affairs that it was made an offence even for a free negro to be found in the territory, for which offence he was ordered to be sold to the lowest bidder, who was obligated to send the unfortunate black out of the territory, as soon as he had paid himself for the expense of doing so, out of his services.

But on the matter of taxes the people were not so well agreed, the general determination being, however, to pay the expenses of the government only by subscription, as agreed to by a vote of the people the previous year.

The American settlers were averse to being taxed for the support of a government which might become a burden to them in this way; and the most politic of the politicians in the American party feared that by taxing the people they should alarm the Canadians, whom they had again invited to join the organization.   As there were dissenters among the voters, there were also two parties in the legislature on this subject.

However, an issue was started this year in the legislature, which governed the election of the next year's legislature. Its purpose was pretty clearly shadowed forth in the following paragraph from the message of the executive committee:

"And we sincerely hope that Oregon, by the special aid of Divine Providence, may set an unprecedented example to the world, of industry, morality, and virtue. And, although we may now be unknown as a state *or power*, yet we have the advantages by united efforts of our increasing population, in a diligent attention to agriculture, arts, and literature, of attaining, at no distant day, to as conspicuous an elevation as any state *or power* on the continent of America."

This feeler put forth by the executive committee, one of whom was the candidate for Governor, of the Independent party, while it struck a responsive chord in the hearts of a portion of the legislative committee, had the effect to alarm the patriotism of the loyal American; an alarm which spread, and which expressed itself in the choice of the legislature of 1845, as well as in the choice of a governor, defeating entirely the hopes and designs of the would-be founders of an Independent Government.

CHAPTER XXIX.

1842–4.   In all the movements which had been made by either party in Oregon the Hudson's Bay Company had not been lost sight of.   Each one had something to gain or lose by the approval or disapproval of that company.   A few individuals, however, belonging to the mission, under the pretence of taking care of the rights of American citizens, made continual war on Dr. McLaughlin as the representative of the Company, and scrupled not to set his rights at defiance.

The Rev. Father Waller, who had in 1840 obtained the Doctor's permission to build a mission school and storehouse on the land claimed by him since 1830, found so many points of merit in the situation of the land that he resolved to set up a counter claim, and hold it by possession.   The first intimation that the Doctor had of such an intention was in 1842, when a rumor of that kind was afloat.   On inquiring of the superintendent of the mission concerning the truth of the matter, he was told that Mr. Waller denied setting up any claim to the land.   Yet when the Doctor, a few days later wished to give a lot to a settler, Mr. Waller would not allow it to be given away, saying he was "very much obliged to Dr. McLaughlin for disposing of *his* property."   Then commenced a tedious and irritating struggle with the Reverend claim-jumper.   On appealing to the superintendent a second time the Doctor was informed that Mr. Lee had "understood Mr.

Waller to say that he had set up no claim in opposition to the Doctor's, but that if the Doctor's claim failed, *and the mission did not put in a claim*, he (Waller) considered that he had a better right than any other man, and should secure the title if he could." It was evident from this admission that Mr. Waller expected that the mission would put in a claim, failing to do which he should do so for himself.

Again, Mr. Lee informed the Doctor that " a citizen of the United States, by becoming a missionary, did not renounce any civil or political rights," therefore he could not control his associates in such matters. Upon which information, Dr. McLaughlin called upon Mr. Waller in order to seek an adjustment of the difficulty. In the interview which followed, Mr. Waller again by implication denied his intention to wrong the Doctor, and agreed that if he were allowed to retain possession of that portion of the Doctor's land which he had cleared and improved, he would give in exchange for it an equal amount of land out of his claim which adjoined the Doctor's. To this Dr. McLaughlin consented, and sent a man to survey and measure the lots which Mr. Waller had improved, or given away to his friends, in order to mark out an equal portion for himself on that portion of Waller's claim adjoining his. But no sooner had he done this than Mr. Waller declared that he would not consent to the arrangement, saying, " keep you yours, I will keep mine ;" a mode of settlement most agreeable to the Doctor, only that while Mr. Waller kept his own, he kept the Doctor's also.

A few months later there came to the Falls a lawyer, who was on his way to the Sandwich Islands, a Mr. Ricord. This gentleman, in a conversation with Mr. McLaughlin, gave it as his opinion that the Doctor could not hold his claim at the Falls, because he was a British subject. Here then, was another and an unexpected bar to his rights, and the Doctor was fain to offer Mr. Ricord a fee if he could show him any way by which he *could* hold his claim. This proposition after some deliberation, and consultation with the mission gentlemen, was entertained on the following terms: That the Doctor was to relinquish his claim to an island in the river whereon the mission had erected a gristmill, that Mr. Waller was to retain two lots on the town site of Oregon City, already occupied by him, and other lots besides, to the amount of five acres, to be chosen by himself: that Rev. Jason Lee should be in like manner secured in regard to certain town lots, in behalf of the Methodist mission, and that for his services in bringing about this exceedingly just and equitable arrangement, and giving his advice, Mr. Ricord was to receive the sum of three hundred pounds sterling.   To such a proposition the Doctor declined to give his assent, and the matter rested for a time.

However, before Mr. Ricord left the colony, which he did on one of the Company's vessels, another conversation was had with him, and also with Mr. Lee, in which the Doctor submitted another proposition, in which he offered the mission two lots for a church, two lots for the clergyman, two lots for the school-house, and two lots for the school-master; said lots to be taken out of a specified portion of the town site.   He also offered to pay for the building occupied by Mr. Abernethy, a member of the mission, and subsequently Governor of the colony, but not for that portion of Mr. Waller's house which had been built out of his own squared timbers, lent for that purpose and never returned or paid for, but for all other improvements which had been made on those lots which he wanted for business purposes.

He further offered to let the milling company go on as they

were doing, until the boundary line was settled, when, if his claim was admitted, he would pay them for the work done and the fair value of the mill as decided by arbitrators. To this proposition Mr. Lee and Mr. Ricord gave their approval, expressing their sense of the Doctor's fairness and generosity. As Mr. Lee was about to set out for Washington, he requested the Doctor to leave the mission in possession until his return, which was agreed to without suspicion.

Nearly four months subsequently, Mr. McLaughlin was presented with a copy of a caveat, made out against him three days previous to the last mentioned conversation, the original of which was in the pocket of one of these gentlemen at the very moment they were expressing their sense of his generosity, and asking for a little time before disturbing the mission, and which ran as follows:

" You will please to take notice that my client, Mr. A. F. Waller, has taken formal measures at Washington to substantiate his claim as a preëmptor and actual settler upon the tract of land, sometimes called the Wallamet Falls settlement and sometimes Oregon City, comprising six hundred and forty acres ; and being aware that, although a foreigner, you claim to exercise acts of ownership over said land, this notice is given to apprise you that all sales you may make of lots or other subdivisions of said farm, after the receipt hereof, will be regarded by my client, and by the government, as absolutely fraudulent, and will be made at your peril. Then followed the grounds upon which the Doctor's claim was denied. *First*, that he was an alien ; *Secondly*, that he was the chief of a foreign corporate monopoly ; *Thirdly*, that he had not resided upon the land in question for a year previous ; *Fourthly*, that he did not hold the land for himself but the company ; *Fifthly*, that his claim, if he had any, arose two years subsequent to Mr. Waller's settlement thereon. This flattering document closed with Mr. Ricord's regrets that he had " failed to make an amicable compromise " of the matter between the Doctor and his client, and also that his " client had been driven to the vexatious proceedings of the law, in order to establish his rights as an American citizen."

Poor old long-suffering Dr. McLaughlin ! it would hardly have been strange had he hated the name of an "American citizen," so often was it assumed only to give countenance to the greatest abuses. At the time, too, that it was so frequently used and abused, there was only a suppositious right to the soil on the side of the Americans, and a British citizen had quite as many rights really as an American. Besides, Mr. Linn's bill, which was the foundation of the colony's assumptions, made no distinction between people of any nationality but provided that every white male citizen might claim six hundred and forty acres of land. Nor had the colonists ever thought of interfering with the Canadians who were settled upon farms in the Wallamet. It was only Dr. McLaughlin, and the gentlemen of the Hudson's Bay Company who were so obnoxious to a portion of the Americans.

We think it was about this time that Meek once surprised the Doctor at his devotions, in his office, where he was probably praying for patience. However that was, Meek was coming in at the door, but seeing the Doctor on his knees, praying and crossing himself—for he was a good Catholic—he paused to await the conclusion. On rising, the Doctor glanced round, and met the mirthful look of the irreverent Joe.

"Oh, Mr. Jo! Mr. Jo! the devil, the devil!" cried the Doctor, greatly surprised at the intrusion, and giving vent to those rapid ejaculations which always escaped him when annoyed. Then immediately repenting of his haste in giving way to his irritability, he exclaimed in the next breath "God forgive me, God forgive me!" rubbing his stomach with a little rapid movement peculiar to him; his fine honest Scotch face flushing in contrast to the long white hair which imparted such distinction to his appearance.

But to finish the story of the Oregon City claim. In April of 1844, Doctor McLaughlin consented that Doctor White should speak to Mr. Waller about the matter, and find whether or not it could be adjusted, because all this discussion was producing delays ruinous to the business of Dr. McLaughlin. It was at last determined to leave the settlement to arbitrators, and Mr. James Douglas, a Chief Factor and associate of the Doctor's, Mr. Gilpin, and Dr. White, were chosen to act for Dr. McLaughlin. The terms exacted by Mr. Waller were five acres and five hundred dollars to himself, and fourteen lots to the Methodist mission. To the credit of the two Americans chosen, be it said, that they opposed this exorbitant demand; and were only persuaded to accede to it by Mr. Douglas.

When the terms were made known to the Doctor, he exclaimed to his arbitrators all, " Gentlemen, you have bound me ;" but Mr. Gilpin instantly disavowed having a hand in the arrangement. Then said the Doctor to Mr. Douglas, " This is your doings!"

" Yes," answered Douglas, who felt how much the constant jarring had annoyed his chief, "I thought it best for your sake to give you one good fever, and have done with it. I have acceded to the terms and signed the papers."

Unfortunately for Mr. Douglas' intentions, this was not the last ' good fever' into which the Methodist mission was to throw the Doctor. Not two months after the settlement was made, it was resolved to dissolve the mission ; and in July Mr. Gary, the new superintendent, began to sell the mission property. Knowing that the lots they held were particularly desirable to Dr. McLaughlin for his own use, Mr. Gary called on him in company with Mr. Hines and one other gentleman of the mission, and offered to sell them back to him for the sum of six thousand dollars, with the improvements ; reserving, however, two lots for the church, all the fruit trees, and garden vegetables then growing, and the use of the warehouse for one year.

In vain the Doctor remonstrated against the valuation put upon the property, and against being made to pay one hundred dollars for Mr. Waller's old house built with timber borrowed from himself; no other terms would the mission consent to. At last, wearied out with contention, and needing them for his own business, Dr. McLaughlin agreed to give them their price for his lots, as he had just before given them the lots.

Thus, with much cost and annoyance, the question of ownership in Oregon City was settled; and after some solicitation the legislative committee passed an incorporation act recognizing its right to be called a town. The island on which the milling company had their grist mill, which had once formed a part of the Doctor's claim, still remained in the hands of the company, more than three-fourths of whom were members of the mission.

But the end was not yet, and we do not choose to anticipate. It is enough to say here, that from this time on, for a period of four years, Dr. McLaughlin was permitted to pursue his business at Oregon City, or Wallamet Falls as it has heretofore been called, without any serious interruption.

The mission party were still opposed to anything which the Hudson's Bay Company might do, thus compelling them to form a party by themselves, between whom and the mission party stood the American party, made up of the more liberal-minded settlers, the late immigrants, and the greater number of the mountain-men. In each of the colonial parties, mission and American, were a few independent individuals, who were friendly to, or at enmity with the Hudson's Bay Company, without consulting party feeling at all. So strong was the prejudice, however, which the mission party, and a few individuals of the American party, indulged towards the Hudson's Bay Company, and

Dr. McLaughlin in particular, that there had always been much uneasiness felt at Vancouver concerning the safety of the fort.

There had been, from the first of the American settlement, some lawless and desperate characters in the country, coming either from California, the mountains, or from trading vessels visiting the Columbia. These persons belonged to no party, nor had any association with the actual settlers. They were frowned down by all good citizens alike. Yet this class of persons invariably took the tone of extravagant Americanism, and refused to be snubbed by the Hudson's Bay Company, whatever slights they were compelled to bear from any other quarter. Many were the threats which had been made against the Hudson's Bay Company's property at Vancouver; and serious, at times, were Dr. McLaughlin's apprehensions lest he should not be able to protect it. While the colonists, in 1843, were memorializing Congress that they were in fear and danger from the Indians and the Hudson's Bay Company, Dr. McLaughlin was writing to the Directors of that Company, that he was in fear of the colonists.

He explained the position of affairs in this wise: there were large numbers of immigrants coming into the territory from that portion of the United States most hostile in feeling to British interests, which hostility was greatly excited by the perusal of Irving's Astoria, and the published letters of Kelly and Spaulding, which represented the Company's conduct in the falsest colors. These immigrants had received such an impression, that they really feared the Company might set the Indians on them, and although they now knew better, it was hard overcoming such prejudices; besides, there were always some who were ready to avail themselves of the prejudices of others to get up an issue. Threats had been uttered against Vancouver, and really the people were encouraged to make an attack, by the public prints in the United States stating that British subjects ought not to be allowed to remain in Oregon. There was no dependence in the common men about the fort to do sentry duty beyond a few nights, nor were there officers enough to be put upon guard without deranging the whole business of the department. To burn the fort would be an easy matter enough in the dry season, everything about it being of combustible material. And so the Doctor asked that a government vessel be sent to protect Fort Vancouver. No answer, however, had come to this demand up to the month of June, 1845.

We have seen how, with affairs in this condition at Vancouver, and with the settled hostility of the Mission party against Dr. McLaughlin, the peace was yet maintained by the constant and unremitting kindness of the Doctor towards the American settlers. He had for some time, in his own mind, yielded the question of the future sovereignty of the country. That the Americans would hold all of Oregon south of the Columbia was beyond a peradventure; how much more, it remained for the heads of government to decide. The only question was, how to keep at peace with them until the boundary should be agreed upon; and how to maintain his own rights in Oregon, as a citizen, until the charter of the Company should expire, leaving him free to choose whether he would be an American or a British subject.

CHAPTER XXX.

1845.   The pressure of all these circumstances induced
Dr. McLaughlin to consider whether it were not best to
unite with the American Organization.   It was true the
Hudson's Bay Company's charter provided for the government of its employes.   But it had no authority over Americans, and if a desperado calling himself an American citizen
chose to destroy the Company's property, as was continually
threatened, he could do so with impunity, so far as the
Company's power to punish was concerned.

There were a few men in the Wallamet colony with
whom Dr. McLaughlin was somewhat confidential, and to
whom he had spoken of his difficulties.   Some of these
were members of the legislature, and determined to use
their influence to remove the chief obstacle to the Doctor's co-operation with the Provisional Government.   Accordingly when the legislature convened in the summer of
1845, the form of the oath of membership was so altered
as to bind the person taking it to support the Organic
Laws only "so far as they were consistent with their duties
as citizens of the United States, *or subjects of Great Britain.*"

The Doctor understood this alteration in the form of the
oath as an invitation to him to join the organization in behalf of the Hudson's Bay Company, and a letter to him from
the gentlemen in the legislature confirmed him in this belief.
Convinced that it was the best thing to do, for the peace
and security of all concerned, the Doctor, after consulting

with his associate, Mr., now Sir James Douglas, became a member of the colonial organization. Now, certainly, it would seem, he might set his mind at rest, since all the people in the country were acting together under one government, which interfered with the allegiance of no one. The Canadians had already united with the Americans, leaving no outsiders except the Indians; the organization itself had been re-modeled and strengthened, the colony had a regular legislature with the full powers usual to such bodies, and had a governor, also clothed with the gubernatorial authority common to that office in the United States.

But just when Dr. McLaughlin was settling down to a somewhat composed state of mind, in view of all the amendments above mentioned, there suddenly appeared at Fort Vancouver two visitors—gentlemen of position—government officers on leave, which perhaps meant in this instance on a secret service. These two gentlemen were Lieut. Peel and Captain Park, and they brought a letter to Dr. McLaughlin from Captain Gordon, of Her Majesty's ship *America*, then in Puget Sound, and this letter was to inform him that the *America* had been sent by Admiral Seymour " to assure Her Majesty's subjects in the country of firm protection."

After the struggle seemed almost over, and light began to dawn on the vexed question of conflicting duties, too late to be of any real service, but seeming rather to be in danger of exciting fresh suspicion, the long-waited-for help had come at last. Dr. McLaughlin had plenty of reason to wish his visitors had staid away, both then and afterwards; so evident was it that their business in Oregon was that of spies—spies upon himself, as well as upon the Americans. What their report was, can only be guessed at. Certain it is, however, that the Doctor was called upon for explanations with regard to his acts encouraging American settlement, and his reasons for joining the American colonial organization, and that he fell under the Company's censure for the same—the misunderstanding ending in his resignation.

Lieut. Peel and Captain Park made their visit to Vancouver agreeable to themselves, as well as serviceable to their Government. They partook not only of the hospitality of the fort, but visited also among the American settlers, taking "pot-luck," and sleeping in a cabin loft, with great good humor. If they sometimes displayed a little native snobishness toward the frontiersmen, it is not to be wondered at.

As our friend Meek was sure to be found wherever there was anything novel or exciting transpiring, so he was sure to fall in with visitors so distinguished as these, and as ready to answer their questions as they were to ask them. The conversation chanced one day to run upon the changes that had taken place in the country since the earliest settlement by the Americans, and Meek, who felt an honest pride in them, was expatiating at some length, to the ill-concealed amusement of the young officers, who probably saw nothing to admire in the rude improvements of the Oregon pioneers.

"Mr. Meek," said one of them, "if you have been so long in the country and have witnessed such wonderful transformations, doubtless you may have observed equally great ones in nature; in the rivers and mountains, for instance?"

Meek gave a lightning glance at the speaker who had so mistaken his respondent:

"I reckon I have," said he slowly. Then waving his hand gracefully toward the majestic Mt. Hood, towering thousands of feet above the summit of the Cascade range, and white with everlasting snows: "When *I* came to this country, Mount Hood was *a hole in the ground !*"

It is hardly necessary to say that the conversation terminated abruptly, amid the universal cachinations of the bystanders.

Notwithstanding the slighting views of Her British Majesty's naval officers, the young colony was making rapid strides. The population had been increased nearly eight hundred by the immigration of 1844, so that now it numbered nearly two thousand. Grain had been raised in considerable quantities, cattle and hogs had multiplied, and the farmers were in the best of spirits. Even our hero, who hated farm labor, began to entertain faith in the resources of his land claim to make him rich.

Such was the promising condition of the colony in the summer of 1845. Much of the real prosperity of the settlers was due to the determination of the majority to exclude ardent spirits and all intoxicating drinks from the country. So well had they succeeded that a gentleman writing of the colony at that time, says: "I attended the last term of the circuit courts in most of the counties, and I found great respect shown to judicial authority everywhere; nor did I see a single *drunken juryman, nor witness, nor spectator.* So much industry, good order, and sobriety I have never seen in any community."

While this was the rule, there were exceptions to it. During the spring term of the Circuit Court, Judge Nesmith being on the bench, a prisoner was arraigned before him for "assault with intent to kill." The witness for the prosecution was called, and was proceeding to give evidence, when, at some statement of his, the prisoner vociferated that he was a "d——d liar," and quickly stripping off his coat demanded a chance to fight it out with the witness.

24

Judge Nesmith called for the interference of Meek, who had been made marshal, but just at that moment he was not to be found. Coming into the room a moment later, Meek saw the Judge down from his bench, holding the prisoner by the collar.

"You can imagine," says Meek, "the bustle in court. But the Judge had the best of it. He fined the rascal, and made him pay it on the spot; while I just stood back to see his honor handle him. That was fun for me."

Such, however, was the good order of the colony at this time, that it was thought important to memorialize Congress on the condition and prospects of Oregon—to remind the Government of the precarious situation of its expectant children, should either the Indians or the Hudson's Bay Company make war on them; but most important of all, to beseech the United States to put an end to the treaty of joint occupation before the expiration of the ten years now nearly concluded.

The memorial being prepared, together with a copy of the Organic Laws, and explanations and assurances to the Government that they were only adopted through necessity, these documents were signed by the members of the House of Representatives and delivered to Dr. White, who was about to leave for the States, to settle up his accounts at Washington.

Connected with this very proper and dignified proceeding, was another not strictly dignified, but on the contrary partaking largely of the ridiculous. It appeared that, although the Speaker of the House opposed the Organic Law, as recently adopted, under the impression it was his duty, he had appended his name to the copy to be transmitted to the Government, and also the resolutions of the House accompanying them. Dr. White was already on his way to Vancouver with the dispatches, when the discovery of this great misdemeanor was made known to the assembly. Immediately thereupon the Speaker was granted leave of absence, to follow and overtake Dr. White, and to erase his name from said documents. Other resolutions were passed, ordering a messenger to be despatched to bring back the documents, and also others not by any means complimentary to Dr. White.

A day or two later, the following note was received from Dr. White:

" August 17, 1845.

To the Honorable, &c.;

GENTLEMEN:—Being on my way, and having but a moment to reflect, I have been at a loss which of your resolutions most to respect or to obey; but at length have become satisfied that the first was taken most soberly, and, as it answers my purpose best, I pledge myself to adhere strictly to that. Sincerely wishing you good luck in legislating,

I am, my dear sirs, very respectfully yours,

E. WHITE.

Not to be outwitted so handsomely by the aspiring Indian Agent, it was subsequently

" *Resolved,* That the Secretary be requested to forward to the United States Government, through the American Consul at the Sandwich Islands, a copy of the articles of compact, as adopted by the people of Oregon Territory, on the last Saturday of July, A. D. 1845; and that the same be signed by the Governor and attested by the Secretary; also, all resolutions adopted by this House, relative to sending said documents by E. White, late Indian Agent of this Territory; also a copy of the letter of E. White to this House."

Whether or not these documents were ever transmitted does not appear; but certain it is, that Dr. White returned not again with either a gubernatorial commission or Indian agency. That he probably hoped to do so may be gathered from an extract taken from the St. Louis *New Era* of that period, which runs as follows:

" OREGON.—Mr. Elijah White is on his way to Washington, *as a delegate from the self-constituted government of Oregon, and goes to ask for a seat in Con-*

*gress, to represent that distant territory.   He carries with him his credentials from
the provisional government of Oregon,* and a large petition from the inhabitants
of that region, asking that the jurisdiction of the United States may extend
over that territory.   *   *   *   *   This delegation to Congress is
to induce that body to take the actual occupancy of Oregon, and on his report
and success will depend the decision of the question, whether or not the people
will establish a separate and independent republic on the shores of the Pacific."

But solemn audacity, like virtue, is sometimes compelled to be its own reward.

The autumn of 1845 was marked less by striking events
than by the energy which the people exhibited in improving the colony by laying out roads and town-sites.   Already quite a number of towns were located, in which
the various branches of business were beginning to develop themselves.   Oregon City was the most populous
and important, but Salem, Champoeg, and Portland were
known as towns, and other settlements were growing up
on the Tualatin Plains and to the south of them, in the
fertile valleys of the numerous tributaries to the Wallamet.

Portland was settled in this year, and received its name
from the game of " heads you lose, tails I win," by which
its joint owners agreed to determine it.   One of them
being a Maine man, was for giving it the name which it
now bears, the other partner being in favor of Boston,
because he was a Massachusetts man.   It was, therefore,
agreed between them that a copper cent should be tossed
to decide the question of the christening, which being
done, heads and Portland won.

The early days of that city were not always safe and
pleasant any more than those of its older rivals; and the
few inhabitants frequently were much annoyed by the
raids they were subject to from the now thoroughly vag-
abondized Indians.   On one occasion, while yet the population was small, they were very much annoyed by the

visit of eight or ten lodges of Indians, who had somewhere obtained liquor enough to get drunk on, and were
enjoying a debauch in that spirit of total abandon which
distinguishes the Indian carousal.

Their performances at length alarmed the people, yet
no one could be found who could put an end to them.
In this dilemma the Marshal came riding into town, splen-
didly mounted on a horse that would turn at the least
touch of the rein. The countenances of the anxious
Portlanders brightened. One of the town proprietors
eagerly besought him to "settle those Indians." "Very
well," answered Meek; "I reckon it won't take me long."
Mounting his horse, after first securing a rawhide rope, he
"charged" the Indian lodges, rope in hand, laying it on
with force, the bare shoulders of the Indians offering
good *back-grounds* for the pictures which he was rapidly
executing.

Not one made any resistance, for they had a wholesome
fear of *tyee* Meek. In twenty minutes not an Indian, man
or woman, was left in Portland. Some jumped into the
river and swam to the opposite side, and some fled to the
thick woods and hid themselves. The next morning,
early, the women cautiously returned and carried away
their property, but the men avoided being seen again by
the marshal who punished drunkenness so severely.

Reader's query. Was it Meek or the Marshal who so
strongly disapproved of spreeing?

Ans. It was the Marshal.

The immigration to Oregon this year much exceeded
that of any previous year; and there was the usual
amount of poverty, sickness, and suffering of every sort,
among the fresh arrivals. Indeed the larger the trains
the greater the amount of suffering generally; since the
grass was more likely to be exhausted, and more hin-

drances of every kind were likely to occur. In any case, a march of several months through an unsettled country was sure to leave the traveler in a most forlorn and exhausted condition every way.

This was the situation of thousands of people who reached the Dalles in the autumn of 1845. Food was very scarce among them, and the difficulties to encounter before reaching the Wallamet just as great as those of the two previous years. As usual the Hudson's Bay Company came to the assistance of the immigrants, furnishing a passage down the river in their boats; the sick, and the women and children being taken first.

Among the crowd of people encamped at the Dalles, was a Mr. Rector, since well known in Oregon and California. Like many others he was destitute of provisions; his supplies having given out. Neither had he any money. In this extremity he did that which was very disagreeable to him, as one of the "prejudiced" American citizens who were instructed beforehand to hate and suspect the Hudson's Bay Company—he applied to the company's agent at the Dalles for some potatoes and flour, confessing his present inability to pay, with much shame and reluctance.

"Do not apologize, sir," said the agent kindly; "take what you need. There is no occasion to starve while our supplies hold out."

Mr. R. found his prejudices in danger of melting away under such treatment; and not liking to receive bounty a second time, he resolved to undertake the crossing of the Cascade mountains while the more feeble of the immigrants were being boated down the Columbia. A few others who were in good health decided to accompany him. They succeeded in getting their wagons forty miles beyond the Dalles; but there they could move no further.

In this dilemma, after consultation, Mr. Rector and Mr. Barlow agreed to go ahead and look out a wagon road. Taking with them two days' provisions, they started on in the direction of Oregon City. But they found road hunting in the Cascade mountains an experience unlike any they had ever had. Not only had they to contend with the usual obstacles of precipices, ravines, mountain torrents, and weary stretches of ascent and descent; but they found the forests standing so thickly that it would have been impossible to have passed between the trees with their wagons had the ground been clear of fallen timber and undergrowth. On the contrary these latter obstacles were the greatest of all. So thickly were the trunks of fallen trees crossed and recrossed everywhere, and so dense the growth of bushes in amongst them, that it was with difficulty they could force their way on foot.

It soon became apparent to the road hunters, that two days' rations would not suffice for what work they had before them. At the first camp it was agreed to live upon half rations the next day; and to divide and subdivide their food each day, only eating half of what was left from the day before, so that there would always still remain a morsel in case of dire extremity.

But the toil of getting through the woods and over the mountains proved excessive; and that, together with insufficient food, had in the course of two or three days reduced the strength of Mr. Barlow so that it was with great effort only that he could keep up with his younger and more robust companion, stumbling and falling at every few steps, and frequently hurting himself considerably.

So wolfish and cruel is the nature of men, under trying circumstances, that instead of feeling pity for his weaker and less fortunate companion, Mr. Rector became impatient, blaming him for causing delays, and often requiring assistance.

To render their situation still more trying, rain began to fall heavily, which with the cold air of the mountains, soon benumbed their exhausted frames. Fearing that should they go to sleep so cold and famished, they might never be able to rise again, on the fourth or fifth evening

they resolved to kindle a fire, if by a n y means they could do so. Dry and broken wood h a d been plenty enough, but for the r a i n, w h i c h was drenching e v e r y-thing. N e i t h e r matches nor flint had they, however, in any case. The night was setting in black with dark-ness; t h e w i n d swayed t h e giant firs over head, and then they h e a r d the thunder of a falling monarch of the forest unpleas-antly near. Search-ing among the bush-

THE ROAD-HUNTERS.

es, and under fallen timber for some dry leaves and sticks, Mr. Rector took a bundle of them to the most sheltered spot he could find, and set himself to work to coax a spark of fire out of two pieces of dry wood which he had split for that purpose. It was a long and weary while before success was attained, by vigorous rubbing together of the dry wood, but it was attained at last; and the stiffening limbs of the road-hunters were warmed by a blazing camp-fire.

The following day, the food being now reduced to a crumb for each, the explorers, weak and dejected, toiled on in silence, Mr. Rector always in advance. On chancing to look back at his companion he observed him to be brushing away a tear. "What now, old man?" asked Mr. R. with most unchristian harshness.

"What would you do with me, Rector, should I fall and break a leg, or become in any way disabled?" inquired Mr. Barlow, nervously.

"Do with you? *I would eat you!*" growled Mr. Rector, stalking on again.

As no more was said for some time, Mr. R.'s conscience rather misgave him that he treated his friend unfeelingly; then he stole a look back at him, and beheld the wan face bathed in tears.

"Come, come, Barlow," said he more kindly, "don't take affairs so much to heart. You will not break a leg, and I should not eat you if you did, for you have'nt any flesh on you to eat."

"Nevertheless, Rector, I want you to promise me that in case I should fall and disable myself, so that I cannot get on, you will not leave me here to die alone, but will kill me with your axe instead."

"Nonsense, Barlow; you are weak and nervous, but you are not going to be disabled, nor eaten, nor killed. Keep up man; we shall reach Oregon City yet."

So, onward, but ever more slowly and painfully, toiled again the pioneers, the wonder being that Mr. Barlow's fears were not realized, for the clambering and descending gave him many a tumble, the tumbles becoming more frequent as his strength declined.

Towards evening of this day as they came to the precipitous bank of a mountain stream which was flowing in the direction they wished to go, suddenly there came to their ears a sound of more than celestial melody; the tinkling of bells, lowing of cattle, the voice of men hallooing to the herds. They had struck the cattle trail, which they had first diverged from in the hope of finding a road passable to wagons. In the overwhelming revulsion of feeling which seized them, neither were able for some moments to command their voices to call for assistance. That night they camped with the herdsmen, and supped in such plenty as an immigrant camp afforded.

Such were the sufferings of two individuals, out of a great crowd of sufferers; some afflicted in one way and some in another. That people who endured so much to reach their El Dorado should be the most locally patriotic people in the world, is not singular. Mr. Barlow lived to construct a wagon road over the Cascades for the use of subsequent immigrations.

CHAPTER XXXI.

EARLY in 1846, Meek resigned his office of marshal of the colony, owing to the difficulty of collecting taxes; for in a thinly inhabited country, where wheat was a legal tender, at sixty cents per bushel, it was rather a burdensome occupation to collect, in so ponderous a currency; and one in which the collector required a granary more than a pocket-book. Besides, Meek had out-grown the marshalship, and aspired to become a legislator at the next June election.

He had always discharged his duty with promptitude and rectitude while sheriff; and to his known courage might be attributed, in many instances, the ready compliance with law which was remarkable in so new and peculiar an organization as that of the Oregon colony. The people had desired not to be taxed, at first; and for a year or more the goverment was sustained by a fund raised by subscription. When at last it was deemed best to make collections by law, the Canadians objected to taxation to support an American government, while they were still subjects of Great Britain; but ultimately yielded the point, by the advice of Dr. McLaughlin.

But it was not always the Canadians who objected to being taxed, as the following anecdote will show. Dr. McLaughlin was one day seated in his office, in conversation with some of his American friends, when the tall form of the sheriff darkened the doorway.

"I have come to tax you, Doctor," said Meek with his

blandest manner, and with a merry twinkle, half suppressed, in his black eyes.

"To tax me, Mr. Jo. I was not aware—I really was not aware—I believed I had paid my tax, Mr. Jo," stammered the Doctor, somewhat annoyed at the prospect of some fresh demand.

"Thar is an old ox out in my neighborhood, Doctor, and he is said to belong to you. Thar is a tax of twenty-five cents on him."

"I do not understand you, Mr. Jo. I have no cattle out in your neighborhood."

"I couldn't say how that may be, Doctor. All I do know about it, is just this. I went to old G—'s to collect the tax on his stock—and he's got a powerful lot of cattle,—and while we war a countin 'em over, he left out that old ox and said it belonged to you."

"Oh, oh, I see, Mr. Jo: yes, yes, I see! So it was Mr. G—," cried the Doctor, getting very red in the face. "I do remember now, since you bring it to my mind, that *I lent Mr. G— that steer six years ago!* Here are the twenty-five cents, Mr. Jo."

The sheriff took his money, and went away laughing; while the Doctor's American friends looked quite as much annoyed as the Doctor himself, over the meanness of some of their countrymen.

The year of 1846 was one of the most exciting in the political history of Oregon. President Polk had at last given the notice required by the Joint occupation treaty, that the Oregon boundary question must be settled. For years the Oregon question had been before Congress, and the people had taken an extraordinary interest in the manner in which it should be arranged. Ever since the emigration to Oregon had set in, the frequent memorials from the far-off colony, and the letters which private individuals were continually writing to friends in the states, concerning the beauty, fertility, and healthfulness of the new territory, kept alive the interest of the people. As the time drew nigh when a notice might be given, thousands were anxiously waiting to learn what course the President would take with regard to it. And when at length the notice appeared, there was equally great anxiety to have the government demand every inch of territory that could be claimed under the most strict construction of the Florida treaty; i. e., as far north as latitude 54° 40′.

So much had the subject been discussed, and so greatly had the feeling against the Hudson's Bay Company's monopoly been strengthened since the colonization of Oregon by the Americans, that the people did not take into consideration the Mexican War, nor the designs of the British government on California, but adopted for their watchword "fifty-four forty or fight," with the greatest enthusiasm; as if the "universal Yankee nation" need not fear the combined attacks of England, Mexico, and California, with twenty or thirty thousand Indians thrown in.

That government was more cautious, was perhaps a gain to our territorial possessions, of California, although by it we lost some degrees of less desirable soil. However that may be, both the British lion and the American eagle kept watch and guard over Oregon in that summer of suspense, 1846. About the close of that year there were fifteen English vessels of war in the Pacific, and eight American war vessels;—there had been nine. The total number of guns in the English squadron was 335; in the American, 310.

Agreeably to the promise which Dr. McLaughlin had received from the British Admiral, H. B. M. Sloop of war *Modeste* had arrived in the Columbia River in the month of October, 1845, and had wintered there. Much as the

Doctor had wished for protection from possible outbreaks, he yet felt that the presence of a British man-of-war in the Columbia, and another one in Puget Sound, was offensive to the colonists.   He set himself to cover up as carefully as possible the disagreeable features of the British lion, by endeavoring to establish social intercourse between the officers of the *Modeste* and the ladies and gentlemen of the colony, and his endeavors were productive of a partial success.

During the summer, however, the United States Schooner *Shark* appeared in the Columbia, thus restoring the balance of power, for the relief of national jealousy.   After remaining for some weeks, the *Shark* took her departure, but was wrecked on the bar at the mouth of the river, according to a prophecy of Meek's, who had a grudge against her commander, Lieut. Howison, for spoiling the sport he was having in company with one of her officers, while Howison was absent at the Cascades.

It appears that Lieut. Schenck was hospitably inclined, and that on receiving a visit from the hero of many bear-fights, who proved to be congenial on the subject of good liquors, he treated both Meek and himself so freely as to render discretion a foreign power to either of them.   Varied and brilliant were the exploits performed by these jolly companions during the continuance of the spree; and still more brilliant were those they talked of performing, even the taking of the *Modeste*, which was lying a little way off, in front of Vancouver.   Fortunately for the good of all concerned, Schenck contented himself with firing a salute as Meek was going over the side of the ship on leaving.   But for this misdemeanor he was put under arrest by Howison, on his return from the Cascades, an indignity which Meek resented for the prisoner, by assuring Lieut. Howison that he would lose his vessel before he got out of the river. And lose her he did. Schenck was released after the vessel struck, escaping with the other officers and crew by means of small boats. Very few articles were saved from the wreck, but among those few was the stand of colors, which Lieut. Howison subsequently presented to Gov. Abernethy for the colony's encouragement and use. News of the Treaty which defined the Oregon boundary having been just received, Lieut. Howison concluded his letter to the Governor by saying: "Nor can I omit the occasion to express my gratification and pride that this relict of my late command should be emphatically the first *United States'* flag to wave over the undisputed and purely American Territory of Oregon."

The long agony was over at last; the boundary question was settled, but not to the satisfaction of the majority of the people in Oregon. They no more liked the terms of the treaty, which granted the free navigation of the Columbia to England until the expiration of the Hudson's Bay Company's charter, than they did the fixing of the boundary line at the 49th parallel. However, there was no help for it now, and after one long sigh of disappointment and chagrin, they submitted to necessity; and, rather sullenly it is true, accepted the fact that seventeen years more they must endure the odious monopoly of the Hudson's Bay Company. While a few malcontents talked quite openly of a design to take Fort Vancouver, and thus end the business of that Company, the wiser portion of the people interested themselves in the future welfare of the colony, and perhaps a few were thoughtful enough to remember that the gentlemen of the Hudson's Bay Company in Oregon had some reason to feel disappointed also, inasmuch as, contrary to their expectations, the United States had taken possession of both sides of the Columbia River.

CHAPTER XXXII

1846.   THERE had been no winter since the commencement of the American settlement which had not had its
own particular causes for agitation, its colonial gossip, and
its party divisions.

The principal subjects on which the agitation, the gossip, and the divisions, were founded, this winter, were
first, the treaty, secondly, the immigration, and lastly, the
usual jealous dislike toward everything that was British.
Formerly, the news of the colony had been carried from
lip to lip alone: but now a newspaper, established in the
beginning of the year, and conducted by the "Oregon
Printing Association" at Oregon City, had become the
medium through which colonial affairs were supposed to
be made known.

And as the editor of the *Oregon Spectator* had as yet
no exchange list, the matter it contained could not but be
that which related almost entirely to Oregon affairs.   From
the following advertisement, which appeared in the first
number of the *Spectator*, we may learn that the facilities for postal communication were, at the best, indifferent.

To PERSONS WISHING TO SEND LETTERS EAST.—The postmaster-general
has contracted with Mr. H. BURNS to carry the mail from Oregon City to
Weston, in Missouri, for one trip only.   Letters mailed at any of the offices,
post paid, will be forwarded to any part of the United States.   As the mail
sent east, by Mr. BURNS, will reach Weston early in the season, it would be
advisable for those wishing to correspond with their friends in the east, to avail
themselves of the opportunity.   Postage only fifty cents on single sheets.

Through the same medium we are informed, by the following notices, that the officers of the *Modeste*, and the Hudson's Bay Company, were still exerting themselves to allay any irritation of feeling which dissatisfaction with the late treaty might have occasioned in the minds of the Americans.

THEATRE AT VANCOUVER.—That happy ship, (H. B. M. S. "Modeste,") was a scene of mirth and amusement upon Tuesday evening, the "Corps Dramatique" again performing before a fashionable and crowded audience. The musical and favorite comedy of "Love in a Village," followed by the "Mock Doctor" and the "Mayor of Garratt," were the plays of the evening, and we have to congratulate the whole performers in having so ably sustained their characters, and to thank these "tars" for the rich treat afforded us, in the *far west*, upon this occasion, as well as for the variety of attractions during the past winter.

THEATRE AT VANCOUVER.—The first performance of this season took place on the evening of the 5th instant, on board H. B. M. S. Modeste, by the same party of sailors who got up the drama so credibly, and afforded so much amusement last winter. The plays were "High life below stairs," "The deuce is in him," and "The Irish Widow;" and to do justice to these companions of the wave, the characters were, if not more ably, equally as well sustained as formerly. A numerous audience attended, (front seats graced by a beauteous circle of the fair sex,) and all appeared much gratified with the fun and mirth of these entertainments.

In addition to the theatrical entertainments, we find mention of balls, races, and picnics, extending through the year-and-a-half during which the *Modeste* remained in the river.

The *Spectator* usually contained articles on the resources of the country, intended to instruct the friends of the colony in the East, and also frequent metrical tributes to the loveliness and excellence of the new territory, contributed by enthusiastic correspondents. The average amount of poetical ability exhibited in these effusions was that of a "happy mediocrity;" and yet the local interest which attached to them made them rather attractive reading at that time. One stanza selected at random, will

25

convey the spirit of these productions, quite as well as a more lengthy quotation :

> " Upon Mount Hood I stand,
>   And with rapt gaze explore
>   The valley, and that patriot band
>   Upon Columbia's shore."

The author of the following, however, was not either a dull or an unobservant writer; and we insert his verses as a comical bit of natural history belonging peculiarly to Oregon.

ADVENTURES OF A COLUMBIA SALMON.

What is yon object which attracts the eye
Of the observing traveler, who ascends
Columbia's waters, when the summer sky
In one soft tint, calm nature's clothing blends:
As glittering in the sunbeams down it floats
'Till some vile vulture on its carcase gloats?

'Tis a poor salmon, which a short time past,
With thousands of her finny sisters came,
By instinct taught, to seek and find at last,
The place that gave her birth, there to remain
'Till nature's offices had been discharged,
And fry from out the ova had emerged.

Her Winter spent amongst the sheltered bays
Of the salt sea, where numerous fish of prey,
With appetite keen, the number of her days
Would soon have put an end to, could but they
Have caught her; but as they could not, she,
Spring having come, resolved to quit the sea:

And moving with the shoal along the coast, at length
She reached the outlet of her native river,
There tarried for a little to recruit her strength,
So tried of late by cold and stormy weather;
Sporting in playful gambols o'er the banks and sands,
Chasing the tiny fish frequenting there in bands.

But ah, how little thought this simple fish,
The toils and perils she had yet to suffer,
The chance she ran of serving as a dish
For hungry white men or for Indian's supper,—
Of enemies in which the stream abounded,
When lo! she's by a fisher's net surrounded.

Partly conscious of her approaching end,
She darts with meteoric swiftness to and fro,
Striking the frail meshes, within which she's penned,
Which bid defiance to her stoutest blow:
To smaller compass by degrees the snare is drawn,
When with a leap she clears it and is gone.

Once more at large with her companions, now
Become more cautious from her late escape,
She keeps in deeper water and thinks how
Foolish she was to get in such a scrape;
As mounting further up the stream, she vies
With other fish in catching gnats and flies.

And as she on her way did thus enjoy
Life's fleeting moments, there arose a panic
Amongst the stragglers, who in haste deploy
Around their elder leaders, quick as magic,
While she unconscious of the untimely rout,
Was by a hungry otter singled out:

Vigorous was the chase, on the marked victim shot
Through the clear water, while in close pursuit
Followed her amphibious foe, who scarce had got
Near enough to grasp her, when with turns acute,
And leaps and revolutions, she so tried the otter,
He gave up the hunt with merely having bit her.

Scarce had she recovered from her weakness, when
An ancient eagle, of the bald-head kind,
Winging his dreary way to'rds some lone glen,
Where was her nest with four plump eaglets lined,
Espied the fish, which he judged quite a treat,
And just the morsel for his little ones to eat:

And sailing in spiral circles o'er the spot,
Where lay his prey, then hovering for a time,
To take his wary aim, he stooped and caught
His booty, which he carried to a lofty pine;
Upon whose topmost branches, he first adjusted
His awkward load, ere with his claws he crushed it.

"Ill is the wind that blows no person good"—
So said the adage, and as luck would have it,
A huge grey eagle out in search of food,
Who just had whet his hunger with a rabbit,
Attacked the other, and the pair together,
In deadly combat fell into the river.

Our friend of course made off, when she'd done falling
Some sixty yards, and well indeed she might;
For ne'er, perhaps, a fish got such a mauling
Since Adam's time, or went up such a height
Into the air, and came down helter-skelter,
As did this poor production of a melter.

All these, with many other dangers, she survived,
Too manifold in this short space to mention;
So we'll suppose her to have now arrived
Safe at *the Falls*, without much more detention
Than one could look for, where so many liked her
Company, and so many Indians spiked her.

And here a mighty barrier stops her way:
The tranquil water, finding in its course
Itself beset with rising rocks, which lay
As though they said, "retire ye to your source,"
Bursts with indignant fury from its bondage, now
Rushes in foaming torrents to the chasm below.

The persevering fish then at the foot arrives,
Laboring with redoubled vigor mid the surging tide,
And finding, by her strength, she vainly strives
To overcome the flood, though o'er and o'er she tried;
Her tail takes in her mouth, and bending like a bow
That's to full compass drawn, aloft herself doth throw;

And spinning in the air, as would a silver wand
That's bended end to end and upwards cast,
Headlong she falls amid the showering waters, and
Gasping for breath, against the rocks is dashed:
Again, again she vaults, again she tries,
And in one last and feeble effort—dies.

There was, in Oregon City, a literary society called the Falls Association," some of whose effusions were occasionally sent to the *Spectator*, and this may have been one of them. At all events, it is plain that with balls, theatres, literary societies, and politics, the colony was not afflicted with dullness, in the winter of 1846.

But the history of the immigration this year, afforded, perhaps, more material for talk than any one other subject. The condition in which the immigrants arrived was one of great distress. A new road into the valley had been that season explored, at great labor and expense, by a company of gentlemen who had in view the aim to lessen the perils usually encountered in descending the Columbia. They believed that a better pass might be discovered through the Cascade range to the south, than that which had been found around the base of Mount Hood, and one which should bring the immigrants in at the upper end of the valley, thus saving them considerable travel and loss of time at a season of the year when the weather was apt to be unsettled.

With this design, a party had set out to explore the Cascades to the south, quite early in the spring ; but failing in their undertaking, had returned. Another company was then immediately formed, headed by a prominent member of society and the legislature. This company followed the old Hudson's Bay Company's trail, crossing all those ranges of mountains perpendicular to the coast, which form a triple wall between Oregon and California, until they came out into the valley of the Humboldt, whence they proceeded along a nearly level, but chiefly barren country to Fort Hall, on the Snake River.

The route was found to be practicable, although there was a scarcity of grass and water along a portion of it ; but as the explorers had with great difficulty found out and marked all the best camping grounds, and encountered first for themselves all the dangers of a hitherto unexplored region, most of which they believed they had overcome, they felt no hesitation in recommending the new road to the emigrants whom they met at Fort Hall.

Being aware of the hardships which the immigrants of the previous years had undergone on the Snake River plains, at the crossing of Snake River, the John Day, and Des Chutes Rivers, and the passage of the Columbia, the travelers gladly accepted the tidings of a safer route to the Wallamet. A portion of the immigration had already gone on by the road to the Dalles; the remainder turned off by the southern route.

Of those who took the new route, a part were destined for California. All, however, after passing through the sage deserts, committed the error of stopping to recruit their cattle and horses in the fresh green valleys among the foot-hills of the mountains. It did not occur to them that they were wasting precious time in this way; but to this indulgence was owing an incredible amount of suffering. The California-bound travelers encountered the season of snow on the Sierras, and such horrors are recorded of their sufferings as it is seldom the task of ears to hear or pen to record. Snow-bound, without food, those who died of starvation were consumed by the living; even children were eaten by their once fond parents, with an indifference horrible to think on: so does the mind become degraded by great physical suffering.

The Oregon immigrants had not to cross the lofty Sierras; but they still found mountains before them which, in the dry season, would have been formidable enough. Instead, however, of the dry weather continuing, very heavy rains set in. The streams became swollen, the mountain sides heavy and slippery with the wet earth. Where the road led through canyons, men and women were sometimes forced to stem a torrent, breast high, and cold enough to chill the life in their veins. The cattle gave out, the wagons broke down, provisions became exhausted, and a few persons perished, while all were in the direst straits.

The first who got through into the valley sent relief to those behind; but it was weeks before the last of the worn, weary, and now impoverished travelers escaped from the horrors of the mountains in which they were so hopelessly entangled, and where most of their worldly goods were left to rot.

This unfortunate termination to their hopes of a southern road had a dispiriting influence on the colony; inasmuch, too, as some of the immigrants who had suffered most loss, were disposed to lay the blame of it upon those gentlemen who, with so much effort, had marked out the new route. It did not soften the acrimony of this class of persons to be assured that those who had arrived by the Cascades were in fully as bad a plight, in many instances, as themselves. They could not forgive the innocent first-cause of their own particular ills. Feuds grew out of their bitter indignation, which only a life-time could heal: and thus it was, that with all these impoverished new-comers making demands on their sympathy, each with the tale of his own peculiar woes to relate, there was plenty of excitement among the colonists that winter.

The Oregon legislature met as usual, to hold its winter session, though the people hoped and expected it would be for the last time under the Provisional Government. There were only two "mountain-men" in the House, at this session—Meek and Newell. There were also two Hudson's Bay Company men, from the counties on the north side of the river, showing an improvement in the public sentiment, since the settlement of the boundary question. In all, there were but fifteen members. Of the three nominees for Speaker of the House, Meek was one, but failed of the election.

There was no very important business before the legislature at this session. Considerable effort was made to get a bill through, regulating the manufacture and sale of wine and distilled spirituous liquors. After considerable discussion the bill passed the House, and was vetoed by the Governor, but finally was passed over the veto, by a two-thirds vote, this being the first successful attempt to legalize the sale of ardent spirits in Oregon.

Wheat still remaining a legal tender, Meek introduced a bill for its inspection, having probably learned from his experience as tax collector, that the people were sometimes inclined to cheat the government.

The Provisional Government had not provided for a divorce law suited to the wants of the country, and it was therefore only by special act of the legislature that divorces could be obtained. Several applications had been made, in the form of bills praying for a release from the bonds of matrimony. In every case but one these applications came from the sterner sex, and with various success. In this one case, the applicant had failed to enlist the sympathies of the committee to whom her case was referred, and there was every prospect that the legislature would adjourn without acting upon her petition.

In this emergency the lady sought out our hero, who could never refuse a lady's request, and entreated him to exert himself in her behalf, to procure her a divorce from her lord no longer loved. Accordingly the bill was prepared, but not presented to the House until the last moment before the close of the session, when it was hurried over, considered engrossed, read a third time, voted on and passed in a very brief space of time, to the entire satisfaction of both Meek and his *protegé*.

CHAPTER XXXIII.

1847. There were no events to make remarkable the spring and summer of 1847. Oregon had a promising commerce growing up with California, the principal articles of export being flour and lumber. In the month of April alone there went out of the Columbia River 1736 barrels of flour, 200,000 feet of lumber, and over 200,000 shingles. Of this amount about half was furnished by the Hudson's Bay Company's mills, the remainder by the mills of the colony. Letters were received from California, giving notice that at least 20,000 barrels of flour would be needed in that country in the fall. Of this quantity the colonists expected to be able to supply one-half. Money now began to come into the colony, and the future looked promising.

To forward the cause of education, the Oregon Printing Association made a reprint of *Webster's Elementary Spelling-Book*, without so much as saying "by your leave" to the owners of the copy-right, and probably justified the theft upon the strength of the adage that "necessity knows no law."

Oregon certainly furnished, in her colonial condition, an example to the world scarcely second in interest to that of the Pilgrims of the New England colonies, such was the determined patriotism, the temperance, the industry, and the wonderful *success* of her undertakings. We have attempted, without being too diffuse, to show by what degrees, assisted by those whom they in their patriotism felt bound to regard as foes, they proceeded step by step toward the goal of their desires—the founding of a new state. Divers were the errors they committed, and rough and unpolished was the material out of which the edifice was to be erected; nevertheless it was well and strongly built, the foundation being civil liberty, the superstructure temperance, good morals, and education. These things the colonists had struggled for, and so far had maintained, and they were now looking for their reward. That Government which they so loved, regarding it as children regard a fond parent, and to which they had addressed so many prayers and entreaties in all these years, was about to take them under its fostering care, and to accept from their hands the filial gift of a vigorous young state.

In the suspense under which they for the present remained, there was nothing to do but to go on in the path of duty as they had heretofore done, keeping up their present form of government until it was supplanted by a better one. So passed the summer until the return of the "Glorious Fourth," which, being the first national anniversary occuring since the news of the treaty had reached the colony, was celebrated with proper enthusiasm.

It chanced that an American ship, the *Brutus*, Capt. Adams, from Boston, was lying in the Wallamet, and that a general invitation had been given to the celebrationists to visit the ship during the day. A party of fifty or sixty, including Meek and some of his mountain associates, had made their calculations to go on board at the same time, and were in fact already alongside in boats, when Captain Adams singled out a boat load of people belonging to the mission clique, and inviting them to come on board, ordered all the others off.

This was an insult too great to be borne by mountain-men, who resented it not only for themselves, but for the people's party of Americans to which they naturally belonged. Their blood was up, and without stopping to deliberate, Meek and Newell hurried off to fetch the twelve-pounder that had a few hours before served to thunder forth the rejoicings of a free people, but with which they now purposed to proclaim their indignation as freeman heinously insulted. The little twelve-pound cannon was loaded with rock, and got into range with the offending ship, and there is little doubt that Capt. Adams would have suffered loss at the hands of the incensed multitude, but for the timely interference of Dr. McLaughlin. On being informed of the warlike intentions of Meek and his associates, the good Doctor came running to the rescue, his white hair flowing back from his noble face with the hurry of his movements.

"Oh, oh, Mr. Joe, Mr. Joe, you must not do this! indeed, you must not do this foolish thing! Come now; come away. You will injure your country, Mr. Joe. How can you expect that ships will come here, if they are fired on? Come away, come away!"

And Meek, ever full of wagishness, even in his wrath, replied:

"Doctor, it is not that I love the Brutus less, but my dignity more."

"Oh, Shakespeare, Mr. Joe! But come with me; come with me."

And so the good Doctor, half in authority, half in kindness, persuaded the resentful colonists to pass by the favoritism of the Boston captain.

Meek was reëlected to the legislature this summer, and swam out to a vessel lying down at the mouth of the Wallamet, to get liquor to treat his constituents; from which circumstance it may be inferred that while Oregon was remarkable for temperance, there were occasions on which conviviality was deemed justifiable by a portion of her people.

Thus passed the summer. The autumn brought news of a large emigration *en route* for the new territory ; but it brought no news of good import from Congress. On the contrary the bill providing for a territorial government for Oregon had failed, because the Organic Laws of that territory excluded slavery forever from the country. The history of its failure is a part and parcel of the record of the long hard struggle of the south to extend slavery into the United States' territories.

One crumb of comfort, however, accompanied the intelligence of this disappointment; and that was a letter from the indefatigable friend of Oregon, Thomas H. Benton, of which the following is a copy :

WASHINGTON CITY, MARCH, 1847.

MY FRIENDS :—(For such I may call many of you from personal acquaintance, and all of you from my thirty years devotion to the interests of your country)—I think it right to make this communication to you at the present moment, when the adjournment of Congress, without passing the bill for your government and protection, seems to have left you in a state of abandonment by your mother country. But such is not the case. You are not abandoned! nor will you be denied protection unless you agree to admit slavery. I, a man of the South, and a slaveholder, tell you this.

The House of Representatives, as early as the middle of January, had passed the bill to give you a Territorial Government; and in that bill had sanctioned and legalized your Provisional Organic Act, one of the clauses of which forever prohibited the existence of slavery in Oregon. An amendment from the Senate's committee, to which this bill was referred, proposed to abrogate that prohibition ; and in the delays and vexations to which that amendment gave rise, the whole bill was laid upon the table, and lost for the session. This will be a great disappointment to you and a real calamity, already five years without law, or legal institutions for the protection of life, liberty, and property, and now doomed to wait a year longer. This is a strange and anomalous condition! almost incredible to contemplate, and most critical to endure! a colony of free men, four thousand miles from the Metropolitan government, and without law or government to preserve them! But do not be alarmed, or desperate. You will not be outlawed for not admitting slavery. Your fundamental act against that institution, copied from the Ordinance of 1787—(the work of the great men of the SOUTH, in the great day of the SOUTH, prohibiting slavery in a TERRITORY far less northern than yours)—will not be abrogated! nor is that the intention of the prime mover of the amendment. Upon the record of the Judiciary committee of the Senate is the author of that amendment; but not so the fact! It is only mid-wife to it. Its author is the same mind that generated the "FIRE BRAND RESOLUTIONS," of which I send you a copy, and of which the amendment is the legitimate derivation. Oregon is not the object. The most rabid propagandist of slavery cannot expect to plant it on the shores of the Pacific, in the latitude of Wisconsin and the Lake of the Woods. A home agitation, for election and disunion purposes, is all that is intended by thrusting this fire-brand question into your bill! and, at the next session, when it is thrust in again, we will scourge it out! and pass your bill as it ought to be. I promise you this in the name of the SOUTH as well as of the NORTH; and the event will not deceive me. In the meantime, the President will give you all the protection which existing laws, and detachments of the army and navy, can enable him to extend to you; and, until Congress has time to act, your friends must rely upon you to continue to govern yourselves, as you have heretofore done, under the provisions of your own voluntary compact, and with the justice, harmony, and moderation which is due to your own character and to the honor of the American name.

I send you, by Mr. Shively, a copy of the bill of the late session, both as it passed the House of Representatives and as proposed to be amended in the Senate, with the Senate's vote upon laying it on the table, and a copy of Mr. Calhoun's resolutions—(posterior in date to the amendment, but, nevertheless, its father)—also a copy of your own Provisional Organic Act, printed by order of the Senate; all which will put you completely in possession of the proceedings of Congress on your Petition for a Territorial Government, and for the protection and security of your rights.

In conclusion, I have to assure you that the same spirit which has made me the friend of Oregon for thirty years—which led me to denounce the joint occupation treaty the day it was made, and to oppose its renewal in 1828, and to labor for its abrogation until it was terminated; the same spirit which led me to reveal the grand destiny of Oregon in articles written in 1818, and to support every measure for her benefit since—this same spirit still animates me, and will continue to do so while I live—which, I hope, will be long enough to see an emporium of Asiatic commerce at the mouth of your river, and a stream of Asiatic trade pouring into the Valley of the Mississippi through the channel of Oregon.

Your friend and fellow citizen,

THOMAS H. BENTON.

In addition to this valuable bit of comfort and of history, another letter, written by James Buchanan, Secretary of State, and conveying President Polk's regrets that no

more had been done for Oregon, was presented to the
colonists by its bearer, who had also brought the communication of Senator Benton.   This gentleman was a Mr.
Shively, one of the two postmasters appointed for Oregon
Territory.   Here was all that Congress, after much effort,
had been able to accomplish—the appropriation of money
for transporting the mails to Oregon *via* the Isthmus of
Panama; the establishment of a post-office at Astoria, and
another at Oregon City; and the appointment of an Indian agent, whose inefficiency was patent· to all Oregon!
Mr. Buchanan's letter, however, contained a promise of a
regiment of mounted riflemen to protect the emigration;
and war vessels to visit Oregon waters as often as practicable.

Justly dissatisfied, but not inconsolable, the colony, now
that hope was extinguished for another season, returned
to its own affairs.   The immigration, which had arrived
early this year, amounted to between four and five thousand.   An unfortunate affray between the immigrants and
the Indians at the Dalles, had frightened away from that
station the Rev. Father Waller; and Dr. Whitman of the
Waiilatpu mission had purchased the station for the Presbyterian mission, and placed a nephew of his in charge.
Although, true to their original bad character, the Dalles
Indians had frequently committed theft upon the passing
emigration, this was the first difficulty resulting in loss
of life, which had taken place.   This quarrel arose out of
some thefts committed by the Indians, and the unwise advice of Mr. Waller, in telling the immigrants to retaliate
by taking some of the Indian horses.   An Indian can see
the justice of taking toll from every traveler passing
through his country; but he cannot see the justice of being robbed in return; and Mr. Waller had been long
enough among them to have known this savage peculiar-

ity.   In the skirmish which followed this act of retaliation,
one of the immigrants was killed, two seriously wounded,
and several others driven into the mountains for safety.
The chief of the Wascopams, or Dalles Indians, was killed,
and several of the tribe wounded.   Fearing the design
of the immigrants was to make war on them, they removed back into the mountains.   And thus was inaugu-
rated a series of Indian difficulties which harrassed the
inhabitants of the territory for the next ten years.

Following the arrival of the immigration and the ex-
tinguishment of the colony's hopes of a territorial government, a movement was put on foot among the members of the Mission party, to send a delegate to Congress,
charged with instructions to that body concerning the
wants and wishes of the future Territory.   The gentleman selected by the Governor, for this mission, was J. Q.
Thornton, at that time Chief Justice of the colony, and a
man of undoubted ability.   But as he did not go as a delegate from the legislature, and only by appointment of
the Governor, with the sanction of the Mission party,
there was considerable dissatisfaction with the action of
Governor Abernethy, and the legislature passed certain
resolutions expressive of its sense of the impropriety of
"secret factions" in the colony.   The event has since
proven that no harm was done, but probably considerable
good, by the extraordinary delegate, who chanced to be
in Washington at a critical time for the interests of Oregon.

But the manner in which the delegate was equipped
for the journey is unprecedented in the annals of the
whole country.   Had he been a regularly chosen delegate
from the legislature,—and had the legislature a right to
send a delegate to Congress, which it had not,—there was
not money enough in the colonial treasury to have paid

his passage out. Nor had the Governor and his friends money enough for this purpose. As might be conjectured in this case, extraordinary measures had to be adopted to raise the passage money. Subscriptions were taken in any and every thing which could be converted into currency. One contributer gave fifteen barrels of flour ; another a little money ; another furnished an outfit of clothing ; and the largest amount of coin raised was one hundred and fifty dollars.

Passage was secured on the bark *Whitton*, Captain Ghelston, who agreed to carry to New York, but failed to do so. At San Francisco the delegate made sale of his flour and other commodities, and Captain Ghelston obtained so favorable an opinion of the profits of a coasting trade, that when he had arrived at San Juan on the Mexican coast, he threw up his contract to carry his passenger to New York, leaving him to proceed as best he could. Fortunately, the United States sloop of war Portsmouth, Captain Montgomery, was lying at this port. She was a part of the squadron which had been guarding the American interests in the Pacific during the previous year ; and when Captain Montgomery learned the situation of the Oregon representative, he took the liberty of construing his instructions to "rescue American ministers in foreign ports" from difficulties into which they might have fallen through various causes, to mean that he was to convey this stranded delegate to his destination, which he immediately proceeded to do. Therefore it may be reckoned that the whole transaction of appointing and conveying the first Oregon delegate to Washington was decidedly unique, as well as somewhat expensive.

Finding that it must continue yet a little longer to look after its own government and welfare, the colony had settled back into its wonted pursuits. The legislature

had convened for its winter session, and had hardly elected
its officers and read the usual message of the Governor,
before there came another, which fell upon their ears like
a thunderbolt. Gov. Abernethy had sent in the following
letter, written at Vancouver the day before:

FORT VANCOUVER, Dec. 7, 1847.

George Abernethy, Esq.;

SIR :—Having received intelligence, last night, by special express from
Walla-Walla, of the destruction of the missionary settlement at Waiilatpu, by
the Cayuse Indians of that place, we hasten to communicate the particulars of
that dreadful event, one of the most atrocious which darkens the annals of Indian crime.

Our lamented friend, Dr. Whitman, his amiable and accomplished lady, with
nine other persons, have fallen victims to the fury of these remorseless savages,
who appear to have been instigated to this appalling crime by a horrible suspicion which had taken possession of their superstitious minds, in consequence
of the number of deaths from dysentery and measles, that Dr. Whitman was
silently working the destruction of their tribe by administering poisonous drugs,
under the semblance of salutary medicines.

With a goodness of heart and benevolence truly his own, Dr. Whitman had
been laboring incessantly since the appearance of the measles and dysentery
among his Indian converts, to relieve their sufferings ; and such has been the
reward of his generous labors.

A copy of Mr. McBean's letter, herewith transmitted, will give you all the
particulars known to us of this indescribably painful event.

Mr. Ogden, with a strong party, will leave this place as soon as possible for
Walla-Walla, to endeavor to prevent further evil ; and we beg to suggest to
you the propriety of taking instant measures for the protection of the Rev. Mr.
Spalding, who, for the sake of his family, ought to abandon the Clear-water
mission without delay, and retire to a place of safety, as he cannot remain at
that isolated station without imminent risk, in the present excited and irritable
state of the Indian population.

I have the honor to be, sir, your most obedient servant,

JAMES DOUGLAS.

26

CHAPTER XXXIV.

1842–7. DOUBTLESS the reader remembers the disquiet
felt and expressed by the Indians in the upper country in
the years 1842–3, when Dr. White was among them, lest the
Americans should take away their lands from them without payment. For the time they had been quieted by
presents, by the advice of the Hudson's Bay Company,
and by the Agent's promise that in good time the United
States would send them blankets, guns, ammunition, food
farming implements, and teachers to show them how to
live like the whites.

In the meantime, five years having passed, these promises had not been kept. Five times a large number of
whites, with their children, their cattle, and wagons, had
passed through their country, and gone down into the
Wallamet Valley to settle. Now they had learned that
the United States claimed the Wallamet valley; yet they
had never heard that the Indians of that country had received any pay for it.

They had accepted the religion of the whites believing
it would do them good; but now they were doubtful.
Had they not accepted laws from the United States agent,
and had not their people been punished for acts which
their ancestors and themselves had always before committed at will ? None of these innovations seemed to do
them any good: they were disappointed. But the whites,
or Bostons, (meaning the Americans) were coming more

and more every year, so that by-and-by there would be all Bostons and no Indians.

Once they had trusted in the words of the Americans; but now they knew how worthless were their promises. The Americans had done them much harm. Years before had not one of the missionaries suffered several of their people, and the son of one of their chiefs, to be slain in his company, yet himself escaped? Had not the son of another chief, who had gone to California to buy cattle, been killed by a party of Americans, for no fault of his own? Their chief's son was killed, the cattle robbed from his party, after having been paid for; and his friends obliged to return poor and in grief.

To be sure, Dr. White had given them some drafts to be used in obtaining cattle from the immigration, as a compensation for their losses in California; but they could not make them available; and those who wanted cattle had to go down to the Wallamet for them. In short, could the Indians have thought of an American epithet to apply to Americans, it would have been that expressive word *humbug*. What they felt and what they thought, was, that they had been cheated. They feared greater frauds in the future, and they were secretly resolved not to submit to them.

So far as regarded the missionaries, Dr. Whitman and his associates, they were divided; yet as so many looked on the Doctor as an agent in promoting the settlement of the country with whites, it was thought best to drive him from the country, together with all the missionaries. Several years before Dr. Whitman had known that the Indians were displeased with his settlement among them. They had told him of it: they had treated him with violence; they had attempted to outrage his wife; had burned his property; and had more recently several times warned him to leave their country, or they should kill him.

Not that all were angry at him alike, or that any were personally very ill-disposed towards him.   Everything that a man could do to instruct and elevate these savage people, he had done, to the best of his ability, together with his wife and assistants.   But he had not been able, or perhaps had not attempted, to conceal the fact, that he looked upon the country as belonging to his people, rather than to the natives, and it was this fact which was at the bottom of their "bad hearts" toward the Doctor.   So often had warnings been given which were disregarded by Dr. Whitman, that his friends, both at Vancouver and in the settlements, had long felt great uneasiness, and often besought him to remove to the Wallamet valley.

But although Dr. Whitman sometimes was half persuaded to give up the mission upon the representations of others, he could not quite bring himself to do so.   So far as the good conduct of the Indians was concerned, they had never behaved better than for the last two years. There had been less violence, less open outrage, than formerly; and their civilization seemed to be progressing; while some few were apparently hopeful converts.   Yet there was ever a whisper in the air—"Dr. Whitman must die."

The mission at Lapwai was peculiarly successful.   Mrs. Spalding, more than any other of the missionaries, had been able to adapt herself to the Indian character, and to gain their confidence.   Besides, the Nez Perces were a better nation than the Cayuses;—more easily controlled by a good counsel; and it seemed like doing a wrong to abandon the work so long as any good was likely to result from it.   There were other reasons too, why the missions could not be abandoned in haste, one of which was the difficulty of disposing of the property.   This might have been done perhaps, to the Catholics, who were establishing missions throughout the upper country; but Dr. Whitman would never have been so false to his own doctrines, as to leave the field of his labors to the Romish Church.

Yet the division of sentiment among the Indians with regard to religion, since the Catholic missionaries had come among them, increased the danger of a revolt: for in the Indian country neither two rival trading companies, nor two rival religions can long prosper side by side. The savage cannot understand the origin of so many religions. He either repudiates all, or he takes that which addresses itself to his understanding through the senses. In the latter respect, the forms of Catholicism, as adapted to the savage understanding, made that religion a dangerous rival to intellectual and idealistic Presbyterianism. But the more dangerous the rival, the greater the firmness with which Dr. Whitman would cling to his duty.

There were so many causes at work to produce a revolution among the Indians, that it would be unfair to name any one as *the* cause. The last and immediate provocation was a season of severe sickness among them. The disease was measels, and was brought in the train of the immigration.

This fact alone was enough to provoke the worst passions of the savage. The immigration in itself was a sufficient offense; the introduction through them of a pestilence, a still weightier one. It did not signify that Dr. Whitman had exerted himself night and day to give them relief. Their peculiar notions about a medicine-man made it the Doctor's duty to cure the sick; or made it the duty of the relatives of the dead and dying to avenge their deaths.

Yet in spite of all and every provocation, perhaps the fatal tragedy might have been postponed, had it not been for the evil influence of one Jo Lewis, a half-breed, who had accompanied the emigration from the vicinity of Fort Hall. This Jo Lewis, with a large party of emigrants, had stopped to winter at the mission, much against Dr. Whitman's wishes; for he feared not having food enough for so many persons. Finding that he could not prevent them, he took some of the men into his employ, and among others the stranger half-breed.

This man was much about the house, and affected to relate to the Indians conversations which he heard between Dr. and Mrs. Whitman, and Mr. Spalding, who with his little daughter, was visiting at Waiilatpu. These conversations related to poisoning the Indians, in order to get them all out of the way, so that the white men could enjoy their country unmolested. Yet this devil incarnate did not convince his hearers at once of the truth of his statements; and it was resolved in the tribe to make a test of Dr. Whitman's medicine. Three persons were selected to experiment upon; two of them already sick, and the third quite well. Whether it was that the medicine was administered in too large quantities, or whether an unhappy chance so ordered it, all those three persons died. Surely it is not singular that in the savage mind this circumstance should have been deemed decisive. It was then that the decree went forth that not only the Doctor and Mrs. Whitman, but all the Americans at the mission must die.

On the 22d of November, Mr. Spalding arrived at Waiilatpu, from his mission, one hundred and twenty miles distant, with his daughter, a child of ten years, bringing with him also several horse-loads of grain, to help feed the emigrants wintering there. He found the Indians suffering very much, dying one, two, three, and sometimes five in a day. Several of the emigrant families, also, were sick with measels and the dysentery, which followed the disease. A child of one of them died the day following Mr. Spalding's arrival.

Dr. Whitman's family consisted of himself and wife, a young man named Rodgers, who was employed as a teacher, and also studying for the ministry, two young people, a brother and sister, named Bulee, seven orphaned children of one family, whose parents had died on the road to Oregon in a previous year, named Sager, Helen Mar, the daughter of Joe Meek, another little half-breed girl, daughter of Bridger the fur-trader, a half-breed Spanish boy whom the Doctor had brought up from infancy, and two sons of a Mr. Manson, of the Hudson's Bay Company.

Besides these, there were half-a-dozen other families at the mission, and at the saw-mill, twenty miles distant, five families more—in all, forty-six persons at Waiilatpu, and fifteen at the mill, who were among those who suffered by the attack. But there were also about the mission, three others, Joe Lewis, Nicholas Finlay, and Joseph Stanfield, who probably knew what was about to take place, and may, therefore be reckoned as among the conspirators.

While Mr. Spalding was at Waiilatpu, a message came from two Walla-Walla chiefs, living on the Umatilla River, to Dr. Whitman, desiring him to visit the sick in their villages, and the two friends set out together to attend to the call, on the evening of the 27th of November. Says Mr. Spalding, referring to that time: "The night was dark, and the wind and rain beat furiously upon us. But our interview was sweet. We little thought it was to be our last. With feelings of the deepest emotion we called to mind the fact, that eleven years before, we crossed this trail before arriving at Walla-Walla, the end of our seven months' journey from New York. We called to mind the high hopes and thrilling interests which had been awakened during the year that followed—of our successful labors and the constant devotedness of the Indians to improvement. True, we remembered the months of deep solicitude we had, occasioned by the increasing menacing demands of the Indians for pay for their wood, their water, their air, their lands. But much of this had passed away, and the Cayuses were in a far more encouraging condition than ever before." Mr. Spalding further relates that himself and Dr. Whitman also conversed on the danger which threatened them from the Catholic influence. " We felt," he says, " that the present sickness afforded them a favorable opportunity to excite the Indians to drive us from the country, and all the movements about us seemed to indicate that this would soon be attempted, if not executed." Such was the suspicion in the minds of the Protestants. Let us hope that it was not so well founded as they believed.

The two friends arrived late at the lodge of *Stickas*, a chief, and laid down before a blazing fire to dry their drenched clothing. In the morning a good breakfast was prepared for them, consisting of beef, vegetables, and bread—all of which showed the improvement of the Indians in the art of living. The day, being Sunday, was observed with as much decorum as in a white man's house. After breakfast, Dr. Whitman crossed the river to visit the chiefs who had sent for him, namely, *Tan-i-tan*, *Five Crows*, and *Yam-ha-wa-lis*, returning about four o'clock in the afternoon, saying he had taken tea with the Catholic bishop and two priests, at their house, which belonged to *Tan-i-tan*, and that they had promised to visit him in a short time. He then departed for the mission, feeling uneasy about the sick ones at home.

Mr. Spalding remained with the intention of visiting

the sick and offering consolation to the dying. But he soon discovered that there was a weighty and uncomfortable secret on the mind of his entertainer, *Stickas*. After much questioning, *Stickas* admitted that the thought which troubled him was that the Americans had been " decreed against" by his people ; more he could not be induced to reveal. Anxious, yet not seriously alarmed,—for these warnings had been given before many times,—he retired to his couch of skins, on the evening of the 29th, being Monday—not to sleep, however; for on either side of him an Indian woman sat down to chant the death-song —that frightful lament which announces danger and death. On being questioned they would reveal nothing.

On the following morning, Mr. Spalding could no longer remain in uncertainty, but set out for Waiilatpu. As he mounted his horse to depart, an Indian woman placed her hand on the neck of his horse to arrest him, and pretending to be arranging his head-gear, said in a low voice to the rider, "Beware of the Cayuses at the mission." Now more than ever disturbed by this intimation that it was the mission which was threatened, he hurried forward, fearing for his daughter and his friends. He proceeded without meeting any one until within sight of the lovely Walla-Walla valley, almost in sight of the mission itself, when suddenly, at a wooded spot where the trail passes through a little hollow, he beheld two horsemen advancing, whom he watched with a fluttering heart, longing for, and yet dreading, the news which the very air seemed whispering.

The two horsemen proved to be the Catholic Vicar General, Brouillet, who, with a party of priests and nuns had arrived in the country only a few months previous, and his half-breed interpreter, both of whom were known

to Mr. Spalding.   They each drew rein as they approached, Mr. Spalding immediately inquiring "what news?"

"There are very many sick at the Whitman station,"
answered Brouillet, with evident embarrassment.

"How are Doctor and Mrs. Whitman?" asked Spalding
anxiously.

"The Doctor is ill—is dead," added the priest reluctantly.

"And Mrs. Whitman?" gasped Spalding.

"Is dead also.   The Indians have killed them."

"My daughter?" murmured the agonized questioner.

"Is safe, with the other prisoners," answered Brouillet.

"And then," says Spalding in speaking of that moment
of infinite horror, when in his imagination a picture of the
massacre, of the anguish of his child, the suffering of the
prisoners, of the probable destruction of his own family
and mission, and his surely impending fate, all rose up
before him—"I felt the world all blotted out at once, and
sat on my horse as rigid as a stone, not knowing or feeling
anything."

While this conversation had been going on the half-
breed interpreter had kept a sinister watch over the communication, and his actions had so suspicious a look that
the priest ordered him to ride on ahead.   When he had
obeyed, Brouillet gave some rapid instructions to Spalding; not to go near the mission, where he could do no
good, but would be certainly murdered; but to fly, to
hide himself until the excitement was over.   The men at
the mission were probably all killed; the women and
children would be spared; nothing could be done at present but to try to save his own life, which the Indians were
resolved to take.

The conversation was hurried, for there was no time to
lose.   Spalding gave his pack-horse to Brouillet, to avoid

being encumbered by it; and taking some provisions which the priest offered, struck off into the woods there to hide until dark.   Nearly a week from this night he arrived at the Lapwai mission, starved, torn, with bleeding feet as well as broken heart.   Obliged to secrete himself by day, his horse had escaped from him, leaving him to perform his night journeys on foot over the sharp rocks and prickly cactus plants, until not only his shoes had been worn out, but his feet had become cruelly lacerated. The constant fear which had preyed upon his heart of finding his family murdered, had produced fearful havoc in the life-forces; and although Mr. Spalding had the happiness of finding that the Nez Perces had been true to Mrs. Spalding, defending her from destruction, yet so great had been the first shock, and so long continued the strain, that his nervous system remained a wreck ever afterward.

CHAPTER XXXV.

1847. WHEN Dr. Whitman reached home on that Sunday night, after parting with Mr. Spalding at the Umatilla, it was already about midnight; yet he visited the sick before retiring to rest; and early in the morning resumed his duties among them. An Indian died that morning. At his burial, which the Doctor attended, he observed that but few of the friends and relatives of the deceased were present but attributed it to the fear which the Indians have of disease.

Everything about the mission was going on as usual. Quite a number of Indians were gathered about the place; but as an ox was being butchered, the crowd was easily accounted for. Three men were dressing the beef in the yard. The afternoon session of the mission school had just commenced. The mechanics belonging to the station were about their various avocations. Young Bulee was sick in the Doctor's house. Three of the orphan children who were recovering from the measles, were with the Doctor and Mrs. Whitman in the sitting-room; and also a Mrs. Osborne, one of the emigrants who had just got up from a sick bed, and who had a sick child in her arms.

The Doctor had just come in, wearied, and dejected as it was possible for his resolute spirit to be, and had seated himself, bible in hand, when several Indians came to a side door, asking permission to come in and get some medicine. The Doctor rose, got his medicines, gave them out, and

MASSACRE OF REV. DR. WHITMAN OF THE PRESBYTERIAN MISSION.

N. ORR. Co.

sat down again. At that moment Mrs. Whitman was in an adjoining room and did not see what followed. *Tam-a-has*, a chief called "the murderer," came behind the Doctor's chair, and raising his tomahawk, struck the Doctor in the back of the head, stunning but not killing him.

Instantly there was a violent commotion. John Sager, one of the adopted children, sprang up with his pistol in his hand, but before he could fire it, he too was struck down, and cut and hacked shockingly. In the meantime Dr. Whitman had received a second blow upon the head, and now laid lifeless on the floor. Cries and confusion filled the house.

At the first sound, Mrs. Whitman, in whose ears that whisper in the air had so long sounded, began in agony to stamp upon the floor, and wring her hands, crying out, "Oh, the Indians, the Indians!" At that moment one of the women from an adjoining building came running in, gasping with terror, for the butchery was going on outside as well, and *Tam-a-has* and his associates were now assisting at it. Going to the room where the Doctor lay insensible, Mrs. Whitman and her terrified neighbor dragged him to the sofa and laid him upon it, doing all they could to revive him. To all their inquiries he answered by a whispered "no," probably not conscious what was said.

While this was being done, the people from every quarter began to crowd into the Doctor's house, many of them wounded. Outside were heard the shrieks of women, the yells of the Indians, the roar of musketry, the noise of furious riding, of meeting war-clubs, groans, and every frightful combination of sound, such as only could be heard at such a carnival of blood. Still Mrs. Whitman sat by her husband's side, intent on trying to rouse him to say one coherent word.

Nearer and nearer came the struggle, and she heard

some one exclaim that two of her friends were being murdered beneath the window. Starting up, she approached the casement to get a view, as if by looking she could save; but that moment she encountered the fiendish gaze of Jo Lewis the half-breed, and comprehended his guilt. "Is it *you*, Jo, who are doing this?" she cried. Before the expression of horror had left her lips, a young Indian who had been a special favorite about the mission, drew up his gun and fired, the ball entering her right breast, when she fell without a groan.

When the people had at first rushed in, Mrs. Whitman had ordered the doors fastened and the sick children removed to a room up stairs. Thither now she was herself conveyed, having first recovered sufficiently to stagger to the sofa where lay her dying husband. Those who witnessed this strange scene, say that she knelt and prayed—prayed for the orphan children she was leaving, and for her aged parents. The only expression of personal regret she was heard to utter, was sorrow that her father and mother should live to know she had perished in such a manner.

In the chamber were now gathered Mrs. Whitman, Mrs. Hayes, Miss Bulee, Catharine Sager, thirteen years of age, and three of the sick children, besides Mr. Rogers and Mr. Kimble. Scarcely had they gained this retreat when the crashing of windows and doors was heard below, and with whoops and yells the savages dashed into the sitting-room where Doctor Whitman still lay dying. While some busied themselves removing from the house the goods and furniture, a chief named *Te-lau-ka-ikt*, a favorite at the mission, and on probation for admission into the church, deliberately chopped and mangled the face of his still breathing teacher and friend with his tomahawk, until every feature was rendered unrecognizable.

The children from the school-house were brought into the kitchen of the Doctor's house about this time, by Jo Lewis, where, he told them, they were going to be shot. Mr. Spalding's little girl Eliza, was among them. Understanding the native language, she was fully aware of the terrible import of what was being said by their tormentors. While the Indians talked of shooting the children huddled together in the kitchen, pointing their guns, and yelling, Eliza covered her face with her apron, and leaned over upon the sink, that she might not see them shoot her. After being tortured in this manner for some time, the children were finally ordered out of doors.

While this was going on, a chief called *Tamt-sak-y*, was trying to induce Mrs. Whitman to come down into the sitting-room.

She replied that she was wounded and could not do so, upon which he professed much sorrow, and still desired her to be brought down, "If you are my friend *Tamt-sak-y*, come up and see me," was her reply to his professions, but he objected, saying there were Americans concealed in the chamber, whom he feared might kill him. Mr. Rogers then went to the head of the stairs and endeavored to have the chief come up, hoping there might be some friendly ones, who would aid them in escaping from the murderers. *Tamt-sak-y*, however, would not come up the stairs, although he persisted in saying that Mrs. Whitman should not be harmed, and that if all would come down and go over to the other house where the families were collected, they might do so in safety.

The Indians below now began to call out that they were going to burn the Doctor's house. Then no alternative remained but to descend and trust to the mercy of the savages. As Mrs. Whitman entered the sitting-room, leaning on one arm of Mr. Rogers, who also was wounded in the head, and had a broken arm, she caught a view of the shockingly mutilated face of her husband and fell fainting upon the sofa, just as Doctor Whitman gave a dying gasp.

Mr. Rogers and Mrs. Hayes now attempted to get the sofa, or settee, out of the house, and had succeeded in moving it through the kitchen to the door. No sooner did they appear in the open door-way than a volley of balls assailed them. Mr. Rogers fell at once, but did not die immediately, for one of the most horrid features in this horrid butchery was, that the victims were murdered by torturing degrees. Mrs. Whitman also received several gunshot wounds, lying on the settee. Francis Sager, the oldest of her adopted boys, was dragged into the group of dying ones and shot down.

The children, who had been turned out of the kitchen were still huddled together about the kitchen door, so near to this awful scene that every incident was known to them, so near that the flashes from the guns of the Indians burnt their hair, and the odor of the blood and the burning powder almost suffocated them.

At two o'clock in the afternoon the massacre had commenced. It was now growing dusk, and the demons were eager to finish their work. Seeing that life still lingered in the mangled bodies of their victims, they finished their atrocities by hurling them in the mud and gore which filled the yard, and beating them upon their faces with whips and clubs, while the air was filled with the noise of their shouting, singing, and dancing—the Indian women and children assisting at these orgies, as if the Bible had never been preached to them. And thus, after eleven years of patient endeavor to save some heathen souls alive, perished Doctor and Mrs. Whitman.

In all that number of Indians who had received daily kindnesses at the hands of the missionaries, only two showed any compassion. These two, *Ups* and *Madpool*, Walla-Wallas, who were employed by the Doctor, took the children away from the sickening sights that surrounded them, into the kitchen pantry, and there in secret tried to comfort them.

When night set in the children and families were all removed to the building called the mansion-house, where they spent a night of horror; all, except those who were left in Mrs. Whitman's chamber, from which they dared not descend, and the family of Mr. Osborne, who escaped.

On the first assault Mr. and Mrs. Osborne ran into their bedroom which adjoined the sitting-room, taking with them their three small children. Raising a plank in the floor, Mr. O. quickly thrust his wife and children into the space beneath, and then following, let the plank down to its place. Here they remained until darkness set in, able to hear all that was passing about them, and fearing to stir. When all was quiet at the Doctor's house, they stole out under cover of darkness and succeeded in reaching Fort Walla-Walla, after a painful journey of several days, or rather nights, for they dared not travel by day.

Another person who escaped was a Mr. Hall, carpenter, who in a hand to hand contest with an Indian, received a wound in the face, but finally reached the cover of some bushes where he remained until dark, and then fled in the direction of Fort Walla-Walla. Mr. Hall was the first to arrive at the fort, where, contrary to his expectations, and to all humanity, he was but coldly received by the gentleman in charge, Mr. McBean.

Whether it was from cowardice or cruelty as some alleged, that Mr. McBean rejoiced in the slaughter of the Protestant missionaries, himself being a Catholic, can never be known. Had that been true, one might have supposed that their death would have been enough, and that he

27

might have sheltered a wounded man fleeing for his life, without grudging him this atom of comfort. Unfortunately for Mr. McBean's reputation, he declined to grant such shelter willingly. Mr. Hall remained, however, twelve hours, until he heard a report that the women and children were murdered, when, knowing how unwelcome he was, and being in a half distracted state, he consented to be set across the Columbia to make his way as best he could to the Wallamet. From this hour he was never seen or heard from, the manner of his death remaining a mystery to his wife and their family of five children, who were among the prisoners at Waiilatpu.

When Mr. Osborne left the mission in the darkness, he was able only to proceed about two miles, before Mrs. Osborne's strength gave way, she lately having been confined by an untimely birth; and he was compelled to stop, secreting himself and family in some bushes. Here they remained, suffering with cold, and insufficient food, having only a little bread and cold mush which they had found in the pantry of the Doctor's house, before leaving it. On Tuesday night, Mrs. O. was able to move about three miles more: and again they were compelled to stop. In this way to proceed, they must all perish of starvation; therefore on Wednesday night Mr. O. took the second child and started with it for the fort, where he arrived before noon on Thursday.

Although Mr. McBean received him with friendliness of manner, he refused him horses to go for Mrs. Osborne and his other children, and even refused to furnish food to re-relieve their hunger, telling him to go to the Umatilla, and forbidding his return to the fort. A little food was given to himself and child, who had been fasting since Monday night. Whether Mr. McBean would have allowed this man to perish is uncertain: but certain it is that some base or cowardly motive made him exceedingly cruel to both Hall and Osborne.

While Mr Osborne was partaking of his tea and crackers, there arrived at the fort Mr. Stanley, the artist, whom the reader will remember having met in the mountains several years before. When the case became known to him, he offered his horses immediately to go for Mrs. Osborne. Shamed into an appearance of humanity, Mr. McBean then furnished an Indian guide to accompany Mr. O. to the Umatilla, where he still insisted the fugitives should go, though this was in the murderer's country.

A little meat and a few crackers were furnished for the supper of the travelers; and with a handkerchief for his hatless head and a pair of socks for his child's naked feet, all furnished by Mr. Stanley, Mr. Osborne set out to return to his suffering wife and children. He and his guide traveled rapidly, arriving in good time near the spot where he believed his family to be concealed. But the darkness had confused his recollection, and after beating the bushes until daylight, the unhappy husband and father was about to give up the search in despair, when his guide at length discovered their retreat.

The poor mother and children were barely alive, having suffered much from famine and exposure, to say nothing of their fears. Mrs. Osborne was compelled to be tied to the Indian in order to sit her horse. In this condition the miserable fugitives turned toward the Umatilla, in obedience to the command of McBean, and were only saved from being murdered by a Cayuse by the scornful words of the guide, who shamed the murderer from his purpose of slaughtering a sick and defenceless family. At a Canadian farm-house, where they stopped to change horses, they were but roughly received; and learning here that *Tamt-sak-y's* lodge was near by, Mrs. Osborne refused to proceed any farther toward the Umatilla. She said, " I doubt if I can live to reach the Umatilla; and if I must die, I may as well die at the gates of the Fort." Let us, then, turn back to the Fort."

To this the guide assented, saying it was not safe going among the Cayuses. The little party, quite exhausted, reached Walla-Walla about ten o'clock at night, and were at once admitted. Contrary to his former course, Mr. McBean now ordered a fire made to warm the benumbed travelers, who, after being made tolerably comfortable, were placed in a secret room of the fort. Again Mr. Osborne was importuned to go away, down to the Walla-met, Mr. McBean promising to take care of his family and furnish him an outfit if he would do so. Upon being asked to furnish a boat, and Indians to man it, in order that the family might accompany him, he replied that his Indians refused to go.

From all this reluctance, not only on the part of Mc-Bean, but of the Indians also, to do any act which appeared like befriending the Americans, it would appear that there was a very general fear of the Cayuse Indians, and a belief that they were about to inaugurate a general war upon the Americans, and their friends and allies. Mr. Osborne, however, refused to leave his family behind, and Mr. McBean was forced to let him remain until relief came. When it did come at last, in the shape of Mr. Ogden's party, *Stickas*, the chief who had warned Mr. Spalding, showed his kind feeling for the sufferers by removing his own cap and placing it on Mr. Osborne's head, and by tying a handkerchief over the ears of Mr. Osborne's little son, as he said, " to keep him warm, going down the river." Sadly indeed, did the little ones who suffered by the massacre at Waiilatpu, stand in need of any Christian kindness.

CHAPTER XXXVI.

1847. A FULL account of the horrors of the Waiilatpu massacre, together with the individual sufferings of
the captives whose lives were spared, would fill a volume,
and be harrowing to the reader; therefore, only so much
of it will be given here as, from its bearing upon Oregon
history, is important to our narrative.

The day following the massacre, being Tuesday, was
the day on which Mr. Spalding was met and warned not
to go to the mission, by the Vicar General, Brouillet.
Happening at the mission on that day, and finding the
bodies of the victims still unburied, Brouillet had them
hastily interred before leaving, if interment it could be
called which left them still a prey to wolves. The reader
of this chapter of Oregon history will always be very much
puzzled to understand by what means the Catholic priests
procured their perfect exemption from harm during this
time of terror to the Americans. Was it that they were
French, and that they came into the country *only* as missionaries of a religion adapted to the savage mind, and
not as settlers? Was it at all owing to the fact that they
were celibates, with no families to excite jealous feelings
of comparison in the minds of their converts?

Through a long and bitter war of words, which followed the massacre at Waiilatpu, terrible sins were charged
upon the priests—no less than inciting the Indians to the
murder of the Protestants, and winking at the atrocities of

every kind committed by the savages.   Whether they feared to enter into the quarrel, and were restrained from showing sympathy solely by this fear, is a question only themselves can determine.   Certain it is, that they preserved a neutral position, when to be neutral was to seem, if not to be, devoid of human sympathies.   That the event would have happened without any other provocation than such as the Americans furnished by their own reckless disregard of Indian prejudices, seems evident. The question, and the only question which is suggested by a knowledge of all the circumstances, is whether the event was helped on by an intelligent outside influence.

It was quite natural that the Protestants should wonder at the immunity from danger which the priests enjoyed; and that, not clearly seeing the reason, they should suspect them of collusion with the Indians.   It was natural, too, for the sufferers from the massacre to look for some expression of sympathy from any and all denominations of Christians; and that, not receiving it, they should have doubts of the motives which prompted such reserve. The story of that time is but an unpleasant record, and had best be lightly touched upon.

The work of death and destruction did not close with the first day at Waiilatpu.   Mr. Kimble, who had remained in the chamber of the Doctor's house all night, had suffered much from the pain of his broken arm.   On Tuesday, driven desperate by his own sufferings, and those of the three sick children with him, one of whom was the little Helen Mar Meek, he resolved to procure some water from the stream which ran near the house.   But he had not proceeded more than a few rods before he was shot down and killed instantly.   The same day, a Mr. Young, from the saw-mill, was also killed.   In the course of the week, Mr. Bulee, who was sick over at the mansion, was brutally murdered.

Meanwhile the female captives and children were enduring such agony as seldom falls to the lot of humanity to suffer. Compelled to work for the Indians, their feelings were continually harrowed up by the terrible sights which everywhere met their eyes in going back and forth between the houses, in carrying water from the stream, or moving in any direction whatever. For the dead were not removed until the setting in of decay made it necessary to the Indians themselves.

The goods belonging to the mission were taken from the store-room, and the older women ordered to make them up into clothing for the Indians. The buildings were plundered of everything which the Indians coveted; all the rest of their contents that could not be made useful to themselves were destroyed. Those of the captives who were sick were not allowed proper attention, and in a day or two Helen Mar Meek died of neglect.

Thus passed four or five days. On Saturday a new horror was added to the others. The savages began to carry off the young women for wives. Three were thus dragged away to Indian lodges to suffer tortures worse than death. One young girl, a daughter of Mr. Kimble, was taken possession of by the murderer of her father, who took daily delight in reminding her of that fact, and when her sorrow could no longer be restrained, only threatened to exchange her for another young girl who was also a wife by compulsion.

Miss Bulee, the eldest of the young women at the mission, and who was a teacher in the mission school, was taken to the Umatilla, to the lodge of *Five-Crows*. As has before been related, there was a house on the Umatilla belonging to *Tan-i-tan*, in which were residing at this time two Catholic priests—the Vicar-General Brouillet, and Blanchet, Bishop of Walla-Walla. To this house Miss Bulee applied

for protection, and was refused, whether from fear, or from
the motives subsequently attributed to them by some
Protestant writers in Oregon, is not known to any but
themselves. The only thing certain about it is, that Miss
Bulee was allowed to be violently dragged from their
presence every night, to return to them weeping in the
morning, and to have her entreaties for their assistance
answered by assurances from them that the wisest course
for her was to submit. And this continued for more than
two weeks, until the news of Mr. Ogden's arrival at Walla-
Walla became known, when Miss Bulee was told that if
Five-Crows would not allow her to remain at their house
altogether, she must remain at the lodge of *Five-Crows*
without coming to their house at all, well knowing what
Five-Crows would do, but wishing to have Miss Bulee's
action seem voluntary, from shame perhaps, at their own
cowardice. Yet the reason they gave ought to go for all
it is worth—that they being priests could not have a
woman about their house. In this unhappy situation did
the female captives spend three most miserable weeks.

In the meantime the mission at Lapwai had been broken
up, but not destroyed, nor had any one suffered death as
was at first feared. The intelligence of the massacre at
Waiilatpu was first conveyed to Mrs. Spalding by a Mr.
Camfield, who at the breaking out of the massacre, fled
with his wife and children to a small room in the attic of
the mansion, from the window of which he was able to
behold the scenes which followed. When night came Mr.
Camfield contrived to elude observation and descend into
the yard, where he encountered a French Canadian long
in the employ of Dr. Whitman, and since suspected to
have been privy to the plan of the murders. To him Mr.
Camfield confided his intention to escape, and obtained a
promise that a horse should be brought to a certain place

at a certain time for his use. But the Canadian failing to appear with his horse, Mr. C. set out on foot, and under cover of night, in the direction of the Lapwai mission. He arrived in the Nez Perce country on Thursday. On the following day he came upon a camp of these people, and procured from them a guide to Lapwai, without, however, speaking of what had occurred at Waiilatpu.

The caution of Mr. Camfield relates to a trait of Indian character which the reader of Indian history must bear in mind, that is, the close relationship and identity of feeling of allied tribes. Why he did not inform the Nez Perces of the deed done by their relatives, the Cayuses, was because in that case he would have expected them to have sympathized with their allies, even to the point of making him a prisoner, or of taking his life. It is this fact concerning the Indian character, which alone furnishes an excuse for the conduct of Mr. McBean and the Catholic priests. Upon it Mr. Camfield acted, making no sign of fear, nor betraying any knowledge of the terrible matter on his mind to the Nez Perces.

On Saturday afternoon Mr. C. arrived at Mrs. Spalding's house and dismissed his guide with the present of a buffalo robe. When he was alone with Mrs. Spalding he told his unhappy secret. It was then that the strength and firmness of Mrs. Spalding's character displayed itself in her decisive action. Well enough she knew the close bond between the Nez Perces and Cayuses, and also the treachery of the Indian character. But she saw that if affairs were left to shape themselves as Mr. Camfield entreated they might be left to do, putting off the evil day,—that when the news came from the Cayuses, there would be an outbreak.

The only chance of averting this danger was to inform the chiefs most attached to her, at once, and throw herself and her family upon their mercy. Her resolution was taken not an hour too soon. Two of the chiefs most relied upon happened to be at the place that very afternoon, one of whom was called *Jacob*, and the other *Eagle*. To these two Mrs. Spalding confided the news without delay, and took counsel of them. According to her hopes, they assumed the responsibility of protecting her. One of them went to inform his camp, and give them orders to stand by Mrs. S., while the other carried a note to Mr. Craig, one of our Rocky Mountain acquaintances, who lived ten miles from the mission.

Jacob and *Eagle*, with two other friendly chiefs, decided that Mrs. S. must go to their camp near Mr. Craig's; because in case the Cayuses came to the mission as was to be expected, she would be safer with them. Mrs. S. however would not consent to make the move on the Sabbath, but begged to be allowed to remain quiet until Monday. Late Saturday evening Mr. Craig came down; and Mrs. Spalding endeavored with his assistance to induce the Indians to carry an express to Cimikain in the country of the Spokanes, where Messrs. Walker and Eells had a station. Not an Indian could be persuaded to go. An effort, also, was made by the heroic and suffering wife and mother, to send an express to Waiilatpu to learn the fate of her daughter, and if possible of her husband. But the Indians were none of them inclined to go. They said, without doubt all the women and children were slain. That Mr. Spalding was alive no one believed.

The reply of Mrs. S. to their objections was that she could not believe that they were her friends if they would not undertake this journey, for the relief of her feelings under such circumstances. At length *Eagle* consented to go; but so much opposed were the others to having anything done which their relations, the Cayuses, might be displeased with, that it was nearly twenty-four hours before *Eagle* got leave to go.

On Monday morning a Nez Perce arrived from Waii-latpu with the news of what the Cayuses had done. With him were a number of Indians from the camp where Mr. Camfield had stopped for a guide, all eager for plunder, and for murder too, had not they found Mrs. Spalding protected by several chiefs. Her removal to their camp probably saved her from the fate of Mrs. Whitman.

Among those foremost in plundering the mission buildings at Lapwai were some of the hitherto most exemplary Indians among the Nez Perces. Even the chief, first in authority after Ellis, who was absent, was prominent in these robberies. For eight years had this chief, Joseph, been a member of the church at Lapwai, and sustained a good reputation during that time. How bitter must have been the feelings of Mrs. Spalding, who had a truly devoted missionary heart, when she beheld the fruit of her life's labor turned to ashes in her sight as it was by the conduct of Joseph and his family.

Shortly after the removal of Mrs. Spalding, and the pillaging of the buildings, Mr. Spalding arrived at Lapwai from his long and painful journey during which he had wandered much out of his way, and suffered many things. His appearance was the signal for earnest consultations among the Nez Perces who were not certain that they might safely give protection to him without the consent of the Cayuses. To his petition that they should carry a letter express to Fort Colville or Fort Walla-Walla, they would not consent. Their reason for refusing seemed to be a fear that such a letter might be answered by an armed body of Americans, who would come to avenge the deaths of their countrymen.

To deprive them of this suspicion, Mr. Spalding told

them that as he had been robbed of everything, he had
no means of paying them for their services to his family,
and that it was necessary to write to Walla-Walla for
blankets, and to the Umatilla for his horses. He assured
them that he would write to his countrymen to keep quiet,
and that they had nothing to fear from the Américans.
The truth was, however, that he had forwarded through
Brouillet, a letter to Gov. Abernethy asking for help
which could only come into that hostile country armed
and equipped for war.   And it was fearing this, that the
Indians detained him and his family as hostages until it
became apparent what the Americans meant to do.

Happily for the captives both at Waiilatpu and elsewhere, the prompt action of the Hudson's Bay Company
averted any collision between the Indians and Americans,
until after they had been ransomed.

Late in the month of December there arrived in Oregon City to be delivered to the governor, sixty-two captives, bought from the Cayuses and Nez Perces by Hudson's Bay blankets and goods; and obtained at that price
by Hudson's Bay influence.   "No other power on earth,"
says Joe Meek, the American, "could have rescued those
prisoners from the hands of the Indians;" and no man
better than Mr. Meek understood the Indian character,
or the Hudson's Bay Company's power over them.

The number of victims to the Waiilatpu massacre was
fourteen.   None escaped who had not to mourn a father,
brother, son, or friend.   If "the blood of the martyrs is
the seed of the church," there ought to arise on the site
of Waiilatpu a generation of extraordinary piety.   As for
the people for whom a noble man and woman, and numbers of innocent persons were sacrificed, they have returned to their traditions; with the exception of the Nez
Perces, who under the leadership of their old teacher Mr.

Spalding, have once more resumed the pursuits of civilized and Christianized nations.

As early in the Spring as possible Messrs. Walker and Eells left the Cimikain mission, and settled in the Wallamet Valley, leaving the upper country entirely in the hands of the Indians for a period of several years, during which Oregon went through her Indian wars.

CHAPTER XXXVII.

1847–8. WHEN the contents of Mr. Douglas' letter to the governor became known to the citizens of the Walla-met settlement, the greatest excitement prevailed. On the reading of that letter, and those accompanying it, before the House, a resolution was immediately introduced authorizing the governor to raise a company of riflemen, not to exceed fifty in number, to occupy and hold the mission station at the Dalles, until a larger force could be raised, and such measures adopted as the government might think advisable. This resolution being sent to the governor without delay, received his approval, when the House adjourned.

A large meeting of the citizens was held that evening, which was addressed by several gentlemen, among whom was Meek, whose taste for Indian fighting was whetted to keenness by the aggravating circumstances of the Waiilat-pu massacre, and the fact that his little Helen Mar was among the captives. Impatient as was Meek to avenge the murders, he was too good a mountain-man to give any rash advice. All that could be done under the existing circumstances was to trust to the Hudson's Bay Company for the rescue of the prisoners, and to take such means for defending the settlements as the people in their unarmed condition could devise.

The legislature undertook the settlement of the question of ways and means. To raise money for the carrying out of the most important measures immediately, was a task which after some consideration was entrusted to three commissioners; and by these commissioners letters were addressed to the Hudson's Bay Company, the superintendent of the Methodist mission, and to the " merchants and citizens of Oregon." The latter communication is valuable as fully explaining the position of affairs at that time in Oregon. It is dated Dec. 17th, and was as follows:

GENTLEMEN :—You are aware that the undersigned have been charged by the legislature of our provisional government with the difficult duty of obtaining the necessary means to arm, equip, and support in the field a force sufficient to obtain full satisfaction of the Cayuse Indians, for the late massacre at Waiilatpu, and to protect the white population of our common country from further aggression.

In furtherance of this object they have deemed it their duty to make immediate application to the merchants and citizens of the country for the requisite assistance.

Though clothed with the power to pledge, to the fullest extent, the faith and means of the present government of Oregon, they do not consider this pledge the only security to those who, in this distressing emergency, may extend to the people of this country the means of protection and redress.

Without claiming any special authority from the government of the United States to contract a debt to be liquidated by that power, yet, from all precedents of like character in the history of our country, the undersigned feel confident that the United States government will regard the murder of the late Dr. Whitman and his lady, as a national wrong, and will fully justify the people of Oregon in taking active measures to obtain redress for that outrage, and for their protection from further aggression.

The right of self-defence is tacitly acknowledged to every body politic in the confederacy to which we claim to belong, and in every case similar to our own, within our knowledge, the general government has promptly assumed the payment of all liabilities growing out of the measures taken by the constituted authorities, to protect the lives and property of those who reside within the limits of their districts.

If the citizens of the States and territories, east of the Rocky mountains, are justified in promptly acting in such emergencies, who are under the immediate protection of the general government, there appears no room for doubt that the lawful acts of the Oregon government will receive a like approval.

Though the Indians of the Columbia have committed a great outrage upon our fellow citizens passing through their country, and residing among them, and their punishment for these murders may, and ought to be, a prime object with every citizen of Oregon, yet, as that duty more particularly devolves upon the government of the United States, and admits of delay, we do not make this the strongest ground upon which to found our earnest appeal to you for pecuniary assistance. It is a fact well known to every person acquainted with the Indian character, that, by passing silently over their repeated thefts, robberies, and murders of our fellow-citizens, they have been emboldened to the commission of the appalling massacre at Waiilatpu. They call us women, destitute of the hearts and courage of men, and if we allow this wholesale murder to pass by as former aggressions, who can tell how long either life or property will be secure in any part of this country, or what moment the Willamette will be the scene of blood and carnage.

The officers of our provisional government have nobly performed their duty. None can doubt the readiness of the patriotic sons of the west to offer their personal services in defence of a cause so righteous. So it now rests with you, gentlemen, to say whether our rights and our fire-sides shall be defended, or not.

Hoping that none will be found to falter in so high and so sacred a duty, we beg leave, gentlemen, to subscribe ourselves,

Your servants and fellow-citizens,

JESSE APPLEGATE,
A. L. LOVEJOY,
GEO. L. CURRY,
Commissioners.

A similar letter had been addressed to the Hudson's Bay Company, and to the Methodist mission. From each of these sources such assistance was obtained as enabled the colony to arm and equip the first regiment of Oregon riflemen, which in the month of January proceeded to the Cayuse country. The amount raised, however, was very small, being less than five thousand dollars, and it became imperatively necessary that the government of the United States should be called upon to extend its aid and protection to the loyal but distressed young territory.

In view of this necessity it was resolved in the legislature to send a messenger to carry the intelligence of the massacre to Gov. Mason of California, and through him to the commander of the United States squadron in the Pacific, that a vessel of war might be sent into the Columbia River, and arms and ammunition borrowed for the present emergency, from the nearest arsenal. For this duty was chosen Jesse Applegate, Esq., a gentleman who combined in his character and person the ability of the statesman with the sagacity and strength of the pioneer. Mr. Applegate, with a small party of brave men, set out in midwinter to cross the mountains into California, but such was the depth of snow they encountered that traveling became impossible, even after abandoning their horses, and they were compelled to return.

The messenger elected to proceed to the United States was Joseph L. Meek, whose Rocky Mountain experiences eminently fitted him to encounter the dangers of such a winter journey, and whose manliness, firmness, and ready wit stood him instead of statesmanship.

On the 17th December Meek resigned his seat in the House in order to prepare for the discharge of his duty as messenger to the United States. On the 4th of January, armed with his credentials from the Oregon legislature, and bearing dispatches from that body and the Governor to the President, he at length set out on the long and perilous expedition, having for traveling companions Mr. John Owens, and Mr. George Ebbarts—the latter having formerly been a Rocky Mountain man, like himself.

At the Dalles they found the first regiment of Oregon Riflemen, under Major Lee, of the newly created army of Oregon. From the reports which the Dalles Indians brought in of the hostility of the Indians beyond the Des Chutes River it was thought best not to proceed before the arrival of the remainder of the army, when all the forces would proceed at once to Waiilatpu. Owing to various delays, the army, consisting of about five hundred men, under Colonel Gilliam, did not reach the Dalles until late in January, when the troops proceeded at once to the seat of war.

28

The reports concerning the warlike disposition of the Indians proved to be correct. Already, the Wascopams or Dalles Indians had begun robbing the mission at that place, when Colonel Lee's arrival among them with troops had compelled them to return the stolen property. As the army advanced they found that all the tribes above the Dalles were holding themselves prepared for hostilities. At Well Springs, beyond the Des Chutes River, they were met by a body of about six hundred Indians to whom they gave battle, soon dispersing them, the superior arms and equipments of the whites tending to render timid those tribes yet unaccustomed to so superior an enemy. From thence to Waiilatpu the course of the army was unobstructed.

In the meantime the captives had been given up to the Hudson's Bay Company, and full particulars of the massacre were obtained by the army, with all the subsequent abuses and atrocities suffered by the prisoners. The horrible details were not calculated to soften the first bitterness of hatred which had animated the volunteers on going into the field. Nor was the appearance of an armed force in their midst likely to allay the hostile feelings with which other causes had inspired the Indians. Had not the captives already been removed out of the country, no influence, not even that of the Hudson's Bay Company, could have prevailed to get them out of the power of their captors then. Indeed, in order to treat with the Cayuses in the first place, Mr. Ogden had been obliged to promise peace to the Indians, and now they found instead of peace, every preparation for war. However, as the army took no immediate action, but only remained in their country to await the appearance of the commissioners appointed by the legislature of Oregon to hold a council with the chiefs of the various tribes, the Cayuses were forced to observe the outward semblance of amity while these councils were pending.

Arrived at Waiilatpu, the friends and acquaintances of Dr. Whitman were shocked to find that the remains of the victims were still unburied, although a little earth had been thrown over them. Meek, to whom, ever since his meeting with her in the train of the fur-trader, Mrs. Whitman had seemed all that was noble and captivating, had the melancholy satisfaction of bestowing, with others, the last sad rite of burial upon such portions of her once fair person as murder and the wolves had not destroyed. Some tresses of golden hair were severed from the brow so terribly disfigured, to be given to her friends in the Wallamet as a last and only memorial. Among the State documents at Salem, Oregon, may still be seen one of these relics of the Waiilatpu tragedy.

Not only had Meek to discover and inter the remains of Dr. and Mrs. Whitman, but also of his little girl, who was being educated at the mission, with a daughter of his former leader, Bridger.

This sad duty performed, he immediately set out, escorted by a company of one hundred men under Adjutant Wilcox, who accompanied him as far as the foot of the Blue Mountains. Here the companies separated, and Meek went on his way to Washington.

CHAPTER XXXVIII.

1848. MEEK's party now consisted of himself, Ebbarts, Owens, and four men, who being desirous of returning to the States took this opportunity. However, as the snow proved to be very deep on the Blue Mountains, and the cold severe, two of these four volunteers became discouraged and concluded to remain at Fort Boise, where was a small trading post of the Hudson's Bay Company.

In order to avoid trouble with the Indians he might meet on the western side of the Rocky mountains, Meek had adopted the red belt and Canadian cap of the employees of the Hudson's Bay Company; and to this precaution was owing the fact of his safe passage through the country now all infected with hostility caught from the Cayuses. About three days' travel beyond Fort Boise, the party met a village of Bannack Indians, who at once made warlike demonstrations; but on seeing Meek's costume, and receiving an invitation to hold a 'talk', desisted, and received the travelers in a friendly manner. Meek informed the chief, with all the gravity which had won for him the name of "*shiam shuspusia*" among the Crows in former years, that he was going on the business of the Hudson's Bay Company to Fort Hall; and that Thomas McKay was a day's march behind with a large trading party, and plenty of goods. On the receipt of this good news, the chief ordered his braves to fall back, and permit the party to pass. Yet, fearing the deception might be discovered,

they thought it prudent to travel day and night until they
reached Fort Hall.

At this post of the Hudson's Bay Company, in charge
of Mr. Grant, they were kindly received, and stopped for
a few hours of rest.   Mr. Grant being absent, his wife provided liberally for the refreshment of the party, who were
glad to find themselves even for a short interval under a
roof, beside a fire and partaking of freshly cooked food.
But they permitted themselves no unnecessary delay. Before night they were once more on their way, though
snow had now commenced to fall afresh, rendering the
traveling very difficult.   For two days they struggled on,
their horses floundering in the soft drifts, until further
progress in that manner became impossible.   The only alternative left was to abandon their horses and proceed on
snow-shoes, which were readily constructed out of willow
sticks.

Taking only a blanket and their rifles, and leaving the
animals to find their way back to Fort Hall, the little party
pushed on.   Meek was now on familiar ground, and the
old mountain spirit which had once enabled him to endure
hunger, cold, and fatigue without murmuring, possessed
him now.   It was not without a certain sense of enjoyment that he found himself reduced to the necessity of
shooting a couple of pole-cats to furnish a supper for himself and party.   How long the enjoyment of feeling want
would have lasted is uncertain, but probably only long
enough to whet the appetite for plenty.

To such a point had the appetites of all the party been
whetted, when, after several days of scarcity and toil, followed by nights of emptiness and cold, Meek had the
agreeable surprise of falling in with an old mountain comrade on the identical ground of many a former adventure,
the head-waters of Bear River. This man, whom Meek

was delighted to meet, was Peg-leg Smith, one of the
most famous of many well-known mountain-men.   He
was engaged in herding cattle in the valley of Thomas'
Fork, where the tall grass was not quite buried under
snow, and had with him a party of ten men.

Meek was as cordially received by his former comrade
as the unbounded hospitality of mountain manners rendered it certain he would be.   A fat cow was immediately
sacrificed, which, though not buffalo meat, as in former
times it would have been, was very good beef, and furnished a luxurious repast to the pole-cat eaters of the
last several days.   Smith's camp did not lack the domestic element of women and chidren, any more than had
the trapper's camps in the flush times of the fur-trade.
Therefore, seeing that the meeting was most joyful, and
full of reminiscences of former winter camps, Smith
thought to celebrate the occasion by a grand entertainment.   Accordingly, after a great deal of roast beef had
been disposed of, a dance was called for, in which white
men and Indian women joined with far more mirth and
jollity than grace or ceremony.   Thus passed some hours
of the night, the bearer of dispatches seizing, in true
mountain style, the passing moment's pleasure, so long as
it did not interfere with the punctilious discharge of his
duty.   And to the honor of our hero be it said, nothing
was ever allowed to interfere with that.

Refreshed and provided with rations for a couple of
days, the party started on again next morning, still on
snow-shoes, and traveled up Bear River to the head-waters
of Green River, crossing from the Muddy fork over to
Fort Bridger, where they arrived very much fatigued but
quite well in little more than three days' travel.   Here
again it was Meek's good fortune to meet with his former
leader, Bridger, to whom he related what had befallen

him since turning pioneer. The meeting was joyful on both sides, clouded only by the remembrance of what had brought it about, and the reflection that both had a personal wrong to avenge in bringing about the punishment of the Cayuse murderers.

Once more Meek's party were generously fed, and furnished with such provisions as they could carry about their persons. In addition to this, Bridger presented them with four good mules, by which means the travelers were mounted four at a time, while the fifth took exercise on foot; so that by riding or walking, turn about, they were enabled to get on very well as far as the South Pass. Here again for some distance the snow was very deep, and two of their mules were lost in it. Their course lay down the Sweetwater River, past many familiar hunting and camping grounds, to the Platte River. Owing to the deep snows, game was very scarce, and a long day of toil was frequently closed by a supperless sleep under shelter of some rock or bank, with only a blanket for cover. At Red Buttes they were so fortunate as to find and kill a single buffalo, which, separated from the distant herd, was left by Providence in the path of the famished travelers.

On reaching the Platte River they found the traveling improved, as well as the supply of game, and proceeded with less difficulty as far as Fort Laramie, a trading post in charge of a French trader named Papillion. Here again fresh mules were obtained, and the little party treated in the most hospitable manner. In parting from his entertainer, Meek was favored with this brief counsel:

"There is a village of Sioux, of about six hundred lodges, a hundred miles from here. Your course will bring you to it. Look out for yourself, and don't make a Gray muss of it!"—which latter clause referred to the

affair of 1837, when the Sioux had killed the Indian escort of Mr. Gray.

When the party arrived at Ash Hollow, which they
meant to have passed in the night, on account of the
Sioux village, the snow was again falling so thickly that
the party had not perceived their nearness to the village
until they were fairly in the midst of it. It was now no
safer to retreat than to proceed; and after a moment's
consultation, the word was given to keep on. In truth,
Meek thought it doubtful whether the Sioux would trouble
themselves to come out in such a tempest, and if they did
so, that the blinding snow-fall was rather in his favor.
Thus reasoning, he was forcing his mule through the
drifts as rapidly as the poor worried animal could make
its way, when a head was protruded from a lodge door,
and "Hallo, Major!" greeted his ear in an accent not
altogether English.

On being thus accosted, the party came to a halt, and
Meek was invited to enter the lodge, with his friends.
His host on this occasion was a French trader named Le
Bean, who, after offering the hospitalities of the lodge,
and learning who were his guests, offered to accompany
the party a few miles on its way. This he did, saying by
way of explanation of this act of courtesy, "The Sioux
are a bad people; I thought it best to see you safe out
of the village." Receiving the thanks of the travelers,
he turned back at night-fall, and they continued on all
night without stopping to camp, going some distance to
the south of their course before turning east again, in
order to avoid any possible pursuers.

Without further adventures, and by dint of almost constant travel, the party arrived at St. Joseph, Mo., in
safety, in a little over two months, from Portland, Oregon.
Soon afterwards, when the circumstances of this journey

became known, a steamboat built for the Missouri River trade was christened the *Joseph L. Meek*, and bore for a motto, on her pilot-house, "The quickest trip yet," in reference both to Meek's overland journey and her own steaming qualities.

As Meek approached the settlements, and knew that he must soon be thrown into society of the highest official grade, and be subjected to such ordeals as he dreaded far more than Indian fighting, or even traveling express across a continent of snow, the subject of how he was to behave in these new and trying positions very frequently occurred to him. He, an uneducated man, trained to mountain life and manners, without money, or even clothes, with nothing to depend on but the importance of his mission and his own mother wit, he felt far more keenly than his careless appearance would suggest, the difficulties and awkwardness of his position.

"I thought a great deal about it," confesses the Col. Joseph L. Meek of to-day, "and I finally concluded that as I had never tried to act like anybody but myself, I would not make myself a fool by beginning to ape other folks now. So I said, 'Joe Meek you always have been, and Joe Meek you shall remain; go ahead, Joe Meek!'"

In fact, it would have been rather difficult putting on fine gentleman airs, in that old worn-out hunting suit of his, and with not a dollar to bless himself. On the contrary, it needed just the devil-may-care temper which naturally belonged to our hero, to carry him through the remainder of his journey to Washington. To be hungry, ill-clad, dirty, and penniless, is sufficient in itself for the subduing of most spirits; how it affected the temper of the messenger from Oregon we shall now learn.

When the weary little party arrived in St. Joseph, they repaired to a hotel, and Meek requested that a meal

should be served for all, but frankly confessing that they
had no money to pay. The landlord, however, declined
furnishing guests of his style upon such terms, and our
travelers were forced to go into camp below the town.
Meek now bethought himself of his letters of introduction. It chanced that he had one from two young men
among the Oregon volunteers, to their father in St. Joseph. Stopping a negro who was passing his camp, he
inquired whether such a gentleman was known to him ;
and on learning that he was, succeeded in inducing the
negro to deliver the letter from his sons.

This movement proved successful. In a short space of
time the gentleman presented himself, and learning the
situation of the party, provided generously for their present wants, and promised any assistance which might be
required in future. Meek, however, chose to accept only
that which was imperatively needed, namely, something
to eat, and transportation to some point on the river
where he could take a steamer for St. Louis. A portion
of his party chose to remain in St. Joseph, and a portion
accompanied him as far as Independence, whither this
same St. Joseph gentleman conveyed them in his carriage.

While Meek was stopping at Independence, he was
recognized by a sister, whom he had not seen for nineteen
years ; who, marrying and emigrating from Virginia, had
settled on the frontier of Missouri. But he gave himself
no time for family reunion and gossip. A steamboat that
had been frozen up in the ice all winter, was just about
starting for St. Louis, and on board of this he went, with
an introduction to the captain, which secured for him
every privilege the boat afforded, together with the kindest attention of its officers.

When the steamer arrived in St. Louis, by one of those
fortuitous circumstances so common in our hero's career,

he was met at the landing by Campbell, a Rocky Mountain trader who had formerly belonged to the St. Louis
Company. This meeting relieved him of any care about
his night's entertainment in St. Louis, and it also had another effect—that of relieving him of any further care
about the remainder of his journey; for, after hearing
Meek's story of the position of affairs in Oregon and his
errand to the United States, Campbell had given the
same to the newspaper reporters, and Meek, like Byron,
waked up next morning to find himself famous.

Having telegraphed to Washington, and received the
President's order to come on, the previous evening, our
hero wended his way to the levee the morning after his

MEEK AS STEAMBOAT RUNNER.

arrival in St. Louis. There were two steamers lying side
by side, both up for Pittsburg, with runners for each,

striving to outdo each other in securing passengers. A bright thought occurred to the moneyless envoy — he would earn his passage!

Walking on board one of the boats, which bore the name of *The Declaration*, himself a figure which attracted all eyes by his size and outlandish dress, he mounted to the hurricane deck and began to harrangue the crowd upon the levee, in the voice of a Stentor:

"This way, gentlemen, if you please. Come right on board the *Declaration*. I am the man from Oregon, with dispatches to the President of these United States, that you all read about in this morning's paper. Come on board, ladies and gentlemen, if you want to hear the news from Oregon. I've just come across the plains, two months from the Columbia River, where the Injuns are killing your missionaries. Those passengers who come aboard the *Declaration* shall hear all about it before they get to Pittsburg. Don't stop thar, looking at my old wolf-skin cap, but just come aboard, and hear what I've got to tell!"

The novelty of this sort of solicitation operated capitally. Many persons crowded on board the *Declaration* only to get a closer look at this picturesque personage who invited them, and many more because they were really interested to know the news from the far off young territory which had fallen into trouble. So it chanced that the *Declaration* was inconveniently crowded on this particular morning.

After the boat had got under way, the captain approached his roughest looking cabin passenger and inquired in a low tone of voice if he were really and truly the messenger from Oregon.

"Thar's what I've got to show for it;" answered Meek, producing his papers.

" Well, all I have to say is, Mr. Meek, that you are the best·runner this boat ever had; and you are welcome to your passage ticket, and anything you desire besides."

Finding that his bright thought had succeeded so well, Meek's spirit rose with the occasion, and the passengers had no reason to complain that he had not kept his word. Before he reached Wheeling his popularity was immense, notwithstanding the condition of his wardrobe. At Cincinnati he had time to present a letter to the celebrated Doctor ——, who gave him another, which proved to be an 'open sesame' wherever he went thereafter.

On the morning of his arrival in Wheeling it happened that the stage which then carried passengers to Cumberland, where they took the train for Washington, had already departed. Elated by his previous good fortune our ragged hero resolved not to be delayed by so trivial a circumstance; but walking pompously into the stage office inquired, with an air which must have smacked strongly of the mock-heroic, if he " could have a stage for Cumberland?"

The nicely dressed, dignified elderly gentleman who managed the business of the office, regarded the man who proffered this modest request for a moment in motionless silence, then slowly raising the spectacles over his eyes to a position on his forehead, finished his survey with unassisted vision. Somewhat impressed by the manner in which Meek bore this scrutiny, he ended by demanding " who are you?"

Tickled by the absurdity of the tableau they were enacting, Meek straightened himself up to his six feet two, and replied with an air of superb self assurance—

" I am Envoy extraordinary and minister plenipotentiary from the Republic of Oregon to the Court of the United States!"

After a pause in which the old gentleman seemed to be recovering from some great surprise, he requested to see the credentials of this extraordinary envoy. Still more surprised he seemed on discovering for himself that the personage before him was really a messenger from Oregon to the government of the United States. But the effect was magical. In a moment the bell-rope was pulled, and in an incredibly short space of time a coach stood at the door ready to convey the waiting messenger on his way to Washington.

In the meantime in a conversation with the stage agent, Meek had explained more fully the circumstances of his mission, and the agent had become much interested. On parting, Meek received a ticket to the Relay House, with many expressions of regret from the agent that he could ticket him no farther.

"But it is all the same," said he; "you are sure to go through."

"Or run a train off the track," rejoined Meek, as he was bowed out of the office.

It happened that there were some other passengers waiting to take the first stage, and they crowded into this one, glad of the unexpected opportunity, but wondering at the queer looking passenger to whom the agent was so polite. This scarcely concealed curiosity was all that was needed to stimulate the mad-cap spirits of our so far "conquering hero." Putting his head out of the window just at the moment of starting, he electrified everybody, horses included, by the utterance of a war-whoop and yell that would have done credit to a wild Camanche. Satisfied with the speed to which this demoniac noise had excited the driver's prancing steeds, he quietly ensconced himself in his corner of the coach and waited for his fellow passengers to recover from their stunned sensations.

When their complete recovery had been effected, there followed the usual questioning and explanations, which ended in the inevitable lionizing that was so much to the taste of this sensational individual.

On the cars at Cumberland, and at the eating-houses, the messenger from Oregon kept up his sensational character, indulging in alternate fits of mountain manners, and again assuming a disproportionate amount of grandeur; but in either view proving himself very amusing. By the time the train reached the Relay House, many of the passengers had become acquainted with Meek, and were prepared to understand and enjoy each new phase of his many-sided comicality.

The ticket with which the stage agent presented him, dead-headed him only to this point. Here again he must make his poverty a jest, and joke himself through to Washington. Accordingly when the conductor came through the car in which he, with several of his new acquaintances were sitting, demanding tickets, he was obliged to tap his blanketed passenger on the shoulder to attract his attention to the "ticket, sir!"

"*Ha ko any me ca, hanch?*" said Meek, starting up and addressing him in the Snake tongue.

"Ticket, sir!" repeated the conductor, staring.

"*Ka hum pa, hanch?*" returned Meek, assuming a look which indicated that English was as puzzling to him, as Snake to other people.

Finding that his time would be wasted on this singular passenger, the conductor went on through the train; returning after a time with a fresh demand for his ticket. But Meek sustained his character admirably, and it was only through the excessive amusement of the passengers that the conductor suspected that he was being made the subject of a practical joke. At this stage of affairs it was

privately explained to him who and what his waggish customer was, and tickets were no more mentioned during
the journey.

On the arrival of the train at Washington, the heart of
our hero became for a brief moment of time "very little."
He felt that the importance of his mission demanded some
dignity of appearance—some conformity to established
rules and precedents.   But of the latter he knew absolutely nothing ; and concerning the former, he realized
the absurdity of a dignitary clothed in blankets and a
wolf-skin cap. 'Joe Meek I must remain,' said he to himself, as he stepped out of the train, and glanced along the
platform at the crowd of porters with the names of their
hotels on their hat-bands.   Learning from inquiry that
Coleman's was the most fashionable place, he decided that
to Coleman's he would go, judging correctly that it was
best to show no littleness of heart even in the matter of
hotels.

CHAPTER XXXIX.

1848. When Meek arrived at Coleman's it was the dinner hour, and following the crowd to the dining saloon, he took the first seat he came to, not without being very much stared at. He had taken his cue and the staring was not unexpected, consequently not so embarrassing as it might otherwise have been. A bill of fare was laid beside his plate. Turning to the colored waiter who placed it there, he startled him first by inquiring in a low growling voice—

"What's that boy?"

"Bill of fare, sah," replied the "boy," who recognized the Southerner in the use of that one word.

"Read!" growled Meek again. "The people in *my* country can't read."

Though taken by surprise, the waiter, politely obedient, proceeded to enumerate the courses on the bill of fare. When he came to game——

"Stop thar, boy!" commanded Meek, "what kind of game?"

"Small game, sah."

"Fetch me a piece of antelope," leaning back in his chair with a look of satisfaction on his face.

"Got none of that sah; don't know what that ar' sah."

"Don't know!" with a look of pretended surprise. "In *my* country antelope and deer ar' small game; bear and buffalo ar' large game. I reckon if you haven't got one,

29

you havn't got the other, either.   In that case you may fetch me some beef."

The waiter disappeared grinning, and soon returned with the customary thin and small cut, which Meek eyed at first contemptuously, and then accepting it in the light of a sample swallowed it at two mouthfuls, returning his plate to the waiter with an approving smile, and saying loud enough to be overheard by a score of people——

"Boy, that will do.   Fetch me about four pounds of the same kind."

By this time the blanketed beef-eater was the recipient of general attention, and the "boy" who served him comprehending with that quickness which distinguishes servants, that he had no ordinary backwoodsman to deal with, was all the time on the alert to make himself useful.   People stared, then smiled, then asked each other "who is it?" loud enough for the stranger to hear.   Meek looked neither to the right nor to the left, pretending not to hear the whispering.   When he had finished his beef, he again addressed himself to the attentive "boy."

"That's better meat than the old mule I eat in the mountains."

Upon this remark the whispering became more general, and louder, and smiles more frequent.

"What have you got to drink, boy?" continued Meek, still unconscious.   "Isn't there a sort of wine called— some kind of *pain*?"

"Champagne, sah?"

"That's the stuff, I reckon; bring me some."

While Meek drank his champagne, with an occasional aside to his faithful attendant, people laughed and wondered "who the devil it was."   At length, having finished his wine, and overhearing many open inquiries as to his identity, the hero of many bear-fights slowly arose, and addressing the company through the before-mentioned " boy," said :

" You want to know who I am ?"

" If you please, sah ; yes, if you please, sah, for the sake of these gentlemen present," replied the " boy," answering for the company.

" Wall then," proclaimed Meek with a grandiloquent air quite at variance with his blanket coat and unkempt hair, yet which displayed his fine person to advantage, " I am Envoy Extraordinary and Minister Plenipotentiary from the Republic of Oregon to the Court of the United States !"

With that he turned and strode from the room. He had not proceeded far, however, before he was overtaken by a party of gentlemen in pursuit. Senator Underwood of Kentucky immediately introduced himself, calling the envoy by name, for the dispatch from St. Louis had prepared the President and the Senate for Meek's appearance in Washington, though it had not advised them of his style of dress and address. Other gentlemen were introduced, and questions followed questions in rapid succession.

When curiosity was somewhat abated, Meek expressed a wish to see the President without delay. To Underwood's question as to whether he did not wish to make his toilet before visiting the White House, his reply was, " business first, and toilet afterwards."

" But," said Underwood, " even your business can wait long enough for that."

" No, that's your mistake, Senator, and I'll tell you why : I can't dress, for two reasons, both good ones. I've not got a cent of money, nor a second suit of clothes."

The generous Kentuckian offered to remove the first of

the objections on the spot, but Meek declined. "I'll see the President first, and hear what he has to say about my mission." Then calling a coach from the stand, he sprang into it, answering the driver's question of where he would be taken, with another inquiry.

"Whar should a man of *my* style want to go?—to the White House, of course!" and so was driven away amid the general laughter of the gentlemen in the portico at Coleman's, who had rather doubted his intention to pay his respects to the President in his dirty blankets.

He was admitted to the Presidential mansion by a mulatto of about his own age, with whom he remembered playing when a lad, for it must be remembered that the Meeks and Polks were related, and this servant had grown up in the family. On inquiring if he could see the President, he was directed to the office of the private Secretary, Knox Walker, also a relative of Meek's on the mother's side.

On entering he found the room filled with gentlemen waiting to see the President, each when his turn to be admitted should arrive. The Secretary sat reading a paper, over the top of which he glanced but once at the new comer, to ask him to be seated. But Meek was not in the humor for sitting. He had not traveled express for more than two months, in storm and cold, on foot and on horseback, by day and by night, with or without food, as it chanced, to sit down quietly now and wait. So he took a few turns up and down the room, and seeing that the Secretary glanced at him a little curiously, stopped and said:

"I should like to see the President immediately. Just tell him if you please that there is a gentleman from Oregon waiting to see him on very important business."

At the word *Oregon*, the Secretary sprang up, dashed his paper to the ground, and crying out "Uncle Joe!" came forward with both hands extended to greet his long lost relative.

"Take care, Knox! don't come too close," said Meek stepping back, "I'm ragged, dirty, and—lousy."

"TAKE CARE, KNOX."

But Walker seized his cousin's hand, without seeming fear of the consequences, and for a few moments there was an animated exchange of questions and answers, which Meek at last interrupted to repeat his request to be admitted to the President without delay. Several times the Secretary turned to leave the room, but as often came back with some fresh inquiry, until Meek fairly refused to say another word, until he had delivered his dispatches.

When once the Secretary got away he soon returned with a request from the President for the appearance of the Oregon messenger, all other visitors being dismissed for that day. Polk's reception proved as cordial as Walker's had been. He seized the hand of his newly found relative, and welcomed him in his own name, as well as that of messenger from the distant, much loved, and long neglected Oregon. The interview lasted for a couple of hours. Oregon affairs and family affairs were talked over together; the President promising to do all for Oregon that he could do; at the same time he bade Meek make himself at home in the Presidential mansion, with true southern hospitality.

But Meek, although he had carried off his poverty and all his deficiencies in so brave a style hitherto, felt his assurance leaving him, when, his errand performed, he stood, in the presence of rank and elegance, a mere mountain-man in ragged blankets, whose only wealth consisted of an order for five hundred dollars on the Methodist mission in New York, unavailable for present emergencies. And so he declined the hospitalities of the White House, saying he "could make himself at home in an Indian wigwam in Oregon, or among the Rocky Mountains, but in the residence of the chief magistrate of a great nation, he felt out of place, and ill at ease."

Polk, however, would listen to no refusal, and still further abashed his Oregon cousin by sending for Mrs. Polk and Mrs. Walker, to make his acquaintance. Says Meek:

"When I heard the silks rustling in the passage, I felt more frightened than if a hundred Blackfeet had whooped in my ear. A mist came over my eyes, and when Mrs. Polk spoke to me I couldn't think of anything to say in return."

But the ladies were so kind and courteous that he soon began to see a little, though not quite plainly while their visit lasted. Before the interview with the President and his family was ended, the poverty of the Oregon envoy became known, which led to the immediate supplying of all his wants. Major Polk was called in and introduced; and to him was deputed the business of seeing Meek "got up" in a style creditable to himself and his relations. Meek avers that when he had gone through the hands of the barber and tailor, and surveyed himself in a full length mirror, he was at first rather embarrassed, being under the impression that he was being introduced to a fashionable and decidedly good-looking gentleman, before whose over. powering style he was disposed to shrink, with the old familiar feeling of being in blankets.

But Meek was not the sort of man to be long in getting used to a situation however novel or difficult. In a very short time he was *au fait* in the customs of the capital. His perfect frankness led people to laugh at his errors as eccentricities; his good looks and natural *bonhomie* procured him plenty of admirers; while his position at the White House caused him to be envied and lionized at once.

On the day following his arrival the President sent in a message to Congress accompanied by the memorial from the Oregon legislature and other documents appertaining to the Oregon cause. Meek was introduced to Benton, Oregon's indefatigable friend, and received from him the kindest treatment; also to Dallas, President of the Senate; Douglas, Fremont, Gen. Houston, and all the men who had identified themselves with the interests of the West.

It will be remembered that only a short time previous to the Waiilatpu massacre a delegate had left Oregon for Washington, by ship around Cape Horn, who had been accredited by the governor of the colony only, and that the legislature had subsequently passed resolutions expressive of their disapproval of "secret factions," by which was meant the mission party, whose delegate Mr. Thornton was.

It so happened that, by reason of the commander of the *Portsmouth* having assumed it to be a duty to convey Mr. Thornton from La Paz, where through the infidelity of the Captain of the *Whitton*, he was stranded, he was enabled to reach the States early in the Spring, arriving in fact a week or two before Meek reached Washington. Thus Oregon had two representatives, although not entitled to any: nor had either a right to a seat in either House; yet to one this courtesy was granted, while the two together controlled more powerful influences than were ever before or since brought to bear on the fate of any single territory of the United States. While Mr. Thornton sat among Senators as a sort of consulting member or referee, but without a vote; Meek had the private ear of the President, and mingled freely among members of both Houses, in a social character, thereby exercising a more immediate influence than his more learned coadjutor. Happily their aims were not dissimilar, although their characters were; and the proper and prudish mission delegate, though he might often be shocked by the private follies of the legislative messenger from Oregon, could find no fault with the manner in which he discharged his duty to their common country.

The bill to admit Oregon as a territory which had been so long before Congress, and failed only because certain southern Senators insisted on an amendment allowing slave property to be introduced into that territory, was again under discussion in the Senate. The following extract from a speech of Benton's, delivered May 31st, before the Senate, shows how his energies were taxed in support of the Oregon cause—a cause which he had fostered from its infancy, and which he never deserted until his efforts to extend the United States government to the Pacific Ocean were crowned with success:—

"Only three or four years ago, the whole United States seemed to be inflamed with a desire to get possession of Oregon. It was one of the absorbing and agitating questions of the continent. To obtain exclusive possession of Oregon, the greatest efforts were made, and it was at length obtained. What next? After this actual occupation of the entire continent, and having thus obtained exclusive possession of Oregon in order that we might govern it, we have seen session after session of Congress pass away without a single thing being done for the government of a country, to obtain possession of which we were willing to go to war with England!

Year after year, and session after session have gone by, and to this day the laws of the United States have not been extended over that Territory. In the mean time, a great community is growing up there, composed at this time of twelve thousand souls—persons from all parts of the world, from Asia as well as from Europe and America—and which, till this time, have been preserved in order by compact among themselves. Great efforts have been made to preserve order—most meritorious efforts, which have evinced their anxiety to maintain their own reputation and that of the country to which they belong. Their efforts have been eminently meritorious; but we all know that voluntary governments cannot last—that they are temporary in their very nature, and must encounter rude shocks and resistance, under which they must fall. Besides the inconvenience resulting from the absence of an organized government, we are to recollect that there never yet has been a civilized settlement in territory occupied by the aboriginal inhabitants, in which a war between the races has not occurred. Down to the present moment, the settlers in Oregon had escaped a conflict with the Indians. Now the war between them is breaking out; and I cannot resist the conviction, that if there had been a regularly organized government in that country, immediately after the treaty with Great Britain, with a military force to sustain it,—for a government in such a region, so remote, would be nothing without military force,—the calamities now impending over that country might have been averted.

But no government was established; and now all these evils are coming upon these people, as everybody must have foreseen they would come; and in the depth of winter, they send to us a special messenger, who makes his way across the Rocky Mountains at a time when almost every living thing perished in the snow—when the snow was at such a depth that nothing could penetrate to the bottom of it. He made his way across, however, and brings these complaints which we now hear. They are in a suffering condition. Not a moment of time is to be lost. If the bill were passed this instant,—this morning, as I hoped it would be,—it would require the utmost degree of vigor in the execution of it to be able to send troops across the Rocky Mountains before the season of deep snow. They should cross the mountains before the month of September. I was in hopes then, that on this occasion, there would be nothing to delay action—that we should all have united in deploring that for years the proposition to give these people government and laws has been defeated by the introduction of a question of no practical consequence, but which has had the effect of depriving these people of all government, and bringing about the massacres which have taken place, and in which the benevolent missionary has fallen in the midst of his labors. All the calamities which have taken place in that country have resulted from mixing up this question, which has not a particle of practical value, with all the measures which have been introduced for the organization of a government in Oregon. All the laws passed by the Congress of the United States can have no effect on the question of slavery there. In that country there is a law superior to any which Congress can pass on the subject of slavery. There is a law of climate, of position, and of Nature herself, against it. Besides, the people of the country itself, by far the largest number of whom have gone out from slave-holding States, many of them from the State of Missouri, in their organic law, communicated to Congress more than a year ago, and printed among our documents at the last session, declare that the law of nature is against slavery in that region. Who would think of carrying slaves to the Lake of the Woods? and what would anybody think of a law of Congress which should say that slavery should or should not exist there ? I was in hopes, then, that this bill would be allowed to pass through this morning. And it was in order to avoid any delay that I did not make a separate bill to raise the regiments necessary to sustain the government there. I did hope, that on this occasion—when a great political measure of the highest importance is pending, which has been delayed for years, and which delay has brought on the massacres of which we now hear—this question, which has already produced these calamities, would not have been introduced, and that some other opportunity would have been taken for its discussion. There will be opportunities enough for its discussion. The doors of legislation are open to it as a separate measure. I trust, even now, that this question will not be permitted to delay our action. The delay of a few days here will be the delay of a year in Oregon. Delay at all now, is delay not for a week or a month, but for a year, during all which time these calamities will continue.

*   *   *   *   *   *   *   *   *   *

With respect to the question itself, I am ready to meet it in every shape and form. Let me here say, that no gentleman on this floor must assume to be the representative of the fifteen slave-holding States. I assume to represent one— no more than one—and if I can satisfy my constituents, my duty is performed. I invade no gentleman's bailiwick, and no one shall invade mine. Let every one speak for himself. This Federal Government was made for something else than to have this pestiferous question constantly thrust upon us to the interruption of the most important business. I am willing to vote down this question at this moment ; I am willing to take it up and act upon it in all its extent and bearings, at the proper time, when its consideration will not interrupt and destroy important measures. What I protest against is, to have the real business of the country—the pressing, urgent, crying business of the country— stopped, prostrated, defeated, by thrusting this question upon us. We read in Holy Writ, that a certain people were cursed by the plague of frogs, and that the plague was everywhere. You could not look upon the table but there were frogs; you could not sit down at the banquet but there were frogs; you could not go to the bridal couch and lift the sheets but there were frogs! We can see nothing, touch nothing, have no measures proposed, without having this pestilence thrust before us. Here it is, this black question, forever on the table, on the nuptial couch—everywhere! So it was not in the better days of the Republic. I remember the time when no one would have thought of asking a public man what his views were on the extension of slavery, any more than what was the length of his foot; and those were happy days which, although gone by, are remembered, and may, perhaps, be brought back.

We ought to vote down this amendment as a thing which should not be allowed to interrupt our action. Our action should not be delayed a single moment. This cruel war, which cannot continue in Oregon without extending to California, must be stopped without delay. Oregon and California must be saved from the desolation of an Indian war. Whatever opinions may be entertained upon the subject of slavery, let us agree on this point, that we will give law and government to the people of Oregon, and stop, if we can, the progress of this Indian war."

This was the tone which the friends of Oregon preserved through that last session of Congress in which the Oregon bill was under discussion.

In the meantime our hero was making the most of his advantages. He went to dinners and champagne suppers, besides giving an occasional one of the latter. At the presidential levees he made himself agreeable to witty and distinguished ladies, answering innumerable questions about Oregon and Indians, generally with a veil of reserve between himself and the questioner whenever the inquiries became, as they sometimes would, disagreeably searching. Again the spirit of perversity and mischief led him to make his answers so very direct as to startle or bewilder the questioner.

On one occasion a lady with whom he was promenading a drawing-room at some Senator's reception, admiring his handsome physique perhaps, and wondering if any woman owned it, finally ventured the question—was he married?

"Yes, indeed," answered Meek, with emphasis, "I have a wife and several children.."

"Oh dear," exclaimed the lady, " I should think your wife would be *so* afraid of the Indians!"

"Afraid of the Indians!" exclaimed Meek in his turn; " why, madam, she is an Indian herself!"

No further remarks on the subject were ventured that evening; and it is doubtful if the lady did not take his answer as a rebuke to her curiosity rather than the plain truth that it was.

Meek found his old comrade, Kit Carson, in Washington, staying with Fremont at the house of Senator Benton. Kit, who had left the mountains as poor as any other of the mountain-men, had no resource at that time except the pay furnished by Fremont for his services as guide and explorer in the California and Oregon expeditions; where, in fact, it was Carson and not Fremont who deserved fame as a path-finder. However that may be, Carson had as little money as men of his class usually have, and needed it as much. So long as Meek's purse was supplied, as it generally was, by some member of the family at the White House, Carson could borrow from him. But one being quite as careless of money as the other, they were sometimes both out of pocket at the same time. In that case the conversation was apt to take a turn like this:

Carson.   Meek, let me have some money, can't you?

Meek.   I hav 'nt got any money, Kit.

Carson.   Go and get some.

Meek.   —— it, whar am I to get money from?

Carson.   Try the " contingent fund," can't you?

Truth to tell the contingent fund was made to pay for a good many things not properly chargeable to the necessary expenditures of " Envoy Extraordinary" like our friend from Oregon.

The favoritism with which our hero was everywhere received was something remarkable, even when all the circumstances of his relationship to the chief magistrate, and the popularity of the Oregon question were considered. Doubtless the novelty of having a bear-fighting and Indian-fighting Rocky Mountain man to lionize, was one great secret of the furore which greeted him wherever he went; but even that fails to account fully for the enthusiasm he awakened, since mountain-men had begun to be pretty well known and understood, from the journal of Fremont and other explorers. It could only have been the social genius of the man which enabled him to overcome the impediments of lack of education, and the associations of half a lifetime. But whatever was the fortunate cause of his success, he enjoyed it to the full. He took excursions about the country in all directions, petted and spoiled like any "curled darling" instead of the six-foot-two Rocky Mountain trapper that he was.

In June he received an invitation to Baltimore, tendered by the city council, and was received by that body with the mayor at its head, in whose carriage he was conveyed to Monument Square, to be welcomed by a thousand ladies, smiling and showering roses upon him as he passed. And kissing the roses because he could not kiss the ladies, he bowed and smiled himself past the festive groups waiting to receive the messenger from Oregon. Music, dining, and the parade usual to such occasions distinguished this day, which Meek declares to have been the proudest of his life; not denying that the beauty of the Baltimore ladies contributed chiefly to produce that impression.

On the fourth of July, Polk laid the corner stone of the National Monument. The occasion was celebrated with great *eclat*, the address being delivered by Winthrop, the military display, and the fire-works in the evening being unusually fine. In the procession General Scott and staff rode on one side of the President's carriage, Col. May and Meek on the other,—Meek making a great display of horsemanship, in which as a mountain-man he excelled.

A little later in the summer Meek joined a party of Congressmen who were making campaign speeches in the principal cities of the north. At Lowell, Mass., he visited the cotton factories, and was equally surprised at the extent of the works, and the number of young women employed in them. Seeing this, the forewoman requested him to stop until noon and see the girls come out. As they passed in review before him, she asked if he had made his choice.

"No," replied the gallant Oregonian, "it would be impossible to choose, out of such a lot as that; I should have to take them all."

If our hero, under all his gaity smothered a sigh of regret that he was not at liberty to take *one*—a woman like those with whom for the first time in his life he was privileged to associate—who shall blame him? The kind of life he was living now was something totally different to anything in the past. It opened to his comprehension delightful possibilities of what might have been done and enjoyed under other circumstances, yet which now never could be done or enjoyed, until sometimes he was ready to fly from all these allurements, and hide himself again in the Rocky Mountains. Then again by a desperate effort, such thoughts were banished, and he rushed more eagerly than before into every pleasure afforded by the present moment, as if to make the present atone for the past and the future.

The kindness of the ladies at the White House, while it was something to be grateful for, as well as to make him envied, often had the effect to disturb his tranquility by the suggestions it gave rise to. Yet he was always de-

A MOUNTAIN-MAN IN CLOVER.

manding it, always accepting it. So constantly was he the attendant of his lady cousins in public and in private, riding and driving, or sauntering in the gardens of the presidential mansion, that the less favored among their acquaintances felt called upon to believe themselves aggrieved. Often, as the tall form of our hero was seen with a lady on either arm promenading the gardens at evening, the question would pass among the curious but uninitiated—"Who is that?" And the reply of some jealous grumbler would be—"It is that —— Rocky Mountain man," so loud sometimes as to be overheard by the careless trio, who smothered a laugh behind a hat or a fan.

And so passed that brief summer of our hero's life. A great deal of experience, of sight-seeing, and enjoyment had been crowded into a short few months of time. He had been introduced to and taken by the hand by the most celebrated men of the day. Nor had he failed to meet with men whom he had known in the mountains and in Oregon. His old employer, Wilkes, who was ill in Washington, sent for him to come and tell "some of those Oregon lies" for his amusement, and Meek, to humor him, stretched some of his good stories to the most wonderful dimensions.

But from the very nature of the enjoyment it could not last long; it was too vivid and sensational for constant wear. Feeling this, he began to weary of Washington, and more particularly since he had for the last few weeks been stopping away from the White House. In one of his restless moods he paid a visit to Polk, who detecting the state of his mind asked laughingly——

" Well, Meek, what do you want now?"

" I want to be franked."

" How long will five hundred dollars last you?"

"About as many days as there ar' hundreds, I reckon."

"You are shockingly extravagant, Meek. Where do you think all this money is to come from?"

"It is not my business to know, Mr. President," replied Meek, laughing, "but it *is* the business of these United States to pay the expenses of the messenger from Oregon, isn't it?"

"I think I will send you to the Secretary of War to be franked, Meek; his frank is better than mine. But no, stay; I will speak to Knox about it this time. And you must not spend your money so recklessly, Meek; it will not do—it will not do."

Meek thanked the President both for the money and the advice, but gave a champagne supper the next night, and in a week's time was as empty-handed as ever. Washington manners were in some respects too much like mountain manners for five hundred dollars to go a great ways.

CHAPTER XL.

We must go back a little way and take up the thread of Oregon's political history as it relates to the persons and events of which we have been writing. However irregular had been the appointment of a delegate for Oregon, while still unrecognized by the general government, and however distasteful as a party measure the appointment of Mr. Thornton had been to a majority of the people of Oregon, there was nevertheless sufficient merit in his acts, since events had turned out as they had, to reconcile even his enemies to them. For what did it concern the people who procured or helped to procure the blessings they asked for, so only that they were made sure of the blessings.

Mr. Thornton had done what he could in Washington to secure for Oregon the things desired by her citizens. Immediately on his arrival he had prepared, at the instance of Mr. Polk, a memorial to Congress setting forth the condition of the country and the wants of the colony. In addition to this he had prayed for the passage of a law organizing a territorial government, and donating land-claims. To be sure Congress had been memorialized on these subjects for years, and all to no purpose. But there was a decided advantage in having a man versed in law and conversant with legal forms as well as territorial wants, to assist in getting up the bills concerning Oregon. Besides, Thornton was a conscientious man, and would not agree to a fraud.

30

The territorial bill was gotten up among the friends of Oregon in the Free-Soil party, and had incorporated into it the ordinance of 1787, prohibiting slavery, and this was so not only because the free-soilers desired it, but because the people of Oregon desired it. But a few sagacious Southern members had conceived the idea of making Mr. Thornton responsible for the expunging of the obnoxious clause, by trying to convince him that the bill could never be passed with the ordinance of 1787 in it, and that would he, Thornton, but consent to have it stricken out, they were assured that the friends of free-soil would allow it to pass for the sake of waiting, expectant Oregon. So reasoned Calhoun and others.

Thornton, however, was both too wise and too faithful to be humbugged in that specious manner. He assured Mr. Calhoun that in the first place he had no authority to consent to the expunging of the ordinance of 1787 ; in the second place, that the people of Oregon would wait for a territorial government until they could obtain one which promised them free institutions ; and in the third place, that he did not believe the free-soil party would ever allow the bill to pass, amended as Mr. Calhoun proposed ; therefore that had he the authority to consent to the amendment, he should gain nothing, but lose all by doing so.

Thus, through the almost entire summer, the friends and the enemies of free-soil quarreled and schemed over Oregon. Not that any were really opposed to the extension of the Government over that territory, but only that the Southern members objected to more free soil.

The President was very anxious that the bill should pass in some shape during his administration. Benton of Missouri, was eager for its passage as it was. Butler of South Carolina, fiercely opposed to it. Numerous were the skirmishes which these two Senators had over the

Oregon question; and a duel would, in one instance, have resulted, had not the arrest of the parties put a termination to the affair.

The land bill too, gave considerable trouble; not from any opposition it encountered, but because nobody knew how much land to give each settler. Some Congressmen, in the magnificence of their generosity and compassion, were for granting one thousand acres to every white male settler of the territory. The committee who had this bill in hand, on consulting the two Oregon representatives, were informed that the proposed donation was altogether too large, and it was subsequently reduced.

The close of the session was at hand and nothing had been done except to talk. Congress was to adjourn at noon on Monday, August 14th, and it was now Saturday the 12th. The friends of Oregon were anxious; the two waiting Oregonians nearly desperate. On this morning of the 12th, the friends of the bill, under Benton's lead, determined upon obtaining a vote on the final passage of the bill; resolving that they would not yield to the usual motions for delay and adjournments, but that they would, if necessary, sit until twelve o'clock Monday.

On the other hand, the southern members, finding that no motion for adjournment could be made to prevail, Butler, of South Carolina, moved that the Senate go into executive session. This was done because under the rules of the Senate, the Oregon bill would necessarily give place to the business of the executive session. And the business to which Senator Butler proposed to call the attention of the senate was certain conduct of the gentleman from Missouri, which he characterized as dishonorable.

At the word "dishonorable" Benton sprang to his feet, exclaiming—"You lie, sir! you lie!! I cram the lie down your throat!!!" at the same time advancing toward Butler with his fist clenched and raised in a threatening manner. Butler on his part seemed very willing to engage in a personal conflict, awaiting his antagonist with the genuine game look which has formerly been supposed to be one of the signs of good southern blood.

But a fight on the floor of the Senate between two of its white-haired members could not be suffered to go on, the combatants being separated by the other Senators, who crowded in between. The eyes of Butler burned fiercely as he said to Benton over the heads of his officious friends,—

"I will see you, sir, at another time and place!"

"Very well, sir;" returned Benton: "but you will do well to understand that when I fight, I fight for a funeral!"

That this affair did not terminate in a funeral was probably owing to the arrest of the parties.

At ten o'clock Saturday evening, order having been restored, and no adjournment having yet prevailed, Senator Foote of Mississippi, arose and commenced to speak in a manner most irritatingly drawling and dull; saying that since there was to be no adjournment before twelve o'clock Monday noon, he proposed to entertain to the best of his ability the grave deliberative body before him.

Commencing at the creation of Adam, he gave the Bible Story—the creation of Eve; the fall of man; the history of the children of Israel; the stories of the prophets; ecclesiastical history,—only yielding the floor for a motion, at intervals of an hour each, continuing to drawl through the time hour after hour.

Sleepy senators betook themselves to the anteroom to lunch, to drink, to talk to the waiting ones, and to sleep. But whenever a motion was made, a page aroused the sleepers and they took their seats and voted.

Thus wore the night away.   The Sabbath morning's sun arose, and still Foote was in the midst of his Bible disquisitions.   At length, two hours after sunrise, a consultation was held between Butler, Mason, Calhoun, Davis and Foote, which resulted in the announcement that no further opposition would be offered to taking the vote upon the final passage of the Oregon bill.   The vote was then taken, the bill passed, and the weary senate adjourned, to meet again on Monday for a final adjournment.

After the adjournment on Sunday morning, Benton in alluding to the scene between himself and the senator from South Carolina, said, "he did not blame Judge Butler so much as he might; because that —— scoundrel Calhoun was urging Butler to it, while he himself sat saying nothing, and doing nothing, but looking as demure as a courtesan at a christening."

Truly "such are the compliments that pass when gentlemen meet."

The Land bill, or Donation act, as it is generally known, failed of being passed at this session, simply because it had to wait for the Territorial bill to be passed, being supplementary to it, and because after the passage of that bill there was no time to take up the other.

As Thornton had been chiefly instrumental in getting the Donation bill into shape, it was a severe disappointment, in not having it passed at the same session with the Territorial bill, and having to return to Oregon without this welcome present to the people of the new territory.

Collamer of Vermont, sympathizing with the failure of the Donation Law, proposed to Thornton to draw up a new bill including some amendments suggested by him, and to forward the same to his (Collamer's) address, promising to see what could be done with it thereafter.   This

Thornton did, and also carried a copy of it home to Oregon, and placed it in the hands of Oregon's first delegate to Congress, who, after making a few alterations in the bill, adopted and claimed it for his own. The bill thus amended and re-amended, became a law in September, 1850; and of that law we shall have occasion to speak hereafter.

CHAPTER XLI.

1848–9.   THE long suspense ended, Meek prepared to return to Oregon, if not without some regrets, at the same time not unwillingly.   His restless temper, and life-long habits of unrestrained freedom began to revolt against the conventionality of his position in Washington.   Besides, in appointing officers for the new territory, Polk had made him United States Marshal, than which no office could have suited him better, and he was as prompt to assume the discharge of its duties, as all his life he had been to undertake any duty to which his fortunes assigned him.

On the 20th of August, only six days after the passage of the territorial bill, he received his papers from Buchanan, and set off for Bedford Springs, whither the family from the White House were flown to escape from the suffocating air of Washington in August.   He had brought his papers to be signed by Polk, and being expected by the President found everything arranged for his speedy departure ; Polk even ordering a seat for him in the upcoming coach, by telegraph.   On learning this from the President, at dinner, when the band was playing, Meek turned to the leader and ordered him to play " Sweet Home," much to the amusement of his lady cousins, who had their own views of the sweets of a home in Oregon. A hurried farewell, spoken to each of his friends separately, and Oregon's new Marshal was ready to proceed on his long journey toward the Pacific.

The occasion of Polk's haste in the matter of getting Meek started, was his anxiety to have the Oregon government become a fact before the expiration of his term of office. The appointment of Governor of the new territory had been offered to Shields, and declined. Another commission had been made out, appointing General Joseph Lane of Indiana, Governor of Oregon, and the commission was that day signed by the President and given to Meek to be delivered to Lane in the shortest possible time. His last words to the Marshal on parting were— "God bless you, Meek. Tell Lane to have a territorial government organized during my administration."

Of the ten thousand dollars appropriated by Congress " to be expended under the direction of the President, in payment for services and expenses of such persons as had been engaged by the provisional government of Oregon in conveying communications to and from the United States; and for purchase of presents for such Indian tribes as the peace and quiet of the country required "— Thornton received two thousand six hundred dollars, Meek seven thousand four hundred, and the Indian tribes none. Whether the President believed that the peace and quiet of the country did not require presents to be made to the Indians, or whether family credit required that Meek should get the lion's share, is not known. However that may be, our hero felt himself to be quite rich, and proceeded to get rid of his superfluity, as will hereafter be seen, with his customary prodigality and enjoyment of the present without regard to the future.

Before midnight on the day of his arrival at the springs, Meek was on his way to Indiana to see General Lane. Arriving at the Newburg landing one morning at day-break, he took horse immediately for the General's residence at Newburg, and presented him with his commission soon after breakfast. Lane sat writing, when Meek, introducing himself, laid his papers before him.

"Do you accept?" asked Meek.

"Yes," answered Lane.

"How soon can you be ready to start?"

"In fifteen minutes!" answered Lane, with military promptness.

Three days, however, were actually required to make the necessary preparations for leaving his farm and proceeding to the most remote corner of the United States territory.

At St. Louis they were detained one day, waiting for a boat to Leavenworth, where they expected to meet their escort. This one day was too precious to be lost in waiting by so business-like a person as our hero, who, when nothing more important was to be done generally was found trying to get rid of his money. So, on this occasion, after having disburdened himself of a small amount in treating the new Governor and all his acquaintances, he entered into negotiations with a peddler who was importuning the passengers to buy everything, from a jack-knife to a silk dress.

Finding that Nat. Lane, the General's son, wanted a knife, but was disposed to beat down the price, Meek made an offer for the lot of a dozen or two, and thereby prevented Lane getting one at any price. Not satisfied with this investment, he next made a purchase of three whole pieces of silk, at one dollar and fifty cents per yard. At this stage of the transaction General Lane interfered sufficiently to inquire "what he expected to do with that stuff?"

"Can't tell," answered Meek; "but I reckon it is worth the money."

"Better save your money," said the more prudent Lane.

But the incorrigible spendthrift only laughed, and threatened to buy out the Jew's entire stock, if Lane persisted in preaching economy.

At St. Louis, besides his son Nat., Lane was met by Lieut. Hawkins, who was appointed to the command of the escort of twenty-five riflemen, and Dr. Hayden, surgeon of the company. This party proceeded to Leavenworth, the point of starting, where the wagons and men of Hawkins' command awaited them. At this place, Meek was met by a brother and two sisters who had come to look on him for the first time in many years. The two days' delay which was necessary to get the train ready for a start, afforded an opportunity for this family reunion, the last that might ever occur between its widely separated branches, new shoots from which extend at this day from Virginia to Alabama, and from Tennessee to California and Oregon.

By the 10th of September the new government was on its way to Oregon in the persons of Lane and Meek. The whole company of officers, men, and teamsters, numbered about fifty-five; the wagons ten; and riding-horses, an extra supply for each rider.

The route taken, with the object to avoid the snows of a northern winter, was from Leavenworth to Santa Fe, and thence down the Rio Grande to near El Paso; thence northwesterly by Tucson, in Arizona; thence to the Pimas village on the Gila River; following the Gila to its junction with the Colorado, thence northwesterly again to the Bay of San Pedro in California. From this place the company were to proceed by ship to San Francisco; and thence again by ship to the Columbia River.

On the Santa Fe trail they met the army returning from Mexico, under Price, and learned from them that they could not proceed with wagons beyond Santa Fe.

The lateness of the season, although it was not attended with snow, as on the northern route it would have been, subjected the travelers nevertheless to the strong, cold winds which blow over the vast extent of open country between the Missouri River and the high mountain range which forms the water-shed of the continent.   It also made it more difficult to subsist the animals, especially after meeting Price's army, which had already swept the country bare.

On coming near Santa Fe, Meek was riding ahead of his party, when he had a most unexpected encounter. Seeing a covered traveling carriage drawn up under the shade of some trees growing beside a small stream, not far off from the trail, he resolved, with his usual love of adventure, to discover for himself the character of the proprietor.   But as he drew nearer, he discovered no one, although a camp-table stood under the trees, spread with refreshments, not only of a solid, but a fluid nature. The sight of a bottle of cognac induced him to dismount, and he was helping himself to a liberal glass, when a head was protruded from a covering of blankets inside the carriage, and a heavy bass voice was heard in a polite protest :

"Seems to me, stranger, you are making free with my property !"

"Here's to you, sir," rejoined the purloiner; "it isn't often I find as good brandy as that,"—holding out the glass admiringly,—"but when I do, I make it a point of honor not to pass it."

"May I inquire your name, sir?" asked the owner of the brandy, forced to smile at the good-humored audacity of his guest.

"I couldn't refuse to give my name after that,"—replacing the glass on the table,—"and I now introduce myself as Joseph L. Meek, Esq., Marshal of Oregon, on my way from Washington to assist General Lane in establishing a territorial Government west of the Rocky Mountains."

"Meek!—what, not the Joe Meek I have heard my brothers tell so much about?"

"Joe Meek is my name; but whar did your brothers know me?" inquired our hero, mystified in his turn.

"I think you must have known Captain William Sublette and his brother Milton, ten or twelve years ago, in the Rocky Mountains," said the gentleman, getting out of the carriage, and approaching Meek with extended hand.

A delighted recognition now took place. From Solomon Sublette, the owner of the carriage and the cognac, Meek learned many particulars of the life and death of his former leaders in the mountains. Neither of them were then living; but this younger brother, Solomon, had inherited Captain Sublette's wife and wealth at the same time. After these explanations, Mr. Sublette raised the curtains of the carriage again, and assisted to descend from it a lady, whom he introduced as his wife, and who exhibited much gratification in becoming acquainted with the hero of many a tale recited to her by her former husband, Captain Sublette.

In the midst of this pleasant exchange of reminiscences, the remainder of Meek's party rode up, were introduced, and invited to regale themselves on the fine liquors with which Mr. Sublette's carriage proved to be well furnished. This little adventure gave our hero much pleasure, as furnishing a link between the past and present, and bringing freshly to mind many incidents already beginning to fade in his memory.

At Santa Fe, the train stopped to be overhauled and reconstructed. The wagons having to be abandoned, their contents had to be packed on mules, after the manner of mountain or of Mexican travel and transportation. This change accomplished, with as little delay as possible, the train proceeded without any other than the usual difficulties, as far as Tucson, when two of the twenty-five riflemen deserted, having become suddenly enamored of liberty, in the dry and dusty region of southern Arizona.

Lieutenant Hawkins, immediately on discovering the desertion, dispatched two men, well armed, to compel their return. One of the men detailed for this duty belonged to the riflemen, but the other was an American, who, with a company of Mexican packers, had joined the train at Santa Fe, and was acting in the capacity of pilot. In order to fit out this volunteer for the service, always dangerous, of retaking deserting soldiers, Meek had lent him his Colt's revolvers. It was a vain precaution, however, both the men being killed in attempting to capture the deserters; and Meek's pistols were never more heard of, having fallen into the murderous hands of the runaways.

Drouth now began to be the serious evil with which the travelers had to contend. From the Pimas villages westward, it continually grew worse, the animals being greatly reduced from the want both of food and water. At the crossing of the Colorado, the animals had to be crossed over by swimming, the officers and men by rafts made of bulrushes. Lane and Meek being the first to be ferried over, were landed unexpectedly in the midst of a Yuma village. The Indians, however, gave them no trouble, and, except the little artifice of drowning some of the mules at the crossing, in order to get their flesh to eat, committed neither murders nor thefts, nor any outrage whatever.

It was quite as well for the unlucky mules to be

drowned and eaten as it was for their fellows to travel on over the arid desert before them until they starved and perished, which they nearly all did. From the Colorado on, the company of Lieut. Hawkins became thoroughly demoralized. Not only would the animals persist in dying, several in a day, but the soldiers also persisted in deserting, until, by the time he reached the coast, his forlorn hope was reduced to three men. But it was not the drouth in their case which caused the desertions: it was rumors which they heard everywhere along the route, of mines of gold and silver, where they flattered themselves they could draw better pay than from Uncle Sam's coffers.

The same difficulty from desertion harassed Lieutenant-Colonel Loring in the following summer, when he attempted to establish a line of posts along the route to Oregon, by the way of Forts Kearney, Laramie, and through the South Pass to Fort Hall. His mounted rifle regiment dwindled down to almost nothing. At one time, over one hundred men deserted in a body: and although he pursued and captured seventy of them, he could not keep them from deserting again at the first favorable moment. The bones of many of those gold-seeking soldiers were left on the plains, where wolves had stripped the flesh from them; and many more finally had rude burial at the hands of fellow gold-seekers: but few indeed ever won or enjoyed that for which they risked everything.

On arriving at Cook's wells, some distance beyond the Colorado, our travelers found that the water at this place was tainted by the body of a mule which had lost its life some days before in endeavoring to get at the water. This was a painful discovery for the thirsty party to make. However, there being no water for some distance ahead, General Lane boiled some of it, and made coffee of it,

GOVERNOR LANE AND MARSHAL MEEK ENROUTE TO OREGON.

remarking that "maggots were more easily swallowed cooked than raw!"

And here the writer, and no doubt, the reader too, is compelled to make a reflection. Was the office of Governor of a Territory at fifteen hundred dollars a year, and Indian agent at fifteen hundred more, worth a journey of over three thousand miles, chiefly by land, even allowing that there had been no maggots in the water? *Quien sabe?*

Not far from this locality our party came upon one hundred wagons abandoned by Major Graham, who had not been able to cross the desert with them. Proceeding onward, the riders eventually found themselves on foot, there being only a few animals left alive to transport the baggage that could not be abandoned. So great was their extremity, that to quench their thirst the stomach of a mule was opened to get at the moisture it contained. In the horror and pain of the thirst-fever, Meek renewed again the sufferings he had undergone years before in the deserts inhabited by Diggers, and on the parched plains of the Snake River.

About the middle of January the Oregon Government, which had started out so gaily from Fort Leavenworth, arrived weary, dusty, foot-sore, famished, and suffering, at William's Ranch on the Santa Anna River, which empties into the Bay of San Pedro. Here they were very kindly received, and their wants ministered to.

At this place Meek developed, in addition to his various accomplishments, a talent for speculation. While overhauling his baggage, the knives and the silk which had been purchased of the *peddler* in St. Louis, were brought to light. No sooner did the senoritas catch a glimpse of the shining fabrics than they went into raptures over them, after the fashion of their sex. Seeing the state of mind

to which these raptures, if unheeded, were likely to reduce the ladies of his house, Mr. Williams approached
Meek delicately on the subject of purchase. But Meek,
in the first flush of speculative shrewdness declared that
as he had bought the goods for his own wife, he could not
find it in his heart to sell them.

However, as the senoritas were likely to prove inconsolable, Mr. Williams again mentioned the desire of his family
to be clad in silk, and the great difficulty, nay, impossi-
bility, of obtaining the much coveted fabric in that part
of the world, and accompanied his remarks with an offer
of ten dollars a yard for the lot.   At this magnificent offer
our hero affected to be overcome by regard for the feelings of the senoritas, and consented to sell his dollar and
a-half silks for ten dollars per yard.

In the same manner, finding that knives were a desirable article in that country, very much wanted by miners
and others, he sold out his dozen or two, for an ounce
each of gold-dust, netting altogether the convenient little
profit of about five hundred dollars.   When Gen. Lane
was informed of the transaction, and reminded of his objections to the original purchase, he laughed heartily.

"Well, Meek," said he, "you were drunk when you
bought them, and by —— I think you must have been
drunk when you sold them; but drunk or sober, I will
own you can beat me at a bargain."

Such bargains, however, became common enough about
this time in California, for this was the year memorable in
California history, of the breaking out of the gold-fever,
and the great rush to the mines which made even the
commonest things worth their weight in gold-dust.

Proceeding to Los Angelos, our party, once more comfortably mounted, found traveling comparatively easy.   At this
place they found quartered the command of Maj. Graham,

whose abandoned wagons had been passed at the *Hornella* on the Colorado River. The town, too, was crowded with miners, men of every class, but chiefly American adventurers, drawn together from every quarter of California and Mexico by the rumor of the gold discovery at Sutter's Fort.

On arriving at San Pedro, a vessel—the *Southampton*, was found ready to sail. She had on board a crowd of fugitives from Mexico, bound to San Francisco, where they hoped to find repose from the troubles which harassed that revolutionary Republic.

At San Francisco, Meek was surprised to meet about two hundred Oregonians, who on the first news of the gold discovery the previous autumn, had fled, as it is said men shall flee on the day of judgment—leaving the wheat ungathered in the fields, the grain unground in the mills, the cattle unherded on the plains, their tools and farming implements rusting on the ground—everything abandoned as if it would never more be needed, to go and seek the shining dust, which is vainly denominated "filthy lucre." The two hundred were on their way home, having all either made something, or lost their health by exposure so that they were obliged to return. But they left many more in the mines.

Such were the tales told in San Francisco of the wonderful fortunes of some of the miners that young Lane became infected with the universal fever and declared his intention to try mining with the rest. Meek too, determined to risk something in gold-seeking, and as some of the teamsters who had left Fort Leavenworth with the company, and had come as far as San Francisco, were very desirous of going to the mines, Meek fitted out two or three with pack-horses, tools, and provisions, to accompany young Lane. For the money expended in the outfit he

31

was to receive half of their first year's profits. The result of this venture was three pickle-jars of gold-dust, which were sent to him by the hands of Nat. Lane, the following year; and which just about reimbursed him for the outlay.

At San Francisco, Gen. Lane found the U. S. Sloop of War, the *St. Mary's;* and Meek insisted that the Oregon government, which was represented in their persons, had a right to require her services in transporting itself to its proper seat. But Lane, whose notions of economy extended, singularly enough, to the affairs of the general government, would not consent to the needless expenditure. Meek was rebellious, and quoted Thornton, by whom he was determined not to be outdone in respect of expense for transportation. Lane insisted that his dignity did not require a government vessel to convey him to Oregon. In short the new government was very much divided against itself, and only escaped a fall by Meek's finding some one, or some others, else, on whom to play his pranks.

The first one was a Jew peddler who had gentlemen's clothes to sell. To him the Marshal represented himself as a United States Custom officer, and after frightening him with a threat of confiscating his entire stock, finally compromised with the terrified Israelite by accepting a suit of clothes for himself. After enjoying the mortification of spirit which the loss inflicted on the Jew, for twenty-four hours, he finally paid him for the clothes, at the same time administering a lecture upon the sin and danger of smuggling.

The party which had left Leavenworth for Oregon nearly six months before, numbering fifty-five, now numbered only seven. Of the original number two had been killed, and all the rest had deserted to go to the mines.

There remained only Gen. Lane, Meek, Lieut. Hawkins and Hayden, surgeon, besides three soldiers. With this small company Gen. Lane went on board the *Jeanette*, a small vessel, crowded with miners, and destined for the Columbia River. As the *Jeanette* dropped down the Bay, a salute was fired from the *St. Mary's* in honor of Gen. Lane, and appropriated to himself by Marshal Meek, who seems to have delighted in appropriating to himself all the honors in whatever circumstances he might be placed; the more especially too, if such assumption annoyed the General.

After a tedious voyage of eighteen days the *Jeanette* arrived in the Columbia River. From Astoria the party took small boats for Oregon City, a voyage of one hundred and twenty miles; so that it was already the 2d of March when they arrived at that place, and only one day was left for the organization of the Territorial Government before the expiration of Polk's term of office. Gen. Lane's economy had nearly defeated Polk's great desire.

CHAPTER XLII.

1849. IF this were a novel which we were writing, we should fix upon this point in our story to write—"And so they were married, and lived together happily ever after;" placing the FINIS directly after that sentence. For have we not brought Oregon through all the romantic adventures and misadventures of her extraordinary youth, and ushered her upon the stage of action a promising young Territory? As for our hero, he too has arrived at the climax of his individual glory and success, a point at which it might be wise to leave him.

But a regard for the eternal fitness of things compels us to gather up again the dropped threads of some portions of our story, and follow them to their proper winding up. We promise, however, to touch as lightly as possible upon the Territorial history of Oregon; for her political record here becomes, what the political record of too many other Territories has been, a history of demagogueism. With this preface we proceed to finish our narrative.

On the 2d of March Gen. Lane arrived at Oregon City, and was introduced to Gov. Abernethy, by Marshal Meek. On the 3d, there appeared the following—

PROCLAMATION.

In pursuance of an act of Congress, approved the 14th of August, in the year of our Lord 1848, establishing a Territorial Government in the Territory of Oregon:

I, Joseph Lane, was, on the 18th day of August, in the year 1848, appointed

Governor in and for the Territory of Oregon. I have therefore thought it proper to issue this, my proclamation, making known that I have this day entered upon the discharge of the duties of my office, and by virtue thereof do declare the laws of the United States extended over, and declared to be in force in said Territory, so far as the same, or any portion thereof, may be applicable.

Given under my hand at Oregon City, in the Territory of Oregon, this 3d day of March, Anno Domini 1849. JOSEPH LANE.

Thus Oregon had one day, under Polk, who, take it all in all, had been a faithful guardian of her interests.

Shortly after the appearance of the proclamation of Gov. Lane, Meek was sworn into office, and gave the required securities. All the other Territorial officers present in the Territory, or as fast as they arrived, took the oath of office; courts were established, and the new government moved on. Of the Presidential appointees who accepted, were William T. Bryant of Indiana, Chief Justice O. C. Pratt of Illinois, and Peter H. Burnett of Oregon, Associate Justices of the District Court: John Adair of Kentucky, Collector for the District of Oregon: and Kintzinge Pritchett of Pennsylvania, Secretary of State.

The condition in which Gov. Lane found the new Territory was not so sad as might reasonably be conjectured from the fears of its inhabitants fifteen months previous. Intimidated by the presence of the volunteers in the upper country, the Indians had remained quiet, and the immigration of 1848 passed through their country without being disturbed in any manner. So little apprehension was felt concerning an Indian war at this time that men did not hesitate to leave their homes and families to go to the gold fields of California.

In the month of August, 1848, the *Honolulu*, a vessel of one hundred and fifty tons, owned in Boston, carrying a consignment of goods to a mercantile house in Portland, arrived at her anchorage in the Wallamet, *via* San Francisco, California. Captain Newell, almost before he had discharged freight, commenced buying up a cargo of flour and other provisions. But what excited the wonder of the Oregonians was the fact that he also bought up all manner of tools such as could be used in digging or cutting, from a spade and pickaxe, to a pocket-knife. This singular proceeding naturally aroused the suspicions of a people accustomed to have something to suspect. A demand was made for the *Honolulu's* papers, and these not being forthcoming, it was proposed by some of the prudent ones to tie her up. When this movement was attempted, the secret came out. Captain Newell, holding up a bag of gold-dust before the astonished eyes of his persecutors, cried out—

"Do you see that gold? D——n you, I will depopulate your country! I know where there is plenty of this stuff, and I am taking these tools where it is to be found."

This was in August, the month of harvest. So great was the excitement which seized the people, that all classes of men were governed by it. Few persons stopped to consider that this was the time for producers to reap golden harvests of precious ore, for the other yellow harvest of grain which was already ripe and waiting to be gathered. Men left their grain standing, and took their teams from the reapers to pack their provisions and tools to the mines.

Some men would have gladly paid double to get back the spades, shovels, or picks, which the shrewd Yankee Captain had purchased from them a week previous. All implements of this nature soon commanded fabulous prices, and he was a lucky man who had a supply.

The story of the gold-fever which began in the fall and winter of '48, and raged with such violence through '49, is too familiar to everybody to need repeating here. Only as it affected the fortunes of Oregon need it be mentioned.

Its immediate effect was to give an impetus to business in the Territory which nothing else ever could have done; to furnish a market for all sorts of produce, and employment for every kind of industry, to bring money into circulation in place of wheat and beaver-skins, and for a time to make the country extremely prosperous.

One of the last acts of the Provisional Government had been to authorize the weighing, assaying, and coining of gold—an act which was rendered necessary by the great amount of "dust" in circulation, and the influx of the debased South American coins. An association of gentlemen taking the matter in hand, bore all the expense of the dies, machinery, and labor, coining only about ten thousand dollars in the summer of '49. They succeeded in raising the price of "dust" from eleven to sixteen dollars per ounce, and stopping the influx of South American coins. The gentlemen who conferred a great benefit on Oregon, were Kilborne, Magruder, Rector,

BEAVER-MONEY.

Campbell, and Smith. This money went by the name of "Beaver-money," owing to the design on the dies, which referred to the previous beaver currency.

But the ultimate effect of the California gold discoveries was to put a check upon the prosperity of Oregon. The emigration from the states, instead of going to Oregon as formerly, now turned off to California. Men soon discovered the fertile quality of California soil, and while the majority dug for gold a sufficient number went to farming to make, together with the imports from the east, almost a supply for the yearly hordes of gold seekers. The fame of the California climate, the fascinations of the ups and downs of fortune's wheel in that country, and many other causes, united to make California, and not Oregon, the object of interest on the Pacific coast; and the rapidity with which California became self-supporting removed from Oregon her importance as a source of supplies. There-fore, after a few years of rather extraordinary usefulness and consequent good fortune, the Territory relapsed into a purely domestic and very quiet young State. This change in its federal status was not altogether acceptable to Oregonians. They had so long been accustomed to regard themselves as the pets of a great and generous, but rather neglectful Republic, from whose hands all manner of favors were to be of right demanded, because they had sustained for so long a time the character of good children, without any immediate reward—that now when a rival darling sprang into vigorous life and excessive favor, almost at once, their jealousy rankled painfully. So naughty and disagreeable a passion as jealousy is its own punishment, as the Oregonian of to-day would do well to remember, while he does what he can to show to the world that his State, by its splendid resources, fully justifies all the outlay of patriotism and ardor which distinguished its early history.

But to return to our mutton. Although Gov. Lane did not find an Indian war on his hands immediately on assuming the duties of his office, there was yet plenty to do in getting the government organized, appointing officers to take the census, ordering elections, and getting the run of Oregon politics, to occupy his attention for the first three months of his administration.

The change in the government had not by any means changed the objects and aims of the different parties in Oregon. Now, as before, there was a Mission party, strong in money and influence; now, as before, the term

"Hudson's Bay man" was used by the Mission party to bring odium upon any aspirant to office, or even business success, who, not being intimidated by their interdict, ventured to be employed professionally by Dr. McLaughlin, or in any way to show regard for him. As there were always a certain number independent enough to act from free will or conviction, there was in consequence still a Hudson's Bay party. Between these two, as before, there stood a third party, who added itself to or subtracted itself from the other two, as its purposes and interests required. As there were haters of Dr. McLaughlin in two of the parties it did not require a great amount of shrewdness to inform a man that on this point might turn his political fortunes.

This discovery was made very early after his arrival in the Territory by Gov. Lane, as well as by Judge Bryant, and others, and used at times by them when there was an object to be gained by it, although neither of these dignitaries declared themselves openly as good haters of the Doctor.

Dr. McLaughlin, on the settlement of the boundary question, seeing that the London Company found much fault with him for having "encouraged the settlement of Oregon by the Americans," went to England to see the Directors and have the matter understood between himself and them. Finding on hearing his explanation, that while doing nothing to encourage settlement, he could not permit the immigrants of the first few years to suffer after their arrival, and that out of charity only he had done what was done for their relief, the Company still blamed him, the Doctor then said to the Directors, "Gentlemen, I will serve you no longer." Sixty thousand dollars, expended in helping American settlers was charged to his private account. This amount was afterwards remitted, but the debt was heavily felt at the time.

On his return to Oregon, and on the establishment of a Territorial government, the Doctor determined to take out naturalization papers, and become an American citizen. But no sooner had the government been organized than new complications arose in the Doctor's case. Judge Bryant had been but a few days in the Territory before he purchased from the Mission Milling Company the Island in the river opposite Oregon City, which was occupied by their mills, but which formed a part of the original claim of Dr. McLaughlin. Thus the Chief Justice assumed at once the same attitude towards him which the Mission and the Milling Company had done; and as the island was contained in Judge Bryant's district, and only two Judges were at that time in the Territory, the Doctor felt constrained to seek advice from such Americans as were his friends. Although some believed that his best chance of holding his original claim, was to depend upon his possessory rights under the treaty of 1846, others counseled him to take out his naturalization papers and secure himself in the rights of an American citizen. This he did at last, on the 30th of May, 1849.

We have spoken in a previous chapter of Mr. Thurston, in connection with the Donation Act. It is related of this gentleman that when he left Iowa for Oregon, he confided to his personal friends his resolve to be "in Congress or in h—" two years after reaching that Territory. Like other ambitious new-comers, he soon discovered what side to take with certain influential persons, concerning the Hudson's Bay Company, which was but another name for Dr. McLaughlin.

Mr. Thurston did not hesitate to ask the Doctor to vote for him, for delegate to Congress, which, however, the Doctor did not do, as one of his friends was up for the same office. But when he was finally elected to Congress, fortunately within the two years to which he had limited himself—Mr. Thurston took ground which betrayed by what influences he had been placed in the coveted position.

Mr. Thornton having returned to Oregon sometime in May had made the acquaintance of the candidate for Congress, and feeling some anxiety with regard to the Land Bill, which he had expended considerable thought and labor upon, conversed freely with Mr. Thurston upon the subject, and finally, on his election, presented him with a copy of his bill; the same, with certain alterations, that could not strictly be called amendments, which afterwards became the Donation Law.

But the notable section of Mr. Thurston's bill, which finally became a law, was that one which was intended to secure him future political favors, by earning him the gratitude of the anti-Hudson's Bay party, and all others whose private interests he subserved. This was the section which exempted from the benefits of the act the Oregon City claim, in the following words. "That there be, and hereby is granted to the Territory of Oregon, two townships, one north and one south of the Columbia River, to aid in establishing a University, to be selected by the Assembly, and approved by the Surveyor General. *Also the Oregon City claim, except those lots sold previous to March 4th,* 1849."

In order to secure the passage of this part of the land bill, Mr. Thurston addressed a letter to the House of Representatives, of which he was a member, containing the following assertions:—that it was the Methodist Mission which first took the Oregon City claim; that they were driven from it by a fear of having the savages of Oregon let loose upon them; that a number of citizens of Oregon had been successively driven from it, by the power of the Hudson's Bay Company; that Dr. McLaughlin had al-

ready sold lots to the amount of $200,000, enough for a
foreigner to make out of American territory; and that
the Doctor had not taken out naturalization papers, but
was an Englishman at heart, and still identified with the
Hudson's Bay Company. Mr. Thurston's letter contained
many more assertions equally false—but those just given
relate more particularly to the eleventh section of the Donation Act.

Mr. Thurston's reason for asking to have all sales of lots
made before the fourth of March, 1849, confirmed, he declared to be to prevent litigation. Dr. McLaughlin, he
said, ought to be made to pay for those lots, but "not
wishing to create any litigation, the committee concluded
to quiet the whole matter by confirming those lots."

He further stated that the Doctor had upon the Oregon
City claim "a flouring mill, granaries, two double saw-
mills, a large number of houses, stores, and other buildings,
to which he *may* be entitled by virtue of his possessory
rights under the treaty of 1846. For only a part of these
improvements, which he may thus hold, he has been urged
during the past year to take $250,000."

Mr. Thurston sees no harm in taking this property, so
valuable in his estimation, which comprises the earnings
of a whole life-time spent in devotion to business in an
Indian country, away from all that men commonly esteem
desirable, from the proper owner. On the contrary he
makes an eloquent appeal to the House to save this valuable estate to the people of Oregon wherewith to educate
the rising generations.

Still further, so great is his fear that some portion of his
property may be left to the Doctor, he asks that the Island
portion of the claim, which he confesses is only a pile of
rocks, of no value except for the improvements on it, may
be " confirmed to George Abernethy, his heirs or assigns;"

assigning as a reason that when the mission was driven from Oregon City, it took refuge on this pile of rocks, and having built a mill, afterwards sold it to Mr. Abernethy, one of the stockholders. Nothing is said about the mill having been resold to Judge Bryant; but Judge Bryant could not object to having the Island confirmed to him through Mr. Abernethy.

And here we may as well sever one of the threads in our story. When it became known that by an act of Congress Oregon City was reserved from the right of even an American citizen to claim, and that only after years of waiting would the title by possessory right be settled either for or against him, the old Doctor's heart was broken.

He still continued to reside upon his claim, but the uncertainty of title prevented any sales of property. The ingratitude of those whom he had assisted when assistance was life itself to them, their refusals to pay what had been lent them, and their constant calumniations, so bore upon his spirits that his strength failed rapidly under them, and for the last few years of his life he fancied himself reduced to poverty, though he was still in possession of his improvements.

An example of the extent to which some men carried their anti-McLaughlin principles may be found in the following story which was related to us by the gentleman mentioned in it. The doctor one day stood upon the street conversing with Mr. Thornton, who had been his legal adviser in some instances, another gentleman also being present. Their conversation was rudely interrupted by a fourth individual, who set upon Mr. Thornton with every manner of abuse and vile epithet for being seen in communication with the " d——d old Hudson's Bay, Jesuitical rascal," and much more to the same effect. To this assault, Thornton, who had a great command of language, replied in a manner which sent the man about his business. Then turning to the Doctor, he said:

"Doctor, I will lay a wager that man is one of your debtors, who never intends to pay, and takes it out in abuse."

"Yes, yes," answered the Doctor, trying to suppress his nervousness; "when he came to Oregon he was naked and hungry. I gave him assistance to the amount of four hundred dollars. He is rich now; has land and herds, and everything in abundance; but he hates me on account of that four hundred dollars. That is the way with most of them!"

Dr. McLaughlin died September, 1857, and is buried in the Catholic church-yard in Oregon City. Five years after his death the State of Oregon restored to his heirs the property which it had so long wrongfully withheld. As for the demagogue who embittered the last days of a good man, for political advancement, he did not live to enjoy his reward. His health, delicate at the best, was very much undermined at last by discovering that he received more blame than praise, even among his former supporters, for the eleventh section of the Donation Law. He became very ill on his return, and died at Acapulco, Mexico, without reaching home.

Very many persons have confirmed what his admirer, Meek, says of Dr. McLaughlin, that he deserved to be called the FATHER OF OREGON.

CHAPTER XLIII.

1850–4. THE Territorial law of Oregon combined the offices of Governòr and Indian Agent. One of the most important acts which marked Lane's administration was that of securing and punishing the murderers of Dr. and Mrs. Whitman. The Indians of the Cayuse tribe to whom the murderers belonged, were assured that the only way in which they could avoid a war with the whites was to deliver up the chiefs who had been engaged in the massacre, to be tried and punished according to the laws of the whites. Of the two hundred Indians implicated in the massacre, five were given up to be dealt with according to law. These were the five chiefs, *Te-lou-i-kite*, *Tam-a-has*, *Klok-a-mas*, *Ki-am-a-sump-kin*, and *I-sa-i-a-cha-lak-is*.

These men might have made their escape; there was no imperative necessity upon them to suffer death, had they chosen to flee to the mountains. But with that strange magnanimity which the savage often shows, to the astonishment of Christians, they resolved to die for their people rather than by their flight to involve them in war.

Early in the summer of 1850, the prisoners were deliv_ ered up to Gov. Lane, and brought down to Oregon City, where they were given into the keeping of the marshal. During their passage down the river, and while they were incarcerated at Oregon City, their bearing was most proud and haughty. Some food, more choice than their prisoner's fare, being offered to one of the chiefs at a camp of the guard, in their transit down the Columbia, the proud savage rejected it with scorn.

"What sort of heart have you," he asked, "that you offer food to me, whose hands are red with your brother's blood?"

And this, after eleven years of missionary labor, was all the comprehension the savage nature knew of the main principle of Christianity,—forgiveness, or charity toward our enemies.

At Oregon City, Meek had many conversations with them. In all of these they gave but one explanation of their crime. They feared that Dr. Whitman intended, with the other whites, to take their land from them; and they were told by Jo Lewis, the half-breed, that the Doctor's medicine was intended to kill them off quickly, in order the sooner to get possession of their country. None of them expressed any sorrow for what had been done; but one of them, *Ki-am-a-sump-kin*, declared his innocence to the last.

In conversations with others, curious to gain some knowledge of the savage moral nature, *Te-lou-i-kite* often puzzled these students of Indian ethics. When questioned as to his motive for allowing himself to be taken, *Te-lou-i-kite* answered:

"Did not your missionaries tell us that Christ died to save his people? So die we, to save our people!"

Notwithstanding the prisoners were pre-doomed to death, a regular form of trial was gone through. The Prosecuting Attorney for the Territory, A. Holbrook, conducted the prosecution: Secretary Pritchett, Major Runnels, and Captain Claiborne, the defence. The fee offered by the chiefs was fifty head of horses. Whether it was compassion, or a love of horses which animated the

defence, quite an effort was made to show that the murderers were not guilty.

The presiding Justice was O. C. Pratt—Bryant having
resigned. Perhaps we cannot do better than to give the
Marshal's own description of the trial and execution,
which is as follows: "Thar war a great many indict-
ments, and a great many people in attendance at this
court. The Grand Jury found true bills against the five
Indians, and they war arraigned for trial. Captain Claiborne led off for the defence. He foamed and ranted
like he war acting a play in some theatre. He knew
about as much law as one of the Indians he war defend
ing; and his gestures were so powerful that he smashed
two tumblers that the Judge had ordered to be filled with
cold water for him. After a time he gave out mentally
and physically. Then came Major Runnels, who made a
very good defence. But the Marshal thought they must
do better, for they would never ride fifty head of horses
with them speeches.

Mr. Pritchett closed for the defence with a very able
argument; for he war a man of brains. But then followed
Mr. Holbrook, for the prosecution, and he laid down the
case so plain that the jury were convinced before they
left the jury-box. When the Judge passed sentence of
death on them, two of the chiefs showed no terror; but
the other three were filled with horror and consternation
that they could not conceal.

After court had adjourned, and Gov. Lane war gone
South on some business with the Rogue River Indians,
Secretary Pritchett came to me and told me that as he
war now acting Governor he meant to reprieve the Indians. Said he to me, 'Now Meek, I want you to liber-
ate them Indians, when you receive the order.'

32

'Pritchett,' said I, 'so far as Meek is concerned, he would do anything for you.'

This talk pleased him; he said he 'war glad to hear it; and would go right off and write the reprieve.'

'But,' said I, 'Pritchett, let us talk now like men. I have got in my pocket the death-warrant of them Indians, signed by Gov. Lane. The Marshal will execute them men, as certain as the day arrives.'

Pritchett looked surprised, and remarked—'That war not what you just said, that you would do anything for me.'

Said I, 'you were talking then to Meek,—not to the Marshal, who always does his duty.' At that he got mad and left.

When the 3d of June, the day of execution, arrived, Oregon City was thronged with people to witness it. I brought forth the five prisoners and placed them on a drop. Here the chief, who always declared his innocence, *Ki-am-i-sump-kin*, begged me to kill him with my knife,— for an Indian fears to be hanged,—but I soon put an end to his entreaties by cutting the rope which held the drop, with my tomahawk. As I said 'The Lord have mercy on your souls,' the trap fell, and the five Cayuses hung in the air. Three of them died instantly. The other two struggled for several minutes; the Little Chief, *Tam-a-has*, the longest. It was he who was cruel to my little girl at the time of the massacre; so I just put my foot on the knot to tighten it, and he got quiet. After thirty-five minutes they were taken down and buried."

Thus terminated a tragic chapter in the history of Oregon. Among the services which Thurston performed for the Territory, was getting an appropriation of $100,000, to pay the expenses of the Cayuse war. From the Spring of 1848, when all the whites, except the Catholic missionaries, were withdrawn from the upper country, for a period of several years, or until Government had made treaties with the tribes east of the Cascades, no settlers were permitted to take up land in Eastern Oregon. During those years, the Indians, dissatisfied with the encroachments which they foresaw the whites would finally make upon their country, and incited by certain individuals who had suffered wrongs, or been punished for their own offences at the hands of the whites, finally combined, as it was supposed from the extent of the insurrection, and Oregon was involved in a three years Indian war, the history of which would fill a volume of considerable size.

When Meek returned to Oregon as marshal, with his fine clothes and his newly acquired social accomplishments, he was greeted with a cordial acknowledgment of his services, as well as admiration for his improved appearance. He was generally acknowledged to be the model of a handsome marshal, when clad in his half-military dress, and placed astride of a fine horse, in the execution of the more festive duties of marshal of a procession on some patriotic occasion.

But no amount of official responsibility could ever change him from a wag into a "grave and reverend seignior." No place nor occasion was sacred to him when the wild humor was on him.

At this same term of court, after the conviction of the Cayuse chiefs, there was a case before Judge Pratt, in which a man was charged with selling liquor to the Indians. In these cases Indian evidence was allowed, but the jury-room being up stairs, caused a good deal of annoyance in court; because when an Indian witness was wanted up stairs, a dozen or more who were not wanted would follow. The Judge's bench was so placed that it commanded a full view of the staircase and every one passing up or down it.

A call for some witness to go before the jury was fol

lowed on this occasion, as on all others, by a general rush
of the Indians, who were curious to witness the proceedings.   One fat old squaw had got part way up the stairs,
when the Marshal, full of wrath, seized her by a leg and
dragged her down flat, at the same time holding the fat

MEEK AS UNITED STATES MARSHAL.

member so that it was pointed directly toward the Judge.
A general explosion followed this *pointed* action, and the
Judge grew very red in the face.

"Mr. Marshal, come within the bar!" thundered the
Judge.

Meek complied, with a very dubious expression of
countenance.

"I must fine you fifty dollars," continued the Judge;
"the dignity of the Court must be maintained."

When court had adjourned that evening, the Judge
and the Marshal were walking toward their respective
lodgings.   Said Meek to his Honor:

" Why did you fine me so heavily to-day ?"

" I *must* do it," returned the Judge. " I must keep up the dignity of the Court ; I must do it, if I pay the fines myself."

" And you *must* pay all the fines you lay on the marshal, of course," answered Meek.

" Very well," said the Judge ; " I shall do so."

" All right, Judge. As I am the proper disbursing officer, you can pay that fifty dollars to me—and I'll take it now."

At this view of the case, his Honor was staggered for one moment, and could only swing his cane and laugh faintly. After a little reflection, he said :

" Marshal, when court is called to-morrow, I shall remit your fine ; but don't you let me have occasion to fine you again !"

After the removal of the capital to Salem, in 1852, court was held in a new building, on which the carpenters were still at work. Judge Nelson, then presiding, was much put out by the noise of hammers, and sent the marshal more than once, to request the men to suspend their work during those hours when court was in session, but all to no purpose. Finally, when his forbearance was quite exhausted, he appealed to the marshal for advice.

" What shall I do, Meek," said he, " to stop that infernal noise ?"

" Put the workmen on the Grand Jury," replied Meek.

" Summon them instantly !" returned the Judge. They were summoned, and quiet secured for that term.

At this same term of court, a great many of the foreign born settlers appeared, to file their intention of becoming American citizens, in order to secure the benefits of the Donation Law. Meek was retained as a witness, to swear to their qualifications, one of which was, that they were possessed of good moral characters. The first day there were about two hundred who made declarations, Meek witnessing for most of them. On the day following, he declined serving any longer.

" What now ?" inquired the Judge; "you made no objections yesterday."

" Very true," replied Meek; "and two hundred lies are enough for me. I swore that all those mountain-men were of 'good moral character,' and I never knew a mountain-man of that description in my life! Let Newell take the job for to-day."

The "job" was turned over to Newell; but whether the second lot was better than the first, has never transpired.

During Lane's administration, there was a murder committed by a party of Indians at the Sound, on the person of a Mr. Wallace. Owing to the sparse settlement of the country, Governor Lane adopted the original measure of exporting not only the officers of the court, but the jury also, to the Sound district. Meek was ordered to find transportation for the court *in toto*, jury and all. Boats were hired and provisioned to take the party to the Cowelitz Landing, and from thence to Fort Steilacoom, horses were hired for the land transportation.

The Indians accused were five in number—two chiefs and three slaves. The Grand Jury found a true bill against the two chiefs, and let the slaves go. So few were the inhabitants of those parts, that the marshal was obliged to take a part of the grand jury to serve on the petite jury. The form of a trial was gone through with, the Judge delivered his charge, and the jury retired.

It was just after night-fall when these worthies betook themselves to the jury-room. One of them curled himself up in a corner of the room, with the injunction to the others to "wake him up when they got ready to hang them —— rascals." The rest of the party spent four or five hours betting against monte, when, being sleepy also, they waked up their associate, spent about ten minutes in arguing their convictions, and returned a verdict of "guilty of murder in the first degree."

The Indians were sentenced to be hung at noon on the following day, and the marshal was at work early in the morning preparing a gallows. A rope was procured from a ship lying in the sound. At half-past eleven o'clock, guarded by a company of artillery from the fort, the miserable savages were marched forth to die. A large number of Indians were collected to witness the execution; and to prevent any attempt at rescue, Captain Hill's artillery formed a ring around the marshal and his prisoners. The execution was interrupted or delayed for some moments, on account of the frantic behavior of an Indian woman, wife of one of the chiefs, whose entreaties for the life of her husband were very affecting. Having exhausted all her eloquence in an appeal to the nobler feelings of the man, she finally promised to leave her husband and become his wife, if he, the marshal, would spare her lord and chief.

She was carried forcibly out of the ring, and the hanging took place. When the bodies were taken down, Meek spoke to the woman, telling her that now she could have her husband; but she only sullenly replied, "You have killed him, and you may bury him."

This excursion of the Oregon court footed up a sum of about $4,000, of which the marshal paid $1,000 out of his own pocket. When, in the following year, Lane was sent to Congress, Meek urged him to ask for an appropriation to pay up the debt. Lane made no effort to do so, probably because he did not care to have the illegality of the proceeding commented upon.

Lane's career in Oregon, before the breaking out of the rebellion, the betrayal of his secession proclivities, and supposed actual conspiracy against the Government, was that of a successful politician. Having been appointed so near the close of Polk's administration, he was succeeded, on the coming into office of General Taylor, by General John P. Gaines, who arrived in Oregon in August, 1850. In 1851, General Lane was elected delegate to Congress, and returned to Oregon as Governor, by Franklin Pierce, in 1853. He was appointed in March, arrived at Salem May 16th, resigned the 19th, was elected to Congress July 7th, returning again to Oregon, where he at present resides, on the expiration of his term. His mileage alone amounted to $10,000, besides the expenses of his first overland journey. John W. Davis was next appointed Governor, by President Pierce. He arrived in Salem April 1st, 1854, and resigned in August. A trip to Oregon, with the mileage, appeared to be quite the fashion of territorial times.

CHAPTER XLIV.

WHILE Meek was in Washington, he had been dubbed with the title of Colonel, which title he still bears, though during the Indian war of 1855–56, it was alternated with that of Major. During his marshalship he was fond of showing off his titles and authority to the discomfiture of that class of people who had "put on airs" with him in former days, when he was in his transition stage from a trapper to a United States Marshal.

While Pratt was Judge of the District Court, a kidnaping case came before him. The writ of *habeas corpus* having been disregarded by the Captain of the *Melvin*, who was implicated in the business, Meek was sent to arrest him, and also the first mate. Five of the *Melvin's* sailors were ordered to be summoned as witnesses, at the same time.

Meek went on board with his summons, marched forward, and called out the names of the men. Every man came up as he was summoned. When they were together, Meek ordered a boat lowered for their conveyance to Oregon City. The men started to obey, when the Captain interfered, saying that the boat should not be taken for such a purpose, as it belonged to him.

" That is of no consequence at all," answered the smiling marshal. " It is a very good boat, and will suit our purpose very well. Lower away, men !"

The men quickly dropped the boat. As it fell, they

were ordered to man it. When they were at the oars, the mate was then invited to take a seat in it, which he did, after a moment's hesitation, and glancing at his superior officer. Meek then turned to the Captain, and extended the same invitation to him. But he was reluctant to accept the courtesy, blustering considerably, and declaring his intention to remain where he was. Meek slowly drew his revolver, all the time cool and smiling.

"I don't like having to urge a gentleman too hard," he said, in a meaning tone; "but thar is an argument that few men ever resist. Take a seat, Captain."

The Captain took a seat; the idlers on shore cheered for "Joe Meek"—which was, after all, his most familiar title; the Captain and mate went to Oregon City, and were fined respectively $500 and $300; the men took advantage of being on shore to desert; and altogether, the master of the *Melvin* felt himself badly used.

About the same time news was received that a British vessel was unloading goods for the Hudson's Bay Company, somewhere on Puget Sound. Under the new order of affairs in Oregon, this was smuggling. Delighted with an opportunity of doing the United States a service, and the British traders an ill turn, Marshal Meek immediately summoned a *posse* of men and started for the Sound. On his way he learned the name of the vessel and Captain, and recognized them as having been in the Columbia River some years before. On that occasion the Captain had ordered Meek ashore, when, led by his curiosity and general love of novelty, he had paid a visit to this vessel. This information was "nuts" to the marshal, who believed that "a turn about was fair play."

With great dispatch and secrecy he arrived entirely unexpected at the point where the vessel was lying, and proceeded to board her without loss of time. The Captain and officers were taken by surprise and were all aghast at this unlooked for appearance. But after the first moment of agitation was over, the Captain recognized Meek, he being a man not likely to be forgotten, and thinking to turn this circumstance to advantage, approached him with the blandest of smiles and the most cordial manner, saying with forced frankness—

" I am sure I have had the pleasure of meeting you before. You must have been at Vancouver when my vessel was in the river, seven or eight years ago. I am very happy to have met with you again."

" Thar is some truth in that remark of yours, Captain," replied Meek, eyeing him with lofty scorn; "you *did* meet me at Vancouver several years ago. But I was nothing but ' Joe Meek ' at that time, and you ordered me ashore. Circumstances are changed since then. I am now Colonel Joseph L. Meek, United States Marshal for Oregon Territory; and you sir, are only a —— smuggler! Go ashore, sir!"

The Captain saw the point of that concluding "go ashore, sir!" and obeyed with quite as bad a grace as ' Joe Meek ' had done in the first instance.

The vessel was confiscated and sold, netting to the Government about $40,000, above expenses. This money, which fell into bad hands, failed to be accounted for. Nobody suspected the integrity of the marshal, but most persons suspected that he placed too much confidence in the District Attorney, who had charge of his accounts. On some one asking him, a short time after, what had become of the money from the sale of the smuggler, he seemed struck with a sudden surprise:

" Why," said he, looking astonished at the question, " thar was barly enough for the officers of the court!"

This answer, given as it was, with such apparent simplicity, became a popular joke; and "barly enough" was quoted on all occasions.

The truth was, that there was a serious deficiency in Meek's account with the Government, resulting entirely from his want of confidence in his own literary accomplishments, which led him to trust all his correspondence and his accounts to the hands of a man whose talents were more eminent than his sense of honor. The result of this misplaced confidence was a loss to the Government, and to himself, whom the Government held accountable. Contrary to the general rule of disbursing officers, the office made him poor instead of rich; and when on the incoming of the Pierce administration he suffered decapitation along with the other Territorial officers, he was forced to retire upon his farm on the Tualatin Plains, and become a rather indifferent tiller of the earth.

The breaking out of the Indian war of 1855–6, was preceded by a long period of uneasiness among the Indians generally. The large emigration which crossed the plains every year for California and Oregon was one cause of the disturbance; not only by exciting their fears for the possession of their lands, but by the temptation which was offered them to take toll of the travelers. Difficulties occurred at first between the emigrants and Indians concerning stolen property. These quarrels were followed, probably the subsequent year, by outrages and murder on the part of the Indians, and retaliation on the part of volunteer soldiers from Oregon. When once this system of outrage and retaliation on either side, was begun, there was an end of security, and war followed as an inevitable consequence. Very horrible indeed were the acts perpetrated by the Indians upon the emigrants to Oregon, during the years from 1852 to 1858.

But when at last the call to arms was made in Oregon,

it was an opportunity sought, and not an alternative forced upon them, by the politicians of that Territory. The occasion was simply this. A party of lawless wretches from the Sound Country, passing over the Cascade Mountains into the Yakima Valley, on their way to the Upper Columbia mines, found some Yakima women digging roots in a lonely place, and abused them. The women fled to their village and told the chiefs of the outrage; and a party followed the guilty whites and killed several of them in a fight.

Mr. Bolin, the Indian sub-agent for Washington went to the Yakima village, and instead of judging of the case impartially, made use of threats in the name of the United States Government, saying that an army should be sent to punish them for killing his people. On his return home, Mr. Bolin was followed and murdered.

The murder of an Indian agent was an act which could not be overlooked. Very properly, the case should have been taken notice of in a manner to convince the Indians that murder must be punished. But, tempted by an opportunity for gain, and encouraged by the somewhat reasonable fears of the white population of Washington and Oregon, Governor G. L. Curry, of the latter, at once proclaimed war, and issued a call for volunteers, without waiting for the sanction or assistance of the general Government. The moment this was done, it was too late to retract. It was as if a torch had been applied to a field of dry grass. So simultaneously did the Indians from Puget Sound to the Rocky Mountains, and from the Rocky Mountains to the southern boundary of Oregon send forth the war-whoop, that there was much justification for the belief which agitated the people, that a combination among the Indians had been secretly agreed to, and that the whites were all to be exterminated.

Volunteer companies were already raised and sent into the Indian country, when Brevet Major G. O. Haller arrived at Vancouver, now a part of the United States. He had been as far east as Fort Boise to protect the incoming immigration; and finding on his return that there was an Indian war on hand, proceeded at once to the Yakima country with his small force of one hundred men, only fifty of whom were mounted. Much solicitude was felt for the result of the first engagement, every one knowing that if the Indians were at first successful, the war would be long and bloody.

Major Haller was defeated with considerable loss, and notwithstanding slight reinforcements, from Fort Vancouver, only succeeded in getting safely out of the country. Major Raines, the commanding officer at Vancouver, seeing the direction of events, made a requisition upon Governor Curry for four of his volunteer companies to go into the field. Then followed applications to Major Raines for horses and arms to equip the volunteers; but the horses at the Fort being unfit for service, and the Major unauthorized to equip volunteer troops, there resulted only misunderstandings and delays. When General Wool, at the head of the Department in San Francisco, was consulted, he also was without authority to employ or receive the volunteers; and when the volunteers, who at length armed and equipped themselves, came to go into the field with the regulars, they could not agree as to the mode of fighting Indians; so that with one thing and another, the war became an exciting topic for more reasons than because the whites were afraid of the Indians. As for General Wool, he was in great disfavor both in Oregon and Washington because he did not believe there ever had existed the necessity for a war; and that therefore he bestowed what assistance was at his command very grudgingly.   General Wool, it was said, was jealous of the volunteers; and the volunteers certainly cared little for the opinion of General Wool.

However all that may be, Col. Meek gives it as his opinion that the old General was right.   "It makes me think," said he, "of a bear-fight I once saw in the Rocky Mountains, where a huge old grizzly was surrounded by a pack of ten or twelve dogs, all snapping at and worrying him. It made him powerful mad, and every now and then he would make a claw at one of them that silenced him at once."

The Indian war in Oregon gave practice to a number of officers, since become famous, most prominent among whom is Sheridan, who served in Oregon as a Lieutenant. Grant himself, was at one time a Captain on that frontier. Col. Wright, afterwards Gen. Wright, succeeded Major Raines at Vancouver, and conducted the war through its most active period.   During a period of three years there were troops constantly occupied in trying to subdue the Indians in one quarter or another.

As for the volunteers they fared badly.   On the first call to arms the people responded liberally.   The proposition which the Governor made for their equipment was accepted, and they turned in their property at a certain valuation.   When the war was over and the property sold, the men who had turned it in could not purchase it without paying more for it in gold and silver than it was valued at when it was placed in the hands of the Quartermaster.   It was sold, however, and the money enjoyed by the shrewd political speculators, who thought an Indian war a very good investment.

Meek was one of the first to volunteer, and went as a private in Company A.   On arriving at the Dalles he was detailed for special service by Col. J. W. Nesmith, and sent out as pilot or messenger, whenever any such duty was required. He was finally placed on Nesmith's staff, and given the title of Major. In this capacity, as in every other, he was still the same alert and willing individual that we have always seen him, and not a whit less inclined to be merry when an opportunity offered.

While the army was in the Yakima country, it being an enemy's country, and provisions scarce, the troops sometimes were in want of rations. But Meek had not forgotten his mountain craft, and always had something to eat, if anybody did. One evening he had killed a fat cow which he had discovered astray, and was proceeding to roast a twenty-pound piece before his camp-fire, when a number of the officers called on him. The sight and savory smell of the beef was very grateful to them.

"Major Meek," said they in a breath, "we will sup with you to-night."

"I am very sorry, gentlemen, to decline the honor," returned Meek with a repetition of the innocent surprise for which he had so often been laughed at, "but I am very hungry, and thar is barly enough beef for one man!"

On hearing this sober assertion, those who had heard the story laughed, but the rest looked rather aggrieved. However, the Major continued his cooking, and when the beef was done to a turn, he invited his visitors to the feast, and the evening passed merrily with jests and camp stories.

After the army went into winter-quarters, Nesmith having resigned, T. R. Cornelius was elected Colonel. One of his orders prohibited firing in camp, an order which as a good mountaineer the Major should have remembered. But having been instructed to proceed to Salem without delay, as bearer of dispatches, the Major committed the error of firing his gun to see if it was in good condition for a trip through the enemy's country. Shortly after he received a message from his Colonel requesting him to repair to his tent. The Colonel received him politely, and invited him to breakfast with him. The aroma of coffee made this invitation peculiarly acceptable—for luxuries were scarce in camp—and the breakfast proceeded for some time very agreeably. When Meek had breakfasted, Colonel Cornelius took occasion to inquire if the Major had not heard his order against firing in camp. " Yes," said Meek. " Then," said the Colonel, " I shall be obliged to make an example of you."

While Meek stood aghast at the idea of punishment, a guard appeared at the door of the tent, and he heard what his punishment was to be, " Mark time for twenty minutes in the presence of the whole regiment."

" When the command "forward! was given," says Meek, " you might have seen somebody step off lively, the officer counting it off, 'left, left.' But some of the regiment grumbled more about it than I did. I just got my horse and my dispatches and left for the lower country, and when I returned I asked for my discharge, and got it."

And here ends the career of our hero as a public man. The history of the young State, of which he is so old a pioneer furnishes ample material for an interesting volume, and will sometime be written by an abler than our sketchy pen. One thing only it occurs to us to state in connection with it, that while many Northern men went, as Gen. Lane did, into the rebellion against the Government, our nobler Virginian was ever sternly loyal.

The chief excitement of Col. Meek's life at present, is in his skirmishes with the Nazerene and other preachers in his neighborhood. They seem not to be able to see him treading so gently the downhill of life, when they

33

fear he may "go to the pit" prepared for mountain-men. In this state of mind they preach at him on every possible occasion, whether suitable or not, and usually he takes it pleasantly enough. But when their attacks become too personal, he does as did the bear to whom he likened Gen. Wool, he "hits one a claw that silences him."

Being very much annoyed on one occasion, not very long since, by the stupid and vulgar speech of a "preacher" whom he complimented by going to hear, he deliberately marched up to the preacher's desk, took the frightened little orator on his hip, and carried him out of the house, to the mingled horror, amazement, and amusement of the congregation.

We think that a man who at fifty-eight is able to perform such a feat, is capable of achieving fresh laurels, and need not retire upon those he has won.

CHAPTER XLV.

It was no part of the original intention of the author of the foregoing narrative to extend the work beyond the personal adventures of one man, and such portions of collateral history as were necessary to a perfect understanding of the times and events spoken of. But since the great interest which the public have taken in the opening of the first Pacific Railroad has become apparent, it has been deemed expedient to subjoin some facts concerning the Western Division of the Northern Pacific Railroad, now in contemplation, and to become a reality, probably, within an early day.

The Northern Pacific Road will have its eastern end somewhere on Lake Superior, and its western terminus at a point on Puget's Sound not yet determined. As that portion of the road lying west of Fort Union, on the Missouri River, traverses much of the country spoken of in the adventures of the fur-traders, as well as all the northern part of what was once the Oregon Territory, whose early history we have already given, it will not be found altogether irrelevant to enter into a brief description of the country so soon to be opened to the traveling public. Hitherto we have roamed it in imagination as the fur-traders did, bent only on beaver-skins and adventure. Now we will briefly consider it as a country fit for the permanent settlement of industrious Peoples seeking homes for themselves and the coming generations.

WESTERN OREGON.—To commence with the oldest settled portion of the original Oregon Territory, we will
first describe that portion of the present State of Oregon
technically known as Western Oregon.   All that portion
of the State of Oregon lying west of the Cascade Mountains, is comprised in three principal valleys—the Wallamet,* the Umpqua, and the Rogue River Valleys—and in
a narrow strip of country lying along the coast, and separated from the valleys by the Coast range of mountains.
These two ranges of mountains, the Cascades, high and
almost inaccessible on the east, and the Coast range, separating it from the sea on the west, make of Western Oregon a country with a very peculiar geography.   With
the Columbia River for a northern boundary, and with
three transverse ranges of mountains to the south, separating the several valleys, the situation of Western Oregon
is isolated and unique.

The Wallamet River takes its rise in the Cascade Mountains, flowing westwardly for some distance, when it takes
a course almost directly north, and falls into the Columbia
in about latitude 45° 30′, and longitude 45° 40′.   The
whole length of this river is probably not over one hundred and seventy-five miles; and the extent of its valley
proper is in the neighborhood of one hundred and twenty-
five miles in length, by from sixty to eighty in breadth.
Numerous tributaries flow into the Wallamet from either
side, making the country both fertile and agreeable.

The Wallamet Valley is mostly open prairie land, ready
for the plowshare.   At the northern end of it, however,
and within a few miles of the Columbia, there are dense
forests of fir, pine, yew, and cedar, on all the high and
dry lands, while the bottom-lands along the streams are

---

* Incorrectly spelled on the maps, *Willamette.*

covered with a fine growth of oak, ash, maple, cotton-wood, alder, and willow. But as we travel southward from the Columbia, the timber along the Wallamet becomes less dense, until finally we come to the beautiful open prairies, only half hidden from view by a thin fringe of low trees. and picturesquely dotted here and there by groves of oak and fir intermingled.

The Prairies of Western Oregon do not resemble the immense flat plains of Illinois ; but are rather gently undulating, and bear a strong likeness to the "oak openings" of Michigan and Wisconsin. Instead of being continuous levels, they are divided by low ranges of hills, covered with oak timber, low and spreading, and draped, like the trees of the Sacramento Valley, with a long hanging gray moss, that floats lightly on the summer wind, as if celebrating the delightful mildness and beauty of the scene.

The Wallamet, although navigable for one hundred and thirty miles from its mouth, is, like all the rivers west of the Rocky Mountains, troubled with rapids, and narrowed in some places to little more than the width of the passing steamer. In the latter part of summer, steamers cannot ascend it beyond Salem, the capital of the State. Of its ten principal tributaries, most of them are navigable for considerable distances, and all of them furnish abundant water-power.

The Falls of the Wallamet, about twenty-five miles from its junction with the Columbia, furnish the greatest water-power in the State, as also some fine scenery. Above the falls, the water spreads out into a wide, deep basin, and runs slowly and smoothly until within a half-mile of the falls, when its width diminishes, its velocity increases, and in its haste it turns back upon itself, forming dangerous eddies, until at length, forced forward, it makes the plunge of more than twenty feet, into a boiling whirlpool below, and breaks into foam along a ledge of volcanic rock stretching from shore to shore. The spray, dashed up by the descent of the water, forms a beautiful rainbow, besides being a means of cooling the hot air of the summer noon at Oregon City, which is situated along the rocky bluffs at this point of the river.

The navigation of the river thus interrupted, formerly necessitated a portage of a couple of miles at Oregon City; but recently the People's Transportation Company have erected a strong basin on the east side of the river, which permits their boats to come so close together that the passengers and freight have only to pass through the Company's warehouse to be transferred.

The amount of agricultural land in the Wallamet Valley is estimated at about three million acres. This estimate leaves out large bodies of land in the foot-hills of the mountains, on either side, more suitable for grazing than for farming purposes.

The Soil of the Wallamet Valley is of excellent quality. Upon the prairies it consists of gray, calcareous, sandy loam, especially adapted to the cultivation of cereals, particularly of wheat, barley, and oats. It is exceedingly mellow and easily worked, and is not affected by drouth. Along the banks of the river, and the streams tributary to it, the soil consists of various decomposed earths, sand, and vegetable matter, deposited there in seasons of freshet, and is of the most fertile description. The soil of the foot-hills is a dark clay loam, mixed with vegetable mold in the small intervening valleys. Excellent grasses are produced, though this kind of soil suffers more from drouth than that of the prairies.

The Climate of the Wallamet Valley is mild and agreeable. The seasons are two,—the wet and the dry. The rainy season usually commences in November, although frequently it holds off, except a few light showers, until December. The rains continue pretty constantly until about the last of January, when there is a clearing up of three or four weeks. This interval is the real winter season, and is sometimes cold, with frozen ground, or snow, though generally the Oregon winters are not characterised either by cold or snow to any great amount. After this "clear spell" comes a second season of rains which may clear up by the first of March, or not until April. It is not an unusual thing for gardening to be commenced in February; but the result of this early gardening is not always sure.

When the rains of winter have passed, there are occasional showers until the first of July, after which there is a dry period of four months. This dry season instead of being oppressive, as would be the case in the Atlantic States, is most delightful. Sufficient moisture is borne in from the sea, over the tops of the Coast range to make the air of a fine coolness and freshness, and not enough to make it humid. Thus there is a fine, dry, cool air, with a moderate temperature, and a dry warm earth, which makes an Oregon summer the most charming season to be experienced in any part of the world. The nights are always cool enough to make a blanket necessary. The mornings bright and not too hot—the heated term during dog-days only extending over the hours from 12 M. to 4 P. M.

That a climate such as this must be healthful is undeniable. During the falling of the rains there is little or no sickness. Just after the rain ceases falling, and before the earth becomes dry, the rapid evaporation causes colds and coughs to the careless or the inexperienced. Through the dry season there is little sickness except in certain localities where, as in all new countries, malaria is formed by the exposure to the sun of new or submerged soils.

One of the faults, so to speak, of Western Oregon, is its mildness of climate. The agricultural population are prone to be negligent in providing for that irregular, and uncertainly certain occasional visitation, a "hard winter." Therefore the stock-raiser who has his several hundred head of cattle and horses ranging his one or two thousand acres of uplands, and who, trusting in Providence, makes no sufficient provision for a month or six weeks of feeding, is liable once in five to eight years, to lose nearly all of his stock. Did this same stock-raiser have to get his cattle through seven months of winter as many eastern farmers do, he might come at last to be willing to provide for the possible six weeks. Cattle in Oregon generally look poor in the spring, because the farmers allow them to shift for themselves all through the rainy season, which they should not do. For this reason, Western Oregon, although naturally the best of dairy countries, furnishes little butter and cheese, and that often of a poor quality. An influx of Central New York dairymen would greatly benefit the state, and develop one of its surest means of wealth.

The Productions of the Wallamet Valley are wheat, oats, barley, rye, wool, and fruits. All of the grains grow abundantly, and are of unusual excellence. The same is true of such fruits as apples, pears, plums, cherries, currants, gooseberries, strawberries, blackberries, raspberries, etc. In fact all fruits do well in Western Oregon, except grapes, peaches, apricots, nectarines, and that class of fruits which love a dry and hot climate. Grapes and peaches can be raised with sufficient care, but are not a natural crop like the first mentioned fruits. Corn is not raised as a crop, on account of the cool nights, which are not favorable to its ripening.

The Umpqua Valley is that portion of Western Oregon

next south of the Wallamet Valley, being divided from it by a range of mountains bearing the Indian name of Cala- pooya. It is a region not so well fitted for grain-raising as the Wallamet valley, but is perhaps superior as a fruit- growing and wool-raising section. The valley is watered by the Umpqua River, and is broken up into numerous hills and valleys, in the most picturesque manner. It is one of the most beautiful portions of the Pacific Coast, being rolling, well, without being densely wooded, and having a very agreeable climate, with rather less rain than falls in the lower altitude of the Wallamet.

The Rogue River Valley is another division of Western Oregon, divided from the Umpqua valley by a range of mountains bearing the name of Umpqua. It resembles the country just described in general, but has a climate which is a happy mixture of Californian dryness and Ore- gonian moisture. It is not considered a grain-growing coun- try to any great extent; not from any inadaptability of the soil, but because it is a very superior grazing and fruit- growing country, and has also a considerable mining noto- riety. It is separated from northern California by the Liskiyou range of mountains, and watered by the Rogue River and its northern tributaries.

The Coast Country consists of a strip of land from five to twelve miles wide, lying between the westernmost range of mountains in Oregon, and the sea. It contains several counties, whose chief agricultural merits consist in the ex- cellence of their grasses and vegetables. Fruit too, grows very well in the Coast counties. Hops and honey, as well as butter, are among their chief farming products. But the greatest wealth of the Coast counties is probably to be derived from the heavy forests of timber which cover the mountain sides; and from the mines of coal and copper which underlie them.

A number of points have already become quite famous for business along the coast; Coose Bay for its coal and lumber; Tilamook for its oysters; and Yaquina for its good harborage, and easy access through a fine natural pass to the heart of the Wallamet valley. The port of Umpqua once promised to become a point of some importance, but latterly has fallen into neglect from the difficulty of communicating thence with the interior.

The climate of the Coast counties is cooler and more moist than that of the valleys to the eastward, on account of their contiguity to the sea. Their soil is deep, black, and rich, supporting an immense growth of shrubbery, and ferns from ten to fourteen feet in height. The prairie spots are covered with grass, and so are the hill-sides wherever the timber is not too dense. Though the mean temperature of the Coast counties is lower than that of the interior, it is also more even; and the sea-fogs in summer as well as the rains in winter serve to keep the natural grasses in excellent condition. In short every circumstance seems to point to the Coast counties of Oregon as the great dairy region of the Pacific Coast, as the valleys of the interior are the granaries, and the hill-sides the sheep-pastures.

Good feed the year round, grain enough for the wants of the farmer, plenty of cold mountain water, abundance of timber, plenty of game and fish, are all inducements to the settler who wishes to make himself a permanent home on the Pacific Slope. These, added to the wealth yet to be developed in mines and lumber at every opening where a vessel of a hundred tons can enter, make the future of these now almost vacant Coast counties look inviting.

Resume of the Soil, Climate and Resources of Western Oregon.—From the foregoing general description of Western Oregon it will be seen that the country lying between the Cascade Mountains and the Coast range, consists of one valley containing about as much agricultural land of the best quality as would make a State of the size of Connecticut, and two other smaller valleys, with a less proportion of farming land, and a greater proportion of hill and pasture lands. Also that between the Coast range and the ocean is a strip of country wide enough for a tier of counties, peculiarly adapted to grazing purposes, yet not without considerable arable land.

No one can survey the Wallamet Valley without being struck with its beauty and its fertility, and many are found who pronounce it the most beautiful spot in America. Its beauty consists in the agreeable intermixture of level or rolling prairies, with ranges of low hills, dotted with oak timber, in the multitude of its winding rivers, along which grow a skirting of graceful trees, and in the grandeur of the mountains which guard it alike from the heat of the eastern deserts, and the cold of the northern ocean. Its fertility is evident from the mighty forests which mantle the hills in everlasting green, and from the grassy plains which year after year clothe the valley with renewed verdure, as well as from the golden harvest fields which man has interspersed among the universal green.

The question which first suggests itself is concerning the durability of the soil which produces so well in a wild state. A sketch of the history of agriculture in Oregon will serve to point to an answer.

Many portions of Oregon have been cultivated for a period of twenty-five years without any of those aids to the soil, or that care in preparation and cultivation which is thought necessary to keep up the quality of soils in other farming States. This thriftless mode of farming was the result, partly of an absence of laborers and good farming utensils, for the first fifteen years of the occupa-

tion of Oregon by a farming community.   From the necessity of poor farming grew the habit.   It was found that the
earth would continue to produce when only half-cultivated,
hence farmers grew indolent from too great security.   The
great regularity of the seasons too, by which the maturing
of crops became a certainty, contributed to this general
indifference, for it is an established fact that in order to
work well, men must be in some sort compelled to work.

Another reason why farmers have not put themselves
upon their mettle in a generous emulation, was, that for
many years farm products were worth little or nothing for
want of a market.   All these reasons conspired to confirm
a habit of indifferent cultivation, which accident and the
condition of the country first forced upon them.   Yet
these same lands do not appear to have suffered very ma-
terially from this long course of impoverishment.

Yet another cause of poor farming has been in the fact
of so large bodies of land having been held as single farms.
It is impossible, of course, for one family to cultivate a
mile square of land.   Hence a little grain was scratched
in on one portion of the claim, and a little more on another,
and all so scattered, and carelessly done that no first-rate
crops could possibly be obtained.

The soil of the prairies is of a dark gray color, is mellow, and not affected by drouth.   It is especially adapted
to cereals, and grows vegetables and fruits well, but not
so well as the more alluvial soil formed immediately along
the banks of the rivers and streams.   It is found, too, that
that portion of the prairie which grows ferns, and the land
which skirts the oak groves, or has been cleared of timber, is more favorable to fruit-growing than the more
compact soil of the prairie.   The timbered lands everywhere are productive, excepting occasional clay ridges
where pines are found.   The prairies still furnish grass in

abundance for hay, but not of such quality nor in such quantity as the swamps, swales, and beaver-dams near the rivers and in the heavy timber when drained and cleared.

Of the several varieties of soil in Western Oregon, there are none that are not sufficiently productive to invite labor with a promise of reward. The whole face of the country is productive, and wherever the hillsides are not too steep to pitch a tent, those things needed by man may be made to grow abundantly.

Climate, however, and the shape of the country govern men in their selection of occupations. The grain-farmer will keep to the valleys; the fruit grower will occupy the gentle slopes of the lowest hills; the stock-raiser will settle among the foot-hills, and take his sheep to the mountains; while the dairy-man will seek those spots where grass is good for the longest period of time, and where the temperature favors the making of good, solid and sweet butter and cheese.

The nights in Western Oregon are always cool, and sleep becomes a regular refreshment. It is owing to the low temperature of the nights that corn and some varieties of fruit have commonly failed. However the proper cultivation will yet produce those things in a sufficient abundance. Good corn has been raised in Western Oregon, and peaches of splendid size and flavor occasionally find their way to market. Apples, cherries, and plums of unequalled size and excellence grow in astonishing profusion.

The winters of Western Oregon, though rainy, are generally mild. The principal hardship of the rainy season consists in simply enduring the monotony of the dull sky and constant rain. It is, however, a favorable climate for the farmer, since he is not forced to work hard all the summer to raise what his stock will need to eat through the winter. A fortnight's feed usually suffices for the wintering of cattle.

The following tables show the comparative mean temperatures of three points in Oregon, with four in other States; also the number of rainy days in Oregon and Illinois, respectively:

TABLE I.—*Showing Comparative Mean Temperatures.*

Time.	Astoria, Oregon.	Corvallis, Oregon.	Dalles, East'n Oregon.	Augusta, Illinois.	Hazelwood, Min.	San Diego, Cal.	Albany, N. Y.	Dubuque, Iowa.
Years of Observation	$1\frac{1}{5}$	$1\frac{1}{8}$	$3\frac{1}{2}$	$11\frac{7}{8}$	2	$5\frac{1}{2}$	24	$3\frac{7}{8}$
Spring Temperature	51.16	52.19	53.00	51.34	42.33	59.97	47.61	47.36
Summer "	61.36	67.13	70.36	72.51	69.95	71.08	70.17	71.42
Autumn "	53.55	53.41	52.21	53.38	42.60	64.36	50.01	50.34
Winter "	42.43	39.27	35.59	29.80	13.06	52.29	25.83	25.88
Whole Time "	52.13	53.00	52.79	51.76	41.97	61.93	48.41	48.75

The only point in Eastern Oregon, whose temperature is exhibited in this table, is Dalles, which, situated as it is, immediately at the base of the Cascade Mountains, does not fairly represent the temperature of the extensive valleys farther east, which constitute the agricultural region of that country. The summer, in most of those valleys, as well as on the table-lands, is much warmer than at the Dalles. The winter temperature, it will be observed, is much higher than that of other States in the same latitude, while that of the spring is nearly the same, and the summer not quite so high.

TABLE II.—*Showing the Number of Rainy Days during the Winter, at Astoria, Oregon, Wallamet Valley, Oregon, and Peoria, Illinois, respectively.*

MONTH.	Astoria, Oregon.			Wallamet Valley, O.	Peoria, Ill.	
	1857–8	1858–9	1859–60	1856–7	1856–7	1857–8
November.........	21	16	19	9	9	16
December.........	25	14	15	13	10	7
January..........	17	19	19	15	4	6
February .... -	9	20	17	6	10	8
Total	72	69	70	43	33	37

This table includes all rainy days, without reference to whether it rained all day, or only a part. It also includes snowy days, very few of which are seen in Oregon, in an ordinary winter.

The climate of Oregon has proven to be a healthful one during a thirty years' residence of some of the earliest missionaries and settlers. So far as natural causes are concerned, there appears to be none for the promotion of disease, if we except the tendency to pulmonary and rheumatic diseases for which both California and Oregon are famed, and which no doubt is to be credited to the cold winds from the ocean. These winds in themselves are a sanitary provision of nature, and serve to give the Pacific coast a climate generally free from miasmatic and pestilential diseases; but it is necessary for sensitive constitutions to guard against the rapid change of temperature which they effect when they come sweeping in from the sea, suddenly displacing the warm air of the valleys. With proper care, and attention to the most manifest laws of health, the physical man has a better opportunity for magnificent development, on the Pacific coast, than in any other part of the American continent.

While the winters of Western Oregon are dull and disagreeable, the summers are proportionately delightful. The general temperature of the days is mild and agreeable, the air bright and clear, warmer in the afternoons than in the mornings, invariably; yet falling again to an invigorating coolness in the evening. *Sultriness* is almost never experienced in this part of Oregon. The greatest heat of summer has not that enervating effect which the summer-heats have in the Atlantic States. It is frequently remarked by the farmers here that their cattle can endure to work right on under the hottest sun of summer without showing signs of exhaustion, as they would have done in those States from which they were brought.

From the peculiarities of the soil, seasons, and climate of Western Oregon, it becomes necessary for the farmer to practice modes of culture especially adapted to it, and to conform to other seed-time than that he may have been accustomed to in other States. Much can undoubtedly be learned from old Oregon farmers; but a careful observation from year to year, with a little judicious experiment, will, we hope, develoᵖ among the newer settlers a better manner of farming than that formerly practiced in Oregon, when one year's cultivation was made to answer for three years' crops—the two latter of which were of course self-sown.

While the yield of wheat is perhaps no greater than that of the Genesee valley, or the rich prairies of Indiana or southwestern Michigan, the crop is far more sure, from the absence of insects, rust, winter-killing, etc. Perhaps not more than twice since the settlement of the Wallamet Valley has the wheat crop been injured by rain in harvest time. As a general thing the straw is short and stout, and the grain is never laid down by summer tempests of wind and rain.

Peas sown broadcast, with or without oats, bring a product about equal to wheat; and are the best crop for fattening hogs, requiring little labor, and producing a fine quality of pork by turning the hogs into the field in the fall and letting them fatten there. Bacon brings a high price in the mines, and is one of the most valuable possessions of the farmer. The rapid increase of sheep in Oregon gives the sheep-raiser a large surplus every year above what he can afford to keep for their wool, and of this surplus quite a number every year may be sold for mutton at home, or driven to the mines, where they command a good price.

The whole country west of the Rocky Mountains is favorably adapted to fruit-growing, and no portion of it more so than Western Oregon. Trees of three years' growth bend to the earth under their burdens of fruit. Before the tree matures its strength it bears at a rate so wonderful that without artificial support the branches split away from the main tree. Apple trees less than two inches in diameter, with branches no more than three-quarters of an inch in thickness are so crowded with apples as to leave very little of the stock visible. We have counted forty large apples on a limb of the thickness mentioned above, and no more than four feet and a half long,—a mere rod. Plum and pear trees bear in the same manner. Cherries are equally prolific, but peaches seldom crowd the tree in Western Oregon, though they do in Eastern Oregon. Probably the best treatment to give young fruit trees in Oregon would be to pull off the greater portion of the fruit for the first year or two in order that the trees might mature their strength. No doubt it would also add to the flavor of the fruit, though that seems to be always excellent.

" Wild berries are very abundant, some of which are peculiarly delicious. The berries are strawberries, dewberries, whortleberries, sallalberries, black and

34

yellow raspberries, gooseberries, juneberries, and cranberries.   The cranberries are good, but found in abundance only in the vicinity of the ocean; the june, salmon, and gooseberries are not particularly desirable; the dew, sallal, and raspberries are choice, and quite abundant; and the straw and whortleberries are extremely abundant and delicious.   The prairies may be truly said to be literally red with strawberries, and the timbered openings blue with whortleberries, in their season.   The season of ripe strawberries is from three to six weeks, and that of whortleberries from six to ten weeks.   The whortleberry bush, except in the mountains, like the Umpqua plum shrub, is borne prostrate upon the earth's grassy covering, from the weight of its delicious fruit.   The wild strawberry of Oregon is larger and better than any we have ever seen, except the largest of the large garden cultivated English strawberry.   The whortleberry has more acidity than those of unshaded growth, growing east of the mountains.   English gooseberries and currants are cultivated here with success."

The native grasses of Western Oregon are blue-grass, and red and white clover.   The grass formerly grew very tall on the prairies but has been so much eaten off and trampled out by numerous herds of cattle, that it is now much shorter.   When sown in favorable situations, timothy will grow to a height of between five and six feet.

The timber of Western Oregon consists of pine, fir, cedar, oak, spruce, hemlock, cotton-wood, cherry, and maple.   Probably there is no country in the world where timber grows so strikingly straight and beautiful, and to such gigantic altitude and dimensions as in Oregon.   Two hundred feet is but a moderate height for the growth of firs, cedars, and spruce, and they frequently attain a much greater altitude.   We have seen elder growing in Oregon three feet in circumference, and hazel thirty inches in circumference, and of the height of forty feet.   Black alder and a species of laurel grow to what would be termed, in most countries, large trees—logs of alder have been obtained thirty-two inches in diameter, and of the laurel four feet in diameter.   In Western Oregon groves of timber are found skirting and separating prairies; but the immense timber districts are mainly confined to the neighborhood of the coast of the Pacific, to the Coast, Cascade and Blue ranges of mountains, and the immediate vicinity of the rivers.

The fir is seen almost solely on the western slope of the Cascade Mountains, along the Columbia River from where it breaks through that range until it passes through the coast range, on the eastern slope of the Coast Mountains, and along the rivers and upon the mountains almost any where between the summits of these two principal ranges. It is everywhere slightly mixed with spruce, hemlock, cedar, and yew. The pine is generally found in ridges or patches by itself, except on the west side of the Coast range where it grows with hemlock, spruce, and cedar. Willow grows along all the streams, and acquires considerable size. Ash, oak, maple, cotton-wood, and alder also grow wherever the ground is low and moist.

The shrubbery of Oregon is very beautiful and in great variety. There are several varieties of alder, bearing, severally, light purple, scarlet and orange colored berries. The wild cherry is a light and graceful tree, having a small, clear scarlet fruit, that is very beautiful, and exceedingly bitter. The tree-whortleberry has a very diminutive leaf, almost round, and a small crimson berry tasting much like a barberry. There are two smaller whortleberry shrubs corresponding to those of the Atlantic States, called swamp and mountain whortleberries. There are several varieties of wild currants, one of which is useless as a fruit, but is most beautiful as a flowering shrub. White spirea, and golden honeysuckle thrust their white or golden blossoms through every thicket, and with the white syringa and wild rose, festoon the river banks and hill sides until they seem one bed of bloom. The handsome shrubbery, and the abundant wild flowers of Oregon, atone greatly for the want of greater variety in the forest tints ; and the ease with which flowers may be cultivated for the adornment of homes is one of the greatest recommendations of the climate. Nature has been lavish, though man may be indifferent. If ever a wilderness might be made to blossom as the rose, that wilderness is Oregon. Few of the old settlers of Oregon have cared, however, to take advantage of the facilities afforded them for beautifying their homesteads, and it is more common to find a house without garden or shrubbery than with either; a peculiarity as strange as it is inexcusable.

Though Western Oregon is especially adapted to agricultural and pastoral pursuits, the present indications of mineral wealth make it almost certain that the miner's pick, as well as the farmer's plow, must furrow the face of mother Earth, west of the Cascade Mountains. This discovery was not sought after by the people of Oregon, who were firmly fixed in their belief that it was as an agricultural and manufacturing State that they were to achieve their highest destiny. But when gold and silver, iron, coal, and copper, are knocking for admittance as State resources, they cannot and will not be denied. They will be accepted as aids to manufactures and commerce ; and will be taken in connection with forests of splendid timber and rivers of unfailing water-power, as the means by which Oregon is to acquire her future status as one of the most important States of the Union.

Since the repeated tests by which the Santiam gold-bearing quartz has been found to yield $160 to the ton, other discoveries have been made, and will continue to be made in the Cascade Mountains. Already the mining town of Quartzville has started up in the Santiam district, and another town called Copperopolis, about ten miles to the southeast has sprung into existence near the copper mines. Discoveries of gold have recently been made in

Clackamas County; but as no actual test has yet been made of the quality of the ores, we cannot speak of their value.

It is sufficient to say that enough is known of the mineral resources of Western Oregon to warrant the investment of large amounts of capital; and that discoveries have only just begun to be made.

As to the price of farming lands in the Wallamet valley, they vary from three to fifteen dollars, including improvements. Many excellent farms may be had at from three to five dollars per acre; the owners selling out in order to remove with their children into towns, where they can be educated. These lands in a few years will be worth fifty dollars per acre, and we trust it will not be long before the population will be sufficiently dense to insure good schools throughout the State. The Oregon Central Railroad, now in course of construction, will do much to bring out the resources of the interior, and the time is not distant when lands in Western Oregon will bring a high price.

Sheep-raising and Manufacture of Woolen Goods. Wm. Lair Hill, in his prize essay, read before the Oregon State Fair, for 1862, says:—

"If Oregon has a specialty, it is her pre-eminence as a wool-growing country. Until recently, very little attention has been paid to the matter of sheep-raising; but it has now become one of the staple interests of the State. Sheep thrive better here than in any other State. Disease amongst them is exceedingly rare. They increase here faster than in the east, and the wool is of excellent quality."

In a similar essay, read before the Oregon State Fair for 1863, by John Minto, Esq., the following passages occur:—

"For the health of sheep, dry upland pasture is necessary. Taking the whole of Oregon into view, nine-tenths of the State may be pronounced of that character. For the feeding of sheep for wool-raising purposes, short sweet grasses and open woodland pastures are deemed best; and full three-fourths of the surface of the State is composed of hills and plains yielding such grasses; and a large portion of it is open woodland. For the growth of a long, even, strong, and flexible staple of wool, a mild, even climate (with proper feeding) is considered best, and that Oregon possesses in a remarkable degree. In fact, the climate and natural grasses of Oregon seem to be a natural combination of the peculiarities of England and Spain, in those particulars, especially the climate.

"Over twenty years ago, Mr. Peale, a naturalist who accompanied Commodore Wilkes' expedition to this coast gave it as his opinion that 'the country would become famous for its production of fine wool,' for the reason that 'the evenness of the climate enables the fur-bearing animals found here to carry their fine covering during the summer months, whereas under greater variations between the seasons, the same animals usually shed their furs, or they become mixed with hair during summer;' and for the further reason that the 'physical geography and natural grasses of the country make it a natural sheep pasture.'

"Experience goes far to show Mr. Peale's opinion correct. In a conversation between the writer and Mr. Henry Perkins, Chief Wool Stapler in the woolen factory at Salem, (a gentleman who has had a large and varied experience in assorting wool,) the latter said that he had never handled the wool from any country, which as a whole, was equal to that of Oregon as a combing wool; and that during a term of three years as wool stapler in a De Laine factory in Boston, Mass., he deemed that he did well when he could get from the bulk assorted 30 per cent. of wool fit for combing and manufacturing into that fabric. Of the wool he was then receiving—the crop of 1863, as it came in indiscriminately—Mr. P. said he could get from 50 to 60 per cent. of good combing wool. He further said if wools were properly assorted here and the combing portion graded and baled and marked according to its quality, and shipped to New York or Boston, it would soon draw the attention of De Laine manufacturers to this country as a source of supply for this most valuable kind of wool. We have further practical proof of the superiority of Oregon wool, in the fact that San Francisco papers as late as July last, quoted Oregon wool as selling three cents per pound above California wool sold on the same day.

"The fact of the superiority of Oregon wool is an encouraging circumstance to those engaged, or about to engage in raising it. But they will never reap the full benefit of it so long as they allow the business men of California to put their crops into market: so long as this is the case, the fact will be used to spread the fame of California, as a wool-producing country, and so long will Oregon dwell in the shadow of California, and feel the blighting influence. This is the inevitable result, even without any effort on the part of California merchants. It goes from their port in their shipping mart; the buyer cares no more but to know that he is receiving a good article for his money, and it would be too much to expect the California merchant to inform his customer that it was the product of another state. * * *

"The success of the woolen manufactory at Salem, started under more adverse circumstances than, it is believed, will ever again exist on this coast, shows plainly that a De Laine factory would be eminently successful here where such goods are worn throughout the year.*

"And there is no doubt that there is many a farmer in the Middle and Western States, who, worn down by the debilitating influences of miasmatic climates, would get a new lease of life by changing his location and becoming a sheep-raiser under the clear skies and pure air of Eastern Oregon. * * * * *

"There are at present more promising inducements for the Oregon farmer to turn his attention to the raising of sheep and wool (where his lands are of a suitable kind,) than any other branch of farming, for the reasons: 1st. That in that occupation the farmer can get along with less hired help, which is always hard to get of a reliable kind, and will continue to be, so long as the discovery of new gold mines continues. 2d. Sheep eat nearer to the ground and a greater variety of plants, and consequently require less labor in providing them food than any other domestic animal which yields anything like the return which they yield. 3d. There are two products from sheep, for either of which there is a greater prospective market than for any other farm product we can raise. We have already glanced at the condition of the market with regard to wool. 'It is the only thing raised by the farmers of Oregon that contains enough value in proportion to its weight to bear the expense of transportation to the Atlantic States. It is the only product that cannot be raised cheaper in the Atlantic States than here. It is the only product of the soil of Oregon (gold excepted) which we can send to the Eastern seaboard in exchange for the clothing, boots and shoes, machinery, iron, etc., etc., which we must buy there or elsewhere until we can build up manufactures of our own.' And manufactures we must have, unless we can contentedly remain utterly dependent upon the manufacturing skill of other communities, subject to the inconveniences of interruption in time of war, and the always increasing cost of transportation, which, as the producers of the raw material and consumers of the manufactured article, we must pay all the cost of, according to the amount of our consumption. The market for good wool-bearing stock sheep is only to be measured by the extent of the country yet unoccupied and fit for grazing purposes lying between the Pacific Ocean and the western base of the Rocky Mountains. The market for mutton will be in accordance with the increase of population; it can be produced cheaper and will always sell higher than beef until the country is glutted with wool-bearing flocks.

"Oregon lies on the western edge of an immense extent of country—reaching from Mexico to the British line; from Kansas to the Pacific Ocean—which, with the exception of the belt between the Cascade Mountains and the ocean, covered by parts of California, Oregon, and Washington Territory, is fitted for pastoral pursuits only. She has within her own borders a large portion of the best of that natural pasture. Within that, and almost surrounded by it, she has the largest compact body of good wheat land on the Pacific slope; which,

* Since the above was written a large factory at Oregon City has commenced manufacturing de laines, and several kinds of cloths.

surrounded and intermingled with never-failing water-power, makes the Willamette Valley adapted by nature for the cheap support of a dense manufacturing population, in a three-fold greater degree than ever was either Old or New England. She may, if her citizens will it, do her full share of first supplying all the region drained by the waters of the Columbia River with stock sheep, and then manufacture the wool raised from them and their increase. She may become to the north-west coast of America what England is now to the world, and what New England is to the United States in the power of their manufacturing commerce—following the settlements as they spread to the East and North with her improved stock and woolen fabrics."

Since Mr. Minto wrote his able essay on Sheep-raising, further facts have come to light concerning the quality of wool raised in the Eastern portion of Oregon. It has been well ascertained that the alkaline properties of the grass on which the sheep feed in some portions of Eastern Oregon, as well as the dust which settles upon them, has a deteriorating effect upon the wool; and that so far no good fleeces have been obtained from those regions. Undoubtedly the very best sheep-pastures are to be found on the Western side of the Cascade Mountains; though many valuable sheep-ranges may yet be discovered in the territory lying east of the Cascades and west of the Rocky Mountains.

Timber and Lumbering.—The State of Oregon, although in reality a prairie State, has immense lumbering resources. The principal timbers made into lumber are the firs and cedars. These grow along the streams and on the mountain ranges, affording fine facilities for milling, and for exporting lumber. A large amount of lumbering is done along the coast, at Coos Bay and Port Orford. All along the Columbia River, from its mouth to the Dalles, a distance of nearly two hundred miles, are dense forests of the most magnificent sized trees, which make superior lumber.

The exports from the Columbia River are about 4,000,-000 feet annually, which find a market at San Francisco, and the Sandwich Islands, chiefly. The lumber trade of Oregon is but in its infancy, being capable of almost unlimited development.

Turpentine, Tar, and Rosin.—Not only do the forests of Oregon furnish exhaustless supplies of lumber, but they offer also an immense source of wealth to the enterprising manufacturer of turpentine, tar, and rosin. T. A. Wood & Co., of Portland, who are engaged in manufacturing these articles, give the following statement on this subject:

" Every day more fully demonstrates the fact that the supply of crude turpentine is inexhaustible, and the probabilities are that this supply will never grow less, from two facts:

1st. The forests best suited for and richest in balsam, are those rough mountain sides that the farmer can never reduce to tillage.

2d. The trees when robbed of their accumulated supply will, like the "busy bee," commence the work of replenishing their stores, or refilling the cavities or "shakes," to be annually or semi-annually robbed.

From the crude article we manufacture turpentine, pitch, bright varnish, rosin, and axle-grease. In the limited time we have been in operation we have consumed 21,000 gallons of crude balsam. From this our manufacture will approximate: turpentine, 5,000 gallons; pitch, 400 barrels; bright varnish, 70 barrels; axle-grease, 25 cases.

We claim that the above articles are equal in quality to any manufactured in the United States, and not without proof. The turpentine being made from balsam of fir, is as far superior to pine turpentine, for medical use, as fir balsam is superior to pine pitch for medical purposes. The Portland physicians who have tried it speak loudly in praise of its medical virtues.

Under date of July 16th, 1864, Mr. P. C. Dart, of San Francisco, says: " Your turpentine is now preferred over California make, and I obtained twenty-five cents on the gallon, in advance of the California article. This fact is certainly encouraging."

The boat pitch is superior to any ever shipped to this coast. Capt. Kellogg said he ' used on the steamer Senator one barrel of States pitch and one of Oregon pitch, and would rather by one hundred dollars have used all Oregon pitch. The calkers said the barrel of Oregon pitch was worth three of the States pitch.'

Though our business has not been very extensive, we have opened a trade with China, Sandwich Islands, Vancouver's Island, California, and are now making a shipment to New York. It is our intention to enlarge our works, and if we do, as now designed, we shall export, from July 1865 to July 1866, over 1,200 tons of manufactured articles. In fact, the crude turpentine is in such abundance as to supply the world, if brought into use."

Fish and Fisheries.—Oregon furnishes some of the finest fisheries in the world. From the roaring mountain torrent, filled with the beautiful speckled trout, to the largest rivers, and the ocean bays, all its waters are alive with fish. In the latter are found cod, sturgeon, carp, flounders, perch, herring, crabs, and oysters. Tillamook, and Yaquina Bays are the principal oyster beds.

All the rivers along the coast furnish salmon, the largest being taken in the Columbia. They run up the rivers twice during the year, commencing in May, and again in October. Notwithstanding their great numbers, but few are taken for commercial purposes, although 100,000 barrels might be secured annually, and sold for ten dollars per barrel.

The following interesting extract is from Father P. J. De Smet's book on the Oregon Missions:

"My presence among the Indians did not interrupt their fine and abundant fishery. An enormous basket was fastened to a projecting rock, and the finest fish of the Columbia, as if by fascination, cast themselves by dozens into the snare. Seven or eight times during the day, these baskets were examined, and each time were found to contain about two hundred and fifty salmon. The Indians, meanwhile, were seen on every projecting rock, piercing the fish with the greatest dexterity.

They who do not know this territory may accuse me of exaggeration, when I affirm, that it would be as easy to count the pebbles so profusely scattered on the shores, as to sum up the number of different kinds of fish which this western river furnishes for man's support; as the buffalo of the north, and the deer from north to east of the mountains furnish daily food for the inhabitants of those regions, so do these fish supply the wants of the western tribes. One may form some idea of the quantity of salmon and other fish, by remarking, that at the time they ascend the rivers, all the tribes inhabiting the shores, choose favorable locations, and not only do they find abundant nutriment during the season, but, if diligent, they dry, and also pulverize and mix with oil a sufficient quantity for the rest of the year. Incalculable shoals of salmon ascend to the river's source, and there die in shallow water. Great quantities of trout and carp follow them and regale themselves on the spawn deposited by the salmon in holes and still water. The following year the young salmon descend to the sea, and I have been told, (I cannot vouch for the authenticity,) that they never return until the fourth year. Six different species are found in the Columbia."

Game. The game of Oregon is principally Bear, Panther, Elk, Deer, Antelope, Squirrel, Geese, Swan, Ducks, Pheasants, Grouse, and Quail. In the Wallamet Valley are found some Bear and Elk, and an abundance of black and white-tailed Deer, and Geese and Ducks.

In the Umpqua, Rogues and Clamet valleys are found an abundance of Elk, Deer, Antelope, Geese, and Ducks. The Deer of this country have been represented by some as small and inferior. Such is not the fact. The meat of the Deer of Oregon is as tender and delicious as the Deer of any other portion of the United States. The meat of the black-tailed Deer of this country is much superior to the meat of the white-tailed Deer of New York, Pennsylvania, or the Western States.

Salt. The salt of Oregon is obtained from springs, and is of very superior quality. The springs are numerous in the western part of Multnomah County, in the valley of the Lower Wallamet, in Columbia County, adjoining, and also in Douglas County, or the Umpqua Valley. Those in Douglas County have been worked for some time, manufacturing about 1,000 pounds per day, which being consumed in the neighborhood of the works, does not offer itself in the Portland market; neither would the distance and difficulties of transportation admit of its seeking a market in this place. There may be other springs in different counties worked in a small way. The salt works lately erected in the Lower Wallamet Valley are situated half way between Portland and St. Helen, at the foot of the hills which skirt the river, and about half a mile distant from it. There are a number of springs in this locality, and extending along near the base of this range of hills from 12 to 20 miles. Only one spring is used at present at the Wallamet Salt Works, and the present works are only experimental. From this one spring, or

well (for it has been deepened 27 feet) with all the surface water in it, and with only one furnace, the company
have been making from 500 to 700 pounds of salt per day
that probably has no superior in any part of the world.
It crystalizes with a handsome, fine grain; is bright, sparkling and as white as snow. It is entirely free from lime,
or any deleterious substance, so that as a dairy salt, or for
curing of meats, fish, etc., it is of the very best quality.
So strong are its preservative qualities that dairymen say
they need use only two-thirds as much of it as of Liverpool
salt; and the Portland butchers who have used it declare
it worth $10 more per ton than any salt in the market,—
that they use the brine over and over. Its quality, then,
is perfectly satisfactory, and the company are about erecting new and extensive works for boiling, beside improving the saline properties of the water in the springs by
boring and piping, to exclude surface or any other fresh
water.

Coal. That there will be found to be a large supply
of coal in Oregon is beyond a doubt. The Coos Bay
coal is not unknown in San Francisco, though its quality
has never gained for it much of a reputation. Other deposits have been discovered on the coast further to the
north. A mine is now being worked on the Cowlitz river,
six or eight miles from its junction with the Columbia,
which bids fair to supersede in merit any yet discovered
on the Pacific Coast. The structure and appearance of the
Oregon coal are peculiar, and at first liable to mislead the
judgment as to its quality. It has a glossy surface, is
rather light in weight, is perfectly clean to handle and
makes no soot in burning, all of which makes it a pleasant
fuel for grates and culinary purposes. It also lights very
readily, burns freely in the open air, and is free from sul-
phur. It shows, or appears to show, a woody structure,

yet is a hard coal, making an intense heat and holding fire for many hours. When burnt it emits a clear white flame, and leaves a white ash, without depositing strong substances, or *clinkers*. It is not anthracite, nor bituminous, though nearly as hard as the first, and quite as inflam able as the latter. Some miners call it cannel; some say it resembles Scotch splinth; but altogether it is easier to say what it is not than what it is. The fossils found in connection with it have created some doubt as to its age, many of them seeming to belong to the tertiary period, while others evidently are palm leaves.

Iron. Extensive beds of iron ore of a very pure quality are known to exist both on the Wallamet and on the Columbia rivers. Those on the Wallamet are situated about six miles south of Portland, and about eighteen above the mouth of the river. Furnaces were erected two years since by a Portland Company, who after sending some iron to San Francisco pronounced equal to the Swedish iron, have stopped manufacturing on account of some difficulty about the land on which the beds are situated, or the water-power used in connection with it. It is to be hoped that the entanglement, from whatever cause it arises, will soon be removed. Very extensive beds of the same kind of ore are found on the Columbia in the county of that name, but so far have not been worked.

Lead. This metal is found in abundance in southern Oregon, and in the Cascade Mountains, but only in conjunction with other metals. No attempt has yet been made to work it on account of the difficulty of separating the ores, and its low price in the market. In the future, however, it will be brought into notice along with other mineral productions.

Copper. The copper mines of Oregon have never yet been worked, yet for richness and favorable location they surpass those on the lower coast. This metal is found on the Rogue, Umpqua, Coquille, and Santiam rivers. Those on the Coquille are the most favorably situated for the shipment of ores. Very rich mines are located in Josephine county, but await the era of railroads for their development.

Gold and Silver. Gold is found in paying quantities on the Umpqua, Rogue, and Illinois rivers, and their tributaries; on the sea-beach at the mouth of the Umpqua and Coquille rivers, and at various places along the coast. But the richest mines have been discovered in a district called the Santiam from the river of that name, about seventy miles east of Salem, in the center of the State. The ore from these mines assays from $20 to $10,000 per ton. Silver is also found in connection with it.

Oregon has never, until within the last five years, been known as a mineral region. The character of the early settlers predisposing them to agricultural pursuits caused them to overlook the possible mineral wealth of the territory, even after the breaking out of the gold excitement in California had made known to the world the existence of rich mineral deposits on the Pacific coast. Those who were taken with the gold fever went to California, leaving unexplored the country nearer home. Gradually, however, and little by little, it became known that there were deposits of the precious metals in Oregon. Placer diggings in Southern Oregon and along the coast began to be worked as early as 1851–2. Copper, iron, and coal were discovered, but with the exception of the coal mines near the sea-coast, remained unworked.

Meanwhile gold continued to be discovered on every side, in British Columbia, Washington Territory, and Idaho, while Oregon, ever slow and deliberate amidst the hurry of events, made no effort to unveil the mysteries of her bosom. In 1861, the mines of Idaho were discovered at the mouth of Oro Fino Creek by E. D. Pierce, an Indian trader, at the head of a prospecting party of ten men. The excitement which followed the published accounts of these mines, caused a rush of explorers in that region of country now known as Idaho, which resulted in the discovery of gold on the head-waters and tributaries of the Clearwater.

Among these adventurers were numbers from the Wallamet valley, who in crossing the country east of the Cascade range, made the discovery of placer diggings on the John Day, Powder, and Burnt rivers, in Eastern Oregon. In 1864, quartz leads were also discovered on Eagle creek between Powder, and Burnt rivers; and towns are already built on each of these rivers. Thus was Oregon at last revealed to the world as a mineral district, unsurpassed in richness by very few districts in the world.

Building Materials. The mountains, in which are probably deposited quarries of different kinds of building stone, have been but little prospected with a view to the discovery of these materials for substantial structures. Lumber has been so abundant, cheap, and excellent in quality, that it has been unnecessary to search out the treasures contained in the bosom of the earth. There is no lack, however, of stone suitable for masonry ; nor of clay to make excellent brick. Limestone deposits exist in the Umpqua valley, in the hills back of the Clatsop Plains, in the highlands back of the Tualatin Plains, and in other parts of the Wallamet valley, and along the Columbia river, especially near its mouth. Southern Oregon furnishes numerous fine ledges of the best crystalline marble, susceptible of the highest polish. Sandstone occurs in the Coast range of mountains.

Bark for Tanning Leather. The forests and plains of Oregon furnish an unlimited supply of oak, fir, and hemlock bark, suitable for tanning purposes, while the extensive pastures of the State can keep supplied, unlimited quantities of hides for manufacturing leather.

Grain Raising and Flour Making. The production of wheat must ever remain one of the greatest resources of the State. Surrounded on every side by pasture lands, Oregon has " the largest compact body of good wheat land on the Pacific slope, which surrounded and intermingled with never-failing water-power, makes the Wallamet valley adapted by nature for the cheap manufacture of breadstuffs."

Wheat yields an average of thirty bushels to the acre, and in cases of good cultivation nearly double that amount. Oats, fifty to seventy-five bushels to the acre. Other grains in proportion ; and all kinds of pulse equally well.

Flax and Hemp. Flax and hemp grow to a great size, and produce a better fibre than in any other country. Flax yields a large amount of seed, and an oil-mill would do well in this State. There is no reason why linen goods may not be profitably manufactured in Oregon.

Tobacco. Tobacco has been grown in Oregon, equal to the best Virginia leaf. Eastern Oregon is peculiarly fitted for the cultivation of this plant ; and only experienced hands to cure it are wanted, to make the Oregon tobacco as celebrated as any in the United States.

Hops. The rainless summers of this country, together with the absence of heavy dews, make it very favorable for hop-raising. The crop is always certain, and may be cured in the open air. Hops will become one of the regular exports of the State.

Fruits—Preserving. The great and steady fruit-crops of Oregon, together with the abundance of berries growing wild in all parts of the State, offer superior inducements for the establishment of preserving houses in the

Wallamet valley. No such establishment exists, though the miners away up in Idaho buy fruits preserved in the Atlantic States and California.

Honey. It is but about five years since bees were introduced into Oregon. They thrive well, and produce a large amount of honey.

Potatoes and Vegetables. Potatoes are excellent in this State, and yield abundantly; from three hundred to four, or even six hundred bushels being grown on an acre of ground. The very best cabbages in the world are grown in Oregon, and in great numbers. The same may be said of Cauliflower. Melons and squashes do well, growing to a great size. Onions, like cabbage are very superior in this soil and climate, being mild and sweet to a degree unknown in the Eastern States. All other vegetables and roots thrive well, and are of good quality.

In short, if an Oregon farmer does not enjoy the comforts of life, he has no one to blame except himself for the lack of these things.

EASTERN OREGON was long regarded as a desert country, unblessed by God and undesired by man. That was when the emigration to Oregon, coming overland all the way from Indiana, Illinois, Missouri, and more southern States, arrived at the South Pass of the Rocky Mountains, with stock and provisions more than half exhausted, to enter upon a country not only more rugged in appearance than that already passed over, but presenting new features and new characteristics, against which, from ignorance of the facts, they had failed to prepare themselves. They found, west of the Rocky Mountains, a totally different climate from any they had ever experienced : delightful enough in summer, on the mountains, but hot and dry on the plains. Their road led them over bare rocks, reflecting strongly the heat of a cloudless sky; over sands

35

burning hot, and terribly heavy for their teams; over alkali deserts, which they knew not how to avoid, and past boiling springs whose disagreeable fumes filled the air. They were too weary to bring much energy to the overcoming of such difficulties as fell in their way, and too discouraged with these difficulties to be fairly thankful for the occasional oases which beautified their desert; so that, when once they had set foot within the ever-verdant valleys west of the Cascade range, the tawny colored hills and plains of Idaho and Eastern Oregon—then all Oregon Territory—were remembered only as " that God-forsaken country." A few emigrants and travelers were intelligent enough to observe the evidences of extensive mineral deposits, but most of these never looked forward to seeing this country occupied, and its minerals made the source of wealth. And least of all did they foresee that much, very much, of this " God-forsaken country " would prove to be of wonderful fertility, so that, in the year 1869, many portions of it have " blossomed like the rose." Such, at all events, is the history of Eastern Oregon.

There is, undoubtedly, a large proportion of waste lands in this part of the State. There are alkali plains and sage deserts, and in some parts, bare rocks coming to the surface. The alkali plains may never be made fit for cultivation. The sage deserts are not quite so hopeless, as some portions of them have been found susceptible of cultivation in California, and they may not prove to be so worthless as has been believed; but the rocks are a foregone conclusion.

In Eastern Oregon, Eastern Washington, and Idaho, the same general aspect of country prevails, except in the most northern portions of the two latter Territories, which are more heavily timbered, and rather better watered. But south of parallel 47, and between the Cas-

cade Mountains and the westernmost divide of the Rocky
Mountains, the country consists entirely of high rolling
plains destitute of timber, and mountain ridges covered
with timber; with the exception, however, of depressions
between the mountains and high table-lands, where lakes
and marshes may sometimes be found. The soil, both of
the plains and the mountains, is excellent. But a small
portion of the plains will ever be cultivated, for want of
the means of irrigation, but they will prove very valuable
for stock-raising purposes, as they are covered with a
natural growth of excellent bunch-grass. The mountain-
sides, when cleared, will produce fruit of the best quality ;
but it is upon the valley lands that the farmer will chiefly
depend for his grain-fields. There is no reason evident
why grapes should not do well east of the Cascades in
Oregon. The soil and climate are quite similar to those
of California, where the grape flourishes best. Corn
grows well in the valleys, and other grains and vegetables
produce remarkably well. It is worthy of mention here,
that, at the late agricultural fair in Eastern Oregon, the
premium for some kinds of vegetables was awarded to an
Indian farmer of the Umatilla tribe.

Eastern Oregon is crossed obliquely by the chain of the
Blue Mountains, which commence about at the eastern
boundary of Washington Territory, where the Snake
River bends to the south, and take a course southwest
to near the centre of Eastern Oregon, where they bend
more to the west, until they connect with the range of
highlands along the Des Chutes River, which runs between these hills and the Cascade range. Where the
Blue Mountains cross the State, they form, with the spurs
which they send out to the east and south, the divide,
or water-shed between the waters which flow into the
Columbia and those which flow into the numerous lakes

of the Oregon portion of the Great Basin, or sink into thirsty sands.

The scenery, the geology, and topography of this portion of Oregon (the Klamath Basin) are alike remarkable. The irregular hills, covered with burnt rock and scoriæ ; the fearful chasms, and sharp, needle-shaped rocks of its basaltic mountains ; its mysterious reservoirs of water ; its salt lakes and alkaline plains, seem to mark it for a country uninhabitable by man, and the resort only of myriads of wild-fowl, which here hatch their young in safety, and the refuge of marauding Indians who retire here after a successful raid into the settlements. Yet it will not be left to these, for the explorer and surveyor are already traversing it everywhere, and roads are being opened in various directions, connecting with the mines of Idaho, and with the towns and mines near the Columbia River. Nor will it be found unfit for settlement. In many parts are very desirable places for farms or stock-raising ; while the excellence of the routes which lead across the southern portion of Oregon, for the use of the emigration and traders to the mines, over those which cross near the Columbia River, will make every available section of land desirable for settlement.

The Great Basin consists of an elevated plateau, raised five thousand feet above the level of the ocean, and varying in surface between low hills, arid plains, marshes, salt and fresh lakes, and occasional fertile valleys. It is bounded by the Cascade Mountains on the west, whose foot-hills, covered with a beautiful growth of pine, extend away nearly to the eastern border of Klamath Lake ; on the north by the divide of the Blue Mountains ; and on the east by another low range of mountains. To the south it extends into California, Nevada, and Utah.

The following extracts from the report of Col. C. S.

Drew, 1st Oregon Cavalry, who made a reconnoisance through Southern Oregon to Fort Boise, in the summer of 1864, will furnish an idea of the cultivable country between Fort Klamath and Fort Boise :

Williamson's River takes its rise in Klamath marsh,—or, as the Indians claim, in Klamath Lake proper,—and running in a southerly course about thirty miles, empties into the east side of Big Klamath Lake, sixteen miles south of Fort Klamath. It is a considerable river—at the ford probably one hundred yards wide. It is somewhat alkaline, and rendered more unpalatable from having its source in swamps and tule marshes. The crossing is over a ledge of volcanic sandstone extending entirely across the river and into the banks on either side. The greatest depth of water is about three feet, and this only for about ten yards. From this ledge the water falls about two feet into a deep eddy below.

The soil immediately along the river, is a dark, sandy loam, but changes to a light granite, or volcanic ash, as we approach the uplands and mountains on either side.

The country between Fort Klamath and the ford of Williamson's River is covered with a fine forest of yellow and sugar pine, with now and then a white or red fir, and occasionally a good sized cedar, cotton-wood, or rather aspen, is frequent around the glades and along the smaller streams. There are also small forests and thickets of a species of pine having as yet no popular name, and seemingly peculiar to the Cascade Mountains. Fort Klamath is built in a beautiful grove of them, and they cover the summit of the Cascade Mountains along the northern base of Mount M'Laughlin, where the road crosses between Fort Klamath and Jacksonville.

* * * * * * * * * *

Sprague's River Valley is about forty miles long, and from two to fifteen miles wide. Its general direction is from southeast to northwest. The banks of the river, and of the numerous streams putting into it on either side, are fringed with willows and cotton-wood, and the entire valley is skirted with a continuous forest of yellow pine, extending back to the summit of the mountains by which it is bounded. It possesses all the natural requisites for a good stock range, its low lands being covered with a fair growth of marsh grasses, while its uplands afford a bountiful supply of the more nutritious bunch-grass, with an occasional spot of wild timothy.

The soil here is a dark, sandy loam, growing lighter and somewhat gravelly towards the mountains. Outcroppings of lava and other volcanic products are general, but there are many tracts of land that offer eligible farm sites, and could be easily cultivated.

The climate is similar to that of Fort Klamath, but the soil is quick and vegetation matures early.

Wild flax grows here so abundantly that in many places it presents the ap-

pearance of tolerably fair cultivation, and produces a fine strong fibre. The
stalk seems to spring from its root and continues to grow until checked by the
frosts of autumn. In this way it seems probable that the old root retains substance enough during the winter to send out new shoots in the spring. * * *

"Passing out of Sprague's river valley in a southeasterly direction, we crossed
the Goose Lake Mountains through a wide and smooth gap, and by an easy
grade, and entered a small fine valley situated to the westward of the northern
extremity of the valley around the upper portion of Goose Lake, but having an
outlet into it some distance down its western border.

"This little valley is about fifteen miles long, having a general direction from
north to south, and has an extreme width of about eight miles. It has a southern exposure and a fertile soil. Its surroundings on the north, east, and west,
are timber-covered mountains, while a low range of grass-covered hills bound it
on the southward, separating it from the basin of Goose Lake. It is well watered by several mountain streams, and by springs, fringed with willow, and in
some places with the cotton-wood, and is covered with a luxuriant growth of
grass. Its soil excels that of Sprague's river valley in its general adaptation to
agricultural purposes. * * * *

"From a point on the east side of the little valley into which we had entered,
and about twelve miles from its head, we diverged to the eastward, and passing
over some low grassy hills and along the bank of a small mountain stream running in a southeasterly direction, we descended into Goose Lake basin by a very
easy grade, through a remarkably smooth depression in its western rim.

"From this pass to the head of Goose Lake, the first four miles was across a
sage desert that extends southward down the western border of the lake as far
as the eye can see.

"From this desert to the head of Goose Lake the surface of the country is
undulating, though from any considerable distance it has the appearance of being entirely level.

"The uplands are generally covered with a luxuriant growth of bunch-grass,
but in many places the outcropping of lava renders them unfit for other than
grazing purposes. For these, however, they excel any portion of the country
yet passed over.

"The lowlands along the numerous little streams, all putting in from the
northward and converging towards the head of the lake, but generally sinking
before they reach it, are extremely fertile, and well adapted for cultivation. A
small portion of them, bordering immediately on the lake, are somewhat alkaline, but produce in many places an excellent growth of rye-grass, and other
vegetation incident to a moderate alkali region.

"The valley is beautifully studded with large willows and some cotton-wood
that fringe its streams, and timber of good quality is abundant and easy of access around its northern extremity and down along its eastern border.

"The main portion of the valley, from its northern extremity down to the
lake, is about twenty miles in length, and from the Sierra Nevada Mountains
which bound it on the east to its western rim, the distance is nearly the same.

In this area is contained the most valuable agricultural land of the Goose Lake basin.

"Along the eastern shore of the lake, however, there is considerable good grazing country, with an occasional tract of good farming land, covered with luxuriant wild clover in addition to all the wild grasses common to the fertile portions of the country.

"Numerous creeks and springs of good water put into the east side of the lake from the Sierra Nevada Mountains.

"Timber is also abundant along the base of the Sierras, up their ravines, and in many places up their sides to the summit.

"In the way of game, antelope and deer are quite plenty, and 'old bruin' is met occasionally. Sand-hill cranes, ducks of every variety, curlew, and all other fowls incident to California, are abundant throughout this region, and along the streams in the upper portion of the valley we saw numerous 'signs' of otter.

"The lake is emphatically alkaline, but abounding with fish near its main inlets. Its surface is beautifully dotted everywhere with flocks of swan, resembling, through mirage, so many fleets under sail.

"Mirage exists here to about the same extent that it does in and around San Jose valley, California. * * * *

"Surprise Valley is a long, narrow strip of land, stretched along the eastern foot-hills of the Sierra Nevada mountains, and sloping down into alkaline lakes, and the sand and sage desert that forms its eastern boundary. These foot-hills and the lower portions of the spurs are generally covered with a bountiful growth of bunch-grass, while between many of them, and sometimes extending out around them toward the dreary waste to the eastward, are small tracts of excellent tillage land, covered with grass, rushes, and spots of clover and wild pea-vine. It is well watered by springs and streams putting down from the Sierras, but these usually sink on reaching the level of the lakes, and the sage fields into which they flow.

"Timber pine is abundant along the Sierras, and of fair quality. Game of all kinds common to California, seems to be plenty.

The Red Bluff *Independent* has the following of Surprise Valley.

"The prospects of the settlers are of the most flattering description. There are about one hundred families now settled down as industrious farmers, besides a large floating population from the Owyhee and Puebla. The recent opening of communication with Red Bluff as a place at which they can obtain supplies has stimulated them to further enterprise, as they have been heretofore almost shut out from the rest of the world; but now they are sending in their teams for their winter supplies and purchasing more advantageously in Red Bluff than at Susanville, and they say the road is about as near to Red Bluff as it is to Susanville. A party of fifteen teams are expected in here this week. Fort

Bidwell, which is established at the north end of the valley, is named after Gen. John Bidwell, our representative in Congress, and is located in one of the finest natural locations. Near the new post are two springs of water, the one hot and the other cold. The hospital is located between these two springs, and so situated that hot and cold baths can be had at all hours. In fact, the water (hot and cold) will be conducted throughout the whole garrison. The health of the valley is excellent, and settlers say they prefer it to the Sacramento valley. The last year's crop of barley has been disposed cf to the soldiers at 3c. per pound. Already parties have been talking of machinery for a grist mill to be put up next spring.

"Warner's Valley is similar to Surprise Valley in point of location, form, and general character. Its direction is from south to north. The Sierras form its western boundary for a distance of about fifteen miles from its southern extremity, thence receding to the westward, and leaving a volcanic table to continue its border northward.

"Springs and streams are found at convenient distances along the base of the Sierras, and two or more streams find their way from the same source, through deep chasms in the table that continues its western rim."

Such are some of the oases in the most desert part of Eastern Oregon. The explorations already made have demonstrated the fact that there is much mineral in the mountains in this portion of Oregon, a circumstance which must lead to its further exploration by experienced miners. A military road is being built from a point in the neighborhood of Diamond Peak to a point in the Owyhee country, which will probably become the popular emigrant road from the east into the Wallamet valley. The Red Bluff route to Idaho City crosses this country, entering it at Goose Lake Valley. Also a road from Yreka, California, to Canyon City on the John Day River, comes in between the Klamath Lakes, and strikes across the country in a general direction northeast to the head-waters of the John Day. Other projected routes will soon be opened, leading from points on the Columbia River to the Owyhee mines.

The northern portion of Eastern Oregon which is drained by the Des Chutes, John Day, Umatilla, and Grande Ronde Rivers; and the extreme eastern portion which is drained by the Powder, Burnt, and Malheur Rivers, consist entirely of rolling grassy plains, wooded mountains, and fertile valleys, the principal ones being those on the rivers already mentioned. These valleys constitute the only inhabited portions at the present time, but the plains are certainly destined to be taken up by stock-raisers.

The *Des Chutes* is a rapid and rocky stream which will never probably be made navigable, rising in the Cascade Mountains near the borders of the Great Basin, and flowing almost directly north into the Columbia. The valley of the Des Chutes has some considerable settlement, but is yet chiefly unoccupied, though capable of supporting a large population. The settlers for the most part are stock-raisers; but the demand for farm products in the neighboring mines is stimulating agricultural improvements. The Des Chutes river abounds with salmon, and has numerous tributaries whose banks are thinly wooded. The Des Chutes, and nearly all the rivers of Eastern Oregon, have high and steep banks which make the crossing difficult except at certain points.

The John Day River, like the Des Chutes, is unnavigable, being one of those swift rivers, full of rocks and rapids, which the salmon love to inhabit. It waters a large valley running in nearly the same direction as the Des Chutes, and only about thirty miles distant to the east. It has only been settled since the gold discoveries in 1862. It is very fertile, and has a good market in its mines. Owing to the mildness of the climate in this region, mining operations can be carried on through the greater portion of the year—the want of water being the only hindrance to mining at any season.

The Umatilla River is a small stream emptying into the Columbia, whose head-waters and southern tributaries flow through a delightful country, fit either for cultivation or grazing. It waters in part the famous pastures of the Nez Perce and Cayuse Indians, where formerly the chiefs sometimes had fifteen hundred or two thousand head of horses in one band.

GRANDE RONDE RIVER rises in the eastern spurs of the Blue Mountains, and has its course a little north of east until it falls into the Snake river. Its valley is of a beautiful round shape, and about twenty-five miles in diameter, having the river running almost directly through the center. It is enclosed between mountain ridges which send down numerous streams of limpid water, keeping the valley ever verdant. These streams are fringed with trees which mark their meanderings, and add a grace and picturesqueness to the landscape, which has gladdened the eyes of thousands of overland emigrants, scorched with travel over sun-burnt plains. In Grande Ronde valley the land is probably all claimed, owing to its nearness to the mines. Considerable grain is raised in this valley, and made into flour in its own mills. The climate of the Grande Ronde is agreeable, though sometimes subject to deep snows in winter.

POWDER RIVER is a small river, not navigable, but affording good water-power. Its valley contains about 200,000 acres of farming land, of which 10,000 acres are under cultivation. The climate is rather warmer and drier than that of Grande Ronde, and the valley is rapidly being settled up. Rich mines both of gold and copper have been discovered, and the gold mines are being extensively worked.

South of Powder River valley the country is rough and broken, not suited to agriculture, but very well adapted to grazing. Burnt river, and Malheur river, flow through this mountain country into the river Snake. Gold has been found in paying quantities on both these rivers, and will doubtless be found on the tributaries of the Owyhee in the less explored region of southeastern Oregon.

The mountains of Eastern Oregon are generally well wooded with forests of fir and birch, spruce and cedar, and some groves of pine. Cotton-wood and willow fringe the smaller streams, and the forests generally extend from the mountains down the foot-hills nearly to the valleys, but never grow along the main rivers.

The climate of this part of the State of Oregon differs entirely from that of the western portion. It is decidedly a dry climate; rather warm in summer, and also somewhat bleak in winter. The snow never falls to any depth on the plains, but does occasionally fall heavily in the valleys. The winters, however, are short, and farmers commence putting in seed in March.

From what has been said of the resources of Eastern Oregon, it will be seen that a great portion of the wealth and importance of the State is in the future to be derived from that portion lying east of the Cascade range, and until recently considered of but little value. As a beef-raising and wool-growing country it will become of very great value, as auxiliary to its mines, which are rapidly becoming known, and already rival those of Idaho and Montana. Although this portion of the State will never, perhaps, become the seat of so dense a population as the western portion, it will be found to contain the means of great wealth and commercial prosperity in its stock-ranches, its fields of corn and sorghum, its fruit orchards, vineyards, flax and wool, as well as in its mines of gold, silver, copper, lead, cinnabar, and plumbago.

The whole State of Oregon, East and West, comprises an area of 102,600 square miles. Its population cannot exceed 110,000.

CHAPTER XLVI.

WASHINGTON TERRITORY is the northern half of the old
Oregon Territory, from the southern half of which its people prayed to be separated in 1852. It has an area of
69,994 square miles; being considerably less than Oregon
in extent. Its population is probably under 20,000.

In general terms Washington and Oregon resemble each
other both in the principal features of the country and in
climate. The chief difference consists in the more open
appearance of the country, it not being so entirely made
up of valleys as Oregon. The principal river is the Cowelitz, which is navigable a distance of only thirty miles;
its valley being narrow and rich, but of very limited extent. Like Oregon, it is divided by the Cascade range of
mountains, with the same relative differences of soil and
climate on the east and west sides. Unlike Oregon, however, it is not so entirely separated from the sea by the
Coast range of mountains, which in Washington are very
much broken. The terminating point of the Coast Mountains is Mount Olympus, which rises to a height of nine
thousand feet, standing forth as a glorious land-mark, visible from the sea; and being closely in view either from
the Straits of Fuca, or Puget's Sound.

The richest agricultural portions of Washington are the
small valleys of its numerous streams, all of which are
well wooded with cotton-wood, maple, oak, ash, fir, cedar,
willow, and alder. The best grain fields of Washington

are contained in a tract of land called the Cowelitz Prairie, commencing about thirty miles north of the Columbia River, and extending only a few miles toward the Sound. Strictly speaking, Washington is not an agricultural country; its peculiar geography pointing it out rather as a commercial than a farming State. A glance at any good map will show the reader at once what is the evident future of Washington Territory. Considering the importance of the inland waters of this Territory, it will be quite apropos of the subject of a Northern Railroad to give a somewhat detailed description of them, taken from the reports of both English and American explorers. From the Pacific Railroad Report of the late Governor I. I. Stevens, we take the following account of *the Strait of San Juan De Fuca:*

"The STRAIT OF JUAN DE FUCA is the most remarkable inlet of the whole Pacific coast of the American continent. It is bounded on the north by the southern shore of Vancouver's Island and other smaller islands, and on the south by the northern shore of the Mount Olympus peninsula. On the east it is terminated to a certain extent by the western shore of Whidby's Island. Its general direction is from east to west, and its length is about eighty nautical miles. The north and south shores of this Strait are parallel as far as the southern end of Vancouver's Island, or to about the middle of its length. Up to this point the Strait has a general width of about eleven nautical miles. From Race Rocks on the north and Freshwater Bay on the south, exactly the middle point of the whole extent, the Strait widens about twenty nautical miles, and afterwards presents more the aspect of a broad interior basin. It is no longer bounded by straight parallel shores, but branches into several broad passages, bays, and channels. De Fuca Strait is very deep throughout its whole extent. In mid-channel its average depth is one hundred fathoms, and this depth is carried near the shore on both sides. It commences shoaling at a distance of two miles from shore; and in all the channels and branches of this Strait the depth is equally great. There are no impediments to navigation through-out the whole extent of this Strait. A deep sea bank is found at the entrance, which is a favorite fishing bank for the Indians in this vicinity." "The southern shores of De Fuca Strait are hills, in the immediate neighborhood of the water, of a moderate height. Many low sandy cliffs fall perpendicularly on beaches of sand and stone. From the top of the cliffy eminences the land takes a further gentle and moderate ascent, and is entirely covered with trees,

chiefly of the pine genus, until the forest reaches a range of high craggy mountains, which seem to rise from the woodland country in a very abrupt manner,
with their summits covered with snow. The northern shore is not quite so
high. , It rises more gradually from the sea-side to the tops of the monntains of
Vancouver's Island, which gives to them the appearance of a compact range,
more uniform and much less covered with snow than those on the southern
side."* The eminences with which the whole coast is lined have nearly all,
more or less, the same form. They form little peninsulas, which all point to
the northwest. The northeastern sides of these peninsulas are long, the northwestern short, and between the two neighboring points usually lies a little bay,
the shores of which are low and sandy."

Passing over the careful accounts of the several ports
along the strait, intended for the benefit of sea-going read-
ers, we come to Port Discovery, at the entrance to Admiralty Inlet, the northern portion of what is now called
in a general way THE SOUND.

" This bay is about six miles long from north to south, and throughout two to
two and a half miles wide from east to west. It is very deep, and has regular
soundings from thirty to thirty-five fathoms in mid-channel, to ten fathoms close
to shore. In some places it is almost too deep for an anchoring place. The
entrance of this port is formed by two low projecting points, Challam Point, to
the west, and Cape George to the east. Wooded cliffs of a middling height
bound the coast of the interior basin. It is protected from all winds, and
especially those of the north, by a little Island, called Protection Island, which
is two miles from its entrance and covers it. " Had this insular production of
nature," says Vancouver, " been designed by the most able engineers, it could
not have been placed more happily for the protection of the port."

From all this it is evident that this bay forms one of
the safest and best harbors in the world. It is also very
easy to fortify it against the attempts of an enemy.

" ADMIRALTY INLET is a most curious, irregular, and complicated compound
of inlets, channels, and bays, which lead to a narrow entrance from the southeastern corner of De Fuca Strait. The principal body of these waters, taking
the whole as one mass, runs in a directly north and south line through more
than a whole degree of latitude; but branches run out from it in all points of
the compass, and fill a region seventy nautical miles in length from north to
south and thirty miles in breadth from east to west. It may be compared to a

---

* Vancouver.

tree, of which the body is recognizable, which is called Admiralty Inlet proper, and the side branches have their particular names. All the water channels of which Admiralty Inlet is composed are comparatively narrow and long. They have all, more or less bold shores, and are throughout deep and abrupt, so much so that in many places a ship's side will strike the shore before the keel will touch the ground."*

Even in the interior and most hidden parts, depths of fifty and a hundred fathoms occur, as broad as De Fuca Strait itself. Vancouver found sixty fathoms near the Vashon Island within a cable's length of the shore, and in Possession Sound he found no soundings with a line of one hundred and ten fathoms. Our modern more extensive soundings prove that this depth diminishes towards the extremities of the inlets and basins. A high tide goes up from De Fuca Strait into all these sounds. Even at Nisqually, the most southern part of the Admiralty Inlet, the spring tides are eighteen feet high and the neaps twelve.

"Nothing can exceed the beauty and safety of these waters for navigation. Not a shoal exists within them; not a hidden rock, no sudden overfalls of the water or the air; no strong flows of the wind as in other narrow waters; for instance, as in those of Magellan's Strait. And there are in this region so many excellent and secure ports, that the commercial marine of the Pacific Ocean may be easily accommodated.

"The country into which these waters enter, and of which they fill the lowest and central parts, may be said to be a broad valley between the Mount Olympus range to the west and the Cascade range to the east; the high, snow-covered peaks of both ranges may be seen from the waters everywhere. They stand at a distance of about a hundred nautical miles from each other. The broad valley between them is, upon the whole, of a moderate elevation, and presents a pretty level depression. The higher spurs of the two mountain ranges do not come down to the water's edge. The shore lands in the immediate neighborhood of the channels may, therefore, be called only hills. They are partly handsomely wooded, partly covered with luxuriant grass."

Puget Sound proper, is that portion of this large inland body of water which extends south of Vashon Island, and

---

* Wilkes.

is a compound of many narrow inlets and sounds like Admiralty Inlet, and differs from it in no particular except in extent.

Hood's Canal is the westernmost arm of this great and complicated sound, the largest portion of which is called on the maps Admiralty Inlet, but which the people of the west coast have named without distinction of boundaries, PUGET SOUND.

When it is remembered that the many arms of the Sound are surrounded with the most valuable timber for ship-building, as well as with many beautiful shrubs and smaller growths of trees, the beauty and the wealth of this favored region may be faintly imagined. On a bright summer's day, when the grand snow-peaks of the Cascade range and of Mount Olympus stand distinctly out to view, a scene is furnished which probably is not surpassed by any in the world—certainly not by any on the American Continent.

The advantages of Puget Sound, as the great Naval Depot of the Pacific coast, cannot be over-rated. Here is the ample room and the safe anchorage; here the timber, the turpentine, tar, rosin, iron, copper, cordage, and a climate favorable to constant labor in the open air. It is impossible to doubt that the United States Government will avail itself of this magnificent gift of nature, or to believe that it will be blind to the necessity of Railroad communication between it and the great commercial marts of the east.

Lumbering Interests. We have already said that agriculture was not the great business of Washington Territory. Its greatest commercial interest at present is the lumber trade. The largest mills of the Pacific coast are located along the shores of Puget Sound. The plain lying north of the Cowelitz Valley and east of the Sound is mostly of a gravelly soil, dotted with scattering timber, and diversified with lakes and streams. It is a country very beautiful to the eye, and with proper care may be made to yield good returns to husbandry, though much less valuable than other portions. But in the immediate vicinity of the Sound the timber is very dense, and grows to a magnificent size, often reaching a height of 250 or 300 feet. This belt of timber which encircles the Sound, is from two to six miles in width, and consists chiefly of fir and cedar—the most valuable timber on the coast. Even the saw-dust of the cedar is valued, on account of its odor, and is carried to San Francisco to be used in saloons, market-places, etc.

The lumbering interests of Washington are controlled by companies who own large tracts of timbered land along the Sound, and at favorable points on the coast. Their market is in San Francisco, the Sandwich Islands, Sitka, and nearly all points on the Pacific coast south of Oregon.

Coal. Another great source of wealth in Washington Territory is the coal which it furnishes. Bellingham Bay coal has long been used in San Francisco as the principal fuel. Later, other mines have been discovered and opened on the Cowelitz River, only four or six miles from its junction with the Columbia. From their extent and thickness the Cowelitz beds are likely to rank high as an opening for the investment of capital.

Fish. Of the rivers which empty into the Sound, are the Skagit, Snohomish, Dwamish, Puyallup, Nisqually, and Skokomish, with their tributaries. Many of these streams are navigable at high tide by vessels drawing eight to ten feet of water, making access to commercial waters easy for the occupants of the land along their course. There are mud-flats of some extent at the mouths of the rivers, and some patches of salt-meadows. The river mouths are choice places for obtaining salmon, cod, and halibut;

salmon and herring are taken in the Sound, and trout in the streams.

The Coast Counties. Of the counties along the coast not much is known except that they have a rich soil, generally covered with a dense growth of timber. Many small streams flow from the Coast Mountains into the Pacific Ocean.

Gray's Harbor, in Chehalis county, together with the fine valley of the Chehalis River, make this portion of the coast a very desirable point for settlement.

Shoalwater Bay, in Pacific county, is an extensive body of water, receiving the waters of numerous small streams, among which the Willopah is the most considerable, having a fine valley like the Chehalis. Both these bays have extensive meadows and natural prairies contiguous, which furnish excellent grass through the whole year. A fine sand beach extends along the coast the whole distance between these bays, making the pleasantest summer drives imaginable. The entrance to Shoalwater Bay is five miles wide, with two channels, each half a mile wide, leading into it. The bay is filled with shoals, mud-flats, and sand pits, all of which are bare at low water; while at high water the tide sets up the rivers from eight to fifteen miles. This bay is the great oyster-bed of the Pacific Coast, and vessels are regularly engaged in the oyster trade between this point and San Francisco. Around the bay the country is heavily covered with fir, spruce, hemlock, and arbor vitae.

From Shoalwater Bay down to Cape Hancock, called on the maps Cape Disappointment, there extends another smooth beach for a distance of twenty miles. This beach is about one hundred yards wide, very even and hard, backed by a range of low, sandy, and wooded hills; and the whole constitutes a narrow peninsula extending to the mouth of the Columbia River. The extreme southern point of this peninsula is Cape Hancock, where the United States has a fortification.

Resume. Western Washington, so far as developed, has been proven to depend chiefly upon its lumber, fish, coal and other minerals, for its commercial position. This is not really on account of the sterility of the country, as

MOUNT RANIER FROM PUGET SOUND.

has been shown, but is owing rather to the habits of the people, and because until lately there existed no market for farm produce in the Territory. Now, however, it is different. Vancouver's Island right at their doors, depends entirely upon Washington and Oregon for grain and vegetables, nor is the opportunity any longer lacking of send-

ing farm products to foreign markets, while the mines of
Eastern Washington, like those of Oregon, make a constant demand on the labor of the farmer.

Western Washington possesses at once the finest inland
harbors in the world, immense forests of valuable lumber,
mines of coal, and precious metals, extensive fisheries, a
healthful and mild climate, and is nearer by seven hundred
miles to the great East Indian marts of trade than any
other harbor of importance on the Pacific Coast.

The Puget Sound country must ultimately become a rich
and thickly inhabited region, and there will undoubtedly
grow up upon the Sound a great maritime city, where
ships from China and Japan will disembark their freight
upon the wharves of a Northern Pacific Railroad, to be
conveyed by the shortest land carriage to the great chain
of inland seas stretching from Lake Superior, by the aid
of a ship-canal, to the Atlantic Ocean; or scattered broadcast over the land along the hundreds of branch roads
that vein the eastern half of the continent in every direction.

Southern and Eastern Washington. That portion of
Washington Territory bordering upon the Columbia River
is not much settled. Farmers are, however, taking up the
land in the valleys of the rivers flowing into the Columbia
on the north side, quite rapidly of late. It is generally
observed that the land seems warmer on that side of the
river than on the Southern or Oregon side. The Cowelitz
Valley and the Lewis River and Lake River Valleys are
now pretty well filled up, and prove to be excellent fruit,
grain, and dairy regions. Farther up the Columbia, and
just west of the foot-hills of the Cascades, is another well-
settled section of the Territory, where some handsome
prairies lie toward the Columbia River, bordered with rich
bottom lands.

East of the Cascades the country is unsettled for a long distance, except here and there a farm near the Columbia.

Walla-Walla. Not until we reach the Walla-Walla Valley, do we find any active life and signs of cultivation. But here, in the southeasternmost corner of the Territory, is a valley of great beauty and fertility, rapidly becoming populated. The productions of this valley are wheat, oats, barley, corn, fruits, and vegetables. Wheat yields thirty to sixty bushels to the acre, oats seventy-five, potatoes four to six hundred bushels, and other garden stuff in proportion. As a grazing country it cannot be excelled, for the quality of either the grass or water. Besides the streams, wells yield excellent cold water at a depth of from twelve to fifteen feet. There is no valley in the whole upper country superior to this in advantages offered for settlement. The climate is dry and healthful, with short winters, and long, warm summers. The chief objection to the climate is the high wind which prevails in summer, in common with all high, open countries.

CHAPTER XLVII.

The Columbia River has no valley proper—that is, continuous levels of agricultural land, commonly known as bottoms. From the junction of its two great forks to its outlet, it flows between high bluffs, which rise into mountains where the river breaks through the Cascade Range.

The mouth of the Columbia forms a large bay, twenty-five miles long by six to eight wide, with numerous smaller bays indenting its shores, and numerous points and promontories, the most conspicuous of which are Tongue Point, four miles above Astoria, Point Adams, which borders on the ocean on the southern entrance, and Cape Disappointment, (or Cape Hancock, as it is known to the Government,) which borders on the northern entrance. These two last named points are fortified. The following mention of these fortifications is from the Astoria "Marine Gazette:"

"Fort Stevens is situated on Point Adams, on the Oregon side, in full view of the ocean, and about one mile from the main channel of the river, and two and a-half or three miles from the ocean. The guns of Fort Stevens will command the channel for several miles above and below the Fort. Next summer a fort is to be built on Chinook Point immediately opposite Fort Stevens and nearly due north of it. The river at this point is about three and a-half miles wide, and is the narrowest point on the river within forty miles of the mouth. Fort Hancock, on Cape Disappointment, is about seven miles northwest of Fort Stevens, and about five and a-half west by north of Chinook Point. Thus the three forts will form a triangle, all commanding the entrance and the channels of the river. When all of these forts are completed, mounted and manned, an enemy would meet with a warm reception, in case he would attempt to pay us a hostile visit.

Fort Stevens is a nonagon, surrounded by a deep ditch thirty feet wide and nineteen hundred feet in length. Beyond the ditch is an outer earth-work, sloping gently back to the surface of the ground, to protect the perpendicular wall of the main work inside of the ditch. From the top of this wall, the earth-works of the main fort slope up to the top where the guns are mounted. An exterior view of the fort exhibits nothing but an inclined plane of earth-works, of so gentle a slope that shot or shell can do it no damage. The magazine in the centre of the fort is a substantial structure, covered deeply with earth, and is bomb-proof. The shell-houses are also bomb-proof, and are interspersed along the line of guns at convenient distances. The entire earth-works, including magazine and shell-houses, except the nice gravel walks through the fort, are covered with sod of sparkling green, and are beautifully pictured upon the broad surface of the deep ditch, as it stretches around the fort, between its parallel walls and numerous angles. Fort Stevens will mount forty-three guns, and some of them are the largest size. The great fifteen-inch pivot gun guards the prominent front facing the approach from sea. Here the grim monster stands sentry, bidding defiance to any foe that dares invade. This is said to be the most substantial and efficient fort on the Pacific Coast, and for beauty and symmetry we doubt if it is surpassed by any similar work in the United States."

There are two channels or entrances to the Columbia, over the celebrated " bar."

The north channel conducts past the light-house on Cape Disappointment, and follows the shore-line of Baker's Bay until abreast of Pacific City, then bears off to the right some distance, where it intersects the south channel which comes in by Point Adams. On the "middle sands" between the north and south channels are lying the bones of many a worthy vessel, and many a gallant sailor also, whom deceitful winds lured on to the bar and suddenly failing, left stranded by the ebbing tide, to go to destruction in the breakers. After the two channels unite in one, that one bears to the south, coming right up to the town of Astoria, where the Custom House is located, and where the first cargo of goods delivered in Oregon was discharged from the ship *Tonquin*, Capt. Thorn, from New York, in the service of John Jacob Astor, in the year 1811. The genius of a great and successful merchant

THE COLUMBIA RIVER.

touched by a wonderful foresight upon the very spot where a mighty People's commerce shall yet be disembarked.

The dangers which once beset the entrance to the Columbia have been overcome by steam. No steamer was ever lost on the bar, and since a proper pilot system has been established, but one or two vessels. The difficulty should be effectually removed by the employment of a steam-tug for sailing vessels.

The vessels which ply on the lower Columbia are the tri-monthly line of ocean steamers from San Francisco, a number of sailing vessels carrying lumber and produce to the same port, a line of vessels to the Sandwich Islands, a steamer connecting with the San Francisco line, taking passengers and freight to Vancouver's Island, and a semi-weekly steamer from Portland to Astoria. All vessels entering the river stop at Astoria to receive their clearances, and proceed to Portland, twelve miles up the mouth of the Wallamet, and one hundred and ten from the ocean, to discharge their cargoes.

Proceeding up the Columbia, the traveler sees little of interest except the great river itself. Like the Hudson, its banks are high and mountainous, but unlike that river, they are not yet dotted with towns, villages, and hamlets, at every accessible point. A few beginnings have been made, where a flouring mill or saw-mill have been established, and where a vessel comes to load with lumber or flour. Oak Point, Cathlamet, and Monticello at the mouth of the Cowelitz, are such examples. A few farms also have been begun where the small valleys of tributary streams come down to the Columbia. St. Helen is the first town which seems to promise a considerable future growth, and that chiefly on account of its fine and favorable situation. It has, however, ample resources, though undeveloped, and has been talked of as the terminus of the Oregon Central Railroad, where it should cross the river toward Puget Sound by way of the Cowelitz Valley. There is a sufficient depth of water at St. Helen to accommodate the largest vessels.

Just above this point the Lower Wallamet falls into the Columbia, the two rivers embracing a fertile island, called Sauvies, about twenty miles in length, where some of the Hudson's Bay Company's people formerly had farms, some of which are still held by them. The Lower Wallamet has a depth of water sufficient for the ocean steamers which sometimes pass this way in going up. At the upper mouth of the Wallamet are a number of small and beautiful islands, and the scene upon a fine summer afternoon is scarcely exceeded anywhere. The wide, blue, majestic Columbia receives the tributary waters of the clear and sparkling Wallamet, which join its nobler flood by several devious outlets among the islands, as if coy and teazing, and reluctant to betray itself all at once for the important adjunct that it is to its grander neighbor with whom it is silently being united, to be recognized no more in its individual character. With a fine sunset sky reflected in these waters, the lovely embowered islands, dotting them over, with the distant bluffs of the Wallamet in view on one hand, and the snowy peaks of Hood and St. Helen standing out grandly on the other, it makes a view scarcely to be surpassed in mingled beauty and sublimity: and must charm the eyes of a sea-weary emigrant with a double charm. It is a very pleasant sail from this point up to Portland on the Wallamet.

The Columbia above the mouth of the Wallamet grows more interesting, and sustains its interest for over a hundred miles. Vancouver on the Washington side, is the old post of the Hudson's Bay Company, and the present head-quarters of the Military Department of Oregon. The situation of Vancouver is charming, as is also the view of the river and the mountains at this place. The Oregon side of the Columbia for some distance is low and well wooded, representing by its depression the valley of the Wallamet. Soon, however, the rise of the foot-hills commences, then the very mountains themselves, until when you have arrived at the Cascades, you are in their very heart—you actually stand in a gap where mighty mountains have been parted. Before arriving at this point, the Lower Cascades village, you have been almost sated with magnificence, but when you leave the steamer and find yourself standing pigmy-like in the midst of the giant cliffs and peaks, nothing is left you but silent awe and delight.

SHERIDAN'S FISRT BATTLE-GROUND, COLUMBIA RIVER.

The "Cascades" are five miles of continuous rapids, where the river forces itself over a rocky inclined bed, through the heart of the Cascade Range. These rapids are passed by six miles of railway portage; and this ride affords such opportunities of wonderful sight-seeing as occur but seldom to the traveler. There is not the wild force to these rapids that you see when the Niagara rushes to its fall; but the variety of play of the water is infinitely greater, and the accessories far more magnificent. At the upper end of the Cascades is another little village, in a most picturesque situation. The river sets back here before rushing through the narrow gorge of the rapids, and forms a beautiful bay with an island or two in it, and beautifully wooded shores. Just above this bay is a sunken forest comprising a belt of timber a mile or two

CASTLE ROCK.

long and half a mile wide, nearly submerged by the waters of the river. Beyond, the first thing that strikes the eye is an immensely high and bald perpendicular cliff of red rock, pointed as a pyramid at the top, which looks as if freshly split off or parted from some other mass of rock, which other mass is nowhere visible.   Here comes in the Indian tradition of a bridge that once existed across the Columbia at this place, and which subsequently fell in, blocking up the river below and forming the rapids.   It looks probable enough to have suggested such an idea, even to an Indian; though the savage must attach a legend of offended spirits to his more natural conclusion in

HORSE-TAIL FALL.

order to account for it. The height and grandeur of the mountains above the Cascades is so great and overpowering that we feel no disposition to attempt anything like a description.   It cannot be described—it can only be felt; and that newspaper correspondent who lately pronounced the scenery of the Columbia River as insignificant, takes rank in our estimation beneath contempt.   The Hudson, which so long has been the pride of America, is but the younger brother of the majestic Columbia.   Place a hundred Dunderbergs side by side, and you have some conception of these stupendous bluffs.   Treble the height of the Palisades, and you can form an idea of these precipitous cliffs. Elevate the dwarfed evergreens of the Hudson Highlands into firs and pines like these, and then you may compare. We confess that we never enjoyed a journey more from the completeness of its impressions. There seemed nothing to desire— we only could gaze and dream; for even these wild Western waters are not without their historical and romantic interest. Down this strong, rapid, high-walled river, fifty years ago, floated the annual "brigade" of the Hudson's Bay Company, bringing the year's accumulation of peltries and the annual express from the Red River settlements and Canada. Ten years earlier, Lewis and Clarke had descended this great river in the service of the Gov-

VIEW ON THE COLUMBIA.

ernment; and a few years later a part of the Astor Expedition suffered all but death passing these rugged mountains in the winter. Only twenty years ago the yearly immigration to Oregon, arriving at the Dalles destitute and sick, late in the season, were dependent on the Hudson's Bay Company's boats to bring them down to the settlements. It was a terrible passage, and many, both of boatmen and immigrants, lost their lives in the fearful rapids. These were the incidents of pioneer life, now passed away; while we, tourists at leisure, dream and gaze from the deck of a first class steamer, with all our wants anticipated. Twenty years more will work marvels, but it is with feelings of satisfaction that we reflect it is not possible to man to intermeddle with the eternal majesty of these mountains. As God made them so they shall remain to be the wonder of all.

"Here," says our captain, "is Wind Mountain. The Indian name answers to our word *enchanted:* probably because the Indians found it so difficult to pass here when the wind was foul." On the opposite, or Oregon side, just where the foot-hills commence, is a fine fruit-farm, in a delightful situation, with Mt. Hood showing just back of it. About thirteen miles above the Cascades is one of the finest, if not quite the finest point on the river. While the steamer lies at a wood-yard taking on fuel, we have time to observe that the view is closed on either side of us by wooded promontories jutting past each other, and that the mountains seem to have attained their highest on either side of the river, thus enclosing us in a little sea, girt round with lofty cliffs of rugged rocks, or forest-crowned mountain ridges. Not far from here Hood river comes in, cold from the snows of the mighty mountain; and the very best view of that mountain is to be obtained. So near does it seem that we can see the glistening of the snow where its cliffs reflect the sun. Nearly opposite, the White Salmon enters the Columbia, and between the cleft heights you catch a passing glimpse of Mount Adams.

On leaving the summit line of the mountains at the

Cascades, the fir begins to disappear and soon the only timber seen on the bluffs, is pine and spruce. Even this becomes scattering, and on coming near the Dalles, the hills are almost bare. The worn basaltic rock which has

MOUNT HOOD FROM THE DALLES.

cropped out all along the river, from its mouth upward, is here everywhere apparent, protruding from the hills and walling in the river on both sides. But the hills are less abrupt, and slope back in long swells and ridges, covered with grass and dotted with scattering pines.

The Dalles (town) is a thriving business place, and a point of importance on the Columbia; the possible terminus of a branch Pacific Railroad. The scenery about the Dalles has a most remarkable wildness and singularity. You stand surrounded with evidences of the time when the region of the Columbia river was one vast field of molten rock and liquid fire. Once burnt by fire, long since worn by the elements into horizontal terraces, or perpendicular columns, and needle-pointed peaks, scored and seamed in every direction, cracked and toppling to their fall, the rocks which characterize the whole region of the Dalles make a very marked impression on the mind and memory of the beholder. The word *Dales* signifies troughs, and was first used by the French voyageurs to describe the narrow passage through which the river is forced at this place. It was easily corrupted into its present agreeable pronunciation, and remains the cognomen, not only of the trough of the Columbia, but has been conferred upon the town which lies just below the *Dale*.

The river narrows on approaching Dalles City, the beginning of a second portage, of sixteen miles, and flows through a sunken channel in solid rock for the whole of that distance. The depth of the fissure which forms its bed may be guessed at, when it is remembered that just above these Dalles the river is over a mile wide, and that in one part of its passage between Celilo and Dalles City, it is not over one hundred and sixty feet! The water has a dark green color, and boils and bubbles like the witches' cauldron in *Macbeth*. A glance at the map will suggest what the tumult must be when a river, whose branches stretch over so vast an extent of country, is compressed within a channel fifty yards wide. Yet the writer has conversed with a lady who passed through this terrible strait in a Hudson's Bay barge, when the oarsmen were thrown from their seats by the violent dashing of the waves made by the fearful eddies—passed in safety, too, though it was a feat seldom attempted, the voyageurs preferring to make the portage at this place.

The geography of the country, and the rapid development of the mining regions above, seem to point to Dalles City as the second great commercial point on the Columbia river. The town stands right on the rocky margin of the river, and extends back over the gradual rise by terraces of the outcropping trap-rock.   There is a thin soil of black mold over the hills, picturesque groves of pines, and a coating of fine grass.   Mt. Hood and Mt. Adams are in full view, and in the cloudless atmosphere of Eastern Oregon, nearly always visible.   A late slight eruption of Mt. Hood, lasting for several hours, must have been distinctly visible from this point.   Some historical interest attaches to the spot where Dalles City stands, from the fact of its having been one of the early Missions, and one of the earliest military posts in Oregon.

A railroad portage conveys the passenger sixteen miles to Celilo; the greater portion of the distance being close along the river, in sight of its rapids and eddies.   There are enormous drifts of sand, which the high winds keep constantly shifting, and which cause much annoyance both to the company who are obliged to employ men to clear the track, and to travelers who wish to see the country. These drifts extend the whole length of the road.   In fact everywhere above the Dalles, sand and wind are the enemies of comfort during the summer months.

Celilo is a little new town, with no pretensions to business except such as the O. S. N. Company's transactions there furnish.   Its distinguishing feature is an immense warehouse, nearly a thousand feet in length, built upon an incline of forty feet, to accommodate boats in all stages of water.   This great warehouse is one of several that will be built at points along the river, if the business of the upper country increases as there is every reason to believe it must increase.

The river at Celilo and for a long distance above is one continuous expanse of foaming rapids.   It hurries over broken torturing rocks, lashing itself into the wildest excitement, which the incline of its bed renders more im-

37

petuous. Such is the rapidity of its flow that the water is apparently, and no doubt actually, piled up higher in the middle of the channel, so that it seems to slope off on either side.

Just above Celilo comes in the Des Chutes River, very rapid and wide at its mouth ; and a little further up on the other side is the town of Columbus, which at present is little more than a wood-yard. Twenty miles above Celilo, on the Oregon side again, John Day River comes by a narrow high-walled mouth which scarcely betrays its locality. A few wood-yards and the Grande Ronde Landing are the only improvements along the river, until we arrive at Umatilla, ninety-six miles above the Dalles. Along this whole distance not a single tree is visible, except such willows and shrubs as grow on the borders of sand-bars and islands. Umatilla, or Utilla, as the Indian name is spelled, is a new and still very small town at the mouth of the Umatilla river, and derives its business from the fact of its being a starting point for the mines of Boise and Owyhee. The banks of the Columbia here are low and smooth, and nothing is in sight from the steamer's deck but extensive rolling plains, covered with bunch-grass. Back ten or twelve miles from the river, however, some timber is found for fuel, and further back in the mountains is timber in abundance for lumbering purposes.

There is the same general aspect all along the Columbia to its forks, and also for the whole length of its southern branch, the Snake or Lewis river. Wallula, situated a few miles below the forks, is the last town of any importance on the Columbia. It is beautifully located at the mouth of the Walla-Walla river, and is a point of considerable importance, where mining outfits are procured, and freight trains started out for the mines. It is a sort of port to Walla-Walla, thirty miles further on the road to

Idaho. Wallula is old Fort Walla-Walla, while Walla-Walla City is near the old Presbyterian mission of Waii-latpu, and the modern Fort Walla-Walla.

" White Bluffs is situated about forty miles above the mouth of Snake river. From Wallula to White Bluffs the river is smooth and deep, offering no obstructions whatever to navigation. From this last named point the river cannot be navigated further until we reach Colville. Between these two places it makes a long detour, so that, following its course, the distance from one point to the other is about 350 miles. The stream is so broken by rapids the whole way that boats cannot run upon it. The bars along the river have long been worked, yielding small pay; but they are now almost abandoned by the whites, who are looking for richer mines, and in their stead are come great numbers of Chinese; some from Oregon, but the greater number from British Columbia. It is believed that there are now above one thousand of these persons working on the river between Priest's Rapids and Colville. They are said to be making from two to five or six dollars per day.

From White Bluffs to Colville by land, the distance is one hundred and fifty miles. The road is excellent, there being no mountains or hills, and but one considerable stream—the Spokane—on the way. White Bluffs is the nearest point to Colville which steamboats can reach, and is now a post of some importance. It seems to be favorably situated to receive a large share of the trade of the upper Columbia river.

Above Colville, for several hundred miles, the river flows through a succession of lakes, rendering navigation easy. A steamer is now running between Colville and Boat Encampment. Rich mines are said to have been discovered, near this latter place, which is about three hundred miles beyond Colville. About fifty miles above Colville the Hudson's Bay Company have established a new trading post which they call Fort Shepherd, by means of which they expect to command the trade of that region. There has been much activity in the search for gold throughout this whole region, and its trade steadily increases.

There has also been strong effort to make a road over from the waters of Fraser river to the Columbia, but the attempt has resulted in nothing. Between these two streams there is an exceedingly high chain of mountains over which it will be forever impossible to carry goods. Hence everything that is consumed east of these high mountains must go by way of the Columbia."

On all the other northern branches of the Columbia, the Kootenai, and head-waters of the Clark especially, gold has been discovered in paying quantities, causing a rush of miners to those districts, and the consequent accompaniment of trade. Already there is competition between the merchants of the Missouri and those of the Columbia as to the profits of trade in the Blackfoot country. Captain Mullan, in his "Miner's and Traveler's Guide," has given so favorable an account of the climate and agricultural resources of this northern region that there is good reason to believe it must soon be settled up by a permanent farming community. The numerous Catholic Missions established through this region confirm the account of its adaptability to settlement, while it is a well established fact that the Hudson's Bay Company's servants have had farms for twenty-five years in this latitude, and have raised the same crops raised in our northwestern States. The yield of wheat was especially good, averaging forty bushels to the acre.

From these facts it will be seen that the Columbia does not rise in a barren, desolate region of country; and that instead, the mighty river flows from first to last through a country rich in mineral and agricultural wealth, only waiting for development.

The Snake, or Southern branch of the Columbia, offers no obstacle to continuous navigation by the Oregon Steam Navigation Company's boats, which line of steamers run regularly, except in low water, from Portland to Lewiston, Idaho, a distance of about four hundred miles. Beyond this point navigation is interrupted for the next one hundred and forty miles, by falls and rapids. Beyond this, however, it is believed there exists no obstacle to navigation for another two hundred miles; and the Oregon Steam Navigation Company have already made roads to, and built steamers on this portion of the Snake river, with the intention of carrying passengers and freight on this route as far as the crossing of the Boise and Owyhee wagon-road. It is expected to bring the boats of the Missouri and Columbia within five hundred miles of each other.   Under these circumstances there must be a lively competition for the trade of the great interior mining territories—a competition which will do much, with that of California and the Colorado river projects, to open up and develop the country, and to hasten on the advent in these mountain regions of the iron horse and the great Pacific Railways.

Very much of the development of Eastern Oregon and Idaho is owing to the well conducted enterprises of the Oregon Steam Navigation Company; and it is only proper in speaking of the resources of the Columbia to make the following extract from the letter of an Oregon gentleman and pioneer:

" Some dozen or more years ago different steamboat projects commenced upon the Columbia.   Then there were no mines found, and the inducement was to carry the freight of the United States Government to military posts and Indian Agencies in the interior; transport the overland emigrations, and have a natural increase of travel with the expected growth of the upper country. Gradually steamboats of primitive make and small dimensions were built on the navigable stretches of the river to connect with the portages, of which there are two—the first at the Cascades, seventy miles from Portland, of five miles; and another, at the Dalles, forty-five miles above, of fifteen miles.   The discovery of gold far north, at Fraser river and Powderway, gave some of these steamboat and railroad men a confidence that the mountains east were all gold-bearing.   On the strength of which rude tramways or railroads were made at great expense around the Cascades on either side of the Columbia river, and indebtedness and expense incurred that would inevitably have ruined the men who undertook them, only that time justified their belief, and the result made them rich, for which they have to thank no one but themselves.   Some eight or ten years ago, all these steamboat interests were consolidated under the present company.   As the business increased, the improvements of the company kept pace with it, and to-day elegant boats are running on each stretch of the river, connected by twenty miles of excellent railroads, one of six miles at the Cascades, and one of fourteen miles at the Dalles.   The Oregon Steam Navigation Company, whose original capital was some $300,000 (or at least the different steamboat lines which were consolidated were assessed at that figure,) now own, by purchase, the railroad lines on each side of the Cascades, which gives them an effective monopoly, and have property valued at not less than $2,000,000.   They have made but few dividends, never more than twelve per cent. per annum, but have constantly kept adding their earnings to their cap-

ital in the way of improvements, until their enterprise has made the difficult
channel of the Columbia one of the most varied and agreeable lines of travel
upon this continent.   Their wharves, warehouses, railroads, and steamers are
magnificent proofs of generous enterprise, and their honorable pride is to extend and improve them constantly in the future.

   Thirteen years ago this spring I ascended the Columbia to the Dalles in row-
boats against the current.   It took us seventeen days of hard labor to make
the up trip.   Now it takes us ten to twelve hours to accomplish the same distance in comfort and safety."

   The scenery of the Snake River resembles that of the
main Columbia above the Dalles, except that it is upon a
smaller scale.   Like the Upper Columbia, it is distinguished for its falls and rapids.   The American Falls furnishes
one of the finest views of the wonderful forms of col-
umnar basalt to be found anywhere.   The river here flows
between high picturesque bluffs of weather-worn trap
rock, and falls over a ledge of the same; the fall being
divided by a rocky island in the middle, around which the
water sweeps in wild haste and is dashed to foam as it de-
scends upon other rocks below, rising again in clouds of
spray from the bosom of the tortured river.

   The Owyhee, the Boise, the Payette, the Salmon, and
the Clearwater, are all more or less important tributaries
of the southern branch of the Columbia; flowing as they
do through the richest mineral districts, watering fertile
valleys, or affording water and water power to the miner.
High divides generally separate the several water-courses,
which mountains are covered with excellent timber.   The
early emigrant to Oregon who traversed the weary road
from the Mississippi to the Lower Columbia, thought all
a desert that laid between the Rocky and Cascade ranges
of mountains.   The aspect of this intermediate territory
will henceforth rapidly be changed.   No more weary
marches over alkali deserts, sage or sand plains; no more
toiling over the Blue and Cascade Mountains.   No more

starvation and misery on the last end of the journey. Boats will meet the emigration somewhere about the Big Camas Prairie at all events before it enters upon the roughest portion of the route, and thence the transit to the Wallamet Valley, or to any other point of settlement will be made easy.

CHAPTER XLVIII.

GOLD was first discovered on the eastern side of the Rocky Mountains, in the month of August, 1862, by a party of miners who wintered on the head-waters of Jefferson's Fork : since which time new discoveries have been constantly made, and Montana seems in a fair way to grow rapidly into a State. Towns are starting up in every part of the Territory, whose growth will not be permanently checked even by a failure of the mining interests of the country.

All writers from Montana agree in pronouncing it to be the most delightful mountain country they have ever visited ; but as successful gold-hunters are not always to be believed by those who have no interests in their favorite region, we have thought best to ignore their opinions entirely, and quote from authorities whose only business in that country has been to explore it. In the Report of Gov. Stevens, on the Pacific Railroad, we find the following :—

"If the voyageur traveling over this country, whatever route he takes, be asked what sort of a country it is, he will tell you, an excellent country for traveling—wood, water, and grass everywhere. But the pine of the Spokane extends nearly to its mouth, and for some miles south of the river. The Spokane is the name of the main stream to its junction with the Coeur d' Alene river, when its name is given to a smaller tributary coming from the north, the Coeur d' Alene being the main stream. One of the most beautiful features of the Coeur d' Alene river and country is the Coeur d' Alene lake, which is embosomed in the midst of gently sloping hills, covered with a dense forest growth ; the irregularity of its form, and the changing aspect of the scenery about it, makes it one of the most picturesque objects in the interior. The Coeur d'

Alene river itself has tributaries flowing from near the main divide of the Bitter Root, the most considerable of which is the St. Joseph's river, which has a general parallel direction with the Coeur d' Alene, and is about twenty miles south of it.

" The whole valley of the Coeur 'd' Alene and Spokane is well adapted to settlement, abounding in timber for building and for fires, exceedingly well watered, and the greater portion of the land arable.—North of the Great Plain, that is from the Spokane to the 49th parallel east of the main Columbia, the country for the most part is densely wooded, although many valleys and open places occur, some of them now occupied by settlers, and all presenting advantages for settlement. Down Clarke's Fork itself there are open patches of considerable size, and so on the Kootenai River. North of the Spokane is a large prairie, known as the Coeur d' Alene prairie, through which the trail passes from Walla-Walla to Lake Pend d' Oreille. This prairie contains some six hundred square miles. * * * * * *

" It is the country, therefore, between these two great backbones of the Rocky Mountains which I now wish to describe, and especially will I first call attention to that beautiful region whose streams, flowing from the great semicircle of the Rocky Mountains before referred to, pass through a delightful grazing and arable country, and find their confluence in the Bitter Boot River, opposite Hell-Gate.

" From Big Hole Prairie, on the south, flows the Bitter Root River, which has also a branch from the southwest, up which a trail is much used by Indians and voyageurs passing to the Nez Perce country and Walla-Walla. The Bitter Root valley, above Hell-Gate river, is about eighty miles long, and from three to ten in width, having a direction north and south from the sources of the Bitter Root river to its junction with the Hell-Gate. Besides the outlet above mentioned,* towards the Kooskooskia, which is the most difficult, it has an excellent wagon-road communication at its head by the Big Hole Pass to Jefferson's Fork, Fort Hall, and other points southward, as well as by the Hell-Gate routes to the eastward. From its lower end, at the junction of the Hell-Gate, it is believed the Bitter Root river is, or can be made, navigable for small steamers for long distances, at least, thus affording an easy outlet to its products in the natural direction. Hell-Gate (Pass) is the debauche of all the considerable streams which flow into the Bitter Root, eighty-five miles below its source at the Big Hole divide. The distance from Hell-Gate to its junction with the Bitter Root is fifteen miles. It must not be understood from the term Hell-Gate that here is a narrow passage with perpendicular bluffs; on the contrary it is a wide, open, and easy pass, in no case being less than half a mile wide, and the banks not subject to overflow. At Hell-Gate is the junction of two streams, the one being the Hell-Gate river, and the other the Big Blackfoot river. The Hell-Gate itself drains the semicircle of the Rocky Mountains from parallel 45° 45' to parallel 46° 30', a distance on the divide of eighty miles. The upper waters

---

* Omitted here.

of this river connect with Wisdom River, over a low and easy divide, across which Lieut. Mullan with his party moved on Dec. 31, 1853.

"Moving down this valley fifteen miles, we come to a most beautiful prairie known as the Deer Lodge, a great resort for game, and a favorite resting place for Indians—mild through the winter, and affording inexhaustible grass the year round. There is a remarkable curiosity in this valley—the Boiling Springs, which have been described by Lieut. Mullan. This Deer Lodge Prairie is watered by many streams, those coming from the east, having their sources also in the Rocky Mountain divide, and these coming from the west in the low, rolling, and open country intervening between the Hell-Gate and Bitter Root rivers.

"The Little Blackfoot, which has been referred to, is one of the most important streams on the line of communication through this whole mountain region. It has an open, well-grassed, and arable valley, with sweet cotton-wood on the streams, and pine generally on the slopes of the hills; but the forests are quite open, and both on its northern and southern slopes there is much prairie country. The Little Blackfoot river furnishes two outlets to the country to the east. It was the southern one of these passes, connecting with the southern tributary of the Prickly Pear creek, that Mr. Tinkham passed over in 1853, and determined a profile of the route. It was also passed over by Lieut. Mullan on his trip from the Muscle Shell, in 1853, but the northern pass was first discovered by Lieut. Mullan when he passed over it with a wagon from Fort Benton, in March, 1854. There is another tributary of the Little Blackfoot flowing into it below the point where Lieut. Mullan struck it with his wagon, which may furnish a good pass to the plains of the Missouri. Its advantages and character were described to him by the Indians.

"Passing down the Hell-Gate river, from the mouth of the Little Blackfoot, we come to several tributaries flowing from the south. Flint Creek, one of them, is a large stream, up the valley of which there is a short route to the Bitter Root valley, in a direction west-southwest from its junction with Hell-Gate. On these rivers are prairies as large as the Deer Lodge prairie, and the whole country between the Deer Lodge Prairie due west to the Bitter Root valley consists much more of prairie than of forest land.

"The Hell-Gate river is thus seen to be one hundred and thirty miles long, flowing for sixty miles through the broad and fertile Deer Lodge Prairie, which is estimated to contain eight hundred square miles of arable land. Then taking a direction more transverse to the mountain, opens its valley, continues from two to five miles wide, until its junction with the Big Blackfoot, at Hell-Gate, after which it widens out to unite with the valley of the Bitter Root. On this part of it there are least one hundred and fifty square miles of fine arable land, and as much grazing prairie on the adjoining hills. * * * * * *

Passing from the Hell-Gate to the Flathead River, we cross over this spur by a low divide, going through the Coriacan defile, and coming upon the waters of the Jocko river. The height of this divide above the Hell-Gate is 560 feet, and above the Flathead river, at the mouth of the Jocko, is 650 feet. From this divide a view of surpassing beauty, looking northward, is presented to the beholder. He sees before him an extraordinarily well-grassed, well-watered, and inviting country. On the East are the divides, clothed with pine, separating the Jocko and its tributaries from the streams running into the Big Blackfoot, and into Flathead Lake. To the North the Flathead Lake, twenty-five miles long and six miles wide, is spread open before you with extensive prairies beyond, and on the West, sloping back from the banks of the Flathead River, a mingled prairie and forest country is seen. Here in a compact body, is one of the most promising countries in this whole region, having at least 2,000 square miles of arable land.

Below the lake the Flathead River flows, following its windings some fifty miles, to its junction with the Bitter Root, where the united streams assume the name of Clarke's Fork. In this distance it is 100 to 200 yards wide, and so deep as to be fordable with difficulty at low water, its depth being three feet in the shallowest places. Its current is rapid, and there is a fall of fifteen feet, five miles below the lake. About eighteen miles below the lake it receives a considerable stream from the northwest called Hot Spring Creek. In its valley, and around it, is also a large extent of fine land. Nearly opposite, a small stream runs in from the East, and another from the same side ten miles below, by which there are routes to the upper part of Big Blackfoot Valley. None of the branches of Clarke's Fork above the junction can be considered navigable, but the river itself, (Flathead,) with the exception of the rapids and falls below the lake, which may be passed by a short canal, gives a navigation of at least seventy-five miles to the head of Flathead Lake.   *   *   *   *

About one hundred and thirty miles above the mouth of Clarke's Fork is the Pend d'Oreille or Kalispelum Lake, which is a beautiful sheet of water about forty-five miles in length, formed by the dilation of the river. The river is sluggish and wide for some twenty-six miles below the lake, where rapids occur during low water. Steamboats could ascend from this point to a point nine miles above the lake, or eighty miles in all. At high water they could ascend much farther. Between the Cabinet (twenty-five miles above the lake) and a point seventy-five miles below the lake, (a total distance of one hundred and forty miles,) the only obstacle which occurs is where the river is divided by rocky islands, with a fall of six and a-half feet on one side. The valley of Clarke's Fork is generally wide, arable, and inviting settlement, though much of it is wooded.   *   *   *   *   *   *   *   *   *

From the divide of the Rocky Mountains to the divide of the Bitter Root Mountains there is an intermediate region, over one-third of which is a cultivable area, and a large portion of it is prairie country, instead of a wooded or mountain country. The following estimate gives in detail the areas of arable land, so far as existing information enables it to be computed: In the region watered by the Bitter Root River and its tributaries, not including Hell-Gate, the prairie region may be estimated at three thousand square miles; in that watered by the Hell-Gate and its tributaries, including the whole country south and west to the Bitter Root, but not including the Big Blackfoot, there is a prairie region of two thousand five hundred square miles; in that watered by the Big Blackfoot and its tributaries, the prairie region is one thousand three hundred square miles. The country watered by the Flathead River, down to its junction with the Bitter Root, and thence down Clarke's Fork to the Cabinet has a prairie region of two thousand five hundred square miles. The country watered by the Kootenai has two thousand square miles of prairie. Thus we have, in round numbers, eleven thousand three hundred square miles of prairie land. The whole area of the mountain region, (from the divide of the Rocky Mountains to the divide of the Bitter Root, and from 45° 30′ to 49°) is about thirty thousand square miles, and it will be a small estimate to put the arable land of the prairie and the forest at twelve thousand square miles. Thus the country in the Forks of the Flathead and Bitter Root, stretching away east above the Blackfoot Canon is mostly table-land, well watered and arable, and on all these tributaries—the Bitter Root, the Hell-Gate, the Big Blackfoot, the Jocko, the Maple River, the Hot Spring River, and the Lou-Lou Fork itself— the timber-land will be found unquestionably better than the prairie-land. It will not be in the immediate bottom or valley of the river where farmers will find their best locations, but on the smaller tributaries some few miles above their junction with the main streams. The traveler passing up these rivers, and seeing a little tributary breaking out in the valley, will on going up it, invariably come to an open and beautiful country. The observer who has passed through this country often, who has had with him intelligent men who have lived in it long, who understands intercourse with the Indians, and knows how to verify information which they give him, will be astonished at the conclusions which he will reach in regard to the agricultural advantages of this country, and it will not be many years before the progress of settlements will establish its superiority as an agricultural region."

The prediction of the late distinguished explorer is about to be realized, more rapidly perhaps than he had ever contemplated. Though owing its rapid settlement to the discovery of mines of gold and silver, Montana Territory is destined to retain a large proportion of its adventurous population, and to invite permanent settlers by the greatness of her varied resources, for besides the precious metals, her valleys abound in the more common and useful materials of marble, limestone, cinnabar, copper, sandstone, lead, plumbago, iron, coal, and the best of timber for lumbering purposes. Add to these a most healthful and delightful climate, and the most agreeable scenery, and there is nothing left to desire which should constitute a happy home for thousands of hardy emigrants.

Remarks on the Climate of Montana. . The first involuntary remark of those who have never considered the
subject, is, that a railroad carried as far north as Montana
would be almost certain to be annually obstructed by
snows. A brief review of the facts, however, will speedily
convince the intelligent reader that of the two roads the
Northern and the Central, the former will not be in as
much danger from a snow blockade as the latter. In the
first place, the actual altitude of the Rocky Mountains is
not so great in the latitude of Montana as it is on the line
of the Central road by about two thousand feet. Secondly,
Montana has a climate modified both by the warm winds
that blow from the hot plains of the southwest, and over
the boiling springs of a large tract of volcanic country to
the south of it, or rather in its southern part. And besides
all these modifying local circumstances the isothermal line
which crosses it, and has its course westwardly to Puget's
Sound, has a mean annual temperature of 50°, thus deter-
mining the question of climate.

Experience, however, is the one authority to which men
safely and confidently refer, and this is in favor of Montana.
If the reader has noted the fact so often mentioned in the
narrative portion of this book, that the hunters and trappers of the Rocky Mountains seldom or never wintered
near the South Pass, but had their favorite wintering
grounds in the bend of the Yellowstone, or upon the borders of one of the affluents of the Missouri nearly directly
east of the Pass talked of for the Northern Railroad, he
must at once have come to the conclusion that the climate
of this region is superior in mildness to that farther south.
It was here that the fur-hunters found grass and sweet cotton-wood for their animals, and it was here that game
resorted for food during the snows of winter in such
numbers as to fairly invade the camps of the companies.

Resources of Montana. Besides the precious metals, which have yielded since 1864 a sum of $80,000,000, Montana contains also an abundance of copper, iron, coal, salt, and other metals and minerals. Its lumbering resources are about equal to those of Washington Territory, and its farming resources probably are superior. Nowhere in the new Territories is there a better opening for regular and legitimate labor, notwithstanding the reputation of Montana is based principally upon its mines.

CHAPTER XLIX.

Climate of the Pacific Coast. The Western coasts of
all large bodies of land have a warmer temperature than
the Eastern.   Latitude on the Pacific coast seems to have
but little influence on climate, compared to its effect on
the coast of the Atlantic.   Astoria, at the mouth of the
Columbia river, has a mean temperature of 54°, while
Nisqually, on Puget Sound, being a degree further north,
but also a considerable distance inland from the ocean, has
a mean temperature of 58.5°.   Frost seldom penetrates
the ground anywhere near the coast, and it never snows at
Astoria, though snow sometimes falls in the northern portion of the Olympic peninsula in Washington Territory.
The places named, be it remembered, are in the same lat-
itude with the Lake Superior region and the Sault St.
Marie of the Western States, and of the frozen coast of
New Brunswick.

As we proceed inland, greater extremes of heat and
cold are experienced.   At Portland, which is in latitude
45° 30', the mean summer temperature is 66.33°, although
there are occasional days, two or three together, when the
thermometer stands at 110° in the shade during three or
four hours of the afternoon, suddenly falling at the approach of evening.   The winters in the interior vary
greatly in degrees of cold.   It is very rarely that the
ground is frozen, or that snow lies upon the ground; yet
the "oldest inhabitants" remember one winter when the

thermometer fell to 15° below zero in the Wallamet valley, and to 26° below zero in the Umpqua valley, which is rather more elevated. It is to elevation in fact that the great differences of climate are due in this region. Sixty miles away from Portland, in the Cascade Mountains, it is cold and snowing heavily, when there is a warm rain at this point. Snow also falls in the Coast Mountains, while on either side of them there is perpetual verdure.

At the Dalles, very nearly east of Portland, but on the other side of the Cascade Mountains, there is an entirely different climate. From the superior elevation of the country we might look for much more severe cold in winter, and a cooler temperature in summer. But here another modifying influence comes in—that of the warm air from the great burning plains of California and the south. The Cascade Mountains intercept the moisture from the ocean, which is discharged in rain on the valleys of Western Oregon, while Eastern Oregon lies under a cloudless sky, and is warmed by the heated air from the rainless country farther to the south. This rarefied air rising, causes the setting in of the strong current of air from the ocean which gives to Western Oregon its steady prevailing winds; these winds blowing from the northwest in summer, and from the southwest in winter. Under these influences while Western Oregon and Washington have a moist climate, Eastern Oregon and Idaho have a very dry climate. The summers are hot and dry, frosts commence in October, but the winter does not begin until quite late, and lasts but a short time, with little rain and snow. Ten degrees below zero is reckoned exceedingly cold on these plains. Nearer to the mountain ranges to the east, there is more rain, and greater variability of climate, though it still continues mild. On the Clearwater, in Northern Idaho, three years observations place the mean temperature at 53°;

and at Ft. Colville the mercury sometimes rises to 100°
in summer, and falls to 12° in winter.   This portion of the
country is subject to heavy frosts in Spring, which makes
the season of planting and harvesting shorter.

Captain Mullan accounts for the mild climate of the
Rocky Mountains in Montana by supposing that the infi-
nite number of hot-springs and geysers which exist at the
head-waters of the Columbia, Missouri, and Yellowstone
Rivers, must modify the climate of this elevated region.
He also says further:

" The meteorological statistics collected during a great number of years have
enabled us to trace an isochimenal line across the continent, from St. Joseph's,
Missouri, to the Pacific, and the direction taken by this line is wonderful and
worthy the most important attention in all future legislation that looks towards
the travel and settlement of this country.   This line which leaves St. Joseph's
in latitude 40°, follows the general line of the Platte to Fort Laramie, where,
from newly introduced causes, it tends northwestwardly between the Wind
River chain and the Black Hills, crossing the summit of the Rocky Mountains in
latitude 47°; showing that in the interval from St. Joseph's it had gained six
degrees of latitude.   Tracing it still further westward it goes as high as 48°,
and developes itself in a fan-like shape in the plains of the Columbia.   From
Fort Laramie to the Clarke's Fork, I call this an atmospheric river of heat, varying in width from one to one hundred miles.   On its either side, north and south,
are walls of cold air, and which are so clearly perceptible, that you always
detect when you are upon its shores.

It would seem natural that the large volume of air in motion between the
Wind River chain and the Black Hills must receive a certain amount of heat as
it passes over the line of hot boiling springs here found, which, added to the
great heat evolved from the large volumes of water here existing, which is constantly cumulative, must all tend to modify its temperature to the extent that
the thermometer detects.   The prevalent direction of the winds, the physical
face of the country, its altitude, and the large volume of water, all, doubtless,
enter to create this modification; but from whatsoever cause it arises, it exists
as a fact that must for all time enter as an element worthy of every attention
in lines of travel and communication from the eastern plains to the north Pacific.   A comparison of the altitude of the South Pass, with the country on its
every side, with Mullan's Pass, further to the north, may be useful in this connection.   The South Pass has an altitude of seven thousand four hundred and
eighty-nine feet above the level of the sea.   The Wind River chain, to its
north, rises till it attains, at Frémont's Peak, an elevation of thirteen thousand
five hundred and seventy feet, while to the north the mountains increase in al-

38

titude till they attain, at Long's Peak, an elevation of fifteen thousand feet; while the plains to the east have an elevation of six thousand feet, and the mountains to the west, forming the east rim of the great basin, have an elevation of eight thousand two hundred and thirty-four feet, and the country between it and the South Pass an elevation of six thousand two hundred and thirty-four feet above the level of the sea. The highest point on the road in the summit line at Mullan's Pass has an elevation of six thousand feet, which is lower by fourteen hundred and eighty-nine feet than the South Pass, and allowing what we find to be here the case, viz: two hundred and eighty feet of altitude for each degree of temperature, we see that Mullan's Pass enjoys six degrees of milder temperature, due to this difference of altitude alone. At the South Pass are many high snow peaks, as Frémont's Peak, Three Tetons, Laramie Peak, Long's Peak, and others, all of which must tend to modify the temperature; whereas, to the north we have no high snow peaks, but the mountains have a general elevation of from seven to eight thousand feet above the level of the sea, and of most marked uniformity in point of altitude.

The high range of the Wind River chain stands as a curvilinear wall to deflect and direct the currents of the atmosphere as they sweep across the continent. All their slopes are well located to reflect back the direct rays of the heat of the sun to the valleys that lay at their bases. These valleys, already warm by virtue of the hot springs existing among them, receive this accumulative heat, which, driven by the new currents of cold air from the plains, rises and moves onward in the form of a river towards the valleys of the Rocky Mountains, where it joins the milder current from the Pacific and diffuses over the whole region a mild, healthy, invigorating, and useful climate."

While the climate of the Valleys, Plains, and Mountains is such as we have described, it is possible to find almost every modification of heat and cold, and moisture and dryness, within these general limits, by seeking certain altitudes or depressions more or less remote from the sea, and having the aid of certain other influences. The vales of Italy, or the glaciers of Switzerland are alike accessible.

Reclamation of Dry Lands by Irrigation. In a recent letter of Hon. John Bidwell, of California, is the following sensible proposition:

" There are millions of acres of dry and apparently sterile land to be found all over the Pacific slope. Is it always to remain in the present condition? There exists no necessity that it should do so. The land possesses in abundance all the elements of fertility. There is one and but one remedy—irrigation. Some have prejudices against irrigation, that must be overcome, because it will require the united effort of all who have a property interest in the State, to begin and carry on such an enterprise upon a scale worthy of the object in view. Once accomplished, lands that are now absolutely worthless would become most valuable. The same encouragement should, in my judgment, be given to bringing water on land that is worthless without it, as to take water from land that is useless with it. The dry, as well as the swamp, lands require reclamation—one will cost relatively as much as the other. Why, then, should not the Government be willing to donate the dry lands to the State as well as the swamp lands?"

to which the *Alta California* adds:

"It is strictly true that there are millions of acres in California now lying unclaimed, unproductive, unoccupied, and worthless, simply because of lack of irrigation, which might be supplied. If our State were as well provided with ditches as was ancient Judea, Spain under the Arabs, or India at the present day, we should have thrice as much land fit for gardens as we actually have. More dry land than swamp needs reclamation in California. The waters of winter and the snows of the Sierras, by careful management, might be made to yield as much treasure as the auriferous sands of the Sacramento basin. Other nations have reclaimed tracts as large and as dry as the San Joaquin and Tulare valleys, and why should we not do as much?"

The same necessity will exist for irrigation in Eastern Oregon and Idaho that exists in California at present, and the means for irrigation are much more abundant, inasmuch as there are thousands of mountain streams of the very best water which might be conveyed and converted to purposes of irrigation. The climate of the West Coast is in all respects very similar to that of ancient Judea, Spain, and other countries where by irrigation the barren plains were made gardens of beauty. The great aqueducts of the Romans, and even those of the Spaniards in Mexico, still remain to testify to the importance and value of irrigation in warm and dry countries. There will yet be some wonderful engineering performed west of the Rocky Mountains, proving that Moderns are nowise inferior in energy or expedients to the Ancients.

Productiveness of the soil. There is no country which will better repay the expense of irrigation than this. Almost every square mile, not entirely naked rock, is rich and productive to a wonderful degree. You have only to cast seed and water upon the loose sand-hills about San Francisco in California, to have them become beds of bloom. Wherever water is given to the soil anywhere, vegetation springs up.

In Western Oregon, where there is plenty of moisture, there is a perfectly wonderful amount of vegetation, from gigantic trees to gigantic ferns; and never has the farmer failed of his harvest since the settlement of the country.

There is no doubt whatever but some method will be found of neutralizing the effect of the too great proportion of alkali in some parts of Eastern Oregon, by which process great results in the way of grain and vegetables may be expected. Those foot-hills of the mountains where the light volcanic ash is found, ought to be put into grape culture, as there is no better soil for the production of that delicious fruit. There are marsh lands for meadows and uplands for sheep-grazing; in short, every reasonable want of humanity may be supplied in this truly wonderful region, which will become in time the glory and pride of the great Republic of the United States.

Scenery of the North-West Coast. Hardly can there be in any one country in the world more of the elements of the grand and wonderful than are to be found among the mountains, and along the rivers of Oregon and the adjacent Territories. The massive size and extent of the Rocky Mountains rather lessens the idea of their superior height, but the steeper slopes of the Cascade Mountains, rising as they do, on one side, from a valley, and made more striking by the numbers of snowy peaks, covered too with magnificent forests far up their rugged sides, all enhances their appearance of grandeur.

But it is when they are explored and their solitary wonders brought to view that their real magnificence is understood.   Notwithstanding their narrow base, the Cascade Mountains are not to be crossed by one dividing ridge, but are formed of many ridges running in all directions, and thrown together in extraordinary confusion, making awful chasms which impede the progress of the explorer, and presenting acclivities up which it is in vain to attempt to proceed.   Once upon their summits, however, and the traveler's toil is repaid.   "In one view he may embrace the rugged steeps of the Green Mountains, the blue, wooded slopes of the Alleghanies, and the ice-crowned peaks of the Alps; the volcanic piles of the Andes, the broad plateaux of Brazil, the fertile prairies of the upper Mississippi, and the lawns, groves and copses of the sunny South.   To the eastward he beholds an immense plateau, or elevated plain, relieved at distant intervals by spurs from the mountain chains, and sloping gently in different directions, toward the various streams, which, wending their way through mountain gorges to the ocean, or to some silent lake, drain the eastern portion of the State. To the west he surveys a country diversified by great rivers, and small streamlets; by tall mountains, and deeply embosomed vale; by gentle undulations, and precipitous, high-walled canons; by dark, frowning forests of pine and fir, spruce and cedar, which the eye fails to penetrate, and natural gardens all carpeted over with luxuriant grasses, redolent with the odors of wild flowers, and full of the music of winged choristers."

Down the precipitous cliffs rush mountain torrents, leaping from rock to rock, by their number giving to this chain of mountains their characteristic name.   And when these mountain torrents have reached the level of the plain below they scarcely lose their mountain peculiarities, but go dashing and foaming over rocky beds, almost to their very mouths; so much disturbed by rocks, and so rapid that very few rivers having their source in the Cascade Mountains can ever be made navigable.

Very many curious things are found on the summits of the Rocky and Cascade Mountains; wonderful lakes, mountains of cinders, fresh as if just from the volcanic forge; sea-shells and corals. One of these wonderful mountain lakes is thus described by a gentleman who visited it:

"Upon rising the slope bounding the lake, the first impression made upon your mind is one of disappointment; it does not come up to your expectations; but this is only momentary. A second look and you begin to comprehend the majestic beauties of the scenery spread out before you, and you sit down on the brink of the precipice, and feast your eyes on the awful grandeur; your thoughts wander back thousands of years to the time when, where now is a placid sheet of water, there was a lake of fire, throwing its cinders and ashes to a vast distance in every direction. The whole surroundings prove this lake to be the crater of an extinct volcano. The appearance of the water in the basin, as seen from the top of the mountain, is that of a vast circular sheet of canvass, upon which some painter had been exercising his art. The color of the water is blue, but in very many different shades, and like the colors in variegated silk, continually changing. Now a spot will be dark blue, almost approaching black, in the next moment it will change to a very pale blue; and it is thus continually changing from one shade to another. I cannot account for this changeableness, as the sky was perfectly clear, and it could not have been caused by any shadows; there was, however, a gentle breeze which caused a ripple of the waters; this may account for it.

At first sight a person would not estimate the surface of the water to be more than two or three hundred feet below the summit of the surrounding bluffs; and it is only after a steady look, almost perpendicularly down into the water, that you begin to comprehend the distance. In looking down into the lake the vision seems to stop before reaching the bottom, and, to use a common expression, you have to look twice before you see the bottom.

Heretofore it has been thought by those who have visited the lake, that it was impossible to get to the water, and this was also my impression at first sight, and I should have been contented to remain on the summit, and view its beauties from that point, without attempting to get to the water, but for Sergeant Stearns and Mr. Ford, who, after gazing awhile from the top, disappeared over the precipice, and in a few minutes were at the bottom, near the water's edge, where no human being ever stood before. Their shouts induced Mr. Coats and myself to attempt the feat, which is in fact only perilous in imagination. A spring of water bursts out of the mountain near the top, on the side where we were, and by following down the channel which the water has made, a good footing may be established all the way down. In all probability, this is the only place in the whole circumference of the lake where the water is accessible, although Sergeant Stearns clambered around the edge of the lake for a short distance, and ascended to the summit by a different route from the one we descended ; yet he does not think he could go down where he came up. The water in the lake is clear as crystal, and about the same temperature with the well water in Rogue River valley. We saw no fish of any kind, nor even insects in the water ; the only thing we saw that indicated that there are fish in the lake was a kingfisher. In ascending, I measured the distance as well as I could, from point to point, by the eye, and conclude that it is from seven to eight hundred feet perpendicular from the water to the summit of the bluff. The lake seems to be very nearly circular, and is from seven to eight miles in diameter ; and except at two or three points, the bluff is about the same altitude. Near the western shore of the lake is an island, about one-half mile in diameter, upon which there is considerable timber growing. The island is not more than one-quarter of a mile from the western shore of the lake, and its shape is a frustrum of a cone : the top seems to be depressed, and I think there is a small crater in the summit of the island. I think a path could be made from the summit to the water's edge, at the western edge of the lake ; for the formation seems to be entirely pomice stone at that point, and to slope to the water's edge at a less angle than any place else around the lake ; at this point also, a boat could be let safely down to the water by a rope.

I do not know who first saw this lake, nor do I think it should be named after the discoverer. Sergeant Stearns and Peyton Ford are the first white men who ever reached its waters, and if named after any person, should be named for them ; but as I do not believe a more majestic sheet of water is to be found upon the face of the globe, I propose the name of " Majesty." It will be visited by thousands hereafter, and some person would do well to build upon its banks a house where visitors could be entertained, and to keep a boat or boats upon its waters, that its beauties might be seen to a better advantage.'

The grandeur of the Columbia River, which has elsewhere been partially described, the wonders of Puget Sound, the splendor of the snow-peaks bathed in sunrise or sunset colors, the noble Mt. Hood blushing like a rose from summit to base—the beautiful blue and purple of the distant ranges, either east or west, all these united, make Oregon and Washington more remarkable for scenery than any other States in the Union, not excepting renowned California, and mountainous Nevada.

Advantages for Commerce. We make use of the following extract copied from a *Report on the Wealth and Resources of Oregon*, and which applies equally well to Washington, only adding to the sections enumerated, the names of other sections north of the Columbia :

" The internal trade of Oregon will always be confined to the trade between the agricultural counties in the Wallamet, Umpqua, and Rogue River valleys, and the mining counties of Eastern Oregon and Idaho Territory, and will consist simply in the transportation of the produce and manufacture of one section to the other, to be exchanged for the bullion or coin of the mines, and will be carried on by means of a railroad to be constructed through the Wallamet valley, terminating at some point on the Columbia, from which river steamers will ply as far up as the centre of Idaho.   To satisfy the most incredulous that this trade will be rapidly and greatly enlarged, we have only to look at its present rapid growth, the territory to be accommodated, and its resources.

The extent of country which is tributary to the agricultural resources of Oregon is embraced in all that country from the summit of the Rocky Mountains westward to the Cascade Range, and between the head-waters of the northern and southern branches of the great Columbia, and reaching from the head of the Owyhee on the south, away to the Kootenai River and its lately discovered rich mines on the border of British America, being an extent of country about eight hundred miles wide, and nine hundred miles long, or seven hundred and twenty thousand square miles.   This vast, and as yet almost unexplored region, is by no means barren or inhospitable.   The Catholic Missionaries have maintained their Missions among the Indians at the farthest point north for many years, raising all the vegetables and grain necessary for their use.   Throughout the whole extent there are now mining settlements spreading in every direction.   What was two years ago a vast, unbroken wilderness, inhabited only by wild beasts and Indians, now contains not less than thirty thousand American citizens, with cities and towns, saw-mills, quartz mills, flouring mills, with all the busy hum of peaceful industry.   And from this great internal, mountain locked basin, is now being shipped down the Columbia one million dollars of gold-dust per month, in exchange for flour, bacon, beans, and merchandise sent up.   This handsome yield of gold will, according to the present rate of progress, be increased to two and a half or three millions per month in the course of another year.

Oregon possesses peculiar facilities for the creation and maintenance of a large foreign commerce.   She possesses unlimited means for building ships— timber, copper, iron, coal, water-power, agricultural productions, a harbor equal to that of New York, and a maritime situation on the direct line of that immense trade carried on by the nations of the West with the nations of the East.   The harbor of the Columbia River looks out upon the ports of Russian America. British Columbia, and Vancouver Island, the west coast of Mexico, Central America, New Granada, Equador, Peru, Chili, and Patagonia on the

American Continent, and on the Eastern ports of the Russian Empire, India, China, Japan, Australia, the Islands of Oceanica, the Sandwich Islands, and the whale fisheries. The ports of all these countries are much nearer to the Columbia River than they are to any of the ports of the Atlantic States. They are all of easy access, and there is no reason why Oregon should not commence competing for their trade. In the year 1860 the United States exported to the above named ports domestic produce amounting to the sum of $19,645,998, and imported from the same places, in exchange, the produce of said countries amounting to $19,551,186. The imports from China alone amounted to $13,566,587. But we are told that the Pacific Coast cannot compete with the Atlantic States for this trade. The custom-house exhibit shows that the Pacific Coast can and does compete for this trade already, and not only this, but also the trade to Liverpool."

Then follow quotations from the "Market Review" of the *San Francisco Bulletin* which show that the export trade from the port of San Francisco for 1864, amounted to $6,337,090.38; an increase of two millions over the year 1862.

" How much of this produce exported from San Francisco should be credited to Oregon, we are unable to say, but that a large portion of it is Oregon produce, we know from the fact that the steamers and sailing vessels plying between San Francisco and the Columbia River, always return to California freighted with Oregon produce. We simply give this report to show what has already been done in foreign exportation from San Francisco, and even admitting that it is all California produce, we know very well that what will pay a California farmer to ship abroad, will also pay an Oregon farmer, with equal advantages.

The only matter which should now prevent the merchants of the Pacific Coast from becoming importers to the United States of the teas, coffee, spices, barks, dye-woods, cotton, sugar, rice, Japanese ware, matting, gold and silver of the above named countries, is, that we have not yet got the ships, or money to do this business. For the year ending June 1st, 1864, Shanghae, China, exported more than $25,000,000 worth of cotton, and now we should endeavor to exchange our produce for this cotton of China, and manufacture it here in Oregon, and build up a Lowell on the Pacific.

This golden harvest of trade is not yet ours, but when the Northern Pacific Railroad shall have been completed, it will become ours from the necessity of the case. What we want most now is a line of ships running direct from New York to the Columbia River, bringing out our merchandise, and carrying back *via* China and the East Indies, our produce, lumber, spars, &c. We are now paying an immense annual tax to California capitalists by receiving and shipping everything through the San Francisco warehouses. All our wheat, wool,

&c., that reaches a foreign market, except what little direct trade we have with the Sandwich Islands, is shipped first to San Francisco, where it has to pay wharfage, drayage, storage and commission, before it can be reshipped. Our merchandise coming to this State has to pass through the same taxing process at San Francisco, in addition to the profits of the importer before it. It is no wonder that Oregon is in the shade of California, and it ought to remain so as long as we will not make some effort to remedy this state of affairs."

The above quotation throws some light upon the commercial condition of the Northwest Coast, and explains pretty clearly the feeling of its people regarding that position. So far the Manufactures of this country have been confined to lumber, flour, woolen goods, some coarse leather, a little turpentine, an inferior article of pottery, a limited quantity of matches, and as much machinery as three or four small foundries and machine shops could turn out. Everything that is used on the farm, in the garden, household, or in the mines, is imported at a great expense. Iron has begun to be manufactured in Oregon, and so has salt, but the complete development of these things must wait, first for capital; secondly, for railroads.

Probable Railroad Routes. The only railroad under construction on the whole Northwest Coast, is the one now building down the Wallamet Valley, and called the Oregon Central. It is intended to connect the Columbia River with San Francisco Bay, and will form a portion of that great line of railway by which Lake Superior, Puget Sound, and San Francisco Bay will eventually be united. Owing to the influence exerted by Portland capital, the Oregon Central has been commenced at that point, but that Portland will long remain the northern terminus is incredible, when its position, and its distance from the Columbia River are considered. A point for the northern terminus of the Oregon Central will undoubtedly be fixed where it will connect by ferriage over the Columbia, with a road down the Cowelitz Valley from Puget Sound, thus making one continuous road through the whole length of Washington, Oregon, and California, as far as San Francisco, if not as far as San Diego.

The question undecided at present by the Oregon Central is, whether to carry the road over the Calapooya, Umpqua, and Siskiyou Mountains, directly south, and open up the Umpqua and Rogue River Valleys to commerce, or to take it by a single easy pass through the Cascade Mountains, at or near Diamond Peak, and thence southward along the almost level country to the headwaters of the Sacramento. The latter would be the cheapest of construction, and might be made to form a branch of the Central Pacific, while the former would take in its course some of the most desirable country in Oregon.

Strong efforts are being made to get a branch road from the Union Pacific to some point on the upper Columbia, either at the Dalles, Umatilla, or Wallula. It is said that in case the road comes to the Dalles it will cross the river there, and pass on down the Columbia to some point below the mouth of the Wallamet, either there to build up a commercial town, or to connect with the road up the Cowelitz Valley going north, and the Oregon Central, going south.

Idaho and Montana are waiting on the action of these railroad projectors, glad to see communication with the coast made easy on any terms, and willing to lend their aid to the first company in the field.

A strong sentiment, however, prevails throughout the Northwest in favor of the Northern Pacific Railroad. To this favorite enterprise, Montana and Idaho, Washington and Oregon, all and each, lend their preference, and so far as it is available, are willing to lend their material aid. All understand that the Columbia River, taken in conjunction with Puget Sound, offers to the commerce of the whole

Pacific the most complete resources which the trade of the world could require. And every intelligent citizen of the Northwest looks forward in fancy to a day when busy millions shall occupy this territory we have so inefficiently described, and when it shall be the most favored portion of the greatest earthly Republic.

When Thomas H. Benton, in a speech delivered at St. Louis, in 1845, prophecied that the men then listening to him should see with living eyes a railroad to the Pacific Ocean, and the trade of China and Japan flowing over it, he was believed to be an enthusiast, if no worse. In twenty-four years his prophecy has been accomplished, and doubtless some of his hearers of that day have enjoyed, or will yet enjoy, a trip by railway across the continent.

But Benton's pet scheme was a railroad which was to connect with the mouth of the Columbia River. It was Oregon, then undivided, that he looked to as the greatest country on the American continent. Perhaps some listener to his speech of 1845, may live to see his judgment vindicated. That is our hope at least.

THE END.